François Bovier, Adeena Mey,
Thomas Schärer, Fred Truniger [eds.]
Minor Cinema:
Experimental Film in Switzerland

JRP|EDITIONS & LES PRESSES DU RÉEL

François Bovier, Adeena Mey,
Thomas Schärer, Fred Truniger [eds.]
Minor Cinema:
Experimental Film in Switzerland

The essays reproduced in this publication and originally written in German and in French can be downloaded at https://blog.zhdk.ch/sfex.

Many resources collected during the research project "Schweizer Filmexperimente 1950–1988," including more than 20 interviews with filmmakers and curators as audio-files and transcripts, are also available on this website.

You can contribute to the "Minor Cinema" research project if you have additional material. Please contact the researchers through the website.

Table of Contents

A Minor History of a Cinema on the Margins
François Bovier and Adeena Mey 6

Fragments of a History of Experimental Filmmaking in Switzerland
Thomas Schärer and Fred Truniger 18

EXPERIMENTAL FILM

HHK Schoenherr's "Broken Cinema"
François Bovier 46

Robert Beavers and Gregory Markopoulos: Time Spent and Time Between
Ian Wooldridge 66

At the Limits of the Visible: Clemens Klopfenstein's Experiments of the 1970s
Simon Koenig 94

The Love of Nature and its Opposite: Staging the Landscape in Peter Liechti's Early Films
Marcy Goldberg 110

Film Forum, *Supervisuell*, and Ciné Circus: Experimental Filmmaking in Zurich in the Late 1960s
Thomas Schärer 120

Notes from *Hors-Champ*: On Experimental Filmmaking in Basel in the 1970s and 1980s
Ute Holl 148

ART SPACES AND EXHIBITIONS

Expanded Kunsthalle: The Role of Cinema
at the Kunsthalle Bern under the Curatorship of
Harald Szeemann (1961–1969)
Nicolas Brulhart 170

Underground Explosion: A Vaudeville of the Avant-Garde
Thomas Schärer and Fred Truniger 196

P.A.P. (Progressive Art Production): A "Film Gallery"
for "Political and Pornographic" Cinema
François Bovier 214

Exhibiting Structural Film? Annette Michelson,
Between Criticism and Curating
Adeena Mey 228

Video Art—Under- and Over-Exposure/Exhibition:
Early Exhibitions in French-Speaking Switzerland
Geneviève Loup 246

Beyond Frontiers: The Singularity of René Bauermeister's
"Moving" Work
Jean-Michel Baconnier 272

Structure and Participation in the Films of Tony Morgan
Renate Buschmann 288

ART SCHOOLS

Serge Stauffer and the *Film de Recherche*:
Traces of a Friendship
Michael Hiltbrunner 300

Experiences of the Experimental in French-Speaking
Switzerland: Ciné-Clubs, Critics, Schools of Art
Interview with François Albera by François Bovier 318

FESTIVALS

From a Debate over a Playground to the Meeting Point for Swiss Video Art: The International Film, Video, and Performance Festival VIPER
Gabriel Flückiger, Siri Peyer, and Fred Truniger 362

INDUSTRIAL FILM

Between Avant-Garde and Sponsor: Kurt Blum's Industrial Films around 1960
Thilo Koenig 378

ON THE MARGINS

An Avant-Garde of Amateurs? The Cinematic Experiments of Jaques Dutoit, Georges Dufaux, and Hans Haldenwang
Vrääth Öhner 398

Cléo Uebelmann, *Mano Destra*, 1985: Coldness and Cruelty
François Bovier and Christian Giuliano Tarabini 412

A Minor History of a Cinema on the Margins
François Bovier and Adeena Mey

Translated from the French by Miranda Stewart

Film Implosion! Experiments in Swiss Cinema and Moving Images, Fri Art Kunsthalle, Fribourg, November 21, 2015–February 21, 2016
Exhibition views; curators: Balthazar Lovay and François Bovier

This publication was born out of a research project supported by the Swiss National Science Foundation between 2010 and 2014,[1] which sought to map experimental cinema in Switzerland. We provided an initial introduction to our research at a talk and film program held at the Cinémathèque suisse in 2012.[2] From a historiographical and methodological point of view, this meeting afforded us the opportunity to position ourselves vis-à-vis the current tendency worldwide to rewrite avant-garde and experimental cinema from the perspective of the history of art. This new slant is closely bound up with the reconstruction of expanded films and installations within major retrospective and solo exhibitions, such as *Into the Light: The Projected Image in American Art 1964–77*, the retrospective by Chrissie Iles at the Whitney Museum of American Art (2001–2002), and the reinstallation of Anthony McCall's *Solid Light Films*[3] at the EYE Filmmusem in Amsterdam (2014). The historical exhibition model has tended to be the primary lens through which experimental cinema has been reassessed, and yet, since the 1960s, experimentation in the medium of film has occupied its own specific independent field; the term "exhibition cinema" did not come into general use until the 1990s. By placing Swiss experimental cinema within a local context, we have been able to shine a spotlight on the advantages and limitations of this historiographical shift.

This approach naturally led us, at a later point, to contrast our research findings and (re)discoveries of forgotten films with actual curatorial practices. These issues underpinned the exhibition *Film Implosion! Experiments in Swiss Cinema and Moving Images* first curated in Fribourg at the Fri Art Kunsthalle in 2015–2016 by François Bovier and Balthazar Lovay, and repeated in 2017 at the Museum für Gestaltung in Zurich, curated by Balthazar Lovay and Andres Janser, and in Cairo in 2018 at Medrar for Contemporary Art, curated by François Bovier and Adeena Mey.[4] In contexts such as these, the exhibition effect can be fully appreciated. When films of vastly different approaches and design are screened side by side in the same space, an experimental Swiss cinema, in terms of a full-fledged national cultural identity, starts to emerge. While the micro-histories reconstructed by a curatorial hand do not always recount an epic tale, they do, at least, describe a rich and pluralistic history. The real success of this approach lies in the use of formal research and all its related conceptual issues to give experimental cinema a special exhibition space through contemporary art and its interstices. Indeed, it serves to map these film practices onto the wider horizon of the moving image from high modernism to the contemporary era.

Nevertheless, we should, perhaps, put the category of experimental cinema into perspective. It initially brings to mind scientific laboratory experiments, and even the model of the experimental novel (the title of an essay by Émile Zola published in 1880), but its core meaning can hardly be said to be stable. Indeed, Dominique Noguez chose to use the term crossed out, much in the style of Jacques Derrida.[5] It is particularly problematic when applied to the Swiss scene and its specificity—a counterintuitive term when we look at the undefined and unrelated nature of all the various experiments in the moving image in this country. The phrase "Schweizer Filmexperimente" (Swiss film experiments), and indeed the more neutral "cinéma expérimental en Suisse" (experimental film in Switzerland), do not even come close to addressing the nature or definition of these practices. They suggest a national focus or, more precisely, a single-nation approach, and yet these practices are pursued in three distinct cultural and linguistic regions. The history of experimental cinema in Switzerland, if we can call it such, comprises a whole series of overlapping elements (including, primarily artists' cinema, commissioned films, *le nouveau cinéma*, amateur films, and militant films), all of which are located, more often than not, on the margins (of the film industry, auteur films, commissioned films, and contemporary art).

It might therefore be preferable to look at these film practices in terms of their different contexts of production and dissemination—where there is an authorial intention, which is not always the case. While this approach has, in part, shaped the structure of this volume, it has not had a bearing on its chapters, which mostly comprise individual case studies. Clearly, it is both possible and justifiable to distinguish between practices—indeed any single one of them could furnish the subject of an entire book. However, even taken as a whole, they do not cover experimental Swiss cinema as a whole. This simple juxtaposition of terms removes all sense of wholeness or unity and runs contrary to the avant-garde predilection for creating movements and forming rival factions.

So, what broadly are these artistic, social, and experimental paradigms? A major history of experimental cinema would cover nonnarrative (or paranarrative, dysnarrative, etc.) experiments with perception phenomena mediated by the camera. These practices are common in the field of independent cinema, in interaction with countercultural spaces, a cinephile culture, and schools of art. Our project initially sought to map out these practices, following a film restoration program led by Fred Truniger. We should not forget that an independent filmmakers' cooperative emerged in 1967, in the very early days of experimental film in Switzerland, at the initiative of Hans-Jakob Siber. This version of events has, nonetheless, been strongly contested by some proponents of this type of cinema, notably HHK Schoenherr. A counter-history of experimental cinema should include militant practices—feminism, antinuclear protests, workers' demands, youth movements, etc. All these strands undeniably exist, but have been played out differently depending on the context and the urgency of the political situation at the time. Another dimension can be found in amateur cinema, or what Fredi M. Murer liked to call "cinéma copain." This takes us to the margins, but significantly, a number of important productions are from this particular field. Institutional practices have also produced experimental film practices—advertising, commissioned films, psychotherapy through the use of the camera, etc. In recent times, these works have started to be taken seriously, but it is probably still too early to come to a considered view of this field. One currently expanding area is that of artists' cinema, which is primarily found in museums, art spaces, and, on occasion, leisure venues. Finally, with the 1960s trend toward intermedia, experimental cinema started to be built on avowedly interdisciplinary performative practices—Expanded Cinema events, screenings of films at concerts, choreography, theater, and artistic performances. This has been accompanied by some more contracted or deliberately reduced versions of this Expanded Cinema, largely linked to visual poetry.

Now that our research is complete, we are in a position to argue that a map of the territory must be drawn full scale, with representation superimposed on the represented space, just like the paradoxical fiction of Lewis Carroll or Jorge Luis Borges.[6] It is not in any case possible to identify any coherent picture of experiments with moving images in Switzerland; nor is it possible to identify any specific characteristics that come into contact and interact. Everything appears, for the most part, to be ad hoc, marginal, fragmentary, and dispersed.

Experimental cinema in Switzerland was never located in a single place; nor did it require cultural actors and filmmakers to serve as its brokers. This absent center, and experimental cinema's concomitant displacement to the periphery, is probably due in no small measure to the relative lack of institutional support that these practices received in Switzerland. It is true that the Federal Department of Home Affairs has awarded ad hoc funding to projects whose artistic quality it recognized, such as *Pazifik – oder die Zufriedenen* (1965) by Murer, *Geschichte der Nacht* (1978) by Clemens Klopfenstein, and *Robert Walser* (1978) by Schoenherr. However, experimental cinema is a catchall category—its definition depends on the aesthetic judgment of the members of the Federal Department of Home Affairs awards board. Consequently, there is no such thing as institutional recognition of a particular artistic or research approach.[7]

Furthermore, all the main practitioners in Switzerland at that time were actually foreign. This was the case of Schoenherr, an emblematic experimental filmmaker working in Switzerland who modeled his approach on the notion of "broken" cinema ("kaputtes Kino"). This was in critical response to the "other" cinema ("das andere Kino"), and the underground. Yet, at the same time, he made a great play of the interval between frames, following musical composition as a model. He was also active in programming films—in 1972, his *Movies Kaputt* selection toured Switzerland, Germany, Holland, and Great Britain—and he published the fanzine *Supervisuell* (1968–1970), which employed German, Italian, Austrian, and American correspondents. Nonetheless, Schoenherr was German and felt most at home in a network of alternative German-speaking filmmakers, who leaned toward Viennese Actionism. Gregory Markopoulos and Robert Beavers were other key players in experimental cinema at an international level. They lived and filmed in Switzerland from 1967. Indeed, they bequeathed their film and documentary archives to this country (Temenos, in Uster). They are, however, both American, and their involvement in the local scene was tenuous to say the least.

Some artists managed to forge a path for their film practices without any particular economic support for cinema production. These included Rolf Winnewisser, the Ecart group, Dieter Meier, Roman Signer, and Dieter Roth. Nevertheless, most of these films, if indeed they were ever presented in public, circulated in contemporary art networks separate from the independent cinema circuit. A notable exception is *Dots* by Roth, which was included by Birgit Hein as a typical example of structuralist cinema in her exhibition *Film als Film* at the Kölnischer Kunstverein in 1977.[8] Dieter Meier, who was at the intersection between independent cinema and contemporary art, particularly with his para-cinema performances, was distributed by one of the rare film galleries in Europe in the late 1960s. This was P.A.P. [Progressive Art Production], which had its head office in the home of its director Karlheinz Hein in Munich. Similarly, particularly in French-speaking Switzerland, a video art scene grew up around René Berger, who became their spokesman. The artists included René Bauermeister, Gérald Minkoff, Muriel Olesen, Jean Otth, and Janos Urban, whom Berger dubbed the "Musketeers of the Invisible." However, there was no real interaction with the experimental cinema scene (with one exception—Bauermeister regularly made experimental films).

While there was clearly a rich production of experimental forms in Switzerland, it could hardly be called a coherent "experimental scene." Given the fragmentary nature of "research cinema" (a term used at that time to refer to experimental cinema) in Switzerland, we have found the most suitable methodology for our purposes to be the "minor history" approach, as applied to history of art in the 1960s by Branden W. Joseph, when working on the Tony Conrad archives.[9] This methodology is based on notion of "minor literature" as advanced by Deleuze and Guattari in connection with Kafka's works, and artist Mike Kelley's idea of a "minor history." Branden Joseph argues that minor history "does not proceed from point to point in clearly articulated relations of development (from minimalism, say, to postminimalism) or of opposition (as in the dialectics of pop and minimalism or Expanded Cinema and structural film)."[10] We are witnessing a reverse phenomenon.

> Appearing at the fringes of major movements or styles, their relation to them is one of deterritorialization, opening these categories up to heterological connections and interactions. These fringes or margins, however, are sometimes found at the very center of major categories or movements; a "minor" figure may—perhaps fleetingly, perhaps not—become essential to the development of a major

category or movement without, however, being fully contained.[11]

It might, at first sight, appear paradoxical to use the category of "minor cinema" insofar as "minor" methodology tends to be used to refer to the careers and approaches of particular artists or groups of artists. Nevertheless, in Switzerland, experimental cinema practices, whatever their nature, have effectively all been "minor" and have never managed to create a "(major) movement." This was not the case for New Swiss Cinema, where, for example, the Group of Five in French-speaking Switzerland—Alain Tanner, Jean-Louis Roy, Claude Goretta, Michel Soutter, and Jean-Jacques Lagrange—was supported by Télévision Suisse Romande. Nor was it the case for "auteur" figures such as Daniel Schmid or Walter Marti and Reni Mertens, who regularly received support from the Federal Cinema Commission from 1963 onward. More peripheral but no less "major" figures such as Jean-Luc Godard negotiated a path for themselves between the New Wave, which quickly garnered international recognition, militant film (particularly the ventures of the Dziga Vertov Group), research cinema, video, and, more sporadically, the world of art. In one sense, experimental cinema in Switzerland can be seen as a fragmentary cinema characterized by dispersed practices which range from amateur cinema to militant, institutional, and commissioned film (films in psychiatric wards, for example, or productions for the pharmaceutical industry). Its relationship with the international independent cinema scene is also clearly evident—when P. Adams Sitney came to Europe to present a film program (taken from the *New American Cinema Exposition* organized by Jonas Mekas), he stopped off in Switzerland; there were discussions with filmmakers in Zurich, Lucerne, Lausanne, and even Solothurn. However, according to the account of his tour published in *Film Culture*,[12] he found the Swiss scene fairly uneven, with the exception of Fredi M. Murer, who he associated with Baudelairean cinema. Presenters from the Swiss filmmakers' cooperative took part in the discussions held at the Knokke Experimental Film Festival in 1967, which was designed to bring together filmmakers' cooperatives from throughout Europe. Schoenherr was also involved in a meeting held at the initiative of Karlheinz Hein in Munich in 1968 to set up a European cooperative. While no real structure emerged on that occasion, there was clearly a desire to create an international federation of alternative and research cinema that included Swiss filmmakers. This was reminiscent of the precedent set by the International Congress of Independent Filmmakers held in 1929 in La Sarraz in Switzerland. The second such Congress, held in Brussels in 1930, proved a failure. It may have been a fertile breeding ground, but it did not manage to produce anything that could remotely be described as a movement.

The London Film-Makers' Co-op was a very different case in point. It provided a space for artists, filmmakers, and experimental poets (indeed, the London Film-Makers' Co-op grew out of the Better Books bookstore run by poet Bob Cobbing, among others). Yet, there does not seem to be any comparable rallying point for experimental cinema in Switzerland—apart from a brief period in 1967–1968, with the Film Forum in Zurich. Experimental cinema and artists' films clustered around alternative production and dissemination platforms, the most famous of which was the New York cooperative set up by Mekas, and rallying points like *EXPRMNTL*, also known as the Knokke Experimental Film Festival, in Knokke-le-Zoute, Belgium. Switzerland had some production sites and alternative screening venues, but they did not screen programs or produce films that subscribed to any particular aesthetic or political principles. The *New Forms in Film* exhibition was organized by American critic Annette Michelson in Montreux in 1974 with the aim of legitimizing experimental cinema as a contemporary art form; however, its most direct effects were felt in Paris, where it led to the creation of the film collection of the Centre Georges-Pompidou, in conjunction with the exhibition *Une histoire du cinéma*, curated by Peter Kubelka. In the 1970s Basel, too, was an ideal place to nurture an experimental scene to bring together the visual arts and cinema. It boasted a theater workshop run by Werner von Mutzenbecher at the Basel School of Art. It also included filmmakers such as André Lehmann and Urs Breitenstein, both of whom had studied at Cooper Union School of Art, New York, a year apart, who were exploring similar issues in their films. However, this particular scene attracted scant attention at an international level.

Underground, as opposed to legitimate, cinema, essentially a heroic, oppositional model, did not figure prominently in Switzerland. It would perhaps be more accurate to say that research cinema was part of the new Swiss cinema and its margins were neither in receipt of institutional support nor viewed as an oppositional practice. Since the 2000s, we have witnessed a gradual reevaluation of the moving image, in relation to other artistic practices, particularly within the field of art history. At the same time, in this age of Media Studies, cinema itself has become a fluid, moving category, and its modes of production and circulation are currently being redefined. In this context, and given the genuine risk that archives and works will be lost, this is surely an appropriate time to provide an initial mapping and critical review of experimental cinema in Switzerland.

[1] The Zürcher Hochschule der Künste (ZHdK) Institute for Performing Arts and Film and the University of Lausanne (UNIL) Department of Cinema History and Aesthetics have jointly supervised two research projects: "Schweizer Filmexperimente" [Swiss experimental films] (2010–2012) and subsequently, "Le cinéma expérimental en Suisse depuis les années 1950" [Experimental cinema in Switzerland since the 1950s] (2012–2014). The researchers involved in the project include Fred Truniger (ZHdK then HSLU), François Bovier (UNIL and ECAL/Lausanne University of Art and Design), Thomas Schärer (ZHdK), and Adeena Mey (UNIL).

[2] "Hors-cadre. Le cinéma expérimental en Suisse depuis les années 1950," Cinémathèque suisse, Lausanne, January 26–29, 2012.

[3] See Christopher Eamon (ed.), *Anthony McCall. The Solid Light Films and Related Works*, Northwestern University Press, Evanston 2005.

[4] See François Bovier, Balthazar Lovay, Sylvain Menétrey, Dan Solbach (eds.), *Film Implosion! Experimental Cinema in Switzerland*, Fri Art/Revolver Publishing, Fribourg/Berlin 2017. Film installations, film stock, and transfers were run non-stop throughout both floors of the Fribourg Kunsthalle. The exhibition was curated by François Bovier and Balthazar Lovay, the director of Fri Art, assisted by the research team and the artists and filmmakers presented at this event.

[5] See Dominique Noguez, *Éloge du cinéma expérimental : définitions, jalons, perspectives*, Centre Georges-Pompidou, Paris 1979 [expanded edition: *Éloge du cinéma expérimental*, Editions Paris Expérimental, Paris 1999; 2010]. The term "avant-garde," which is regularly used in English-speaking countries, is also problematic insofar as it has strong connotations of the historical avant-garde movements of the 1910–1930 period, and of the military (in the literal sense of "advance guard").

[6] Lewis Carroll wrote: "'That's another thing we've learned from your Nation,' said Mein Herr, 'map making. But we've carried it much further than you. What do you consider the largest maps that would be really useful [...] We actually made a map of the country, on the scale of a mile to the mile!' 'Have you used it much?' I enquired. 'It has never been spread out, yet,' said Mein Herr. 'The farmers objected: they said that it would cover the whole country, and shut out the sunlight! So now we use the country itself, as its own map, and I assure you it does nearly as well.'" Lewis Carroll, *Sylvie and Bruno Concluded*, Macmillan and Co, London/New York 1889.

Jorge Luis Borges attributes this short text to an imaginary author: "In that Empire, the Art of Cartography attained such Perfection that the map of a single Province occupied the entirety of the City, and the map of the Empire, the entirety of a Province. In time, those Unconscionable Maps no longer satisfied, and the Cartographers Guilds struck a Map of the Empire whose size was that of the Empire, and which coincided point for point with it. The following Generations, who were not so fond of the Study of Cartography as their Forebears had been, saw that that vast map was Useless, and not without some Pitilessness was it, that they delivered it up to the inclemencies of Sun and Winters [...]" Jorge Luis Borges, "On Exactitude in Science," *Collected Fictions*, trans. Andrew Hurley, Viking Penguin, New York 1998, p.199 [*El Hacedor*, Emece Editores, Buenos Aires 1960].

[7] On this subject, see Olivier Moeschler's doctoral thesis, *Cinéastes indépendants, politique fédérale du cinéma et co-production du "Nouveau cinéma suisse," 1963–1970. Contribution à une sociologie de l'innovation artistique*, supervised by Jean-Yves Pidoux, University of Lausanne, 2008. See also Olivier Moeschler, *Cinéma suisse. Une politique culturelle en action: l'État, les professionnels, les publics*, Presses polytechniques et universitaires romandes, Lausanne 2011.

[8] See Birgit Hein, Wulf Hergozenrath (eds.), *Film als Film. 1910 bis heute: Vom Animationsfilm der zwanziger zum Filmenvironment der siebziger Jahre*, Kölnischer Kunstverein, Cologne 1977.

[9] See Branden W. Joseph, *Beyond the Dream Syndicate. Tony Conrad and the Arts after Cage*, Zone Books, New York 2008. We invited Branden W. Joseph to talk about these issues at the "Hors Cadre: Swiss Film Experiments" symposium, held at the Cinémathèque suisse from January 26–29, 2012.

[10] Ibid., p. 50.

[11] Ibid., p. 51–52.

[12] P. Adams Sitney, "The New American Cinema Exposition," *Film Culture*, no. 46 (Autumn 1967), p. 22–32.

Poster for the *Der Film* exhibition, Kunstgewerbemuseum Zürich, Zurich, January 10–April 30, 1960; graphic design by Josef Müller-Brockmann

Fragments of a History of Experimental Filmmaking in Switzerland
Thomas Schärer and Fred Truniger

Translated from the German by Steven Lindberg

A Bolex H16 belonging to the Gruppe AKS

The research project "Swiss Film Experiments 1950–1988" ran from 2010 to 2014 and explored a buried history of Swiss film. Its goal was to look at the significance of experimental filmmaking for the history of film from a narrower perspective, and its involvement with the history of art more generally. "Experimental Swiss film has no specific national characteristics," wrote Swiss experimental filmmaker and video artist René Bauermeister in 1980 in a treatise on the situation of experimental film in Switzerland.[1] The evolution of avant-garde cinema in Switzerland was largely parallel and analogous to the international evolution of this marginal cinema, albeit fragmentary, often delayed, and with a history that is characterized by powerful personal, institutional, and geographic rifts. These rifts, which can be called, following Branden W. Joseph, characteristic of a "minor cinema,"[2] make it virtually impossible to talk about an experimental film scene in Switzerland. Nevertheless, we attempt here to offer an overview of the development of experimental film practices in Switzerland by tracing the distinct and diverse discourses that link the history of film, video, art, and social events, and that intersect in the field of the artistic avant-garde. Any claim to completeness is ruled out not only by the limited size of the article and by the fragility and ramifications of the historical strands, but also by the extensiveness of the discourses that would need to be connected. Experimental film of the 1960s, for example, is intimately connected to the emergence of a self-confident youth culture, which began to claim its own spaces. It found its expression primarily in pop and jazz music, which were in turn linked to artistic practices. Working on the history of experimental films necessarily means taking note of artistic discourses in the broader sense as well. From a specifically cinematic-artistic perspective, it can be placed with related works that address nonconformity in Zurich, the Swiss art and music scene of the 1960s and 1970s, the 1960s counterculture, punk culture, and the history of video, among other topics.[3]

    Historical interpretation of Swiss experimental film is particularly difficult due to the precarious state of the source material. Concrete traces left by more established art forms—program schedules and flyers, (press) reviews, and journal and book publications—are largely lacking. The data on which this article and the publication as a whole are based are thus taken from a wide variety of sources, sometimes transmitted in writing and sometimes orally, spread across many media, and usually omitted from archives, or at least not compiled with the necessary rigor. These sources include, among others, hand-copied program leaflets; newspaper clippings with reviews of programs or portraits of filmmakers; unpublished manuscripts by the filmmakers themselves; fragmentary film histories of experimental cinema by contemporaries; fanzine-like magazines, usually short-lived; film catalogues from festivals and distributors; and, finally, perhaps the most important source, the personal memories of those involved from interviews we conducted ourselves. Only a fraction of the material on which this historical overview is based can be found in public archives. Most of it was collected informally, and it has now been compiled in a research blog to be double-checked and further studied: blog.zhdk.ch/sfex.

Sometimes these disparate sources shed light on one another, making it possible to connect films, people, places, leaflets, invitations, texts, and cameras originally found without context, and to understand them as actors within a lived practice. One of our most important research paths was therefore examining the meeting places, and more or less informal film screenings, which sometimes evolved into festivals, and which left sources behind in the form of letters, program announcements, newspaper reviews, and catalogues. In addition to the films themselves, these sparse traces were our central sources. The randomness of historical records undoubtedly led to us place too much weight on certain facts or aspects. Events, films, and developments that were seen as important by contemporaries may have escaped our notice simply because no documentation has survived. We attempted to address that risk by interviewing 26 former exponents of this film culture.[4] Despite this multi-perspectival, comparative approach, however, we are aware that blind spots inevitability remain. For example, formal analyses of the films themselves get short shrift in this anthology, even though we did not intend to write a "history of film without films."[5] From this perspective, it becomes clear that the interpretations made here are provisional.

The degree to which various historical moments have been concentrated differs in our attempt at a thematic introduction. Themes that are treated in greater detail in the individual essays in this volume are mentioned only with suitable brevity, and those that the essays do not touch on, or only briefly, are discussed at greater length.

Early Experimental Films

Just how rudimentary knowledge of the avant-garde was in Switzerland in the early 1950s, and how unclear the contours of cinematic genres sometimes were, is evident from the program for the second Festival du film de demain, which had been held by the Association of International Film Archives in Antibes for the first time in 1950 and subsequently in Basel in 1954. Over ten days, with up to five program points per day, it not only featured lectures and film programs, for example, on medical and scientific films (Jean Painlevé) and travel films (*Polarexpeditionen* [Polar Expeditions] and *Die höchsten Gipfel der Welt* [The World's Highest Peaks]); there was also a cross section of the repertoire dedicated to artistic and experimental cinematic practices, including films by Rudy Burckhardt of Basel, who had been making films since emigrating to New York in the 1930s, and a retrospective of films by Man Ray, who introduced the program personally.[6] This festival was one of the first documented large-scale events in Switzerland that presented a panorama of the cinematic avant-garde.

Because relatively few artistic and "free" films were produced, with very heterogeneous conditions and ambitions, it is not correct, even in the 1950s, to speak of a clearly distinguished genre of experimental film. Rather, free films have to be looked for in commissioned films; in commercial films in the broad sense; in artists' films; in installations with projectors, concerts, or performances; and in amateur films, if one wants to assess cinematic creativity beyond the well-trodden paths.

In the 1950s, free films could succeed only as contraband within established structures as an expensive leisure-time activity with more or less high aspirations. To our knowledge, experimental films in the strict sense were produced only sporadically. At the *EXPRMNTL* film festival, which was a festival of central importance for experimental film in Europe, held in Knokke-le-Zoute in 1958—on the occasion of the World's Fair in Brussels—three films with Swiss participation were presented: Claude Goretta and Alain Tanner showed their debut film, *Nice Time* of 1957, an insightful essay that is considered part of the British Free Cinema movement, which was financed by the Experimental Production Committee of the British Film Institute, and which won the prize for the best experimental film at the Venice Film Festival in 1958. Fred Schmid of Biel was represented in the program by his *Über Zink/Sur le Zinc*, a formal study on light reflections, and young filmmaker Gérard Vallet of Geneva presented *Une lettre*, an experiment with film positive and film negative.

One path to experimental film was to explore new forms within the bread-and-butter work of corporate film (Kurt Blum) or to oscillate between classic commissioned films and unpaid "free films" (Erwin Huppert, Ferry Radax, and later Urs Graf). With his commissioned film *L'Uomo, il fuoco e il ferro* (The Man, the Fire, and the Iron) of 1960, Bernese photographer Kurt Blum produced a radically abstract form of commissioned film,[7] which he continued to pursue, along with others such as Alexander J. Seiler and Rob Gnant, in *À fleur d'eau* (Switzerland, 1962, for the Swiss Tourism Office), which won a prize in Cannes in 1962, and in *via Zürich…* (1967). Cameraman and maker of commissioned films Erwin Huppert shot, in addition to his professional work, private, experimental works such as the bizarre collage *Recherche dans l'intérêt des familles* of 1958. Visual artists who used film as a means of expression could be found in Switzerland from the 1950s onward (Guido Haas, Franz Fedier, Bernhard Luginbühl, Leonardo Bezzola, Dieter Roth). In Basel, painter Franz Fedier scratched and drew his experimental work *Filmographie* (1959) directly onto the celluloid stock, and had his friend, boxer Fritz Chervet, box for the soundtrack in 1976. Guido Haas of Bern left his homeland in the late 1950s to study with Fernand Léger in Paris and, at the Cinémathèque française, first came into contact with the films of the classic avant-garde. With his life partner, Eva Haas, he produced camera-less films from 1958 onward (*Abstrakt 1 und 2*, 1958–1959; *Inclinations* 1962–1966; *Anamorphosis* 1968), which were shown at the *EXPRMNTL* festival in Knokke-le-Zoute. In 1958 Bernese iron sculptor Bernhard Luginbühl and photographer Leonardo Bezzola shot their short film *Isognomik 59*, which was orchestrated with animated pieces of iron.

Fragmentation, Meeting Places, and Ephemeral Networks

Amateur filmmakers in the 1950s were largely from the affluent classes: they recorded their private lives, celebratory moments with family or friends, impressions from holidays and travels. Several of them pursued personal interests; served as cinematic chroniclers of their sports club or community; systematically filmed animals, trains, or, for a symbolic fee, vanishing trades for the Schweizerische Gesellschaft für Volkskunde (Swiss Society for Folklore Studies).[8] Clubs for amateur filmmakers organized competitions on community, national, and international levels, in which technical mastery of cinematic means and the professional film model were central. The position of these filmmakers between professional and individual production—the primary profession of many amateur filmmakers was that of film technician—and their complete reliance on their own work and creative energy, makes it difficult to draw a clear boundary between "amateur film" and "experimental film": now and again, free, playful works were produced, such as those of the maker of animated films Hans Haldenwang, who cannot be adequately placed in either of these two categories, as the chapter by Vrääth Öhner in the present volume reveals.

Meanwhile, artistic practices in filmmaking were marked by fragmentation. In addition to the difficulties of making and screening films and seeing the films of colleagues, the linguistic diversity of Switzerland was a crucial factor, since filmmakers were largely limited to their section of the country. Contacts across linguistic borders remained limited and were usually on a personal level. In the larger cities—Bern, Basel, Lausanne, Geneva, and Zurich—often short-lived informal groups began to form from the 1960s onward, whose members would regularly exchange ideas, screen films, or produce magazines, but as a rule their influence remained limited to their small circles and brief lifespan.

    The fact that fragmentation and atomization made the development of networks and friendships more difficult applied to the entire period being studied, and was at best less true in the rare periods when individual and later institutional activities grew more intense, when temporary "fields," and specifically "fields of art" in Pierre Bourdieu's sense, formed[9]—for example, in Zurich in the late 1960s, in Geneva in the 1970s, and in Basel from the late 1970s to the late 1980s.[10] The short-term networks of experimental film can only be understood by focusing on other forms of articulation in music or in the visual and performing arts or on developments within the culture as a whole, beyond the cultural field, as the present volume proposes. One indication of this is that the careers of filmmakers who expressed themselves in several areas and were oriented toward the visual arts (Tony Morgan, Werner von Mutzenbecher, Clemens Klopfenstein, Dieter Meier, Rolf Winnewisser,

Dieter Roth) or music (Dieter Meier) were more successful and enduring than those of their colleagues who dedicated themselves exclusively to experimental film.[11]

One exhibition repeatedly mentioned by the (future) filmmakers of the 1960s as a starting point in their biographies is *Der Film*, shown at the Kunstgewerbemuseum (Museum of Applied Arts) in Zurich in 1960.[12] Avant-garde classics such as *Entr'acte* (René Clair, 1924), *Man with a Movie Camera* (Dziga Vertov, 1929), *Berlin – Die Sinfonie der Grossstadt* (*Berlin: Symphony of a Great City*, Walter Ruttmann, 1927), and *Un chien andalou* (Luis Buñuel and Salvador Dali, 1928) influenced many cinephiles. For young people interested in the arts, it was a first contact with artistic film. The film program that accompanied the exhibition, however, clearly showed that the approach to the medium at the time was still largely influenced by classical auteur films and their precursors, and experimental film played only a subordinate role.

Another important event was the first of the Filmarbeitswochen (Film Work Weeks) of the Mittelschulclub (High School Club), under the direction of Alex Bänninger in Engelberg in 1961. This festival became an important meeting place, screening annually until 1974 not only important auteur films and, in later years, also films of the avant-garde, but also bringing high-school students from the whole of Switzerland together for discussions in a kind of weeklong intensive curriculum. Budding Swiss filmmakers met and then continued to see each other annually. The personal contact among high-school students established by the Filmarbeitswochen was more significant to the developments in Swiss film in the new decade than all the screenings, lectures, and discussions there and elsewhere. Some of these contacts evolved further in the context of institutions such as the Kunstgewerbeschule (School of Applied Arts) in Zurich. New courses of study were established temporarily that would help the young generation of designers at the school to develop a new self-confidence as artists: in 1965 Serge Stauffer and Hansjörg Mattmüller established the F+F course, which quickly became a course in the free arts and a catalyst for the Zurich scene of independent filmmakers.[13] From 1967 to 1969, the Filmarbeitskursen (Film Work Courses) headed by Hans Heinrich Egger at the same institution offered the first educational program in film in Switzerland.[14]

Also important for the development of networks were the informal places and objects that varied from filmmaker to filmmaker. Anyone who owned or had access to a small-gauge film camera (Bolex or Beaulieu, 8mm or 16mm), like, for example, Rolf Niederer, Clemens Klopfenstein, Hansjakob Siber, and Fredi M. Murer, would lend it to colleagues. With a borrowed camera, a love of cinema could be transformed into one's own practice of searching and experimenting. The cinematic experiments that resulted were tickets to the film programs being organized by the emerging networks, which in turn encouraged them. By looking at these wandering cameras, it is possible to follow recurring formal qualities of cinematic practice: technical possibilities such as single-frame release, manual rewinding, multiple exposures, and, for example, the hand-cranked spring drive (limited to 22–24 seconds) of a Bolex H16 defined a shared formal foundation. Sometimes out-and-out manipulation mistakes and chance would spur the exploration of experimental visual languages.[15]

In parallel to a growing interest in auteur film, art film, and cinematic avant-garde, nonconformist forces were fermenting in the 1960s. They created places where urban cultures could network. One of the most influential meeting places of the early subculture in Switzerland was the club Platte 27, founded by Herbi Wertli and Eduard Stöckli in Zurich in 1965. Hans-Jakob Siber founded Film Forum in Zurich in the spring of 1966, and Platte 27 was one of its venues. Film Forum was one of the first filmmaker cooperatives in Europe[16]; it was run until 1969 by Beat Kuert, Hans Helmut Klaus Schoenherr, Robert Boner, Peter Weiller, and others. During the first three years of its existence, Film Forum was the central organization, whose film programs and film distribution turned Zurich into a visible hub in the experimental filmmaking network in Europe, and took over the function of a structure parallel to the commercial film business. On the one hand, it showed films by the international avant-garde and by young Swiss filmmakers; on the other hand, its distribution concentrated solely on local filmmakers. Film Forum was expanded by Ciné Circus, a touring program that from late 1967 spent a weekend each in Basel and Bern annually and, for one year, in Lucerne and Winterthur as well.[17]

Groups similar to Film Forum also formed in French-speaking Switzerland, such as the one founded by journalist Marcel Leiser and run by him with Frédéric Gonseth and Marcel Schüpbach: Cinéma Marginal Distribution (Lausanne, 1968–1973).[18] Like the film cooperatives in Germany, it was established as a consequence of the festival in Knokke-le-Zoute in 1967–1968, to be a distributor of films in the substandard formats of 8mm and 16mm, to make this "minor" cinema profitable for filmmakers.[19] Leiser was the editor of the western Swiss film magazine *Travelling*, and thus had privileged access to a publication he could use as a megaphone for marginal forms of film. Cinéma Marginal's first program took place in the spring of 1968 with films by young western Swiss directors, as part of Film Forum's programs in the banquet hall of the Weisser Wind restaurant in Zurich. In Geneva, artist John M. Armleder, who was connected to the Fluxus movement, formed the Ecart group with Patrick Lucchini and Claude Rychner in 1969. The group's activities were limited neither to film nor solely to production, but included a broader framework of art actions and performances, as well as dissemination of work through the Galerie Ecart in Geneva and its bookshop. That was characteristic of the artist-run spaces of the 1960s.

Festivals as Places for Networking and Exchanging Information

In the era before websites such as ubu.com (founded 1996) and youtube.com (founded 2005), that is, until just a few years ago, watching the films of the international avant-garde was something reserved for audiences of specialized film screenings (usually in film clubs or museums) or at film festivals. Independent filmmaking was "invisible,"[20] and this was often described as a problem in writing about experimental film: "writing about movies that you can't see anywhere."[21] Without knowledge of the films and without the acquaintance of likeminded colleagues, experimental filmmakers remained isolated, and their films purely personal experiments. It is thus central for any history of experimental film to look at places that showed independently produced films, so that networks of filmmakers and film fans could form on the basis of seeing films together.

If one can speak of a real movement of experimental film in Europe, it is only from 1968 onward, and it was made possible by the experiences and contacts that resulted from the fourth *EXPRMNTL* festival. This was one of the most important movements in the history of the experimental film internationally, and it took place over Christmas and New Year's Day of 1967–1968. The audience was primarily young, had traveled from all over Europe, and was specifically interested in experimental film. In addition to American films, the third *EXPRMNTL* festival in 1963–1964 had screened a few Asian and Australian colleagues as well. For many filmmakers, this may not have been their first contact with avant-garde films, but the breadth of forms of expression it revealed did trigger ideas among those watching that would bear fruit in Swiss filmmaking in subsequent years.[22] HHK Schoenherr emphatically described his experiences in the first issue of his journal *Supervisuell* in 1968: "In Knokke, opinions were split, and I made friends, images, saw never-seen worlds, received the criticism I had long been searching for. There were people who understood my films. Loved my images. Loved my film images."[23] The isolation of independent filmmakers and their varied, small, unconnected places had ended for the time being, and from now on would be limited only by the fact that many filmmakers lacked the funds to travel and by the prohibitive costs of international telephone calls.

Following a meeting on the margins of the festival that had been proposed by Jonas Mekas and P. Adams Sitney, and at which the two Americans encouraged the founding of a European film cooperative, the experimental film scene in Europe developed in leaps and bounds, with the establishment of many different film coops and distributors. Among others, immediately following the festival the influential Hamburger Filmmacher Cooperative was founded in 1968, after the Hamburger Filmschau inaugurated in 1967, along with X-Screen in Cologne, the "Cologne studio for independent film." In February 1968, the first Hamburger Filmschau was held, and it was followed in November 1968 by the "first meeting of independent filmmakers," which had been inspired by discussions in Knokke-le-Zoute and was coorganized by the Zurich filmmaker HHK Schoenherr.

Contacts between filmmakers were clearly increasing as a result of acquaintanceships established in Knokke-le-Zoute.

In Switzerland, too, discourse on experimental film and on art generally grew more intense from the autumn of 1967. Alongside the founding of Cinéma Marginal in Lausanne, Film Forum also expanded its activities with the founding of its own distribution company.[24] Gregory Markopoulos, a well-respected American avant-garde filmmaker with Greek roots, settled in Zurich for a time with Robert Beavers.[25] Zurich and Switzerland generally became a stop for experimental filmmakers touring Europe. The multiday film program that has become famous as the *New American Cinema Exposition*, which P. Adams Sitney presented at the Kunstgewerbeschule in September 1967 with the help of Hans-Jakob Siber, as a cooperation between Film Forum and the Zürcher Film Club, as well as the program of films by Robert Nelson at the Solothurner Filmtage in 1968, are evidence of the increasing networking of the scene in the second half of the 1960s.

Traces of the Swiss culture of the experimental film can also be found in the regular program of the Solothurner Filmtage, which was founded in 1966 by the Film-Gilde Solothurn as a place to discuss Swiss film, and which is still in existence today. Whereas the program of the first two years of this festival was characterized by works from more or less established filmmakers, the list of filmmakers for the third festival in 1968 exploded; it included the names of young filmmakers, whose brief, often experimental or essayistic films dominated the festival until 1972. Stephan Portmann, the director of the Filmtage, actively encouraged visual artists who were making films, such as Werner von Mutzenbecher and Guido and Gorgon Haas, to show their films in Solothurn.[26] In those years Peter Bichsel in Solothurn coined the term "Waldläuferfilme" (forest-walker films) for the often-playful debut works.[27] From 1972 to 1975 these films were increasingly displaced by ever longer documentary and fictional films before disappearing from the programs entirely.

Even more explicitly than the Solothurner Filmtage, the recently founded Luzerner Filminformationstage (*Film-In*), under the direction of Peter A. Stocker and Felix Bucher, put underground film on its program. The three programs were curated by distributor and organizer Progressive Art Productions (P.A.P.), which had been founded by Karlheinz Hein of Munich and Dieter Meier.[28] The Kunstmuseum Luzern under the directorship of Jean-Christophe Ammann, and the Kleintheater Luzern, run by Emil Steinberger, were partners from the first year. The majority of the films shown were from the distributor's immediate circles, supplemented by a work by American filmmaker Paul Sharits. Switzerland was represented by only one film and one performance, by P.A.P. cofounder Dieter Meier and by HHK Schoenherr. The *Sélection Suisse* program of seven films had apparently been canceled because the filmmakers involved were disappointed by the program's location on the edge of the festival.[29] The following year one of the festival co-organizers, Marcel Boucard, was personally involved in organizing a program with "progressive films" that ran parallel to *Film-In* proper. A greatly enlarged program was shown in collaboration with P.A.P. and in the spaces of the Kunstmuseum and the Kleintheater. In addition to independent productions by young Swiss filmmakers, the program listed the film *Schweizer Künstler in 21 Minuten* (*Swiss Artists in 21 Minutes*) (1969), which had been produced by Balthasar Burkhard (in collaboration with Peter von Gunten) for an exhibition at the Stedelijk Museum in Amsterdam, as well as the Gerry Schum's television exhibition *Land Art* from his "television gallery"—mentioned in the preface to the program but not listed in the program itself.[30] This makes it clear that the integration of experimental film into the art scene was beginning to be accepted by institutions, a goal which Jean-Christophe Ammann was also pursuing in Lucerne with other events and presentations.[31]

By 1971 the program of independently produced films had shrunk to just three dates, announced as "Progressiver Film Schweiz" (Progressive Film Switzerland), which had, apparently, been organized without the cooperation of either P.A.P. or the two local institutions. Apart from Dieter Meier's Expanded Cinema work, *Echter Diskussionsfilm* (*Genuine Discussion Film*)—the projectionist was instructed to turn on the lights for eight minutes, and the resulting discussion between the attendees gave the film its title—

the program exclusively lists documentary works. In 1972, the year Marcel Boucard resigned, *Film-In* removed experimental film from its program entirely, with a justification that is worth noting: "underground film and also agitprop film in its traditional form no longer exist."[32] In a meeting on November 14, 1973, the association in charge of running the Luzerner Filminformationstage was dissolved in a two-page communiqué, with reference to "financial and organizational difficulties."[33] The last initiative during this phase of the (re-)discovery of experimental film in Switzerland was the *New Forms in Film* Festival,[34] which, for three weeks in August 1974, showed 44 film programs with examples from the American avant-garde. Following its debut in 1972 at the Solomon R. Guggenheim Museum in New York, the festival was organized for the second time in Montreux by René Berger and curated by American film critic Annette Michelson at his invitation.[35] It brought together works by 15 mostly American independent filmmakers, some of who attended the screenings, but unlike P. Adams Sitney's touring program, *New American Cinema,* of 1967, this program met with no response from the local film scene.[36]

The End of the First Wave of Experimental Films from Switzerland

One crucial development was already heralded at the 1967–1968 *EXPRMNTL* festival: young Berlin filmmakers, including Harun Farocki, protested at the heart of the festival against the "meaningless camera exercises" and the "American cine aggression" that they claimed characterized the festival. They called instead for film with specifically political subject matter[37]—an ambition that seized the film scene in Switzerland at almost exactly the same time, and became an important factor in the ebbing of the wave of experimental film in the early 1970s. The events in 1968 in Paris, Berlin, and the United States met with a response in Switzerland as well, and led to the politicization of art, but also accelerated the discovery of young people as a group of consumers. Youth culture was already being exploited economically by 1969, and "underground" became a label. The tour of happenings and events entitled *Underground*

Explosion,[38] which presented the underground as a monster show for enormous audiences, heralded the end of a brief window of time, while its openness, curiosity, yearning, and the echoed momentum of a new dawn had made possible an experimental and ephemeral coalition of various radical artistic forms and forces. Thereafter interests quickly fanned out: politically, aesthetically, psychedelically, psychologically, and ecologically oriented formats and groups began to distinguish themselves from one another.

The heyday of experimental film in Switzerland ended in the early years of the 1970s, and the final Ciné Circus in Basel in October 1970 was no longer organized by Film Forum, which had closed in 1969, but by the Nationales Filmzentrum. Cinéma Marginal Distribution in Lausanne ceased its activities in 1973,[39] and P.A.P. restricted itself to film programming and participation in art fairs, amounting to a de facto nonexistence. But like the finale before the fireworks fade, two long films were produced that can be considered examples of efforts to participate in the new structures with full-length experimental formats: Hans-Jakob Siber completed his 60-minute film *Die Sage vom alten Hirten Xeudi und seinem Freund Reiman* (*The Saga of the Old Herdsman Xeudi and his Friend Reiman*) in 1973, which he was invited to present at the Berlinale as part of the Forum des Jungen Films (Forum of New Cinema), and which received a subsidy for quality from the Eidgenössisches Departement des Innern (Federal Department of Home Affairs). Dieter Meier completed a long film titled *81,000 Units*, which he showed at the fifth and final *EXPRMNTL* festival in Knokke-le-Zoute in 1974–1975, and which is now considered to be one of the most astonishing works from this period.[40] In both cases these were the authors' final films (for a time): Siber was disappointed by the audience's lack of interest in his film and turned to his business selling minerals, and subsequently as a dinosaur expert and museum operator, while Meier worked first as a visual artist with performances and video, and then made pop music history in the late 1970s with the band Yello.

Following a phase of free development, cooperation across artistic genres, and the founding of regional groups for the production and distribution of films, longer-lived, more institutional structures were built. Filmmaking became established as autonomous artistic work, gained an audience, and financially secured the existence of those involved. The Solothurner Filmtage and the Nationales Filmzentrum, as well as the foundation of Film-Pool in 1970 as a distributor throughout Switzerland of independently produced Swiss films, are all expressions of this consolidation of a view of film that—unlike neighboring Austria, for example—favored a "universally understandable film language,"[41] promoted politically relevant films, and slowly displaced the filmmakers of the avant-garde: many filmmakers soon turned to longer documentary or fictional forms and were thus embraced by the new structures for subsidies—although these remained precarious. Reto Savoldelli with his *Stella da Falla* (1971), Georg Radanowicz with *Alfred R. – Ein Leben und ein Film* (*Alfred R.—A Life and a Movie*, 1972), and the Gruppe AKS with *Die Fabrikanten* (*The Factory Owners*, 1973) tried making long feature films with the help of the Swiss Televisions' "Aktion Jungfilmer" (Young Filmmakers Action) subsidy program—and in the assessment of the public, they failed. A group of young filmmakers in Zurich founded Nemo Film AG, the first independent film production company in Switzerland founded by directors.

From 1972 to 1988: Video and Moving Closer to the Art Scene

The artistic and experimental filmmaking of the 1970s was marked by the aforementioned politicizing of the film scene as well as by two trends whose full effects would only become tangible decades later: the arrival of the medium of video in the art context, and the acceptance of the medium of film in museums. From 1970 to 1972, P.A.P. tried to introduce film to the art market by a direct path. It was the first company in the German-speaking world to try to provide an economically viable basis for experimental film, but it soon ended after it failed to achieve success.[42]
The idea seemed right, but the moment chosen was too early. Various parallel developments, however, encouraged the gradual integration of film into the art scene and, from the late 1960s, the rising medium of video. In Switzerland, that development began in the French-speaking region. In 1969 René Berger, director of the Musée cantonal des Beaux-Arts in Lausanne at the time, organized courses at the Université

de Lausanne that provided an introduction to the medium,[43] and three years later, also in Lausanne, the Galerie Impact presented *ACTION/FILM/VIDEO*, the first exhibition to bring together video and film.[44] It was followed by another exhibition in 1974 by the Groupe Impact at the Musée des Arts décoratifs, which was dedicated exclusively to the medium of video: *Impact Art Video Art 74*.[45] Both exhibitions brought together Swiss and international audiences, and made clear the astonishing speed with which the independent Swiss scene had been internationalized— in just ten years. At the same time, *ACTION/FILM/VIDEO* also revealed a trench that had opened up between the representatives of the 1960s and those of the scene that had been forming in Lausanne: the film section included only René Bauermeister, Erwin Huppert, and Eva Lurati, who had already been shown in the programs of the "Zurich" scene and the Cinéma Marginal.[46] Galerie Impact initially employed the same cinematographic apparatus as their precursors, but at the same time their selection of filmmakers and works was clearly distinct.

The creation of a separate collection for video at the Kunsthaus Zürich in 1980, and a series of exhibitions in Lucerne, Bern, and Basel established this new genre of art in German-speaking Switzerland as well.[47] Video as a medium was spreading not only in the visual arts, but also becoming an important means of expression for those with political and documentary interests who saw themselves as part of a new countercultural youth movement. A reference to elitism and a concern for the urban neighborhood went hand in hand with an attitude of emancipation, self-empowerment, political agitation, and the search for autonomous forms. The most famous work in this context is the 100-minute tape *Züri brännt* (*Zurich is Burning*) by the Videoladen Zürich, which documented the youth riots in Zurich in the spring of 1980 from the perspective of a protagonist.

From the mid-1970s onward video groups began to form in many of the larger Swiss cities to show works in their communities, often inspired by corresponding initiatives in large European and American cities.[48] Beginning in the 1980s, video was increasingly shown at festivals as well.

Joint participation in film festivals, and campaigns for the recognition of 8mm, 16mm, and video formats by those offering subsidies created the basis for a short-lived cooperation between video makers and independent filmmakers, one example of which was the formation of the Verein für das unabhängige Filmschaffen (VuF; Association for Independent Filmmaking) in 1977. The circles around VuF, which was officially founded in Basel on March 4, 1978, quickly evolved into a lively new scene of independent filmmakers and those interested in experimental film who struggled to gain recognition for small-format film and video. Another goal—one that had also been pursued by their precursors in the 1960s—was to create structures for the distribution and screening of independently produced films and videos. A working group within the VuF led by Pius Morger and Arc Trionfini (soon replaced by Ruedi Bind and Urs Berger) began publishing the *Filmfront* journal in the spring of 1978, and reported pragmatically on VuF's activities, past and future film screenings, and technical aspects of filmmaking, as well as publishing theoretical articles about independent filmmaking.[49] Soon this platform and its name became synonymous with the scene of young filmmakers forming in Basel.

The Filmfront scene in Basel in the 1970s was probably the most successful and certainly most diverse network linking experimental film and art. It produced Werner von Mutzenbecher, André Lehmann, and Urs Breitenstein, who saw themselves as part of an expanded field of art, and who were probably the most distinguished exponents of experimental filmmaking in Switzerland in the 1970s.[50]

When Filmfront came to an end in 1988, there were only a few filmmakers remaining in Switzerland whose work could still be categorized as experimental film. Hannes Schüpbach in Winterthur, who had studied with André Lehmann and Werner von Mutzenbecher in Basel, is clearly indebted to the experimental form. Véronique Goël in Geneva has combined documentary and experimental practice in her films since 1979, and as a result she has found a place both in the cinema and in the art worlds. Peter Liechti, who from 1984 established himself in cinema with experimental short films, remained faithful all his life to the stance of the experimental filmmaker, even in his documentary films, especially in the way he approached archival materials he had filmed himself.[51] In the mid-1980s, however, careers began to develop in the art world based on the medium of video, most famously that of Pipilotti Rist.

Another expression of the acceptance of experimental film in the art world was the founding of festivals dedicated to experimental and art film and video. In 1980, the Krienser Filmtage was founded in a town near Lucerne: a festival dedicated to independently produced, political, and increasingly experimental and artistic film. In 1985 the festival moved to Lucerne, having changed its name the year before to Film Video Performance Tage Kriens. The festival evolved as a result of a drive to professionalize in the late 1980s, which pushed it further in the direction of an academically inclined approach to experimental film, making it one of the central hubs in the European network of the cinematic avant-garde for around a decade.

Also in 1980, gallerist Rinaldo Bianda founded the VideoArt Festival in Locarno.[52] Unlike the Krienser Filmtage, which saw itself as part of the Swiss film and art scene, the VideoArt Festival primarily saw itself as international, inviting an impressive number of renowned video artists such as Nam June Paik, Robert Cahen, and Gianni Toti. In 2001, four years before the VIPER festival came to an end, the VideoArt Festival took place for the last time. VIPER had moved from Lucerne to Basel in 1999.

The focus of video art in the 1980s resulted in the founding of other festivals, some of which were even shorter-lived. From 1984 to 1988 the Biennale Videowochen im Wenkenpark was held three times in Basel, and it included video performances. In Geneva the Semaine Internationale de Vidéo was another video biennial that started in 1985 and continued until 2008 after changing its name to the Biennale de l'image en movement; after a long interruption, it was revived in 2014 and continues today.

The medium of video managed to achieve what had been denied film a decade earlier: as a simple, handy medium, it offered an image of lesser quality, but before the arrival of affordable video projectors, its visible technology represented a clear break with the practice of cinema, which carefully conceals its projection and production apparatus in black boxes. With video, technology was always present, and in the form of television sets it claimed physical space, making video art predestined for the museum space.[53] From the 1990s onward the medium was so well established in the art context that the original distinction between cinematic practices gave way to the increasing adoption of cinematic conventions by "artists' cinema," blurring the boundaries more and more between respective practices in the cinema and in the art context.[54] It was, however, not just that the approaches of filmmakers on the art scene moved in the direction of cinematic conventions; the works of experimental filmmakers also began to orient themselves around the apparatuses of the art space, as is revealed, for example, by the work of Basel filmmakers André Lehmann and Urs Breitenstein. The distinction between the two practices no longer seems relevant today.

Participation and Recognition: Between Subculture and Institutionalization

Independent and experimental film and video was torn between individual realization and public and institutional recognition, not only in Switzerland. Despite the sometimes aggressively represented "underground" existence, and demarcation from everything "established," most clearly seen in Switzerland in HHK Schoenherr's stance, many experimental filmmakers hoped for a response and recognition from outside their inner circle, either from the press, from festivals and museums, from education, or from other institutions.

At least in the second half of the 1960s, and hence during the birth of New Swiss Film, filmmakers working experimentally were not always marginalized, but rather sometimes appeared in places central to contemporaneous art making. That is demonstrated, for example, by the participation of filmmakers such as Murer and Guido Haas in *Expo 64* in Lausanne. Haas not only produced a large mural (2.4 × 14.08 m) for "La Voie Suisse / La nature et l'homme" (*The Swiss Way/Nature and Man*) using stills from *Inclinations* (1962–1966, made with his wife, Eva Haas), but was also assigned the exhibition scenography for that section.[55] Murer, too, who had attended the photography class at the Kunstgewerbeschule in Zurich, was responsible for the conception and realization of the large slide projections in the *L'École et l'éducation* pavilion of the Swiss exhibition. Siber collaborated with dance choreographer Jean Deroc on *Fahrt durch die Nacht* (*Journey through the Night*), which was invited to be the Swiss submission at the World's Fair in Osaka, Japan, in 1970. Despite the debacle he experienced with the film *Die Fabrikanten* in 1973, Clemens Klopfenstein received an art scholarship in the form of a sojourn at the Instituto Svizzero in Rome, where he gradually moved away from painting and returned to cinematic work. In Basel, Werner von Mutzenbecher was appointed acting curator at the Kunsthalle Basel in 1977, and from 1973 he taught at the Kunstgewerbeschule Basel, where from 1987 to 2000 he headed the Fachklasse für freies bildnerisches Gestalten (Course for Free Painterly Design). The Pro Helvetia cultural funding institution made independent-to-marginal filmmaking the focus of its film education efforts especially in the late 1970s and the 1980s with programs such as *Espaces* and *Cinéma en marge* (1977–1980), which enabled Schoenherr to make an extensive tour of the cinemas of London, Amsterdam, Hamburg, Berlin, Cologne, Mannheim, and Berlin in 1972, where he presented a program he had compiled of decidedly experimental films by Swiss filmmakers.[56]

In the central areas of Swiss filmmaking, the subsidies for quality awarded by the Eidgenössisches Departement des Innern (Federal Department of Home Affairs), and the Scotoni-Prize, which was funded privately and awarded by the cultural authorities of the City of Zurich, became yardsticks for the recognition of filmmakers' work. For example, at the suggestion of Alex Bänninger, who was working as a film journalist at the time, Murer submitted his film *Chicorée* as a candidate for the subsidies for quality in 1966 to test how liberal the federal government's funding program was. He received a subsidy only after challenging its rejection.[57] Such subsidies for emphatically experimental forms remained rare, with the exception of the phase of relatively generous subsidies in the late 1960s and early 1970s.[58]

Schoenherr was already thinking internationally at this time. In July 1972 he made an effort to get his film

Das kaputte Kino (*Broken Cinema*) rated "especially valuable" by the Filmbewertungstelle Wiesbaden (Wiesbaden Film Evaluation Office), and he put up with considerable bureaucracy to do so. This evaluation committee classified the work as a "cultural film" and as "valuable," and proposed it for a subsidy from the Federal Minister of Home Affairs "for the production of short films and full-length films without plot."[59] The background for this request was a short film planned as a coproduction by Schoenherr with Film Deutschland and Nemo Film Schweiz. Schoenherr presumably submitted his film to the Filmbewertungsstelle Wiesbaden in order to be able to apply to the Federal Minister of Home Affairs for funding, despite the fact that his official place of residence was in Switzerland. The tone of the cover letter suggests that his motivation went beyond the material, to include a search for recognition: "To judge from our telephone conversation, knowledge of my film work has not yet made it to Wiesbaden."[60]

Looking back at the history of experimental film in Switzerland, the cinematic practices that are still considered the cornerstone of the avant-garde show, in the brief period from the mid-1960s to early 1970s, the initial signs of a "minor" cinema,[61] which produced exponents of experimental works who, though they have always remained on the margins of writing on the history of film, have never been forgotten entirely, and were directly present in various places and times as central figures of a different kind of historical writing. This is probably most clearly the case with Dieter Meier, whose music videos for the pop band Yello contributed crucially to the group's popularity in the early phase of the MTV music cable channel. The videos can scarcely be categorized without reference to his earlier experimental works and video art. When he was "rediscovered" in several solo exhibitions in museums from 2011 to 2013, all these videos were accepted as part of the corpus of his work. Another example of the presence of experimental practice in a (more) mainstream field is Peter Liechti, whose roots lay in small experimental works. Liechti used shots that had often originally been made as a kind of diary as found footage in many of his later documentary films, which he often also accompanied with experimental music.

The approach of an experimental filmmaker was the basis for many of his later films, and was particularly clearly manifested in his 80-minute film *The Sound of Insects* (2009), for which he won the European Documentary Film Award.

Terms such as "experimental," "underground," "avant-garde," and "progressive" are largely just historical today. The practices they describe continue to exist in the works of Hannes Schüpbach and Robert Beavers, for example, but they do not receive much attention in cinemas. Experimental film in Switzerland today is cultivated more in the visual arts, whose institutions are showing a more lasting concern for its legacy, and are creating an audience for it.

[1] René Bauermeister, "Un cinéma inscrit dans la mouvance d'un courant international," François Bovier et al. (eds.), *Film Implosion! Experimental Cinema in Switzerland*, exh. cat., FriArt/Revolver, Fribourg/Berlin 2017, p. 9.
[2] Branden W. Joseph, *Beyond the Dream Syndicate: Tony Conrad and the Arts after Cage*, Zone, New York 2008, p. 50.
[3] Erika Hebeisen, Elisabeth Joris, Angela Zimmermann, *Zürich 68: Kollektive Aufbrüche ins Ungewisse*, Hier + Jetzt, Baden 2008. Fritz Billeter, Peter Killer, *1968 Zürich steht Kopf: Rebellion, Verweigerung, Utopie*, Scheidegger & Spiess, Zurich 2008. Irene Schubiger (ed.), *Schweizer Videokunst der 1970er und 1980er Jahre: Eine Rekonstruktion/Reconstructing Swiss Video Art from the 1970s and 1980s*, JRP|Ringier, Zurich 2009. Sabine Gebhard-Fink, Muda Mathis, Margarit von Büren (eds.), *Floating Gaps: Performance Chronik Basel, 1968–1986*, Diaphanes, Zurich 2011.
[4] Urs Breitenstein, Basel, October 5, 2012; Jacques Dutoit, Biel, September 2, 2013; Guido Haas, Kaltacker, April 17, 2013; Karlheinz Hein (telephone), May 23, 2012; Clemens Klopfenstein, Bevagna, June 8, 2012; Beat Kuert (telephone) April 12, 2013; André Lehmann, Basel, March 13, 2013; Dieter Meier, Zurich, June 19 and July 7, 2011; Fredi M. Murer, Zurich, December 19, 2012; Reto Andrea Savoldelli, Zurich, November 14, 2012; HHK Schoenherr, Zurich, March 28, 2012; Sebastian Schroeder, Kilchberg, November 14, 2011; Hans Jakob Siber, Aathal, May 10 and July 13, 2011; Tjerk Wicky, Lausanne, March 27, 2012; Bernhard Uhlmann and Giorgio Frapolli, Zurich, June 6, 2012; Peter von Gunten, Bern, July 5, 2013; Werner von Mutzenbecher, Basel, March 13, 2013; Jaques Dutoit, Biel, September 3, 2013; Charles Moser, Lucerne, February 5, 2016; Cecilia Hausheer, Zurich, December 8, 2015; Valerian Maly, Bern, March 18, 2016.
[5] Michèle Lagny, "'… man kann keine Filmgeschichte ohne Filme betreiben!' Ein Gespräch mit Michèle Lagny," *Montage AV* 5, no. 1 (1996), p. 5–22.
[6] A.S., "Die Avantgarde von gestern: Eindrücke vom Basler 'Festival des Films von Morgen,'" *Basler Woche*, November 8, 1954.
[7] See the chapter by Thilo König in this volume.
[8] Amateur filmmakers such as Hans Heinrich Heer and also professional filmmakers such as Erwin Huppert, Yves Yersin, and Claude Champion were commissioned by this Society to make films about traditional crafts and manufacturing methods. On this, see Thomas Schärer, "Dokumentarfilmpraxen der Schweizerischen Gesellschaft für Volkskunde," Edmund Ballhaus (ed.), *Dokumentarfilm: Schulen, Projekte, Konzepte*, Reimer, Berlin 2013, p. 265–279.
[9] Pierre Bourdieu, *The Rules of Art: The Genesis and Structure of the Literary Field*, trans. Susan Emanuel, Stanford University Press, Stanford, California 1996.
[10] See the chapter by Ute Holl in this volume.
[11] See the chapter by Renate Buschmann in this volume.
[12] Fredi M. Murer worked for the exhibition as a photographer; Georg Radanowicz made his first film, *Elemente des Films* (1960), for this exhibition.
[13] See the chapter by Michael Hiltbrunner in this volume.
[14] Thomas Schärer, *"Wir wollten den Film neu erfinden": Die Filmarbeitskurse an der Kunstgewerbeschule Zürich, 1967–1969*, book and DVD, Limmat, Zurich 2005.
[15] Hans-Jakob Siber, for example, received a roll of film that had been improperly exposed and was completely black from the laboratory, and therefore began to work the emulsion side with knives and pins. It became the first version of his film *Jalousie* in 1967.
[16] See HHK Schoenherr, "Europe," *Filmmaker's Newsletter*, vol. 1, no. 12 (1968), p. 10–11; and Theophil Dänzer, "Ein Forum für den jungen Schweizer Film," *Zürichseezeitung*, April 6, 1967.
[17] On the situation in Zurich in the 1960s, see the chapter by Thomas Schärer in this volume.
[18] Marthe Porret, "Pour un jeune cinéma romand: Maison de production et territoire: Freddy Landry et Milos Films, 1968–1972," *Revue historique vaudoise* (115–2007), p. 127–141. Marthe Porret, "Diffuser le jeune cinéma romand partout! Marcel Leiser et Cinéma Marginal Distribution (1968–1974)," Alain Boillat, Philipp Brunner, & Barbara Flückiger (eds.), *Kino CH / Cinéma CH: Rezeption, Ästhetik, Geschichte*, Schüren, Marburg 2008, p. 221–231.
[19] Marcel Leiser et Cinéma Marginal: Un début d'expérience en Suisse romande," *Travelling* (December 1968–January 1969), p. 13–16, esp. p. 14 ; and Marcel Leiser, "Cinéma Marginal est mort, vive le cinéma," *Travelling*, no. 40 (January–February 1974), p. 5–7.
[20] David E. James, *Allegories of Cinema: American Film in the Sixties*, Princeton University Press, Princeton 1989, p. ix.
[21] Jonas Mekas, *Movie Journal: The Rise of the New American Cinema, 1959–71*, Columbia University Press, New York 2011, p. 84.
[22] On Schoenherr's films, see the chapter by François Bovier in this volume.
[23] HHK Schoenherr, "Filmmaker Schoenherr über sein isoliertes Filmmakerdasein," *Supervisuell*, no. 1, 1968, unpaginated. The complete series of *Supervisuell* can be accessed at blog.zhdk.ch/sfex.
[24] See the statement on the awarding of the prize by its founders Eric and Attila Scotoni in the *Neue Zürcher Zeitung* of November 7, 1968.
[25] See the chapter by Ian Wooldridge in this volume.
[26] "Stephan said, 'That is a niche. Swiss film needs you. You have to be in it.' And when he was no longer part of it, things changed quickly." Werner von Mutzenbecher, interviewed by Thomas Schärer and Fred Truniger, Basel, March 13, 2013. Guido Haas: "Then he [Stephan Portmann] said, 'Why haven't you already registered it for Solothurn?' And I said, 'It's an amateur, a child.' And he said, 'That doesn't matter, it's interesting.' I should send it. Then we sent it. And it ran there. And then, of course, Gorgon was immediately in the newspapers. He was the youngest Swiss filmmaker. And after that he was invited to Oberhausen." Guido Haas, interviewed by Thomas Schärer and Fred Truniger, Kaltacker, April 17, 2013.
[27] "Several years later Peter Bichsel wrote an article in *Die Weltwoche*: 'Abschied von den Waldläufern' [Farewell to the Forest Walkers] […] "AKS was a proper Gruppe. Reto Savoldelli, the miracle kid from Solothurn […] If it had not been for the Solothurner Filmtage, he would never have made a film." Alexander J. Seiler, interviewed by Thomas Schärer, September 4, 2007. "The main character, Hans Suter, was working on a head that was Giacometti-like, and then a young woman ran through the forest in slow motion, I assume. We were probably all doing the same shots." Robert Boner, interviewed by Thomas Schärer [Zurich], May 14, 2009.
[28] On the situation in Zurich in the 1960s, see the chapter by Thomas Schärer in this volume.
[29] H. F. (Hanns Fuchs?), "Die Schweizer fehlen beim Luzerner Film-In: Sonderveranstaltung 'Sélection Suisse' fällt ins Wasser," *Tages-Anzeiger*, June 7, 1969. Hanns Fuchs, "In Frage gestellt: Luzerner Film-In in der Krise," *NZ*, March 12, 1972, p. viii.
[30] J. C. Ammann, E. Steinberger, M. Boucard, Preface in *Dokumente und Manifeste zu den im Kunsthaus und Kleintheater gezeigten Filmen*, programs from *Film-In* (Lucerne 1970), p. 1.
[31] See, for example, the participation of Dieter Meier and Balthasar Burkhard in the *Visualisierte Denkprozesse* exhibition at the Kunstmuseum Luzern in 1970.

[32] See "fsch," "Ein gestraffteres, aber weniger profiliertes Programm: Notizen zum vierten Luzerner Film-In," *NZZ*, June 17, 1972, p. 25.
[33] Film-In Luzern chairman's communiqué to the representatives of the Schweizer Massenmedien (Swiss Mass Media) and the different Vertreter der Filmwirtschaft (Swiss Film Economies).
[34] An extensive catalogue was published for this "exhibition." Annette Michelson (ed.), *New Forms in Film*, Corbaz, Montreux 1974.
[35] See the chapter by Adeena Mey in this volume.
[36] A lengthy article on the festival appeared in *Le Monde* in Paris: Louis Marcorelles, "Une 'exposition' du septième art," *Le Monde*, August 27, 1974, 1 and 13. In the *NZZ* on August 3, 1974, Martin Schlappner (ms) had a brief report on the imminent opening of the festival, which, as he noted with regret, was taking place at the same time as the festival in Locarno. Martin Schlappner, "Musste das sein?" *NZZ*, August 3, 1974.
[37] Anonymous, "Knokke: Preschendes Bild," *Der Spiegel*, (August 2, 1968), p. 82–83. See also Xavier Garcia-Bardon (ed.), "EXPRMNTL: Festival hors-normes, Knokke 1963 1967 1974," *Revue belge du cinéma*, no. 43 (December 2002), p. 36.
[38] See the essay by Thomas Schärer and Fred Truniger in this volume.
[39] Marcel Leiser, "Cinéma Marginal est mort, vive le cinema," *Travelling*, vol. 40 (January–February 1974), p. 5–7.
[40] The material for the film had largely been shot by 1969 when Meier showed the film in an earlier cut under the title *100,800 Units*.
[41] In *NZZ*, June 17, 1972 (see note 32).
[42] See François Bovier, "P.A.P. [Progressive Art Production]: Eine 'Filmgalerie' für 'politische und pornografische' Filme," in *Film Implosion* (see note 1), p. 21–33.
[43] See René Berger, "L'Art vidéo: Défis et paradoxes," *Impact Art Vidéo – 8 jours de vidéo*, Galerie Impact and Musée des Arts décoratifs, Lausanne 1974, p. 7.
[44] The exhibition was accompanied by the catalogue *ACTION/FILM/VIDEO*, exh. cat., Galerie Impact, Lausanne 1972. In it, the medium in question for the works shown was indicated as "Video Tapes" (AKAI ¼" and SONY ½"), and "Films 8mm," "Films Super 8mm," and "Films 16mm."
[45] See the chapter by Geneviève Loup in this volume.
[46] On René Bauermeister's work, see the chapter by Jean-Michel Baconnier in this volume.
[47] For a brief history of the medium of video in Switzerland, see the chapter by Gabriel Flückiger, Siri Peyer, and Fred Truniger in this volume.
[48] Heinz Nigg, *Rebel Video: The Video Movement of the 1970s and 1980s; London, Basel, Bern, Lausanne, Zurich*, Scheidegger & Spiess, Zurich 2017.
[49] Thirty-four issues were published continuously until 1988. They are all accessible at blog.zhdk.ch/sfex.
[50] On the Filmfront circle, see the chapter by Ute Holl in this volume.
[51] On Peter Liechti, see the chapter by Marcy Goldberg in this volume.
[52] Vittorio Fagone (ed.), *L'Art vidéo, 1980–1999: Vingt ans du VideoArt Festival, Locarno; Recherches, théories, perspectives*, Edizioni Gabriele Mazzotta, Milan 1999.
[53] Beginning in the 1970s, films were also presented as installations in museums, as infinite loops, for example, but the video format gained acceptance. See Franziska Stöhr, *Endlos: Zur Geschichte des Films- und Videoloops im Zusammenspiel von Technik, Kunst und Ausstellung*, Transcript, Bielefeld 2016, p. 94–101.
[54] Erika Balsom, *Exhibiting Art in Contemporary Cinema*, Amsterdam University Press, Amsterdam 2013, p. 12.
[55] Guido Haas, interviewed by Thomas Schärer and Fred Truniger, Kaltacker, April 17, 2013; and *Manifest X: Guido Haas*, serielle manifeste 66, Édition Galerie Press, St. Gallen 1966.
[56] "Cinéma en marge, zum ersten Mal durchgeführt 1977 im Rahmen von Pro Helvetia organisierten 'Espaces' in Paris und wiederholt im Februar 1978. Versuch: Präsentation von 16mm- und Super 8-Filmen bei freier Beteiligung schweizerischer und französischer Filmautoren," anonymous, *Filmfront* (5–1979). Schoenherr's touring program of 1972 had the title "Movies Kaputt/Das kaputte Kino." See also the reprint of the program in Patrizia Landgraf & Hans Helmut Klaus Schoenherr (eds.), *bbk Schoenherr: das kaputte kino*, dossier film 4, Pro Helvetia, Zurich; Zytglogge, Gümligen 1986, p. 19; a French edition was also published.
[57] "The rejection used the words 'pure anarchy.' I had to look up what it meant. That made me bristle like mad. I met Alex Bänninger and said to him that my film had been rejected. As a young lawyer, he offered to write an appeal. But that was a year later for *Chicorée*. And then, thanks to his appeal, I did indeed get a subsidy for quality. I received 10,000 francs and made my next film with it. For me, of course, that was a fortune." Fredi M. Murer, interviewed by Thomas Schärer, Zurich, January 31, 2008.
[58] A list of subsidies for quality recognized several films with an experimental character. Unless otherwise indicated, the year in parenthesis is the year the award was granted: *Chicorée* (produced in 1966) by Fredi M. Murer; *Lydia* (1969) by Reto Andrea Savoldelli; *Mondo Karies* (1969) by Kurt Gloor; *Luigi Crippa* (1979) by Robert Schär; *Z.B. Uniformen* (1969) by Urs and Marlies Graf; *Sad-is-fiction* (1969) by Fredi M. Murer; *Warten auf…* (1969) by Beat Kuert; *Krawall* (1970) by Jürg Hassler; *22 Fragen an Max Bill* (1970) by Georg Radanowicz; *Kleiner Emmentalfilm* (1970) by Bernhard Luginbühl and Leonardo Bezzola; *Eine Linie ist eine Linie ist eine Linie* (1970) by Urs Graf; *Arise Like A Fire* (produced in 1972) by Hans-Jakob Siber; *Die Sage vom alten Hirten Xeudi* (produced in 1973) by Hans-Jakob Siber; *das schlesische Tor* (produced in 1980–82) by Clemens Klopfenstein; *Robert Walser* (produced in 1974–1978) by HHK Schoenherr.
[59] "The evaluation committee considers the idea noteworthy. The way the motif of destruction is realized cleverly with the medium of film, which looks at itself ironically, is, in the view of the evaluation committee, an unmistakable indication of the director's inventiveness. Nevertheless, the evaluation committee believes it has *longueurs* (especially at the end), with the effect that the invention more or less grows dull." Filmbewertungsstelle to HHK Schoenherr, August 25, 1972, Archiv Schoenherr.
[60] HHK Schoenherr to the Filmbewertungsstelle, July 24, 1972, Archiv Schoenherr.
[61] Joseph, *Beyond the Dream Syndicate* (see note 2).

Luzerner Filminformationstage flyer, Lucerne, 1970

EXPERIMENTAL FILM

HHK Schoenherr's "Broken Cinema"
François Bovier

MOVIES KAPUTT
DAS KAPUTTE KINO

MANNHEIM	MI	3-5-72	KINO ROYALE CINEMA QUADRAT	20h30
KOELN	FR	5-5-72	KINO CITY XSCREEN	22h30
AMSTERDAM	ZA	6-5-72	ELECTRIC CINEMA	21h00
AMSTERDAM	ZA	6-5-72	THE MOVIES HAARLEMMER DIJK	24h00
HAMBURG	DI	23-5-72	ABATON KINO	18h00 + 20h30
BERLIN	FR	26-5-72	ARSENAL	22h30
BERLIN	SA	27-5-72	ARSENAL	20h00
FRANKFURT	SA	3-6-72	T A T KOMMUNALES KINO	22h30
MUENCHEN	FR	9-6-72	ROTTMANN KINO UNDEPENDENT F.C.	22h30
MUENCHEN	SA	10-6-72	CINEMONDE CITTA 2000 UNDEP. F.C.	23h00
LONDON	SAT	17-6-72	LONDON FILM COOP CINEMA	8.00 pm
LONDON	WED	21-6-72	ELECTRIC CINEMA PORTOBELLO RD	7.00 + 9.00 pm
LONDON	THU	22-6-72	ELECTRIC CINEMA PORTOBELLO RD	7.00 + 9.00 pm
LONDON	FRI	23-6-72	NATIONAL FILM THEATRE	6.15 + 8.30 pm

NO 1/68 BY WERNER V. MUTZENBECHER & NO III/71A BY MUTZENBECHER
ARISE LIKE A FIRE BY HANS-JAKOB SIBER & MR. EICHORN'S GOLFBALL BY
SEBASTIAN C. SCHROEDER & STATUS SYMBOL BY SEBASTIAN C. SCHROEDER
METERMASS KAPUTT BY RAPHAELA SCHOENHERR & X - BILDER BY KURT KUEHN
POINT ZERO BY CHARLES-ANDRE VOSER & ELKOFASEIHELE BY WERNER OTT
PLAY 4 & 5 BY HHK SCHOENHERR & DAS KAPUTTE KINO BY HHK SCHOENHERR

Movies Kaputt film program, 1972

Hans Helmut Klaus (HHK) Schoenherr belonged to an international network of experimental filmmakers through his publishing activities (*Supervisuell*, more of which later) and his personal links with the German and Austrian avant-garde scene—primarily Birgit and Wilhelm Hein and Kurt Kren, to whom he dedicated the film portrait *Portrait: Kurt Kren* (1970). The aim of this essay is two-fold. I would like to contextualize the work of HHK Schoenherr as a programmer, publisher, and filmmaker within the broader perspective of international independent cinema, with Hamburg, Cologne, Vienna, and London as its main venues in Western Europe. To this we must add the *EXPRMNTL* film festival at Knokke-le-Zoute. I would also like to explore Schoenherr's work using isolated frames and film screening materials.

Schoenherr's films have much more in common with the formal

and performative film scene in Germany (i.e. *Das andere Kino* and Progressive Art Production) and with Gregory Markopoulos' film portraits of places and people than they do with other Swiss filmmakers.[1] Hence the distance between Schoenherr and Film Forum and Ciné Circus, a Zurich film cooperative directed in the mid-1960s by Hans-Jakob Siber and a film club screening movies in different cities (in particular Lucerne in 1967, Bern in 1968, and Basel in 1967, 1968, and 1970) respectively. In the first issue of *Supervisuell* (1968), HHK Schoenherr was quick to publish a letter of protest, arguing that no creative film had been produced in Switzerland through a cooperative structure of this nature:

> [Beat] Kuert + [Hans-Jakob] Siber want an organization, a big fat organization. The individual interests of the filmmaker aren't taken into account. The filmmaker must be at the service of the organization, not the other way around [...] Long live the organization, and Siber, its organizer; however, if this mindset doesn't change, no better films will be made at all.[2]

This belligerent stance explains why Schoenherr withdrew his films from the Film Forum catalogue. A year earlier, he had argued in a similar vein in *Filmmakers' Newsletter*:

> The oldest [European] cooperative is the one in Switzerland, but they have no good films at all; and usually pay nothing to the filmmaker.[3]

Indeed, the goals of a production cooperative such as Cinéma Marginal,[4] the equivalent of Film Forum in French-speaking Switzerland, were diametrically opposed to Schoenherr's approach. Schoenherr was more interested in giving visibility to the experimental film movement throughout Europe than in shaping tools for the production of essay films on a national scale or becoming an "auteur" filmmaker. His intentions can best be grasped in his article on European independent cinema published in *Filmmakers' Newsletter* in 1968, where he claimed that what was really needed was a "real" European film cooperative.[5] Internationalism such as this was at the core of his publishing and programming activities. He presented *Supervisuell*, which he edited from 1968 to 1970, as "the only exclusive magazine for independent films produced with international cooperation"[6]; and in 1972 he toured his film program *Movies Kaputt* to different European cities.[7]

Notwithstanding the fact that Schoenherr worked outside Film Forum and Ciné Circus, his films have clearly become landmarks in Swiss experimental cinema. His work garnered a local reputation, as attested by the publication of a monograph on his films in 1986 by Pro Helvetia—The Swiss Arts Council,[8] and was praised abroad, as can be seen from a film retrospective of his work at Anthology Film Archives in 1991.[9] Experimentation with the formal features of film materials and the unfolding of an open structure do not, in themselves, constitute a first step toward a more professional cinema—as in the films of Clemens Klopfenstein[10] and Fredi M. Murer.[11] From 1964, when he arrived in Zurich with a film project about writer Robert Walser, which was eventually completed in 1978, up to the early 1990s Schoenherr systematically investigated the materiality of the moving image, but eschewed a medium-specific dogma.[12] He saw his films in terms of a succession of isolated frames generating flickering effects, and projected them through performative devices, inviting the audience, for instance, to use microphones during the screening of *Daydream* (1969) in Zurich and later in Hamburg in 1970.[13] In any case, he was deeply attracted to the mechanical rhythm of the handheld camera and the ways in which its footage could be printed. In *Das kaputte Kino* (*Broken Cinema*) (1971), for instance, he printed the footage directly inside an old Debrie 35mm camera, a process that allowed him to play with contrasts and under- and over-exposure, and invert positive and negative pictures. More generally, he saw the camera as an artisan's tool with the mechanical precision of a clock, and used the reverse function to superimpose different layers of pictures while shooting 16mm footage. His *Plays* (1968–1990) series, to take another example, used predetermined montage diagrams.

Schoenherr promoted his own work through the notion of "broken cinema" ("kaputtes Kino"). His films are deconstructive, and seek to use the camera and, later, the projector, to isolate the discontinuous movement of single frames. This brings his work close to experiments with isolated frames conducted at that time in Germany, where he was born,[14] and in the United States, as can be seen in Gregory Markopoulos' impressive body of film portraits.[15] Markopoulos was working in Switzerland with Robert Beavers at that time. First, however, I would like to turn to Schoenherr's activities as an editor and programmer.

From *Supervisuell*, a Minor Magazine, to *Movies Kaputt*, a Touring Program

Schoenherr's involvement in the organization of the first European Meeting of Independent Filmmakers [*Europäisches Treffen unabhängiger Filmemacher*] in November 1968 in Munich (with Birgit and Whilhem Hein, Karlheinz Hein, and others)[16] is clear evidence of his desire to establish oppositional experimental filmmakers in the public sphere. Nevertheless, this meeting failed to lead to any practical independent international production organization, much as the first and second International Congresses of Independent Cinema held in La Sarraz in 1929 and in Brussels in 1930 had also failed in this respect.[17] In any case, for Schoenherr, the creation of a counter-public sphere depended more on the exhibition and discussion of experimental cinema than on the financing of films. His most visible public actions consisted of publishing a minor international magazine, *Supervisuell*, from 1968 to 1970, and touring the *Movies Kaputt* film program from May to June 1972.

The six issues of *Supervisuell* offer tangible evidence of an experimental network linking Switzerland to Germany, Austria, Italy, and indirectly the USA. Ernst Schmidt was its Vienna correspondent, with Birgit Hein for Germany, Alfredo Leonardi for Italy, and Robert Nelson and Jonas Mekas for the USA. The first pages of the first issue set Ciné Circus and Film Forum alongside the Hamburger Filmmacher Cooperative and the Hamburg Film Show (with Werner Nekes, Dore O., Hellmuth Costard, among others), the XSCREEN projection space in Cologne (founded and run mainly by Willem and Birgit Hein), the Austria Filmmakers' Cooperative (led by Kurt Kren, Ernst Schmidt, Peter Weibel, and Hans Scheugl), and a French magazine,

Approches (published by Julien Blaine and Jean-François Bory). There is also mention of the *EXPRMNTL* film festival in Knokke-le-Zoute in Belgium, and of screenings planned for documenta 4 to be held in Kassel. From the outset, *Supervisuell* was designed as a forum to promote a European network of independent film theaters and alternative projection spaces.[18]

The magazine published regular accounts of the situation of independent cinema in Austria, Germany, and Italy. *Supervisuell* heralded European filmic experimentation, which can be compared with the New American Cinema, notwithstanding Schoenherr's unrelenting, sporadic attacks on the underground. The magazine can best be described as a platform for the exchange of practical information about European and American independent filmmaker cooperatives. Jonas Mekas outlined the situation of American film cooperatives in the third issue, while Robert Nelson regularly reported on American independent film. Both Gregory Markopoulos[19] and Viennese activist Otto Muehl[20] featured as special guests, describing their film practices and latest projects. The magazine showcased articles that were not strictly informational. In a provocative spirit of the avant-garde, the fourth issue was overwritten throughout by an empty manifesto, with the words "Blah Blah" repeated endlessly (there is a table of contents, but no articles follow[21]). Among the most important contributions to *Supervisuell* are Schoenherr's film frame scripts.

In the third issue, for instance, Schoenherr published his diagrams for *Variationen ABC*.[22] He presented the principles behind this film in an almost "scientific," objective way through film frame scripts.[23] His diagram showed different series of figurative motifs, which were distributed along two axes: the number of frames and the levels of superposition. Films thus illustrated can literally be read by using these diagrams. The score respects the linear order of appearance of the shots (a is followed by b and optionally by c, or followed by ab or abc grouped into a superimposed shot); shot length is determined by a standard multiple of 3 or 4 frames (including 6, 8, 12, 16, 24, 32—up to 96); each cadenza forms a unit that enters into a relationship with another cadenza. Sequences of frames, rhymes, and echoes recur and are repeated between successive bars, reducing the fragmentation of the representation. The patterns themselves, in this case of a sexual nature, are elementary, organized through color codas and form: in the first stanza, under the color red, a child's head is associated with the eyes of a beautiful woman; under the color green, oranges are linked to the vulva of a beautiful woman; under the color blue, a doll is compared with the face of a beautiful woman; in the second stanza, a newspaper, a tree, binoculars, and Dracula are combined through the color red; through green, a tank, a penis, scissors, and a child's head; through blue, Stalin, beer, radio, and soup; etc. A third organizational factor is movement inside the frames. The desired effect is shock and a superposition of frames—the basic figurative motifs fuse together, or reverberate in unison. Isomorphy and contrast between forms (the circle set against erectile forms) facilitate this aesthetics of fusion, which is further enhanced by the use of inversion and reciprocity (the various motifs are twofold: the face of a child and the eyes of a woman; oranges and a vulva; a doll and the face of a woman). The symbolism is at once sexual (face and sexual organs of a woman, doll, penis) and warlike (scissors, camera, soldier, pen, Stalin, and later a battleship explicitly alluding to Eisenstein's *Potemkin*). The syncopated rhythm of the frames leads to generalized equivalence between forms, while maintaining harmony between the frames. We could argue that these diagrams represent a film skeleton or a matrix for a potential series of films, a set of axiomatic principles, as it were: that is, a theoretical approch to film, where jump cuts are both highlighted and neutralized (hence the discontinuous movement of the frames and general sense of harmony). These diagrams determine in advance the rhythmic structure and formal composition of the movie: the length of the frames and layers of superposition are strictly calculated. The model here is the musical score, but the material itself predominates—neither the concept or the overall structure prevail over a pattern arrangement. Not only is the creative act based on montage (as is the case with Peter Kubelka's metric films, more of which below), editing choices and figurative patterns are crucial. In any case, *Supervisuell* not only provided an information-exchange platform, but also a forum for the promotion of an ideal cinema linked to music and interval theory.

The *Movies Kaputt* touring program was similar in intent. Funded by Pro Helvetia (to the tune of CHF 12,000/~10,500 euros), it toured Switzerland[24] and held screenings in 12 regular movie theaters in Holland, Germany, and Great Britain,[25] over a period of seven weeks from May to June 1972. Schoenherr selected experimental short films from recent Swiss work, including his own, along with a film made by his young daughter Raphaela.[26] Schoenherr's curatorial principles were open and not systematic—he juxtaposed animation films (Hans-Jakob Siber, and, partly, Kurt Kühn), artists' films exploring public spaces (Werner von Mutzenbecher), Fluxus or conceptual-art-oriented films (Charles-André Voser and René Bauermeister), and collage work (Sebastian Schroeder). Yet his own films set the main direction of the program, as can be seen by the way he incorporated the title of his own film, *Das Kaputte Kino*, into the banner headline for the event, *Movies Kaputt. Das Kaputte Kino*. Schoenherr exported his own idea of cinema to the rest of Europe, with the financial support of an official Swiss institution. This selection was motivated by a desire to return to the materiality of the projection of discontinuous moving pictures, focusing on the craft quality of the work. *X-Bilder* (Kurt Kühn) is a good illustration of this, as it links together a reading of the pages of a book, flickering screen images, and the movement of zoetropes and other precinematographic tools. Schoenherr's films, *Play 4 and 5* (1969) and *Das Kaputte Kino* (1971), highlight the presence of isolated frames assembled into short sequences, and the jump-cut quality of the image. *Das Kaputte Kino* draws on the reversible nature of shooting and projecting moving pictures. Using an old Debrie 35mm camera, Schoenherr printed the copy directly into the camera (two prints were superimposed inside the camera, one exposed, and one blank).[27] When the 35mm print was projected, there was a speed-up effect, with many gaps and cuts—"broken cinema," precisely what this program sought to promote and demonstrate.

Schoenherr was, however, quite suspicious of the notion of "underground cinema," which he basically saw as a phenomenon of the American press.[28] He preferred to speak of "independent cinema" and "creative films":

> I call my films "creative films" [...] Creative films all have the same production features: the author, narrator, sound technician, and cameraman are all the same person [...] They have a second important feature—creative films reject the perfection that typifies the film industry.[29]

He was reluctant to offer any strict definitions, yet was apparently opposed to the widespread mediatization of underground cinema:

> How do you define "creative film"? I give up. I don't know. (I am writing this article to discover what a "creative film" actually is.) "Creative film" has nothing to do with the underground. *The underground is a woolly sign for exceptionally woolly things. The undeground is toast. The underground has had it* [...] How do you define "creative film"? I still don't know. "Creative film" has nothing to do with [the] "other cinema" (other sex). The other sex is impotent. The other sex has been castrated.[30]

Schoenherr also wanted to dissociate his own production from "Das andere Kino," the German equivalent of underground cinema:

> The press uses underground for these new kinds of films; in German-speaking countries, they are also called "the other cinema." From now on, only the terms "independent films" and "creative avant-garde" will be used.[31]

It can be argued that his intention was not to *go underground*, but to occupy the public sphere—even if his ideal audience had yet to be created. I would like to turn now to a brief topology of the use of the isolated frames, in light of critical debate on this subject, and try to further circumscribe Schoenherr's approach.

The Aesthetics of Isolated Frames

Photogrammatic montage can be distinguished from ultra-fast cutting characterized by a fluid and plastic montage that generates hypnagogic images and suspends the possibility of memory and anticipation (see, for instance, Annette Michelson on Stan Brakhage's hyperbolic montage[32]). On the contrary, photogrammatic montage exacerbates the discontinuity of the film-editing process as exemplified by flicker films and Muybridge and Marey's chronophotography—entirely in line with Bergson's critique of the cinematographical mechanism.[33] In any case, this seems to provide an account of and explanation for artistic work with isolated frames. However, this is too simple an account.

When critics, historians, or filmmakers think of photogrammatic montage, they see in it an implicit genealogy. The main accounts of this approach can be traced back to "metrical film" theory as propounded by Peter Kubelka in lectures in the 1970s,[34] in reference to the fugue as a musical model and to his own films shot in the late 1950s (*Adebar*, 1957; *Schwechater*, 1958; and *Arnulf Rainer*, 1960). From Kubelka's point of view, the shot in itself hardly matters—the creative process relies exlusively on the way in which individual frames are edited, following montage "scores." This founding myth is directly connected to "structural film" as described by P. Adams Sitney in 1969,[35] a Minimalist cinema that explores two opposing devices, the aesthetics of the long shot and the flickering of isolated frames. The aim here is to create objective, impersonal structures that seek to reduce the work to its basic components (not without a degree of theatricality).

No sooner was this history written, than opposing voices were heard. In Great Britain, Peter Gidal proposed, through "Structural/Materialist film," a more Marxist-oriented practice, in a break with the phenomenological model that still underpinned Minimalism.[36] An alternative history, stretching back to George Maciunas in 1969,[37] contrasted the Fluxus approach with Sitney's modernist-oriented account (Maciunas linked Paul Sharits' and Tony Conrad's flicker films to Andy Warhol's and Yoko Ono's long mechanized shots). Here, the frames are seen as aggressive, and generate a shock effect. The theatricality of the projected images in the flicker films by Paul Sharits (particularly in *Ray Gun Virus*, 1966) and Tony Conrad (*The Flicker*, 1966), prevents the viewer from becoming absorbed into the scene.

The projector beam acquires a sculptural quality (as can be seen in Anthony McCall's *Line Describing a Cone*, 1973, a further example inspired by Minimal art).

There is a European version of this history, which links metrical films with the 1960s–1970s German formal scene (*Das andere Kino*, principally led by Werner Nekes) and later with 1980s–1990s Austrian independent cinema (mainly Martin Arnold and Peter Tscherkassky). This configuration focuses not so much on structures or forms, antiforms, and conceptual gestures, as on interaction with the spectator; the most striking defining feature of the German scene, or, at least, of Werner Nekes' theory and practice, from a Structural/Materialist point of view, was its subjective use of isolated frames to generate mental images. This overview could be further complicated, if we add a forgotten history. Gil J. Wolman's *L'Anticoncept*, in 1951, alternated black-and-white frames on an expanded screen to generate the physiological effect of shock through flickering images.[38] We could even go back to Charles Dekeukeleire's work in the early 1930s: in *Impatience* (1928), for instance, he uses four series of isolated frames, and fast rhythms (woman, engine, motorcycle, landscape in movement, figurative patterns that evoke the fusion of the woman and the engine). Schoenherr is part of this tradition, particularly in terms of the musical construction of the montage. This explains the central role played by film frame scripts which can be read independently of the completed film (if it is ever completed—indeed the protocol statement is potentially self-sufficient). It is not so much the materiality of the frames that is highlighted, as in Peter Kubelka's metric films that have been exhibited literally as scores, but the readibilty of the rhythm of the projected film (showing a potential affinity with conceptual art).

The common feature that links these (Metrical, Structural or Materialist, Anti-Art, traumatic, or afterimage) accounts can be found in the absolutizing of the montage. It can be argued that the instantaneous movement of the isolated frames contrasts with the continuous movement of the shot. In this sense, it could be seen as a positive return to Henri Bergson's critique of the cinematograph, in *Creative Evolution*.[39] Werner Nekes illustrates precisely this point with irony in *Jüm-Jüm* (1967): here, the brief sequences

of four frames randomly extracted from a continuous shot
go against the grain of the natural movement of the woman
on the swing (again a sexual metaphor). In another sense,
instantaneous isolated frames can be related to the dense
texture of superimposed images, as is the case with
Markopoulos' film portraits, Schoenherr, and even Nekes'
later films (*T-WO-MEN*, 1972, for instance). Essentially,
the opposition between fixed and animated images can be
positioned differently if we add a distinction between single
and multiple images on a single frame.

Schoenherr's "Broken Cinema," or Superimposed Frames Seen Through the Musical Prism of the Cluster

I would argue that Schoenherr's "broken cinema," an
exemplary case of "minor history" set against the backdrop
of experimental cinema at an international level, features
two principal components: brief sequences of isolated frames
which conflict with the stillness of relatively stable shots,
and even the blank or black leader; and single frames, which
contrast with multiple layers of images in a sequence of
frames or longer shots. The musical model of the "cluster"
can be used here: superimposed frames generate a dissonant
chord, which interacts with the rhythm of the sequence
of frames. Two levels are relevant: the ryhthm of the isolated
or amalgamated frames over a brief period of time; and the
cluster of images that still reverberates after it has occurred.
"Kine," as propounded by Nekes,[40] and "overtonality"
as proposed by Paul Sharits,[41] are both theories centered
around the same basic idea, even if the intentions of filmmakers differ. The cluster of frames generates new textures,
colors, and sonorities, which cannot be reduced to a
combination of single frames or layers of frames in itself
(this has potential shades of Eisenstein's theory of "overtonal
montage"[42]). Schoenherr himself provided no precise
definition of this phenomenon, but suggested an analogy
when he mentioned as a model the drama-oratorios with
spoken chorus composed by Wladimir Vogel[43]: as he says,
Vogel showed him a new way to "rhythmically organize the
play of images." More precisely, a dodecaphonic, rather than
diatonic, composition model offered a means of generating
the effect of blending isolated frames, following the principle

of the cluster. In the case of Schoenherr, this homologous structure of superimposed frames and clusters was most probably influenced by Markopoulos' film portraits and theoretical essays.

As previously noted, the projection of Markopoulos' *Through A Lens Brightly: Mark Turbyfill* in Zurich in the autumn of 1967 was a major event and proved a revelation to Schoenherr. In this portrait, Markopoulos uses in-camera photogrammatic montage, superimposing different layers of images. Dancer and poet Mark Turbyfill describes the precise effect of this film portrait, quoting from the chapter entitled "The Cinematographical Mechanism of Thought and the Mechanistic Illusion" in Henri Bergson's *Creative Evolution*:

> Whether we would think becoming, or express it, or even perceive it, we hardly do anything else than set going a kind of cinematograph inside us [...] There is, between our body and other bodies, an arrangement like that of pieces of glass that compose a kaleidoscope picture. Our activity goes from an arrangement to a rearrangement, each time no doubt giving the kaleidoscope a new shake, but not interesting itself in the shake, and seeing only the new picture.[44]

Turbyfill constructively reactivates the Bergsonian critique of the reproduction of movement in his understanding of the kaleidoscopic structure of the film portrait: "It was as if a jigsaw puzzle had fallen into a well-proportioned pattern." Bergson's "kaleidoscope picture" or Turbyfill's "jigsaw puzzle" refer to the isolated frames and multiple layers of superposition that generate a discontinuous movement, and evoke a rigid decomposition of the moving figure through grids. The viewing of the film inverts this feeling, generating an impression of fluidity and absorption. This is what is intended to happen with the transition from Schoenherr's film frame scripts to the actual films themselves—a subjective image emerges in contradistinction to the mathematically measured structure of the grid.

In a widely published manifesto Markopoulos summed up a similar idea. He wrote,

I propose a new narrative film form through [...]
the use of short film phrases which evoke thought–
images. Each film phrase is composed of certain
selected frames that are similar to the harmonic units
found in musical composition. The film phrases
establish ulterior relationships among themselves [...]
in my abstract system there is a complex of differing
frames being repeated.[45]

The letter that Schoenherr wrote to Markopoulos to explain his own montage scores indicates that they are closer in spirit.[46] Schoenherr isolates different parameters: rhythmic (the number of frames: 6 or 12), graphic (direction of movement and contrast between objects), and symbolic (the dramaturgy of the photography). Nevertheless, it cannot be denied that the filmic universes of Schoenherr and Markopoulos are at odds: Markopoulos opts for the neo-classical, directing his actors in Romantic landscapes; Schoenherr is more interested in a new form of self-portraiture, depicting even his own family. It can be argued that Dieter Meier's fictional wandering in the late 1960s, as in *100,800 Units* (1969, with Herbert Lachmayer), has more than one feature in common with Schoenherr's films. Home movies seem to provide a reference point, and frame scores would appear to have been used to structure these family portraits dynamically; they could legitimately be called "structural home movies."

Schoenherr designed prototypes of montage diagrams, frequently using the same grid for different films, as is the case with the score published in an article for *Tages–Anzeiger Magazin*, in December 1971.[47] The first shot of *Das nervöse Kino* (1974) cites this score verbatim, giving user instructions to the audience. Schoenherr further employs this magazine page both as a formal motif and a self-referential sign in the film. This self-potrait alternates between basic motifs, framing details of objects and his hands (a to f) in close up; the final motif is a medium shot of Schoenherr at his table (g). The rhythm of the amalgamated frames alternates from relatively slow to very fast, with a common denominator of eight frames used as a structuring device. *Das nervöse Kino* plays with these basic contrasts—the brief appearance of a shape out of black

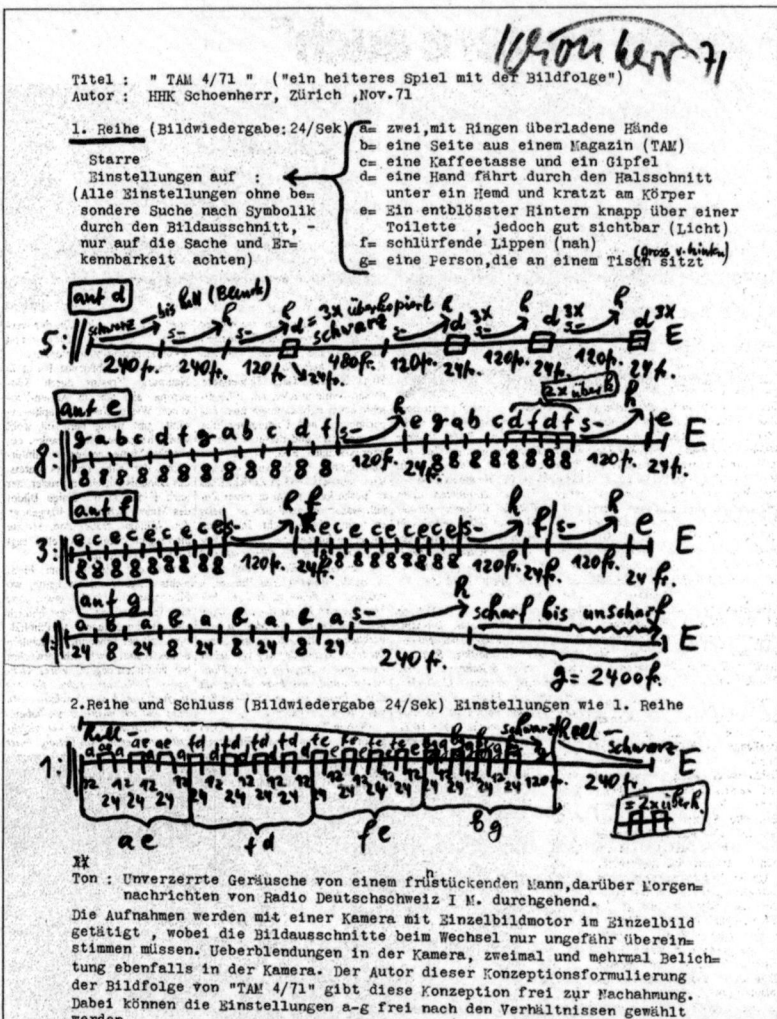

HHK Schoenherr's montage diagram published in *Tages-Anzeiger Magazin*, Zurich, December 1971

or white background; the immobility of the image/
movement through photogrammatic montage or the superposition of layers of frames. The objectivity of the film
frame script contrasts with the subjective mood or nightmare-
like state of an early-morning breakfast that it expresses,
which can be irritating. Nervous editing uses filmic devices
to convey a physical sensation of unease (indeed the author
is repeatedly seen to scratch his chest) and self-destructive
behavior. Here, although the script is predetermined, it
can be updated with different patterns which take it in one
direction or another.

Essentially, I would like to argue that many of Schoenherr's
films cannot be classified as processual cinema, guided
by preconceived rules and subject to formal constraints.
In some cases, the subject of the film is actually suited to
its structure. In other words, the subjects in his "formula"
films could arguably be designed for a preconceived grid.
Schoenherr, for instance, in the aforementioned series
Play, reused footage that he had previously discarded. In
Das Portrait der Cordua (1969), to take the most obvious
example, the rhythm of the score cannot be distinguished
from actual movements inside the frame or between shots.
With two Bolex cameras and only four reels of film,[48]
Schoenherr composed a portrait of dancer Beatrice Cordua
during her training sessions, both alone and with other
dancers, and at home, with her husband Peter Schoenherr,
during their daily lives. Cordua's precisely framed gestures,
the movements of the camera following the dancer's
training, or making its way through her apartment, and
scrutinizing her sometimes naked body, along with the
energy of the frames, work closely together. Layers of
superposed images, it should be noted, add another level
to the structure of the film, without competing with it.
Outdoor signs (billboards, etc.) are progressively superimposed onto the bodies, and yet there is no blurring of
the image. What we see here is, to all intents and purposes,
a choreography for the camera, and a dance of both the
camera and of isolated frames. As is frequently the case
in Schoenherr's fims, there is a homology between the
woman's skin and the materiality of the print. Indeed, this
analogy is not devoid of a male voyeuristic gaze, as is clearly

the case with *Gedanken beim Befühlen einer Mädchenhaut* (1968), a film that focuses fetichistically on a young woman's skin. This, of course, was a limitation inherent to a generation of mainly male filmmakers (under the influence of "sexual liberation," which, all too often, in the late 1960s and 1970s, was seen as the liberation of the female body to become an object to be desired and consumed, or exhibited and fetishized). Nonetheless, Schoenherr's work is not devoid of enigmas when it comes to its structure, which proves both systematic *and* loose—and is undeniably extremely consistent in its formal/rythmical/hypnotic resonances. His films are also striking insofar as their performative dimension is akin to that of Live Art. This is not limited to his use of a live cello in front of the screen and on the soundtrack. The vibration of his sequences of frames, irregularly reiterated, which creates physical sensations during the projection, causes spectator-observers to suspend their attention, and become caught up in the rhythm of the film.

[1] See J. G. Hanhardt & M. Yokobosky (eds.), *Gregory J. Markopoulos: Mythic Themes, Portraiture, and Films of Place*, Whitney Museum of American Art, New York 1996; Mark Webber (ed.), *Film as Film: The Collected Writings of Gregory J. Markopoulos*, The Visible Press, London 2014. Schoenherr wrote in *Filmmakers' Newsletter*: "The traveling film exposition to which Sitney exposed the European cities was a great success [...] The films were surprising. I was overwhelmed and stunned when I saw Markopoulos' *Through a Lens Brightly: Mark Turbyfill* in the autumn of 1967 in Zurich. I could no longer concentrate anymore on the subsequent films that evening." (HHK Schoenherr, "Europe," *Filmmakers' Newsletter*, vol. 1, no. 12 (1968), p. 10.)
[2] HHK Schoenherr, "Aus Protest gegen die *Geistesbaltung* und das *Finanzgebaren* von Kuert + Siber (einflussreichste Leute des Film Forum Zürich) zieht Schönherr seine Filme zurück," *Supervisuell*, no. 1 (1968), n.p., my translation. The complete series of *Supervisuell* can be accessed at blog.zhdk.ch/sfex.
[3] HHK Schoenherr, "Europe," p. 11.
[4] Cinéma Marginal Distribution was an association founded by Marcel Leiser and François Pasche in 1968. Its structure was akin to the New York Film-Makers' Cooperative, but the filmmakers involved in this association produced amateur films that favored "auteur" cinema, while still aspiring toward inclusion in professional cinema. See Marthe Porret, "Diffuser le jeune cinéma romand partout! Marcel Leiser et Cinéma Marginal Distribution (1968-1974)",

in Alain Boillat, Philipp Brunner, Barbara Flückiger (eds.), *Kino CH: Rezeption, Ästhetik, Geschichte / Cinéma CH: Réception, esthétique, histoire*, Schüren Verlag, Marburg 2008, p. 221–231.
[5] HHK Schoenherr, "Europe," p. 10. See too the letter he published in the first issue of *Cinébulletin*, where he asked for the coordinated national distribution of experimental films: "Who will assume the task of representing the interests of experimental cinema, of promoting it and organizing tours? Absolutely nothing has been done in the last three years [...] This problem should be resolved as soon as possible, since the Filmcenter intends to set itself up as a foundation." ("Ein Brief von HHK Schoenherr," [June 12, 1975] *Ciné bulletin*, issue 1 October 1975, my translation).
[6] HHK Schoenherr, "Europe."
[7] See the announcement for the *Movies Kaputt: Das kaputte Kino* touring program, in Otto Ceresa and Max Nyffeler (eds.), *HHK Schoenherr: Movies Kaputt*, Pro Helvetia/L'Age d'Homme, Zurich/Lausanne 1985, p. 33.
[8] *Ibid*. It should be noted that few monographs have been written about experimental Swiss filmmakers.
[9] See *HHK Schoenherr Retrospective: at Anthology Film Archives, October 3 to October 6, 1991*, Pro Helvetia, Zurich 1991. It should be noted that this publication consists of extracts from *HHK Schoenherr: Movies Kaputt*. Earlier major retrospectives of Schoenherr's work were held at the Centre Georges-Pompidou (Paris), in 1979, after his participation in the "Cinéma en marge" event, and at the Swiss Cultural Center in Paris, in 1985.

[10] With *Geschichte der Nacht* (1978), Clemens Klopfenstein made one of the most radical, experimental full-length feature films ever produced in Switzerland, shooting in 50 different European towns at night for 150 days. However, he later turned to fiction films and comedies.

[11] Fredi M. Murer produced different film portraits, sometimes described as "private movies," culminating with *Pazifik* (1966), a full-length feature film. He then moved into making ethnographic documentaries, with *Wir Bergler in den Bergen sind eigentlich nicht schuld, dass wir da sind* (1974). In 1985, his dramatic fiction film *Höhenfeuer* was a great success, and received very favorable press reviews. See *Fredi M. Murer*, Pro Helvetia, Zurich 1980. For a critical analysis of his first films, see my article "De l'art du portrait au documentaire ethnographique," *Décadrages. Cinéma, à travers champs*, "Fredi M. Murer," no. 12, Spring 2008, p. 21–30.

[12] *4 Minutennachmittag* (1967) and *Was Suchst du in der Schublade?* (1967) are Schoenherr's first films in Super-8; *Thaler's, Meier's, Sakowsky's Life in the Evening* (1967) is his first 16mm film, shown at EXPRMNTL in Knokke-le-Zoute in 1967, at the Hamburg Filmshow in 1968, and at Avignon Festival in 1969. *Play 33* (1990) is one of his last 16mm films, shown at the Anthology Film Archives in 1991, among other screenings. He produced four full-length feature films, which have been screened widely: *Autoportrait* (1968, 16mm), *Daydream* (1970, 16mm), *Robert Walser* (1974–1978, 35mm with 16mm copies for distribution) and *Innen & Aussen* (1979-1984, 16mm). His last film was also a full-length feature film: *Kinderkrieg & Kinderfrieden oder J.S. Bach: Die Kunst der Fuge* (1996, 16mm); it was screened at Viper Festival in Luzern in 1996, but not, to my knowledge, on any other occasion (the 16mm copies, stored in Schoenherr's archives at Lichtspiel, Bern, show no traces of wear).

[13] See the program for *Daydream*, reproduced in Otto Ceresa & Max Nyffeler (eds.), *HHK Schoenherr: Movies Kaputt*, p. 64–65.

[14] HHK Schoenherr (1936–2014) studied at Hamburg University of the Arts, from 1956 to 1961. He lived and worked in Zurich from 1963 up to his sudden death in 2014. He maintained close contacts with the Hamburger Filmmacher Cooperative, founded in 1968 by Werner Nekes, Dore O., Hellmuth Costard, Klaus Wyborny, and Thomas Struck, and with XSCREEN, the independent projection space in Cologne, created in 1968 by Birgit and Wilhelm Hein, Lutz Mommartz, and Wilfried Reichart. Nevertheless, in his articles, he regularly rejected "das andere Kino," centered around the Hamburg Film Coop, and took a stand against both the American underground and particular protagonists of the German independent scene, especially Werner Nekes and his wife Dore O. (he even accused Nekes, in his correspondence, of stealing his film soundtracks).

[15] Schoenherr financially assisted Markopoulos to release *Political Portraits* (1969), in which Schoenherr and his family appear among portraits of Giorgio de Chirico, Dieter Meier, Giorgio Frapolli, Wilhelm and Birgit Hein, Hans-Jakob Siber, and Jacques Doniol-Valcroze. It should be noted that this film was produced by Dieter Meier through Progressive Art Production (a structure founded by Karlheinz Hein in 1969; for further details, see my article on P.A.P. in the present volume). In return, Markopoulos sent a letter of support to Schoenherr, highlighting his technical and artistic abilities as a filmmaker.

[16] See *Kinematagraph*, no. 3 ["W+B Hein: Dokumente 1967–1985. Fotos, Briefe, Texte"], 1985, p. 23.

[17] See Christophe Gauthier, *La passion du cinéma: cinéphiles, ciné-clubs et salles spécialisées à Paris de 1920 à 1929*, Ecole nationale des Chartes/Association française de recherche sur l'histoire du cinéma, Paris 1999, p. 198–202.

[18] That is why the Ciné Circus international program was published in this issue, with films by Alfredo Leonardi, Wilhelm and Birgit Hein, Werner Nekes, Lutz Mommartz, Hans Scheugl, Kurt Kren, and Ernst Schmidt. Film Forum and Ciné Circus participated in a European network of filmmakers' cooperatives, whose scope and financial ambitions became the target for Schoenherr's criticism.

[19] Gregory Markopoulos, "Sto Palikari," *Supervisuell*, no. 3 (1968), "Note from Zurich of a Work in Progress," *Supervisuell*, no. 5 (Spring 1969), not paginated.

[20] Otto Muehl, "Materialaktion und Materialaktionsfilme von Otto Muehl," *Supervisuell*, no. 6, 1970, not paginated.

[21] Interventions by Alfredo Leonardi, Wilhelm and Birgit Hein, HHK Schoenherr, Raj Marbres, Dieter Meier, Thomas Alva, and Jonas Mekas were listed in the table of contents, but were removed in Schoenherr's "Manifesto."

[22] HHK Schoenherr, "Konzeption für *Variationen ABC*," *Supervisuell*, no. 3 (1968), p. 4.

[23] See also "Schema der rythmischen und arythmischen Abläufe von Schoenherr's *Sonate: Graubild Fraubild Blaubild und Weisskader*," *Supervisuell*, no. 2 (August 1968), p. 7.

[24] See "Le Cinéma Kaputt à Zurich," *La Suisse*, April 25, 1972.

[25] *Movies Kapputt* was shown in Mannheim (May 3), Cologne (May 5), Amsterdam (May 6), Hamburg (May 23), Berlin (May 26–27), Frankfurt (June 3), Munich (June 9–10), and London (June 17 and 21–23).

[26] *Movies Kaputt* is composed of the following films: *No. 1* and *No. 3* by Werner von Mutzenbecher; *Arise Like a Fire* by Hans-Jakob Siber; *Mr. Eichorn's Golfball* and *Status Symbol* by Sebastian Schroeder; *Metermass Kaputt* by Raphaela Schoenherr; *X-Bilder* by Kurt Kuen; *Point Zero* by Charles-Andre Voser (and René Bauermeister); *Elkofaseibele* by Werner Ott; *Play 4 & 5* and *Das kaputte Kino* by HHK Schoenherr.

[27] See the photograph of his Debrie camera reproduced in Otto Ceresa & Max Nyffeler (eds.), *HHK Schoenherr: Movies Kaputt*, and his diagram ("Schema des kopierens von Lichtton") in P.A.P. [Progressive Art Production], *Lagerkatalog 1969*, P.A.P., Munich/Zurich 1969, n.p.

[28] "'Underground,' as a word, is broken. For me, Underground Music, Underground Cinema, Underground Family are broken concepts [...] The word is an invention of the American press, and the press wants to use the word 'underground' to reduce Music/Film/Theater to a small, despicable form that apparently epitomises the notion of perfection for the Music/Film/Theater industry." HHK Schoenherr, letter to Martin Höllen, around 1968, my translation.

[29] HHK Schoenherr, "Experimentalfilme III am Sonntag, 8 November 1970," *Nationales Filmzentrum der Schweiz*, typescript, my translation.

[30] HHK Schoenherr, "'Kreativer Film', die neue Filmrichtung," *Supervisuell*, no. 5 (Spring 1969), n.p.

[31] HHK Schoenherr, "Der unabhängige Film in Europa," my translation.

[32] "In his filmic perpetual present, inspired by the poetics of Gertrude Stein, images and sequences thus follow in the most rapid and hyperbolic fluidity of editing, eliminating anticipation as vector of cinematic construction. Both memory and anticipation are annuled by images as immediate and fugitive as those we call hypnagogic, that come to us in a half-waking state." Annette Michelson, "Where Is Your Rupture? Mass Culture and the Gesamtkunstwerk," *October*, vol. 56 (Spring 1991), p. 60–61.

[33] See for instance Mary Ann Doane, *The Emergence of Cinematic Time: Modernity, Contingency, the Archive*, Harvard University Press, Cambridge/London 2002.

[34] Peter Kubelka, "The Theory of Metrical Film," P. Adams Sitney (ed.), *The Avant-Garde Film: A Reader of Theory and*

Criticism, New York Univerity Press, New York 1978, p. 139–159.
[35] See P. Adams Sitney, "Structural Film," *Film Culture 47* (Summer 1969), p. 1–10.
[36] See Peter Gidal, "Definition and Theory of the Current Avant-Garde: Materialist/Structural Film," *Studio International*, vol. 187, issue no. 963 (February 1974), p. 53–56; Peter Gidal (ed.), *Structural Film Anthology*, BFI, London 1976. See also Peter Wollen, "'Materialism' and 'Ontology' in Film," *Screen*, vol. 17, no. 1 (Spring 1976), p. 7–23. It should be noted that Malcolm Le Grice holds an intermediate and more open position on Sitney's and Gidal's points of view (see Malcolm Le Grice, "The History We Need," in *Film as Film: Formal Experiment in Film, 1910–1975*, exh. cat., Hayward Gallery, London 1979, p. 113–117).
[37] See George Maciunas, "Some Comments on 'Structural Film' (by P. Adams Sitney)," P. Adams Sitney (ed.), *Film Culture Reader*, Praeger, New York 1970, p. 349.
[38] "In *L'Anticoncept*, Gil J. Wolman created a primary movement which entirely covered the screen and alternated between black and white over time on the screen. In optics, we know that the eye perceives relationships and not differences. The relationships between black and white generate a subjective 'physical movement.' Effectively, when the retina observes a brief flash of light it does not rest immediately after the stimulus ceases [...] The intensity of these rhythms was such that during the first showing, spectators who chose to close their eyes could perceive the movement through their eyelids. Even those who turned away could not escape: the movement became part of the room itself [...] *L'Anticoncept* makes concepts subjective and fluid through spectator reaction, and triggers a physical reaction." Gil Joseph Wolman, "Le cinématochrone–nouvelle amplitude," *Ur*, (2–1952) (Gil J. Wolman, *Défense de mourir*, ed. Gérard Berréby, Allia, Paris 2001, my translation).
[39] See Henri Bergson, *Creative Evolution*, Henry Holt and Company, New York 1911 (first edition: *L'Évolution créatrice*, Presses universitaires de France, Paris 1907).
[40] See Werner Nekes, "Whatever Happens Between the Pictures," *Afterimage*, no. 5, (November 1977), p. 7–13: 8: "Out of which elements is film built up? Or, what is the smallest filmic element? I came to the answer that *cinema is the difference between two frames*: the work the brain has to do to produce the fusion of the two frames. This small unit which I call kine is the smallest particle of a film one can think of [...] If you, for example, take this big unit: a single frame, you have a photographic information; if you take two frames, the difference between them defines the smallest unit of filmic language that is possible, one filmic information. Every film can be regarded under the principle of this difference, which is a construct of a time/space relation. The analysis of the kine enables us to come to conclusions over the language used, to determine the level of filmic information connected to the work the spectator has to do."

[41] See Paul Sharits, "Hearing: Seeing," *Ausgabe*, no. 2, (Summer 1976); see also "Words per Page" (1970), *Afterimage*, no. 4 (Autumn 1972): "My early 'flicker' films—wherein clusters of differentiated single frames of solid colour can appear to almost blend, or, each frame, insisting upon its discreteness, can appear to aggressively vibrate—are filled with attempts to allow vision to function in ways usually particular to hearing. In those films of 1965 to 1968, the matters of 'psychological theme' and perceptual analysis of filmic information were part of a set which included regard for the way in which rapidly alternating color frames can generate, in vision, horizontal-temporal 'chords' (as well as the more expected 'melodic lines' and 'tonal centers') [...] It was obvious that it was necessary to somehow divide the frame into 'parts,' to introduce enough complexity into the instantaneous image so that overtones could be legibly generated [...] In S:STREAM:S:S:SECTION:S:S:ECTION :S:S:ECTIONED I finally came to use superimposition, as a way of attaining both 'chordal depth' and the possibility of 'counterpoint'; united with these 'musical' motivations, there was the larger concern with the relationship of water's directionalities and the flow of film through a projector."

[42] See especially S. M. Eisenstein, "The Fourth Dimension in Cinema" [1929], *Selected Works, vol. 1: Writings 1922–1934*, ed. and trans. Richard Taylor, I. B. Tauris, London 2010, p. 181–194.

[43] Raphaël Bassan, "Schoenherr/Walser: un autre regard sur la Suisse," *Canal*, June 1979, Otto Ceresa and Max Nyffeler (eds.), *HHK Schoenherr: Movies Kaputt*, p. 30.

[44] Mark Turbyfill, "Being Myself in a Markopoulos Biography," *Film Culture*, no. 46 (Autumn 1967), p. 18–19.

[45] Gregory Markopoulos, "Towards a New Narrative Film Form," *Film Culture*, no. 31 (Winter 1963–1964), p. 11.

[46] HHK Schoenherr, letter to Gregory Markopoulos, around September 1968.

[47] Alexander J. Seiler, "Film ist ein Material wie jedes andere auch," *Tages-Anzeiger Magazine*, December 24, 1971.

[48] See HHK Schoenherr, typewritten document, June 1971, Otto Ceresa and Max Nyffeler (eds.), *HHK Schoenherr: Movies Kaputt*, p. 55–59.

HHK Schoenherr, *Portrait der Cordua*, 1969 (Switzerland)
16mm film, 16 minutes

Robert Beavers and Gregory Markopoulos: Time Spent and Time Between
Ian Wooldridge

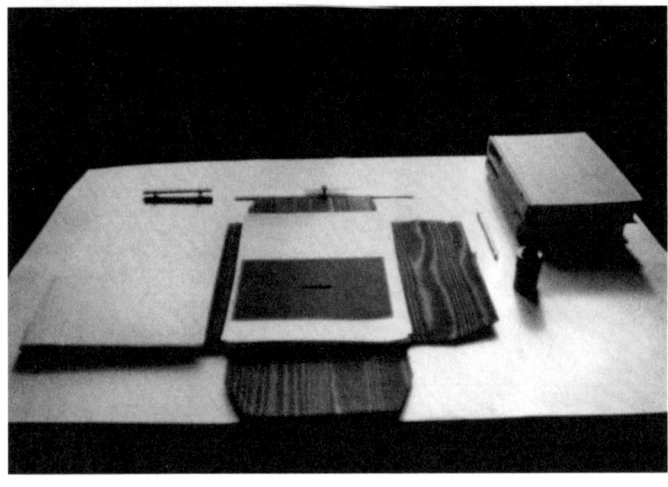

Robert Beavers, *From the Notebook of...*, 1971/1998 (USA)
16mm film, 48 minutes

The year 1967 marked the relocation of Robert Beavers and Gregory Markopoulos and set them on the path toward a different way of working, living, and being. It was the year that they located themselves primarily in Europe and formed a lasting tie to Switzerland in the pursuit of Markopoulos' uncompromisingly idealized conditions for creating their films. This pursuit of and persistence in realizing these ideal conditions for work and life, both viewed as one, led to a relentlessly nomadic existence, which bore fruit within the aesthetic, poetic, and compositional forms of both their trajectories. Switzerland became the lynch pin, the magnet for their circumnavigational positioning.

    Beavers and Markopoulos' time in Switzerland can be divided into three periods—an initial period in Zurich and Basel between 1968 and 1970, a middle period nomadically returning time and again to various remote Alpine locations throughout the 1970s and 1980s, and the period after Markopoulos' death in 1992 when Beavers returned predominantly to Zurich to set up structures for their archive and films.

Gregory Markopoulos (1928–1992) was born in Toledo, Ohio, USA, to Greek immigrant parents. In 1945, he enrolled on a film course at the University of Southern California, but quit after two years. In 1959, Jonas Mekas cofounded the New American Cinema Group in New York, and Markopoulos joined as the only member who had a "genuine pedigree" in filmmaking.[1] Prior to living in New York, Markopoulos had been working, for five difficult years, on an ambitious 35mm film, *Serenity* (1961). His funding was eventually withdrawn and the edited copies of the film disappeared, leaving Markopoulos with a very poor impression of the film industry. Markopoulos moved to New York City during the production of *Serenity*, and this is where he created his most celebrated films: *Twice a Man* (1963) and *The Illiac Passion* (1964–1967). The cast for *The Illiac Passion* included Andy Warhol, Taylor Mead, Gregory Battcock, and Jack Smith among others.

Robert Beavers was born in Brookline, Massachusetts, USA, in 1949. Beavers attended Deerfield Academy, a boys-only boarding school in western Massachusetts. In the summer of 1965, Beavers traveled to New York City to carry out research for a film club he wished to establish at the school. In New York, Beavers met Markopoulos. Beavers' first film program, to be screened to inaugurate the film club at Deerfield, was rejected due to its inclusion of Kenneth Anger's *Scorpio Rising* (1963), on the grounds that it contained nudity and homosexuality. Beavers dropped out of Deerfield, and by 1966, aged 15, was living in a small loft on the Bowery in Manhattan.

Markopoulos' text, *Inherent Limitations*, offers an early insight into the coming together of Beavers and Markopoulos. Markopoulos quotes a tenacious young Beavers: "I am interested in your opinion of what a 'filmmaker's education' should consist of."[2] Within *Inherent Limitations*, Markopoulos seems set on furthering a disparate existence, never directly answering Beavers, yet musing over wild happenstance in quoting Nikos Kazantzakis: "The creator's responsibility is a great one; he opens a road that may entice the future and force it to make up its mind."³

This romantic ideal is relayed into a single vision where work, life and the craftsmanship of "personal filmmaking"⁴ constitute a single constant. No prominence given to time captured, time spent, and time projected.

> [T]he signs that enable the filmmaker to chant his always measured, monotonous song as he must, are unmistakable. Direct, inflexible, precise, unyielding as Man, Woman, Child, the filmmaker lays stress upon himself toward the great deep of primordial matter; and this act or condition becomes the multiplying unit of his craftsmanship.⁵

In 1967 Markopoulos filmed Beavers in New York in Beavers' loft on the Bowery for *Eros, O Basileus* (1967); Beavers was Eros. Markopoulos connected everything and saw all as a whole: myth, film, editing, projection, and life.

> The film moves very, very slowly. One sequence has a shot where somebody is sitting at a desk, he's really not doing anything at all. I take this sequence and I cut it into four sections. What happens in the first section, I fade in and then I fade out and then the person is still sitting at the desk. The composition doesn't change. In the second section I fade in and fade out at the same time, the essential part of it is that each one is measured, that each one is equal to the other. Again, it fades in, you have the scene, it fades out and then you have a space with apparently no content and yet you do have content.⁶

The "space with apparently no content ... yet content" became a fixation both formally and metaphysically for Markopoulos and in turn informed Beavers: queer space, hermetic space, sealed uncompromising conditions, and external factors nullified.

It is important to note the shifting form of Markopoulos' work prior to leaving the United States for Europe. Markopoulos identified with neo-Dada and the

Abstract Expressionists—Agnes Martin, Jasper Johns, and Robert Rauschenberg, who lived in downtown Manhattan, were often visited by Markopoulos.[7] Jasper Johns sat for Markopoulos for the *Galaxie* (1966) series of film portraits. Markopoulos steered away from the rise of Pop art, as he was closer to the homosexual Abstract Expressionist group of artists. He became less interested in narrative film and his writing became less psychological. "I have been communing with my innermost Anticipations of what must be. For me, the film as film; and this among the civilized chasms today called Pop culture or otherwise the Modern."[8] Markopoulos' focus and direction shifted to the film material itself and to abstraction. What drew Markopoulos to Martin, Johns, and Rauschenberg was the "other homoerotic."[9] Markopoulos saw the "other homoerotic" as a need to work and a need for isolation, counter to the view of the homoerotic reflected in Pop art. Markopoulos became intrigued by the "enigmatic, secretive atmosphere" that Martin, Johns, and Rauschenberg created.[10] This positioning informed the film form of his work, a form with sealed conditions, and eventually the removal of sound.

In 1966 Markopoulos completed a series of film portraits in New York entitled *Galaxie* (1966). *Galaxie* included portraits of the aforementioned Jasper Johns, Parker Tyler, Storm de Hirsch, Amy Taubin, Donald Droll, Harry Koursaros and Gordon Herzig, Ben Weber, George and Mike Kuchar, Erick Hawkins, Louise Grady, Frances Steloff, Charles Boultenhouse, Alfonso Ossorio, Jasper Johns, Jonas Mekas, W. H. Auden, Jerome Hill, Allen Ginsberg and Peter Orlovsky, Robert Ossorio, Gregory Battcock, Hendrik Ruitenbeek, Shirley Clarke, Jan Cremer, Kenneth Kelman, Maurice Sendak, Paul Thek, Susan Sontag, Tom Chomont, Gian Carlo Menotti, Ed Emshwiller and family, and Robert C. Scull. The film portraits were each shot on a single cartridge of 16mm film, approximately 3 minutes in length.

Under similar conditions, Markopoulos created a second series of portraits in Europe entitled *Political Portraits* (1969), which he dedicated to Dieter Meier. His cast included the Schoenherr family, Claudia Honegger, Dieter Meier, Alfredo Leonardi, Massimo Bacigalupo, Hulda Zumsteg, Giorgio Frapolli, Gunnar Parelius, Berit Hiff, Wilhelm and Birgit Hein, Franco Quadri, Giorgio di Chirico, Frieda

Honneger, Ulrich Herzog, Karlheinz Hein, Marcia Haydée, Rudolf Nureyev, Bruno Bischofberger, Felix Baumann, Anna Giroux, Hans-Jakob Siber, Jacques Doniol-Valcroze, and Jack Siler. It was filmed in Zurich, Rome, Bergen, Cologne, Munich, and the Cote d'Azur. Markopoulos continued to make portraits until very late in his life, although *Galaxie* and *Political Portraits* are his only series. Beavers was present at many of the sittings and described Markopoulos as having an "ambivalence toward the person sitting"; rather Markopoulos focused on what surrounded the person, light, and rhythm.[11]

Markopoulos' approach to creating film portraits treated the multiple exposure of the film collage as static and rhythmic with light transferring constantly to different areas of the composed multi-layered still frame. The premise for Markopoulos was similar to that of a photographic still, capturing a single moment. Markopoulos would select an object or an activity with personal significance to the subject. Carefully watching the frame-counter on his camera, he then exposed a number of takes of one image, interspersed with blackness achieved by covering the lens with his hands or the lens cap for as long as he liked, or by using the automatic fading mechanism of his Bolex camera. Each method of covering the lens had a different nuance. The portrait needed no editing after filming as it had been created entirely in the camera—"in-camera editing."[12]

Markopoulos found that the measured black film between the exposed film had the effect of awakening the next exposure's film image. He would rewind the film and expose the next view, detail, or object with a second exposure. Black gaps in the film made by covering the lens in the first exposure were exposed in either the second or third exposures, as well as in later exposures overlapping the first exposed film image, thus creating a form of stasis— "time captured is not time released, but time suspended."[13]

Prior to leaving the United States, Markopoulos snubbed the underground New York film scene. In Europe, Markopoulos removed all of his films from circulation and insisted that "From Trance to Myth," the chapter dedicated to Markopoulos in P. Adams Sitney's seminal study of American avant-garde cinema, *Visionary Film*,[14] be removed from the second edition. Markopoulos had chosen to isolate and erase himself from avant-garde film history. In Europe, Markopoulos believed that one of the small European countries like Belgium or Switzerland would be more nurturing, and the best structural place for experimental film thinking. He believed that these nations could not facilitate a major film industry, and should thus focus on experimental film.

> How has film developed between 1960 and 1968? What has become of the character of film, film-making, and filmmakers in the period mentioned? What is the illusion which has been fostered? What is a filmmaker working apart? What is a filmmaker relying upon the immediate contact with other filmmakers? What is the publicity of the New Cinema? What has been the publicity of the New Cinema? Who has profited aesthetically from the publicity of the New Cinema? Who has profited politically from the publicity of the New Cinema? Why has publicity replaced what might be the New Cinema?[15]

Markopoulos' relentless questioning goes on to disregard cooperatives and public funding systems, and set the tone for his abandonment of the USA.

Beavers traveled from New York to Greece in February 1967. By the end of July he moved on to Rome and then, a couple of months later, to Vienna. Markopoulos intermittently joined Beavers, and on one of these visits Beavers filmed Markopoulos in Hydra, Greece, for his film *Winged Dialogue* (1967/2000). Together they saw out 1967 in Belgium at *EXPRMNTL 4*, the experimental film festival in Knokke-le-Zoute, which ran from Christmas through to the New Year of 1968. *EXPRMNTL 4* screened Markopoulos' film *The Illiac Passion* and premiered *Spiracle* (1966), Beavers' first film featuring Tom Chomont.

As a result of the inclusion of *The Illiac Passion* in *EXPRMNTL 4*, Markopoulos was invited to tour his work in Switzerland in May 1968. The tour was proposed by Giorgio Frapolli who was active in Switzerland during the Zurich youth movement and punk period of 1968–1969; Bernhard Ullmann who became the head of Film Podium in Zurich and then moved on to the Cinémathèque suisse in Lausanne; Hans-Jakob Siber, a young filmmaker at the time; and Harald Szeemann, the director of the Kunsthalle Bern. Giorgio Frapolli finalized the tour, which consisted of screenings at the Filmklub Zürich, Le Bon Film Basel, the Kunsthalle Bern, and the Cinémathèque suisse de Lausanne. Markopoulos presented *The Illiac Passion*, *Galaxie* (1966), and *Gammelion* (1968). This was the first time Markopoulos had screened his films in Switzerland, and this tour also brought Beavers to Switzerland indirectly.

In late spring 1968, after the tour in Switzerland, Beavers and Markopoulos traveled back to Greece, only to return to Zurich a couple of months later. By the autumn of that same year, 1968, they had more or less settled in Switzerland.

HHK Schoenherr, Hans-Jakob Siber, and Dieter Meier were crucial during this first period. Meier had started getting involved in film at this time and had starred in Schoenherr's film *Thaler's, Meier's, Sadkowsky's Life in the Evening* (1967), which was included in the program for EXPRMNTL 4 at Knokke-le-Zoute alongside *The Illiac Passion* and *Spiracle*. Dieter Meier and Eduard Stöckli were interested in running film programs at the Platte 27 club, and they hosted an organization called P.A.P. founded by Karlheinz Hein, which was active from 1968 to 1970. It was the most consistent period in Zurich for Markopoulos and Beavers. During this time Schoenherr, Meier, and Markopoulos tried to organize a large exhibition of experimental film at the Kunsthaus Zürich but to no avail; the director of the Kunsthaus at that time was Felix Baumann.

The first films that Beavers made in Europe included *Winged Dialogue*, filmed in Hydra, Greece, *Plan of Brussels* (1968), and *Early Monthly Segments* (1968–1970). Their filmic language had an erratic sense of curiosity in the way the camera moved, the rhythm, or simply what was within the frame. These forms arose from a freedom based on a very special situation. This was not a freedom formed from the closeness of the relationship with Markopoulos, but rather freedom through it: "These curious aspects, it almost feels like they are testing a conversation, perhaps conversation is not the right word, but maybe testing a dialogue. It felt like a two-person society, like a dialogue."[16]

Plan of Brussels (1968/2000), shot when Beavers was 19 years old, is erotically charged, almost feverishly so, and connects to the work he had viewed in New York, and to New American Cinema.

> The outburst and connection between that moment of social erotic and free invention in film. One can say it's like dividing the atom. The energy that comes out of that can either be positive or negative depending on how it's used. In that moment, historically, there were two sides to it. I don't see many of those filmmakers as positive individuals. Producing breakthroughs perhaps in filmmaking but being destructive and negative otherwise. It's synonymous in some cases. So that's always a question of utopian things.[17]

Tom Chomont, a filmmaker and acquaintance of Beavers, who is in Beavers' film *Spiracle*, described *Wing Dialogue* in the following terms: "[It] details with growing clarity the desperate beauty and sexuality of the body animated by its soul, essence blindly reaching out, touching, in brilliant patterns through and beyond those of the vanishing images, expressed vividly in the after-image on the mind, on the soul's eye."[18] Susan Oxtoby describes *Early Monthly Segments* as a

> highly stylized work of self-portraiture, depicting the filmmaker and his companion Gregory Markopoulos. The film functions as diary, capturing aspects of home life with precise attention to detail, documenting the familiar with great love, and transforming objects and ordinary personal effects into a highly charged work of homoeroticism.[19]

Both Chomont and Oxtoby align Beavers' early work with the "personal" notion of "objects" and the sentiment of "ordinary personal effects" permeated with homoeroticism; the space around and between objects, captured through a stasis in time, evokes an atmosphere of homoeroticism. The "other" in fruition not through descriptive verse, but through evocation of rhythm and air, or a lack thereof.

Three films by Beavers, made between 1969 and 1970 were shot in Zurich—*The Count of Days* (1969/2001), *View*

(1969), and *Palinode* (1970/2001). These films present "various erotic and spiritual themes in the context of the places where I had been living." Chomont noted that *The Count of Days*

> is seen as though upon and through the structure of its spiritual partitions. One might say that there are three elements or levels to the images: narrative, descriptive or analytic, and abstract. *The Count of Days* is not an account so much as an accounting of the essence of the days in which three separate persons are related at points ... a penetration through the masks and habits of these days to reveal the nature of the charade and the arena in which it is enacted.[20]

Spiritual partitions, masks, habits, and illicit patterns form a charade within a place. Beavers' early works articulated a filmic language that was uniquely positioned, not aligned with but informed by, Markopoulos.

In 1967 Markopoulos wrote "The Filmmaker as Physician of the Future," an essay in which he stated the importance of "a sense of communion, as opposed to deliberate communication."[21] Markopoulos' "lyrical" montage and film form espoused the ideal of the subliminal image. Markopoulos quoted philologist Friedrich Creuzer: "In a flash the motion springs out from the symbol and grips all senses. It is a ray which comes directly from the depths of being and thinking, pierces our eye, and permeates our entire nature: immediate perception."[22]

Gammelion (1968) was the first film that Markopoulos made after choosing to permanently relocate to Europe from the United States. *Gammelion* is the name of the month the ancient Greeks thought suitable for marriage. Markopoulos went to Il Castello Roccasinibalda, in the Rieti Province in Italy, with two rolls of approximately seven-minute 16mm color film. When editing *Gammelion*, Markopoulos interspersed very brief images with a thousand fades to a black or white leader, extending the final film to a total of 55 minutes.

> Each shot that I took, I took only a few frames, and so what I've done is I've extended the film through

the use of white leader. The film is an hour long. It's 60 minutes, though I only used 270 feet of film. The shots are more or less static, there's no movement.[23]

In the later period of his life, Markopoulos focused almost entirely on the production of *Eniaios* (1948–1991), a radically minimal ordering of his entire film oeuvre. The structure of *Gammelion* transforms seven minutes of film footage into almost an hour; P. Adams Sitney describes *Gammelion* as the "germ" of *Eniaios*, in which flashes of image appear within passages of white and black.[24]

The impression of *Gammelion* is unlike that of any other Markopoulos film. It is at once terribly spare and very rich. The unmoving images (there may be a slight flutter in the castle's flag, but that would be all), the lack of figures other than the couple in the fresco, who first appear so quickly they might be actual, and the total lack of incident in the film, create the aura of a fiction without elaborating any specific fiction.[25]

Markopoulos had begun to work with film as an entirely static medium. After *Gammelion*, he stopped moving the camera during filming. The methodology Markopoulos formed was that of projecting images at intervals. The intervals were created either by "in-camera" editing by blocking the lens, or by editing black leader between spliced film images. "For hours the screen flashes and winks with gorgeous vestiges of ancient ruins, mythical narratives, and figures from the art world."[26] Markopoulos related the measured intervals to a creation myth, and Beavers commented on the film form of *Eniaios*, with blank intervals, in the following words: "what may appear as mere fragmentary elements in a film can speak to us through the pattern of the intervals as it rests upon the screen and articulates the extended phrases of image."[27] The film form that Markopoulos developed throughout his work as a whole, and that ultimately led to *Eniaios*, derives from the fact that he did not view his films until their completion. Markopoulos saw significance in the film medium's relation to memory, and used memory and harnessed intuition for the editing process. Memory became central to the film assembly, and in projection, the viewer's memory was now tasked with questioning the film images. Markopoulos' belief in the process of editing from memory paved the way for the logistical opportunity to work remotely and in solitude.

Markopoulos filmed *Sorrows* (1969) on January 22, 1969, in Tribschen, Switzerland, at the house where Richard Wagner had sought refuge on Lake Lucerne. The film was dedicated to Wilhelm and Birgit Hein, and Markopoulos added a soundtrack by Ludwig van Beethoven—an excerpt from the *Overture to Fidelio*. According to Markopoulos "Wagner is one of the few very creative individuals that the world has ever known, everything that he said has been very true."[28] Markopoulos insisted that *Sorrows* was not intended to be a Wagnerian project. He said that he had simply gone to the location as he believed in "the house as a refuge ... that's why it's so extraordinary."[29] Markopoulos used the "in-camera" technique, filming once and frequently blocking the lens, then rewinding the film cartridge and doing the same again with different measured patterns. He felt that it was a mistake to describe the film rhythm in *Sorrows* as a musical rhythm. "It's not a musical rhythm, it's a movement that has to do with the reasoning that takes place in the packing together of so much material and yet allowing it to have a wonderful existence or wonder in itself."[30]

In the late 1960s there was still excellent technical support for 16mm filmmaking in Switzerland. This deteriorated later with the rise in value of the Swiss Franc and the loss of the market for film labs when digital media sprang up. Between 1968 and the mid-to-late 1980s, Robert Beavers and Gregory Markopoulos lived in various locations across Switzerland. These ranged from the formative period between 1968 and 1970 in Zurich and Basel, to the alpine locations of Gstaad and Soglio in the later 1970s, and thereafter to other more remote points in Switzerland. They saw the advantage of Switzerland, not in the cities, but in the mountains, very often editing their films in mountain villages. They were determined to create under what they thought were the best conditions. The Bolex office in New York gifted them a camera, and the Schwarz film labs in Ostermundigen Bern and Cinegram accommodated their needs, often beyond the call of duty. Figures such as Athanase Ghertsos in Zurich were essential in helping them sustain this way of work, of life.

When Markopoulos and Beavers relocated to the Swiss Alps, they had in mind poets such as Rainer Maria Rilke, who spent the latter part of his life in the canton of Valais, and who also visited Soglio, where Beavers and Markopoulos had resided. "Rilke being just one of many venturing there for solitude; the major ones are the German Romantics."[31] The lyrical form of Rilke's poetry was part of Beavers' and Markopoulos' favored consciousness. Editing the film works in a wilderness, with a picturesque view of the mountains and isolation affected their states of mind and concentration.

Soglio was the high point of Beavers' and Markopoulos' time in Switzerland. The age gap of 21 years between them meant that Beavers, in his mid-20s during this period, was very young to be cutting himself off from more urban locations, although this time was balanced by periods spent in Italy and Greece.

Upon locating to the Alps, Beavers created a number of films: *The Painting* (1972/1999) which interwove the traffic around Theaterplatz in Bern with details from a 15th-century altarpiece, The Martyrdom of Saint Hippolytus; *Work Done* (1972/1999) filmed in Florence, Italy, and Grisons, Switzerland ("*Work Done* is based on a series of textual or transformative equivalences: the workshop and the field, the book and the forest, the mound of cobblestones and a distant mountain"[32]); *Ruskin* (1975/1997) containing the sites of John Ruskin's work in London, the Alps, and Venice ("The sound of pages turning and the image of a book, Ruskin's *Unto This Last*, forcibly remind us that a poet's perceptions, and in this case his political economy, are preserved and reawakened through acts of reading and writing"[33]); *Sotiros* (1976–1978/1996) filmed in Athens, Sparta, and Leonidio in Greece; Graz and Rein in Austria; and Bern, Switzerland (Sotiros, meaning healer, redeemer, is one of many designations of Apollo[34]). Beavers stated that there is an unspoken dialogue and a seen dialogue. "The first is held between the intertitles and the images; the second is moved by the tripod and by the emotions of the filmmaker. Both dialogues are interwoven with the sunlight's movement as it circles the room, touching each wall and corner,

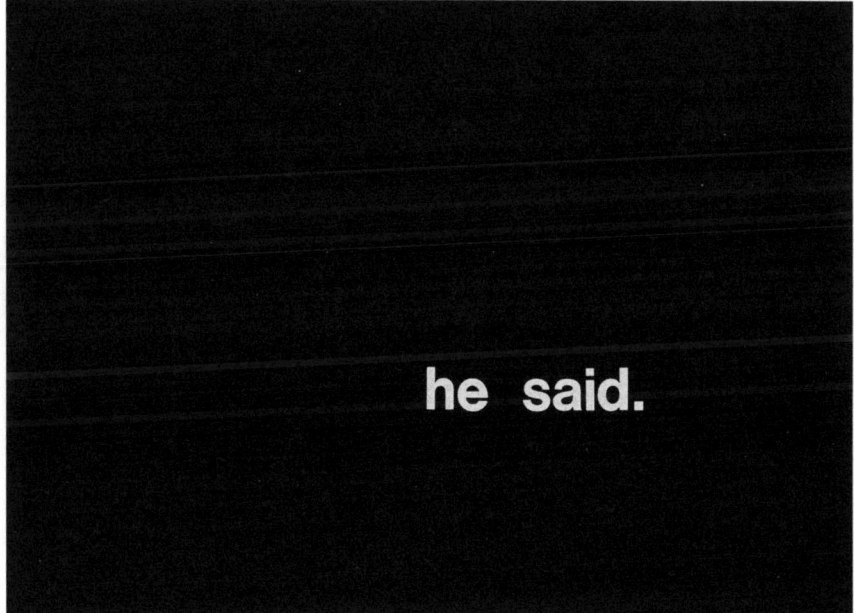

Robert Beavers, *Sotiros*, 1976–1978/1996 (USA)
16mm film, 25 minutes

detached and intimate." Beavers wrote notes on *Sotiros*, within which are profound sentences:

> Each film is a step toward a more solid and clear time element.
> A pattern of camera movements away from fixed points becomes a measure of the interval. The pattern *rests* upon the screen as the film is projected. If the camera movement is into the film cut, an opening is made into darkness or light; it negates, in part, the closure of the film cut or at least carries it differently.
> The voice of the film, the dialogue of its images, speaks more directly than performance. Its simplicity merely appears elliptical.
> The new relation of image and sound in the Self is the measure.[35]

Work and life, seen as one by Markopoulos in New York, were lived as such by both Beavers and Markopoulos in Switzerland.
 Celebrating one of Apollo's primary attributes, the film is suffused with the presence and mobility of light, which is delineated by crosscutting between the hotel room and landscapes, cityscapes, and worksites. No secondary player to human action, the god of light is center stage, revealing his manifold manifestations: time-teller, space-marker, shape-changer, adjutant of the eye as well as its deceiver.[36]
 After *Sotiros*, Beavers did not create any film works located in Switzerland for over 30 years, until *Listening to the Space in My Room* (2013), which was filmed in Zumikon at a time when he was editing his film *The Suppliant* (2010). Switzerland became more a place to edit, to consolidate, to do postproduction, than to film.

The technique Markopoulos used for editing 16mm film was to edit on two rolls, an A roll and a B roll, alternating the image with black leader. When the image is on roll A, roll B has black leader and vice versa. This technique avoids a splice being seen when printing the two rolls together, and is called checkerboard editing or "A&Bing."[37] Markopoulos' concept of "Film as Film," his use of checkerboard editing, and his shift of focus to film materiality and abstraction determined the structure for *Eniaios*. "A&Bing is a process that is best suited to an editing situation in which one is not viewing the film while editing."[38] Markopoulos created the form of the film during the editing process, not planning sequences, but finding them while working with the medium, listening to the film, not viewing the film. In 1973, in a piece called "The Intuition Space," he wrote:

> The question must be asked: what does the filmmaker see? What does the film spectator see? What does the film projectionist see? The filmmaker, if he is truly a filmmaker, looks at a film image on a table—a sparse table. He views by hand, using a small magnifying piece, a single frame, a film image. This constant instant of contact produces the undisturbed vision, which becomes the meaning of the work. What is the meaning of the work? The Work Is the Meaning ... For the filmmaker to refrain from viewing his film rolls as images in movement is to imbue them with a far greater and extraordinary Movement.[39]

Unlike Stan Brakhage who sought to form film as a moving plastic medium, Markopoulos reacted to single frames, not as movement, but as conceptually separate ideal forms that are static. A solipsism of two, the two selves being all that is known to exist, physicality is heightened, a silent queer otherness, remote and nomadic:

> It's always a question of: how formative is sexuality? A question that would take very careful thinking. One could connect Judd's use of numbers to Markopoulos' use of numbers in editing and to the proportions. The idea of proportion and Judd's connection to Greek philosophy, or philosophy in general.[40]

Switzerland did not always appear in the work directly as a location even though it was extremely important in the whole structure of the work. Beavers and Markopoulos worked together in a symbiotic manner. "There was an attunement, so of course we were in conversation. A society of two. Which is slightly more social than a society of one."[41]

The term "film as film" eventually became identified exclusively with Markopoulos and his work and with Beavers. Metaphysical assertions, which had always been a factor in Markopoulos' theoretical speculations, assumed "Blakean proportions" by the 1970s.[42] In "The Intuition Space," Markopoulos suggests an enigmatic duality in "reality," and posits that its apocalyptic meaning will be revealed to the initiated through "film as film."

> The Content of a film image is like a magnificent, super terrestrial, chlorophyllic process (in constant Evolution), which creates, and at the same time preserves or imbues, enforces, a sense of human reality. A human reality, always, incomprehensible. Incomprehensible because of the existence of the Gigantic Reality; with both Human Reality and the Gigantic Reality forever doomed in a state of illusion as opposites. In this state of the illusions of opposites, the Human Reality retains its state only so long as it remains unresolved; and, the Gigantic Reality forbids any communication with Human Reality, or Meaning itself, until the ultimate moment is achieved or revealed.[43]

Markopoulos aligned himself with romanticism and, in *Eniaios*, created a film form with a mythic ideal that was contrary to conceptual and postmodern art present in the 1970s and 1980s.

> We move in accelerated Time with our vision and movements reduced (probably retarded) before what we know as our time, and what we know through intuition or moments in science, of other more universal times. The film image is a crystallization of time ... in time.[44]

He engaged with poetic structures and rhythms, likening his film structures and the use of lengths of black and clear leader to punctuation. He likened film-editing craftsmanship to writing poetry in terms of the pauses that the lengths of leader would create around the image.

It's the same as seeing very, very quickly, but we don't talk about it when you're reading poetry and you have a comma, a comma or a semi colon or a dash or a space, it's that kind of thing. It's something which I think is very, very important.[45]

Eniaios places all of Markopoulos's previous film work into a system of orders, the structure and radical minimalization of which was of personal spiritual significance to Markopoulos. The film form of *Eniaios* has a theme of resurging memory. Markopoulos saw the resurgence of memory as "being simultaneous and in mass instead of linear and successive."[46]

The position both Beavers and Markopoulos took within Switzerland intertwined with the film form they used for their work, which was different for both of them.

Markopoulos showed an extraordinary sense of mission and absolute faith in his instincts throughout his life, which proved crucial to the ambitious plans he had in making *Eniaios*. The Greek title translates into English as "uniform," and has connotations of coming together and uniting. It has been suggested that the title "indicates both the 'singularity' and the 'uniqueness' of the film."[47] *Eniaios* is a single film work in 22 cycles, or orders, as Markopoulos called them, which unite his known filmography with 67 previously unseen films. The unseen films far outnumber Markopoulos's known film work, but the most celebrated of all his films, *The Illiac Passion*, is given the most prominence, appearing in every single order once, and in the last order four times. *Eros, O Basileus* appears in eight orders, with three sections alternating with *The Illiac Passion* in the final order. *The Mysteries* (1968) and *Twice A Man*, are each included in four orders, but never together. *Himself as Herself* (1967) is also in four of the 67 later works, most unseen not only by the public, but also by Markopoulos himself due to a lack of funds to print the films. Markopoulos chose to call the sections "orders" rather than "cycles" in an allusion to the composer François Couperin.[48]

The complete running time for all 22 orders of *Eniaios* is estimated at over 80 hours. The 16mm film orders have a formal structure inspired by Wagner's Ring Cycle, and refer to the transformation of Prometheus and the healing by sleep of Asclepius. Each order is divided up into reels, which act as chapters, with each chapter being a strategic reedit of a single film. No single chapter within *Eniaios* edits together more than one of his previous film works. There are between five and 13 reels, or chapters, in each order, with Order I containing the largest number—13 reels. Markopoulos perceived *Eniaios* as his sole film work and wanted the previous edited oeuvre to be either destroyed or forgotten.[49] After Markopoulos' death, Beavers made the older, known films available for selected screenings.

Eniaios was created for a specific site, to be the sole location where the work would be projected. The idea to have complete control of the projection and location for Markopoulos' work was both inspired by Wagner, and grew from a dissatisfaction with the way that art films were screened at public institutions. In 1980 Markopoulos, along with Beavers, held the first of seven annual outdoor screenings at a site he named Temenos.[50] It was during this period that Markopoulos began editing a complete order of his films. The initial intention for *Eniaios* was for the whole work to be screened over a period of several weeks in the 1990s, and then later shown at regular intervals at the Temenos site. The Temenos is located outside the village of Lyssaraia in the Peloponnese and was chosen as it was the birthplace of Markopoulos' father. Had circumstances been different, the chosen site could well have been in Switzerland, despite the fact that Markopoulos felt strongly drawn to his Greek roots: "Arcadia, the idyllic pastoral landscape of classical Greece, and a place where ritual and religion had been intertwined with the natural world for thousands of years."[51]

Markopoulos managed to complete the edit for all 22 orders before his death in 1992; it took over a decade, but he did not view or screen a single reel, as the orders remained unprinted. In 2004, orders I and II were shown for the first time at the Temenos, followed by orders III, IV and V in 2008; orders VI, VII, and VIII in 2012; and orders IX, X and XI in 2016. The 45-minute dedicatory preface work, *Pyra Heracleous* (date unknown), was projected at the 2008 screening. It begins with its title in code format, alternating black and clear leader, showing the title of the film with each clear section measured to represent different letters of the Greek alphabet. The black-and-white measured flashes on the screen continue after the title has finished, and are then occasionally punctuated by images of the ruins on Mount Oeta, traditionally described as the funeral pyre of Hercules, from which, according to myth, his immortal being rose to Mount Olympus.[52] Each reel of each order starts with its title in the same black-and-clear leader code. These coded titles build a rhythm for the film. When the film images are projected, each image is heavily surrounded by either a clear or a black leader, or a pattern of both, usually placed symmetrically with each side of the image. The audience is not meant to be "able to decipher the cryptogram, but the cinematic rhythms it produces tutor the eye for the hours to follow."[53]

Eniaios and the Temenos are reminiscent of Wagner's *Ring des Niebelungen* (*Ring Cycle*, 1874), and the Bayreuther Festspielhaus (Bayreuth Festival Theatre). Wagner created the Bayreuth Festival Theatre while composing the *Ring Cycle*, with the intention that the building be solely used for his work. The Bayreuth Festival Theatre differed from the traditional opera house, which has several tiers of seating in a horseshoe shaped auditorium. The design at Bayreuth arranged the seating in a single, steeply shaped wedge, with no galleries or boxes. Markopoulos theorized the spectator similarly to Wagner as can be seen in Wagner's design of Bayreuth; there was an unseen recessed orchestra pit that would create a "mystic abyss."[54]

The idea for the Temenos site can be traced back to the late 1960s and it has been suggested that the notion of the Temenos was in "dialectical opposition" to the Anthology Film Archives, which initiated its utopian phase in 1970.[55] Anthology's original conception was to house the Essential Cinema Repertory, a selection of films that were to be screened continuously in a cycle intended to define the art of cinema. The Invisible Cinema at Anthology was designed by Peter Kubelka, with panels between the chairs to enhance the spectator's immersion by blocking the view from either side. The design of The Invisible Cinema as an enclosed cinematic space with only a view of the screen, contrasts with Markopoulos' vision of an outdoors cinema under the stars with the natural sounds of the Peloponnese.

Eniaios was created as a film to harmonize with Markopoulos' vision of the Temenos site. *Eniaios* may indeed be the longest film ever made, but it was clearly not the only grand-scale project to come out of New American Cinema. Another system-building approach to film can be seen in Hollis Frampton's *Magellan* project. Frampton created a system for a film work to be viewed in sections each day of the year. As Frampton wrote in "A Statement of Plans for *Magellan*": "It's not a work that can be diagrammed in linear fashion, since it uses the grid—among many others—of the cycle of the solar year. In other words, it's a calendar."[56] The plans included "The malleability of the sense and notion of time in film. Investigating of the temporal plasticity proper to an art that subsists at once within the colliding modes of memory, absolute 'presentness,' and anticipation."[57] Frampton voiced concern for *Mallegan* in the "empirical retrieval of its scheme," and, like Markopoulos, wanted the work to be in "the immediate, the present, and not to show structure."[58]

Frampton's essay, "Notes on Composing Film," postulates two modes of examining the process of artistic composition: the first is "reading"; and the second, "misreading."[59] "The mode we call reading entails a correct extrapolation of the axiomatic substructure from the artist's immediately apprehensible tradition."[60] Frampton further divides the mode of reading into four categories, one of which is "constriction."[61] In an essay on Beavers, P. Adams Sitney makes an association between Frampton's idea of "constriction," and the environment in which Beavers grew up as a filmmaker. "Joyce: 'the works from which he derived the laws that govern his writing were those of another, Gustave Flaubert.' Surely this is a hyperbole, but an instructive one. A similar case in the American avant-garde cinema would be that of Beavers himself: a parallel hyperbolic statement might usefully claim that he constricted the history of cinema to the films of Gregory Markopoulos."[62]

The isolation and metaphysical process Markopoulos procured for *Eniaios* are similar to the idea of constriction as the reduction of a canon to a single author. Frampton theorized film as being comparable to "metahistories" of events.[63] The structure of *Eniaios* can literally be compared to Frampton's concept of metahistory in that *Eniaios* projects and repeats Markopoulos' metahistories. The similarity of thinking between Markopoulos and Frampton with regard to Frampton's mode of constriction and metahistory perhaps reflects the zeitgeist and the trend at this time toward creating grand, scale-built systems for film. Despite Markopoulos' chosen isolation and disassociation, parallels can still be drawn between him and other filmmakers in his materialist, structural thinking of film.

When Markopoulos conceived of the Temenos, he renounced the psychological analogy of the single frame, evoking "thought images." The narrative aspect of Markopoulos' film development ceased to be an essential dimension of his films. Instead, the "rhythmic and connotative" forces of the film frame would become the center of his work.[64] Markopoulos was not the first filmmaker to make extensive use of very brief shots, including single frames, but he was the first to give the matter theoretical expression. Robert Breer, Stan Brakhage, and Peter Kubelka had made such editing strategies signature aspects of their filmmaking. Breer never entered the domain of film theory, Brakhage never addressed the issue of the single frame editing directly, and Kubelka maintained silence about his working methods and ideas on cinema until he was first welcomed by American audiences in 1965. The theoretical work for which Kubelka is known was largely formulated in the 1970s.[65] Kubelka's theories often intersect with those of Markopoulos in fascinating ways. *What Is Film*, is a cyclical film program created by Kubelka in 1996 on the centenary of cinema, as a series seeking to define "film as an independent art form, as a tool that cultivates new ways of thinking."[66] *What Is Film* was screened at the Austrian Film Museum in Vienna and consists of 63 curated programs, three of which are dedicated solely to Markopoulos, and two to Robert Beavers. Kubelka and Markopoulos both theorize personal numeric systems and the importance of hand craftsmanship in filmmaking. The personal numeric systems are defined by Kubelka as "Metric Films," and by Markopoulos in his writings as "Personal Mathematics." Both approaches to film editing see film as "measured rhythm."[67] During a lecture at the Rotterdam International Film Festival in 2000, Kubelka announced:

> I introduced something into cinema that has had a history of millions of years in music, and that's measured rhythm. Which until cinema came, was not possible to handle, because we could not master visual information with the necessary speed.[68]

Kubelka's theory of measured rhythm differs from Markopoulos' similar theories in that Kubelka takes an anthropomorphic, and Markopoulos an esoteric, approach.

In describing his anthropomorphic film theory, Kubelka makes the point: "Human thought is static. We think in static elements. Be it images, be it sound."[69] Through viewing film as a series of static images and likening the projection of film to the brain's recognition of movement, Kubelka concludes that film "imitates the situation of the human organism."[70] Kubelka's numeric relationship with film is similar to Markopoulos' approach, as can be seen in the measured film length that structures *Eniaios*. Markopoulos' esoteric approach to measured rhythm in film can be seen in his numerous writings and interviews.

> The secret language is that you have seen one of my films before. It is like looking at Egyptian hieroglyphics or some advance mathematical scheme and having no way of relating to it.[71]

Both Markopoulos and Kubelka thought in similar ways about the poetics of film repetition through measured rhythm in contrast to the more literary tendency of commercial film.

> There are two usual ways of looking at the world. There are novels and there are poems. Novels have a chronological progress, they start with a birth and end with death or whatever, it's chronological. One thing after the other, linear. Then there is another view of the world, which is the ecstasy of repetition, the knowledge of the cyclic. The fact that everything repeats itself, we ourselves are a symphony of repeating events.[72]

Beavers revisited his early work, reediting it and recording new sound. This was in dialogue with Markopoulos, who was reediting his filmography into *Eniaos* and deciding upon no sound. Beavers removed certain layers and superimpositions.

> About 20 years after I made *The Count of Days* in Zurich, I was at the Cinémathèque suisse de Lausanne, they have a copy of the film and I looked at it and thought, "Oh, I can do this better." And because I owned the films, I had the freedom, I could do this. And I decided to invest the time and that's a very important thing to decide whether you want to invest your time in a new direction or by revisiting. I probably wouldn't have done it if I hadn't had that time, connection, and judgment about the work as it was. It can be very important, and this I learnt from the extreme New American filmmakers. With Gregory as a main example. To extreme individuality and independence. But how to protect that. Because that alone can be a very dangerous state. Which also comes from the medium of film coming from the outside of art systems. So I saw something in it that was somehow mannered, and I wanted to make it clearer and simpler.[73]

Beavers revisited his filmography in parallel to Markopoulos, although this restructuring was considerably more fragmentary for Markopoulos.

> Gregory was more speculative, the theories behind what are animating his decisions are more speculative. His ideas of Hellenism and healing, etc. I'm not so interested in placing the spectator in such an extreme position. Which is not to say I don't think it's wonderful, it's just not me. And I'm more interested also in the human voice. But we still share a lot.[74]

Just before Markopoulos' death in 1992, Beavers and Markopoulos were living between Switzerland and Munich and Freiburg in Germany. In 1993 Beavers relocated to Zug in Switzerland, and was a guest of Ulrich Straub for five years. This was an important period for Beavers, as he edited and created new soundtracks for his films working with Christian Beusch. He launched all the structures of the Temenos, creating an archive with the aid of Thomas and Ruedi Bechtler, establishing Temenos Inc., a nonprofit charity in New York, and preparing for the first retrospectives of Markopoulos' work, and screenings of his own. Christoph von Graffenried, David Streiff, and Daniel Schedler were instrumental in aiding and advising Beavers, while creating and sustaining the structures put in place.

> I gave 10 years to reediting my soundtracks in an editing room on the Röntgenstrasse in Zurich, except for one or two. For some reason the soundtrack for *Amor* I didn't change. I found it was fine as it was.[75]

In creating the new soundtracks, Beavers revisited many of the locations of his films to record new sound, combining these new recordings with the original older recordings, mixing together the space from the past and present. Beavers also shot the film *The Ground* (1993/2001) during this period when he was rerecording sound. *The Ground* was shot in Hydra in Greece, and Beavers captured the same tower in *The Ground* as appeared in *Winged Dialogue*, the first film Beavers shot in Europe.

> Recognition. How does one recognize one filmmaker from another filmmaker? I pose this question to myself amid the din of the small craft named *Aegina*, which at the moment is speeding toward the island of Aegina, the first stop on its way to the island of Hydra. The laughter and spray of the sea is conducive to this afternoon's extravagant gesture.[76]

[1] P. Adams Sitney stated that Markopoulos was the only filmmaker with a genuine pedigree to join the New American Cinema during a lecture at the American Academy, Berlin, on May 5, 2011.
[2] Letter dated October 6, 1965 from Robert Beavers to Gregory Markopoulos. Gregory Markopoulos, "Inherent Limitations" (1966), Mark Webber (ed.), *Film As Film: The Collected Writings of Gregory J. Markopoulos*, The Visible Press, London 2014, p. 64.
[3] Nikos Kazantzakis, "Report to Greco" (1961), Gregory Markopoulos, "Inherent Limitations" (1966), *Film As Film: The Collected Writings of Gregory J. Markopoulos*, p. 64.
[4] "Personal filmmaking," a term Beavers used in an interview with Ian Wooldridge, Berlin 2017.
[5] Gregory Markopoulos, "Inherent Limitations" (1966), *Film As Film: The Collected Writings of Gregory J. Markopoulos*, p. 64–65.
[6] Markopoulos interviewed in Knokke-le-Zoute, Belgium, in 1968. Interview audio file at Temenos Archive shelf number: 12_1_68_KNOKKE_INT.01_02-01.
[7] Robert Beavers interviewed by Ian Wooldridge, Berlin 2017.
[8] Gregory Markopoulos, "A Solemn Pause" (1971), *Film As Film: The Collected Writings of Gregory J. Markopoulos*, p. 349.
[9] Robert Beavers interviewed by Ian Wooldridge, Berlin 2017.
[10] Ibid.
[11] Personal correspondence with Robert Beavers, August 2011.
[12] Ibid.
[13] Gregory Markopoulos, "The Complex Illusion," *Boustrophedon*, printed edition of 100, Pioda, Rome November 1977, p. 73, Temenos Archive.
[14] It has been well documented that when he lived in Europe Markopoulos withdrew his permission to print this chapter in the second edition of *Visionary Film*. The chapter has been restored to the current edition. P. Adams Sitney, *Visionary Film: The American Avant-Garde 1943–2000* [1974], 3rd ed., Oxford University Press, Oxford 2002.
[15] Gregory Markopoulos, "Sto Palikari" (1968), *Film As Film: The Collected Writings of Gregory J. Markopoulos*, p. 50.
[16] Robert Beavers interviewed by Ian Wooldridge, Berlin 2017.
[17] Ibid.
[18] Tom S. Chomont, "A Note on *The Count of Days*, a Film by Robert Beavers 1970," Rebekah Rutkoff (ed.), *Robert Beavers*, Österreichisches Filmmuseum SYNEMA-Gesellschaft für Film und Media, Vienna 2017, p. 15.
[19] Susan Oxtoby, "Toronto International Film Festival program notes, 2003," Rebekah Rutkoff (ed.), *Robert Beavers*, p. 206.
[20] Tom S. Chomont, "A Note on *The Count of Days*, a Film by Robert Beavers 1970," p. 15.
[21] Gregory Markopoulos, "The Filmmaker as Physician of the Future 1967," *Film As Film: The Collected Writings of Gregory J. Markopoulos*, p. 231.
[22] Ibid., p. 32.
[23] Gregory Markopoulos interviewed in Louvain, 1968. Audio file from the Temenos Archive: II_68_Louvain_Illiac_P_1_01_01.
[24] P. Adams Sitney, "Further Orders," *Artforum*, October 2008, p. 135–140.
[25] Ibid.
[26] Ibid.
[27] Robert Beavers, "Em.blem," *The Searching Measure: Writings by Robert Beavers*, University of California, Berkeley 2004.
[28] Gregory Markopoulos interviewed in Frankfurt in 1985. Temenos Archive audio file: 28_II_85_FRANKFURT_DICKENBERGER_03-01.
[29] Gregory Markopoulos interviewed in Zurich in 1969. Temenos Archive audio file: 21_1_69_ZURICH_INT.
[30] Ibid.
[31] Robert Beavers interviewed by Ian Wooldridge, Berlin 2017.
[32] James Hoberman, "The Village Voice," Rebekah Rutkoff (ed.), *Robert Beavers*, p. 208.
[33] P. Adams Sitney, "Majestic Images," *Film Comment*, March/April 2001.
[34] Tony Pipolo, "The Films of Robert Beavers, Berkeley Art Museum and Pacific Film Archive," Rebekah Rutkoff (ed.), *Robert Beavers*, p. 209.
[35] Robert Beavers, "Sotiros A Sequence of Notes" (1978), Rebekah Rutkoff (ed.), *Robert Beavers*, p.181–192.
[36] Ibid.
[37] "A&Bing" was a term commonly used for checkerboard editing and was the term that Brakhage used.
[38] Brakhage, letter to Markopoulos published in "On Splicing," Stan Brakhage, *A Moving Picture Giving and Taking Book*, Frontier Press, West Newbury 1971.
[39] Gregory Markopoulos, "The Intuition Space" (1973), *Film As Film: The Collected Writings of Gregory J. Markopoulos*, p. 76.
[40] Robert Beavers interviewed by Ian Wooldridge, Berlin 2017.
[41] Ibid.
[42] P. Adams Sitney, "Foreword," *Film As Film: The Collected Writings of Gregory J. Markopoulos*, p. 36.
[43] Gregory Markopoulos, "The Intuition Space" (1973), *Film As Film: The Collected Writings of Gregory J. Markopoulos*, p. 75.
[44] Ibid.
[45] Markopoulos interviewed in Knokke-le-Zoute, Belgium, in 1968. Interview audio file at the Temenos Archive with shelf number: 12_1_68_KNOKKE_INT.01_02-01.
[46] Edward Carpenter, *The Drama of Love and Death*, Mitchell Kennerly, New York/London 1912, cited in Gregory Markopoulos, "The Filmmaker as Physician of the Future," p. 234.
[47] Michael Wang, "Silent Nights," *Artforum*, 12.07.08, http://www.artforum.com/film/id=20697, last accessed March 2020.
[48] François Couperin, 1668–1733, French Baroque composer, organist, and harpsichordist. Personal communication with Robert Beavers, August 24, 2011.
[49] Ibid.
[50] In calling his projection space "Temenos," the filmmaker was invoking the religious traditions of ancient Greece, where a portion of land was set aside for the ritual worship of a god. The original meaning of the term "Temenos" is "a piece of land set apart."
[51] P. Adams Sitney, "Further Orders," *Artforum*, October 2008, p. 135–140.
[52] Ibid.
[53] Ibid.
[54] Richard Wagner, "Bayreuth (The Stage Festival Hall)," *Collected Writings and Poems*, 4th edition, Röder, Leipzig 1907, p. 336.
[55] P. Adams Sitney, "Foreword," Gregory Markopoulos, *Film As Film: The Collected Writings of Gregory J. Markopoulos*, p. 31.
[56] Deke Dusinberre, Ian Christie, "Episodes from a Lost History of Movie Serialism. Interview with Hollis Frampton," *Film Studies*, no. 4, Summer 2004.
[57] Hollis Frampton, "A Statement of Plans for *Magellan*," Bruce Jenkins (ed.), *On the Camera Arts and Consecutive Matters: The Writings of Hollis Frampton*, MIT Press, Cambridge, Massachusetts 2009, p. 226.
[58] Deke Dusinberre & Ian Christie, "Episodes from a Lost History of Movie Serialism. Interview with Hollis Frampton."
[59] Hollis Frampton, "Notes on Composing Films" (1976), Bruce Jenkins (ed.), *On the Camera Arts and Consecutive Matters: The Writings of Hollis Frampton*, p. 151
[60] Ibid.
[61] Ibid.

[62] P. Adams Sitney, "Majestic Images," *Film Comment*, vol. 37, no. 2, March–April 2001, in relation to Hollis Frampton's "Notes on Composing Films."
[63] Hollis Frampton, "For a Metahistory of Film: Commonplace Notes and Hypotheses" [1971], Bruce Jenkins (ed.), *On the Camera Arts and Consecutive Matters: The Writings of Hollis Frampton*, p. 131.
[64] P. Adams Sitney, "Foreword," *Film As Film: The Collected Writings of Gregory J. Markopoulos*, p. 31.
[65] *Ibid.*
[66] *What is Film / Was ist Film*, Peter Kubelka's cyclical programme at Österreichischen Filmmuseum.
[67] Rotterdam International Film Festival 2000. PK _ 020000 _ Rotterdam What is Cinema, by Peter Kubelka, recorded by Mark Webber.
[68] *Ibid.*
[69] *Ibid.*
[70] *Ibid.*
[71] *Ibid.*
[72] *Ibid.*
[73] Robert Beavers interviewed by Ian Wooldridge, Berlin 2017.
[74] *Ibid.*
[75] *Ibid.*
[76] July 10, 1967, *Film As Film: The Collected Writings of Gregory J. Markopoulos*, p. 285.

At the Limits of the Visible: Clemens Klopfenstein's Experiments of the 1970s
Simon Koenig

Translated from the German by Steven Lindberg

Clemens Klopfenstein, *Geschichte der Nacht* (*Story of the Night*), 1978 (Switzerland)
16mm film, 63 minutes

The 1970s were a crucial period in Clemens Klopfenstein's life and work, a time marked by a new productivity that enabled Klopfenstein to establish an artistic foundation, reorient himself, and, thanks to great independence and a lack of constraints, develop freely.

In the early 1960s, Klopfenstein, who was born in Täuffelen in the Canton of Bern in 1944, made his first cinematic efforts using his father's 8mm Keystone camera. Impressed by Alain Resnais' *L'Année dernière à Marienbad* (*Last Year at Marienbad*, 1961), he made his first film, *René*, in 1962. An internship at the Schwarz Film laboratory in Ostermundigen made the secondary-school student sensitive to the technical and yet creative process of developing film, and established important contacts for his key work *Geschichte der Nacht* (*Story of the Night*, 1978). In 1963 he realized *La Condition humaine* (*The Human Condition*) and in 1964 *Darf die Schweiz nicht verlassen*

(*May Not Leave Switzerland*). In 1966 Klopfenstein cofounded, with Urs Aebersold and Philip Schaad, the AKS artists' collective. Together they made several short experimental films and organized screenings of films by the international avant-garde. In 1973, in the wake of the financial debacle of and the legal battles over the lavishly produced feature film *Die Fabrikanten* (*The Factory Owners*, 1974), the group broke up. The end of AKS did not mean Klopfenstein's farewell to filmmaking, but he did put down his camera for a time and began to draw, returning to the medium he had studied at the Kunstgewerbeschule (Applied Arts School) in Basel in the 1960s. The drawings he made at this time led him to a new, productive, and artistically formative period in his life.[1]

With Drawings to New Shores[2]

The *Pandesowna* drawings of the early 1970s years grew out of the failure of the major project *Die Fabrikanten*, and reflected Klopfenstein's search for a new form of artistic expression. The cycle alludes to Jan Potocki's novel *Manuscrit trouvé à Saragosse* (*The Manuscript Found in Saragossa*, 1814). They were initial studies for the production of a large-scale history film, intended to provide the visual, atmospheric foundation for that project. The preparatory sketches for this large planned project, which had presumably been discussed euphorically among friends, became an autonomous work, and ultimately a crucial point in the biography of the filmmaker. The large-format drawings (70 × 100 cm) show fragments of monumental buildings, labyrinthine sequences of spaces situated in bleak architectonic settings, occupied but not animated by several figures that seem lost. The images, which are highly reminiscent of Giorgio de Chirico's *Pittura metafisica* or the Surrealist paintings of Salvador Dalí, also depict deserts: arid, extinct wastelands. They express a tormented wilderness and reveal memories of a collapsed world, whose inhabitants are lonely and abandoned prisoners of an environment that can no longer be reanimated and is doomed to destruction. No redemptive ending will appear in its blank gaze. High walls that close off access to a world behind them illustrate this oppressive captivity. The white paper support itself also becomes an unarticulated prison wall. The unmarked areas of the sheet seem like an unbounded, unstructured place, and thus become a suffocating, seemingly opaque space or even the projection screen for the psychotic, depressive worlds of ideas of the apathetic-looking figures and their viewers. The pencil strokes become lost in the white of the background, a *non finito* that does not mean, as that phrase might suggest, a lack of production time, but rather a degeneration and hence a superfluity of time. That work was already a manifestation of Klopfenstein's interest in integrating the support, and in its visible dovetailing with the motif and the diegesis of the image.

The theme of ruins made Klopfenstein a suitable candidate for the Swiss Art Competition organized annually by the Federal Office of Culture. The grant he received as a result of his entry enabled him to stay in Rome from 1973 to 1974 at the Istituto Svizzero, a villa in the center of the city, a place for artists and scientists. Klopfenstein lived in the tower room, which enjoyed a panorama over the city and intense sunshine from morning to evening—a situation that had a crucial effect on his work. During this stay he produced the cycle *Blast of Silence*—ink drawings with a certain cinematic look of nighttime dreams, and dungeons with scaffold-like constructions in wood that vanish into an immense depth. These works recall the architectural phantasies of Giovanni Battista Piranesi's *Carceri* (Prisons, 1745–1761). They are focused, detail-obsessed drawings that are dedicated to complex perspective and dystopian effect.

The untitled ink drawings Klopfenstein produced in 1974, by contrast, are much less inhibited. He explored the spatial behavior of utopian-looking spaces, architecture, and snail- and mollusk-like shells with rapid strokes, although here too the desertedness leaves the impression of an unconditional abandonment. Here too he was sketching the atmosphere that the draftsman, painter, photographer, and filmmaker would bring to its full potential in his later experimental photographs and films shot at night.

Living in the Roman Lighthouse

In 1975 Klopfenstein produced the cycle *Der Tag isch vergange* (*The Day Has Passed*). He studied the path of the daylight, the state of twilight, the effect of light and darkness on space and architecture. Although he was not working on any specific film projects, he never set his Bolex camera aside entirely. That same year he made the short film *La luce romana vista da Ferraniacolor* (*The Light of Rome as Seen in Ferraniacolor*),[3] a cinematic sketch with no ambition to be a formally perfect work. As the film's title suggests, it focuses on Roman light—a topos of Western art—and its effect on film stock. The Ferraniacolor amateur film stock captures light in a characteristic way and stores it and reproduces it in a specific way. In Klopfenstein's experimental film *Geschichte der Nacht* (1978), too, the artist's grappling with the materiality of the medium is crucial.

La luce romana vista da Ferraniacolor was made directly from the apparatus of the studio—from its immediate horizon. The tower room served Klopfenstein as a frame, the balcony a place to position the 16mm Bolex camera, and the city and the sky as his protagonists and objects of study, which he captured with lenses of different focal lengths. The changing light of day and night made Rome seem always new and different. The camera and the film stock reacted in different ways to the changing light, and hence the prospect changed constantly. Klopfenstein did not systematically compile a collection of lighting situations; rather, he gave in to the existing moods of the light and captured them in numerous panning shots. There is no chronological sequence, but rather a potpourri of distinct shots whose duration was always limited by the maximum shooting time of his hand-wound Bolex.

Another crucial visual feature of this film is the movement of rotation. The spring-driven 16mm Bolex had to be wound with a crank. Perhaps it was this cranking motion of winding it up and the subsequent whirring sound of the film winding through when shooting that inspired Klopfenstein to transfer the rotating motion to his own body and to his motifs: the repetitive pans over the city lie within an angle of 120 to 160 degrees. Only in the second half of the film are these perspectives mirrored by shots of a monk absorbed in reading while walking in a circle. He makes his repetitive rounds on the roof terrace of the building next to the Istituto Svizzero, the Sant'Isidoro a Capo le Case monastery, while Klopfenstein records the

monk with his cinematic eye. Seemingly affected by this movement, in the final shot of the film Klopfenstein steps from the balcony into the tower room and ends the brief sketch-like film with a quick pan around his own axis.
It looks as if, by turning wildly, he wanted to expand his view from the balcony and his own angle of view. The tower's balcony offers a view of the city, but its limited width restricts the field of vision, transfixes the gaze, even, by means of deflecting barriers. Moreover, its separation divides people from the urban space, since at best the balcony permits an inevitable approximation. Klopfenstein seems to want to liberate himself from this limit: by stepping through the balcony door into the room and then turning 360 degrees wildly several times, he breaks through the limits he has set himself. Not only the real space of the studio, but also the image—and its specific directedness and format—seem to break down.

Under the belated gaze of science, which seeks ordering patterns, a metaphor for Klopfenstein's transformative artistic practice can be found in these various qualities of movement: the car traveling through the streets of Rome with which the film opens, the panning and turning of the camera, and the rapidly fading Roman light reproduced in moving cinematic images can be interpreted as a rediscovery of movement. Already in the AKS films, even in *Nach Rio* (*To Rio*, 1968), that is to say, already in his earliest films, car trips play an important role; in Klopfenstein's later films they almost become a leitmotif. On the one hand, they give the image a direction and a depth, and offer the viewers and the protagonists room for reflection through this basic photogenic quality,[4] and, on the other hand, they are action-filled entertainment, albeit in extremely reduced form, thanks to the maelstrom of movement. The free pans of the rotating handheld camera also become Klopfenstein's trademark and stand prototypically for his films, since they sum up two basic features of his aesthetics and poetics: freedom when making films, and the visibility of the process of producing a film. The distanced gaze from the balcony over the city of Rome is followed in later works by the real world lying directly before our eyes. The step back and the rotation made possible by the expanded surroundings of the studio seem like a blow for freedom from the gloomy fantasy worlds in Klopfenstein's drawings, as a transition and physical entry into a real space. The sketch-like film is also interesting because Klopfenstein once again exchanged pencil, brush, and pen for the Bolex; his images are produced with light and set in motion. It seems as if Klopfenstein had had enough of sitting still in front of the drawing paper, and the gloomy worlds that emerged on it. As if he, filled with light, noise, and lust for life, had reached a state of extreme tension like the wound Bolex spring, and had to transfer this energy onto film: renouncing all limits and, rotating freely, finding a new language. In the dark cinema, Klopfenstein becomes a lighthouse keeper awakening the light of the Roman cityscape to new life in the darkness of space. Life in the musty, condemned buildings of Kleinbasel, which plagued the artist, who suffered from asthma, was past.[5] The joy of the light, the glare, and hence the exploitation of the material—an amusing fiasco that manages to capture the light of Rome but also destroys the image—all prevail.

Rome at his Feet

This shift, which can be followed in the film, returns—albeit not in quite such a linear form—in Klopfenstein's later artistic practice. The flat space of the drawing paper, which achieves an illusion of depth in drawings of fantasy landscapes, leads to the photograph, which freezes the real space of Rome and reproduces it almost as flatly. Only the film medium, and filming in the city bring movement and expand the experience of a sense of space. When drawing imaginary worlds, Klopfenstein was able to move by imagination in virtual worlds alone, whereas as a photographer and cameraman he can actually spend time in the spaces around him. Installed at the Istituto Svizzero, Klopfenstein turned to the motifs that lay at his feet: the actual city of Rome. His works now no longer came solely from his imagination; the real but nonetheless stage-like, apparently utopian space of Rome now became the foundation and point of departure for Klopfenstein's work. The city, which draws its present day from the presence of the past, seemed almost predestined for his interest in utopian-dystopian orders. The perplexing simultaneity of architectural epochs and styles is heightened in the darkness of late night when the urban space is washed clean of its traces of everyday life and freed of loud, smelly traffic, that is to say, of the unromantic facts that give the city its contemporaneity. In such moments Rome reveals itself to the flâneurs strolling through the city, as at once a stage and a scenery storage room. At night the sparsely lit buildings are reduced to their facades and thus in a sense to the radiant cinematic image that can set passersby in motion: time travel and a quasi-cinematic experience, and not only because of the memory of the many movies filmed in this setting.

Soon after arriving at the Istituto Svizzero, Klopfenstein began to work on reproducing the night. In 1974 he produced the photographic series *Paese Sera* (*Night Pieces*), with *Roma Notte 74* (*Rome at Night 74*) and, a year later, *Umbria Notte 75* (*Umbria at Night 75*). Very much in contrast to the sober aesthetic and the photojournalism of the documentary style that had secured Klopfenstein an income during the politically troubled 1970s,[6] and enabled him to make additional trips to Italy, these night photographs anticipated the poetics of the cinematic experiments of *Geschichte der Nacht* and *Transes – Reiter auf dem toten Pferd* (*Trances—Rider on the Dead Horse*, 1982). Klopfenstein "experienced" the nocturnal Roman urban space on his moped; he traveled to the rural villages of Umbria, experimented with the high-speed still film Kodak Tri-X, indulged his vagrancy, sounded out and developed his liberated experimentation and unprejudiced approach to the world before him and his Pentax or Bolex. Slowly but surely his filmic language became close to the characteristic language of photography and film that evolved from the documentary eye and experimental, artistic alienation. During this period he established the foundation for the artistic practice of his later cinematic night shots.

Filming in the Dark

Klopfenstein had a great love of classical narrative cinema. The frequent but brief night scenes typical of the genre of film noir, and the atmospheric night scenes of the films of Jean-Pierre Melville, Michelangelo Antonioni, and Federico Fellini won Klopfenstein over to cinematically reproducing darkness. The night scenes in classical narrative cinema and in European art house films particularly inspired Klopfenstein. Just as important, however, were his interests specific to the medium and to the aesthetic of the material, which could be explored experimentally by working with the paradoxical relationship of film, as a medium of light, to darkness: like all other cinematic images, darkness is reproduced with light.

Working with darkness and its reproduction using photosensitive materials had preoccupied Klopfenstein since the late 1960s. In addition to his film *copains* from the AKS artists' collective, he made the short documentary film *Variété Clara* in 1969, in collaboration with Georg Janett. The themes of decline and former glory resonated here as well, since the eponymous theater building was about to be demolished, and the goal to use no additional light sources to illuminate the setting made high-speed film stock necessary. In 1972 he produced *White Night*, another important experiment on this subject. In a hunting magazine to which his father had subscribed, Klopfenstein came across a residual light intensifier, a passive night-vision instrument— a piece of technical equipment that had originally been developed for military purposes, but was appreciated in the civilian world for, among other things, tracking game. Fascinated by this technical possibility, he contacted Eltro GmbH, a radiation technology company that produced the device, and was able to convince them to let him take test photographs. With the help of their engineers, he mounted the night-vision device in front of the lens of a rented 16mm Arriflex, supplementing the camera's lens with an intermediary lens. This resulted in bright shots with lots of noise due to the specific technology of the device—images that referred to the real space in front of the camera and made things visible that would be hidden to the naked eye. But the world reproduced in this way is subject to powerful distortion by the medium. The filmed objects joined with the noise of the medium and created a new, surreal world. This striking discrepancy between the image, and pre-cinematic reality, was what fascinated Klopfenstein.

Several years later Klopfenstein was experimenting again, this time with Kodak 4-X reversal film stock, which had only recently been made available in Switzerland. As the field for his experiments he chose the night of the Thursday morning of Basel's Fasnacht carnival, which ends at 4:00 am. Snow flurries and film grain, motifs and the materiality of the medium seem to fuse. Enthusiastic about the result, Klopfenstein submitted the film to the Solothurner Filmtage under the title *Ceremony* (1977). This was a crucial step, since the ZDF producer Sibylle Hubatschek-Rahn saw the film there and offered Klopfenstein partial funding for a full-length experimental film in this style to be shown as part of the series *Das kleine Fernsehspiel* (*The Short Television Play*). (In 1978, Klopfenstein integrated fragments of the ten-minute short film into *Geschichte der Nacht*.) In Schweizerische Radio- und Fernsehgesellschaft (SRG) and the Institut national de l'audiovisuel (INA), he found additional partners who were very important for the dissemination and visibility of nascent experimental film. Working with his friend and sound engineer Hugo Sigrist, he planned a European trip for the filming, and the majority of the material was shot and developed within two years.

Story of the Night

Although the title might suggest otherwise, *Geschichte der Nacht* does not really have a narrative. Neither spoken nor narrated, it is purely the effect of the images and the sound, which plunge the viewers into a cinematic, unreal world and cause them to stroll like flâneurs through a night full of contradictions. Ruins appear, lost plazas, contrasted with illuminated monuments, palaces, deserted train stations—misery, wealth, the harsh power of the state, and yet also traces of humanity. Processions, masquerades, fireworks, and celebrations, populated by ghostly figures in isolated sociability. The viewers stroll out of mild summer nights and cool mornings into ice-cold snow flurries, damp, and cold, surrounded by noises, murmurs, the echo of final melodies. A journey through the night, not just dark but also bright as day, evolves from jet-black darkness to the gray morning sky of the city. But the city remains dominated by the atmosphere of night. Here and there figures are seen, but they are shadows, silhouettes, ghostly beings without faces, forms, or words. The slow, regular, and yet disturbing breathing of the images taken with a camera rotated without a tripod reveal, when viewed subjectively, a living gaze, which becomes our own and enables us to look into a strange timeless and placeless night, into a melancholy, beautiful world. Klopfenstein turns the labyrinth that he had already made a theme of his drawings into an experience in this work. The film's title makes us think it shows a single night. But the images allow the viewers to experience the state of the night, without time or space, edited in an inconsistent unity. In a single night, the rhythms of the year pass; big cities gather with small ones; southern architecture is replaced by northern and eastern architecture. The recognition of famous monuments or views leaves false trails and cause the viewers lost in the cinematic labyrinth to grope around, confused, in the dark.[7]

    The matching of the images with noises recorded by Hugo Sigrist and music by Uşşak Mevlevi Ayini and by the Third Ear Band produces the dreamlike atmosphere of this experimental film. It is, however, chiefly the result of Klopfenstein's artistic ambition not to show the world as we know it. The profilmic real world, already alienated by darkness, was altered and manipulated by means of the high-speed film stock and specific technical procedures and operations during the shooting and developing of the film. The decision to dispense entirely with additional light sources when filming forced Klopfenstein to use the highest-speed film he could find. The 16mm Kodak Eastman 4× film that he used featured a higher percentage of large silver-bromide crystals. The resulting surface has increased photosensitivity that ensures that entire crystals change color even under poor light conditions. Even during the shooting Klopfenstein tried to ensure through various technical measures that as much residual light from the dark night dream as possible reached the photosensitive reversal film. First, he opened the camera aperture as wide as possible; second, he reduced the speed of the camera from the usual 24 frames per second to 23. This enabled him to further counter the underexposure of the material resulting from poor lighting conditions.

    The Swiss film laboratory Schwarz Film, which over time came to specialize in developing reversal film,[8] granted Klopfenstein experiments that could intensify the traces in the latent image on the reversal film. Developing the film is subject to rules that differ according to the type and manufacture of the film stock. These are set by the makers of the stock. The specifications are based to a certain extent on an ideal image that is neither under- nor overexposed, does not cause grain noise, and does not result in other artifacts becoming visible. It was crucial to Klopfenstein's artistic practice that he was not primarily interested in producing such standard images. He did not just put up with flaws, but declared them to be part of the poetics of his images. This ambition meant that the machines at Schwarz Film's laboratory had to be manipulated as well. Because their settings were relatively fixed during the day in order to develop conventional films, the developing work in the laboratory could only begin when the workday ended. For this work at night, Klopfenstein changed the developing speed and temperature to push the film and its photo-sensitive emulsion to the limits of their tolerance. By slowing the speed of the developing machine, and increasing the temperature of the developer baths, the film could be pushed and the latently present, but invisible traces of exposure could be made visible: in the places richer in silver nuclei, that is, the ones with greater exposure, more bromine precipitates from the silver bromide halogens during the developing process than it does in places with a smaller number of silver nuclei.[9] By manipulating the temperature and duration of the development, this photochemical process can be reinforced, and the density of the blackened silver grains also increases in places that were hardly exposed at all. This intensified developing makes the negative in general darker, and the positive correspondingly brighter. With these technical interventions, the parameters established by the film's manufacturer are exceeded, and the ideal appearance of the photograph defined by it are avoided. This intensified developing not only makes nuances of the objects reproduced in the film visible, but also qualities of the structure of the film's support. These qualities do not relate to the profilmic world, but as film grain, distort the likeness of the image. The increased visibility of the individual grains of the film achieved by overdeveloping the film stock results in a merging of the motifs by means of the units that constitute the image; the grain noise becomes part of the motif. This effect recalls the *Pointillist* painting technique of Georges Seurat. The ruins visible in the photograph are extended by the dancing grains, by the flaking emulsion of the support. Their ephemeral status is subliminally made meaningful, on the one hand, by the visible support and, on the other hand, on the diegetic level. It is no longer the grain of the photograph, but rather the cinematic world before our eyes that is sent into a bizarre ecstasy. At the same time, the visible support calls the unity of the photograph into question; the images seem to break down or build up, depending on how one looks at it. The final shot of *Geschichte der Nacht* ends with a freeze frame, the grains that were dancing stand still; the images suddenly seem flat. This reduced effect of depth throws the viewers back on themselves and on the apparatus of visibility. The removal of the visible mechanism of the material's movement causes not only the effect of the image but also, as it were, the overall effect of the film to collapse.

The image of the profilmic world is thus permeated by external structures that are caused by the support itself— a photochemical reaction that Klopfenstein very crucially determines in its poetics and aesthetics. Not only the filming, but also the developing of the film stock are done blind, as it were: decisions have to be made based on optical, technical settings, that is, in a sense abstractly, without it being possible for their effect on the images to be determined directly and hence controlled. Nor could any interventions be undone: when the developing goes wrong, it is not possible to revert to copies of the same material. With *Geschichte der Nacht*, Klopfenstein evolved into a pioneer with a penchant for experiment.

In the summer of 1978, Klopfenstein and Sigrist edited the film and created the soundtrack. They rented a house in Montefalco, edited during the day, and organized night-time screenings. They simply projected the current edit of the 16mm film on a wall of the house. The reactions of their friends and fellow artists during the screening and the discussions that followed led to the final version of the film. Images exclusively, accompanied and supported by atmospheric noises and music, were supposed to achieve the effect of the cinematic experience; all narrative was to be prohibited. That experimental decision not to tell a specific story turned out to be the greatest difficulty.

The limited filming time of the spring-driven Bolex established fixed parameters to which Klopfenstein and Sigrist had to adjust. They could make the shots shorter, but they were bound by the films' relatively short duration. Although the duration of the shots varies, viewers do not necessarily perceive these differences. Rather, they believe they are following a regular flow of impressions that seems to be subject to a constant rhythm. This impression points not only to an inherent quality of the images, but also to the precision of the montage, which is distinguished by a subtle sense of rhythm, timing, and beat.

The international success of *Geschichte der Nacht* provided Klopfenstein with the foundation for his later filmmaking. In the years that followed, he made *Transes* and *Das Schlesische Tor* (*The Silesian Gate*, 1983), films of a similar poetics; he also worked as the cameraman on Christian Schocher's night film *Reisender Krieger* (*Traveling Warrior*, 1981). The stay in Rome that the drawings had originally made possible was in retrospect a crucial turning point in Klopfenstein's work and life. During his Italian years he developed his own artistic practice, which would also shape his work in the long term. Although distortions of the medium were no longer a direct theme, the visible traces of production in his later feature films can certainly be seen in that context: for example, the handheld camera; autofocus, which sometimes results in imprecise and at times even arbitrary areas of focus; and the noise of the grain and later the pixel. His paintings and drawings changed as a result of formative experiences with different media in the 1970s.

Moreover, filmmaker, painter, and author Clemens Klopfenstein never lost interest in the fantastic and the surreal—traces of the unreal quality of *Geschichte der Nacht* and *Pandesowna* can also be found in his later films, texts, and paintings. The pleasure taken in strolling, in the unknown and the random, that can be found in his work from the 1970s—especially in *Geschichte der Nacht*—could be affirmed as typical features of Klopfenstein's aesthetic practice.

[1] In the spring of 2013 and 2015, the author conducted two long interviews on this subject with Clemens Klopfenstein. Additional important reference material includes the interviews conducted with the filmmaker by Fred Truniger and Thomas Schärer in the summer of 2012, which they kindly made available to me.

[2] For reproductions and an overview of Klopfenstein's drawings, see *Paese Sera: Zur Ausstellung "Clemens Klopfenstein," vom 1. bis zum 23. November 1975 im Kunsthauskeller Biel*, Kunstverein, Biel 1975.

[3] According to information from Klopfenstein, the version of *La luce romana vista da Ferraniacolor* with which I am familiar, the one in the archive of the Cinémathèque suisse, is not complete. Klopfenstein is currently working with the Lichtspiel cinema in Bern on a longer, restored, digital version of this short film, for which he also wants to create a new soundtrack.

[4] See Louis Delluc, *Photogénie*, M. de Brunoff, Paris 1920. Jean Epstein, *Bonjour cinéma*, Sirène, Paris 1921.

[5] See Rolf Eichenberger, "Junge Schweizer Filmrebellen, 2. Teil," *Schweizer Illustrierte*, no. 20 (May 13, 1968), p. 69. Martin Schaub, "Der Schattenspieler: Der Zeichner, Maler, Fotograf, Filmer und Schriftsteller Clemens Klopfenstein," *Tages-Anzeiger-Magazin*, no. 42 (1982), p. 34.

[6] His photojournalism was published in the *Basler Nachrichten*, *Der Bund* and the *Tages Anzeiger*.

[7] See Jörg Becker, *Sehnsucht nach dem Unendlichen: Die Filme von Clemens Klopfenstein*, FilmwärtsTexte 1, Filmwärts, Hannover 1991. Thomas Pfister, "Clemens Klopfenstein's Night & Trance Films/The Longing for Times Lost," André Iten, Peter Stohler (eds.), *12th Biennial of Moving Images*, JRP|Ringier, Zurich 2007, p. 130–134. Schaub, "Der Schattenspieler" (see note 5), p. 28–34 and 158.

[8] See André Amsler, *Rückblende: Vom Schwarzweissfilm zum Digitalvideo; Fünfzig Jahre Produktionstechnik*, Chronos, Zurich 2004, p. 78.

[9] See Johannes Weber, *Handbuch der Film- und Videotechnik*, Franzis, Munich 1993, p. 68.

The Love of Nature and its Opposite: Staging the Landscape in Peter Liechti's Early Films
Marcy Goldberg

Peter Liechti, *Ausflug ins Gebirg* (*Alpine Forays*), 1986 (Switzerland)
16mm film, 33 minutes

At the time of his death at 63 in 2014, Peter Liechti had established himself as one of Switzerland's most important and internationally recognized contemporary filmmakers, celebrated for his boundary-blurring blend of experimental, documentary, and fiction forms in works such as *The Sound of Insects: Record of a Mummy* (2009) and *Vaters Garten – Die Liebe meiner Eltern (Father's Garden—The Love of My Parents*, 2013).[1] His otherwise diverse body of work is linked by three intertwined themes or motifs: an ongoing interrogation of (Swiss) local identity and belonging; the search for a corresponding audio-visual language through which to conduct that interrogation; and the role of the filmmaker/artist as a critical figure on the margins of his or her own culture.

Liechti began making films in the mid-1980s, and it is astonishing how much of his oeuvre as a whole is prefigured in those early works, most particularly in the experimental shorts *Sommerhügel* (*Summer Hills*, 1984, 50 minutes) and *Ausflug ins Gebirg* (*Alpine Forays*, 1986, 33 minutes). It is as if he burst onto the scene fully formed, ready to take on the task of simultaneously reinventing both the *Heimatfilm* genre and Swiss experimental film practice.

Landscape as Provocation

The Swiss landscape, in particular the Alpine landscape, has long been a provocation for artists and writers. However, it is especially challenging for the photographic arts, since the most stunning vistas are often transformed into hopelessly kitsch clichés as soon as they pass through the lens of a camera. Liechti possessed two main advantages in tackling this daunting task—a lack of interest in conventional image making, and a highly ambivalent relationship with the natural landscape and the folkloric traditions often associated with it.

Originally trained in art history and art education, his filmmaker's gaze tended to reject the naturalistic in favor of painterly, abstract, or arranged images. Playful staging was a part of his repertoire from the very beginning. Liechti was undogmatically committed to documentary practice, but always with an eye to capturing real-life scenes in unusual, unexpected compositions and juxtapositions. Using his camera to refresh or renew perceptions of the visible world beyond the banality of everyday ways of seeing—what the Russian Formalists called the "aesthetic function"—was also part of Liechti's modus operandi.

However, beyond his distinctive aesthetic position, Liechti also possessed a third advantage. He was part of a generation in Switzerland that sought a new, more nuanced connection to the folkloric tradition and the concept of *Heimat*, in contrast to previous generations. *Heimat*, a near-untranslatable German word, means something much more fundamental and rooted than simply "homeland," and is often used in connection with certain kinds of patriotic political positions. During the Nazi period in Germany, neutral Switzerland's strategy of resistance against its fascist neighbor had included using Alpine imagery and customs to represent a distinctly Swiss national vision of freedom and independence. The cinema of the time reflected this

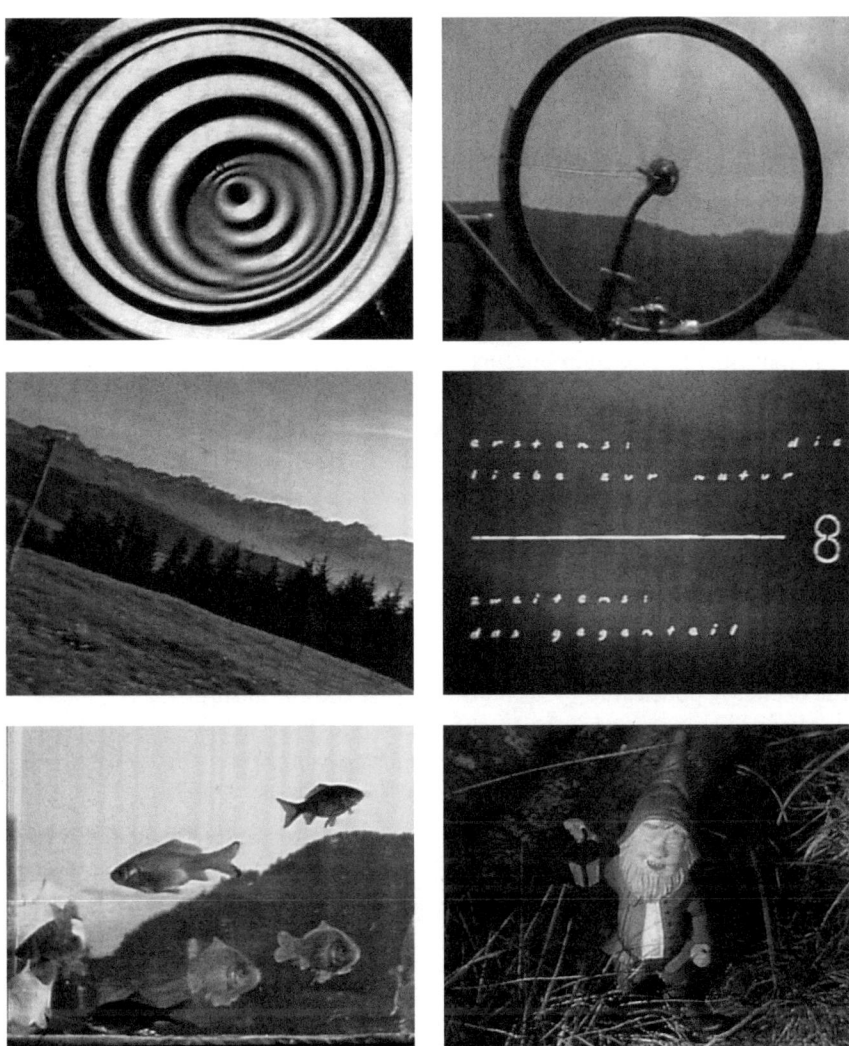

Peter Liechti, *Sommerhügel* (*Summer Hills*), 1984 (Switzerland)
Super-8 and video, 50 minutes

strategy with idyllic representations of the natural landscape and rural culture known as *Heimatfilme*.[2] This explosion of patriotism during the Second World War was followed by a postwar backlash, as the rebellious youth of the 1968 generation (the European parallel to the American baby boomers, named after the political protests of that turbulent year) rejected the conservative, conformist values of their parents' generation.

In the films of the Swiss New Wave of the 1960s, 1970s, and 1980s, whose proponents were closely linked with the 1968 movement, mountain imagery was to be avoided or disparaged. Filmmakers such as Alain Tanner and Fredi M. Murer, Yves Yersin and Christian Schocher tended to present the mountain regions as bleak, dreary, and desolate—the ideal backdrop for the *anomie* and existential crises of their characters. While they and other fiction filmmakers did their best to deconstruct the idyllic postcard image of Switzerland in more or less earnest, if not downright angry, ways, the experimental filmmakers of the period took more playful approaches, distancing themselves from the explicitly political to focus on the surreal and the absurd (for example, *Der rechte Weg* by Fischli/Weiss, 1983), or the mysterious and magical (for example the 1973 psychedelic odyssey *Die Sage vom alten Hirten Xeudi und seinem Freund Reiman* by Hans-Jakob Siber).

The Landscape of Ambivalence

One of the most distinctive aspects of Liechti's work, from the very beginning, is the way he was able to integrate the angry rants of the politically-committed filmmakers with the whimsical, visionary aesthetic of the experimental artists in order to offer his own oppositional vision of *Heimat*. It is likely that he was influenced in this approach by the work of the visual artist Roman Signer who, like Liechti, was born and raised in the town of St. Gallen in Eastern Switzerland. The two men were friends and colleagues, and Signer was later the subject of Liechti's first mainstream success, the experimental documentary portrait *Signers Koffer* (*Signer's Suitcase*, 1996). Signer is best known for his "time-sculptures" or "actions" in which everyday objects are misappropriated (or, to use a Situationist term, "detourned") for dramatic, and often comic, effect. Several of Liechti's earliest films feature his "actions." In *Tauwetter* (*Spring Thaw*, 1987), for example, Signer hung buckets full of water onto the T-bars of a moving ski lift and then shot holes in them with a pistol, causing the water to drip down and create ice formations. Playful destruction against the backdrop of Alpine tourism: this typical Signer motif is found again and again in Liechti's work.

Signer is also featured in the prologue to Liechti's first film *Sommerhügel* (*Summer Hills*, 1984). Here he tosses a wooden stool attached to a bungee cord off a swaying bridge and lets it dangle in mid-air: a resonant image that links daring with self-destruction. Liechti made the film together with a group of artist friends, all of whom happened to be living or working in the rural Appenzell region at the time: Walter Grawit, Felix Kälin, Hugo Keller, Johanna Liechti, and Walter Siering. The project arose from their shared sense of ambivalence at living as outsiders in a closed-off rural society, and their shared fascination with the landscape in spite of its association with the canton's highly conservative values and customs. In order to understand the region's uniquely retrograde reputation, it is worth mentioning here that the half-canton of Appenzell Innerrhoden did not grant women the right to vote until 1990, and that Appenzell Ausserrhoden boasts an unusual number of faith healers and natural-remedy "magicians."

The film's second title is *Eine Inszenierung der appenzellischen Landschaft in zehn Akten* (*The Staging of the Appenzell Landscape in Ten Acts*). As the filmmaking collective observes in their statement about the film (featured on Liechti's website), the local scenery offered them an undeniably fascinating backdrop and thus begged to become the backdrop for their happenings, even if their own interests were otherwise unrelated to the traditional rural lifestyle. Dressed in eccentric costumes, the film's characters ride through the terrain by bicycle or moped, set up picnics with tables, chairs, and crockery in meadows full of artificial flowers, and go hunting for garden gnomes in the woods. In creating these scenes, they distanced themselves from both traditional folk culture and their generation's primarily urban aesthetic. This amounted to a quietly radical artistic position in the politically-contested mood of the time, amid the Swiss youth rebellion of the early 1980s and its slogan *Nieder mit den Alpen, freie Sicht aufs Mittelmeer* (*Down with the Alps, for a Clear View of the Mediterranean*). Their very ambivalence *is* their position, and is captured in the titles of the individual acts, most notably number eight: "Firstly: the love of nature. Secondly: the opposite" (*erstens: die liebe zur natur, zweitens: das gegenteil*).

In spite of the essentially activist background to the work, its tone is not strident. With its incongruous characters and brightly colored Super-8 footage of sunny meadows and snow-capped peaks, *Sommerhügel* seeks to develop an aesthetic response through an idiosyncratic and very distinctive personal style. Dada and Surrealism are clear influences here. The liner notes confirm that Liechti and his colleagues were inspired by the work of Marcel Duchamp; the film includes a spinning spiral in homage to Duchamp *Anemic Cinema* (1926) as well as a shot of an upside-down bicycle wheel that quotes the notorious Duchamp sculpture. With its visual trickery and absurd, dreamlike scenes, *Sommerhügel* also recalls other experimental films of the 1920s, including Hans Richter's *Vormittagsspuk* (*Ghosts Before Breakfast*, 1928) and René Clair's *Entr'acte* (1924).

Surrealist, or at least incongruous, juxtapositions, such as an aquarium full of goldfish seeming to swim against a mountain landscape, or dreamlike shots of shadows moving across the cliffs became a defining feature of Liechti's unmistakable visual style. Canted camera angles or even upside-down shots serve to defamiliarize the landscape. This aesthetic of incongruities is emphasized by the film's soundtrack, which ranges from deliberately out-of-tune recordings of Alpine folk music to free jazz. In spite of the nod to the 1920s, the film, with its mix of Super-8 and video formats, and its free jazz soundtrack, is firmly rooted in its own time. Ultimately, these formal experiments do not only deconstruct the undeniable beauty of the landscape, they also refresh the representation and thus the perception of it.

The Landscape of Transition

Ausflug ins Gebirg (1986), on the other hand, tells another story. Liechti's third film and first solo work—the second being the eight-minute short *Senkrecht/Waagrecht* (*Vertical/ Horizontal*, 1985), a collaboration with Roman Signer—takes the form of an extended rant about Alpine hiking and the tourist culture of the mountains. Shot during a trip through the Austrian Vorarlberg, the film begins with a recitation of some of the region's more absurd place names. Saustein, Schrottenkopf, Schmalzberg, and Ritzenspitzen sound more like parodies of Germanic names, and in Liechti's pronunciation, take on the tones of a desperate lament. Later in the film he curses the mountains for robbing him of the ability to think clearly in the thinner air of the peaks. "The mountain destroys my thoughts and makes me stupid" (*Der Berg zerstört meine Gedanken, der Berg macht blöd*), he says scornfully, in a poetic voiceover text reminiscent of the Austrian dramatist Thomas Bernhard's critical monologues.[3] Liechti's tone and phrasing here also recall the tension-filled text performances of Swiss artist Dieter Roth, who was a friend of his; Liechti later quoted footage of Roth reading his "Scheissgedicht" (shit poem) in *Hans im Glück* (*Lucky Jack*, 2003).

Throughout the film, Liechti emphasizes the monotony and repetitiveness of his hiking holiday, most notably in an extended sequence in which he robotically eats a gelatinous slice of raspberry torte, sips his drink, doffs his Tyrolean hat, and then begins all over again, as a sort of sarcastic performance of desperation before the camera. In the film, the scene appears both in the original color footage and in pixelated monochromatic shots filmed off the editing monitor. This reframing of the self-portrait footage—an extension of what was already a self-reflexive device—feeds into his ongoing project of establishing an audiovisual vocabulary to parallel his thematic interrogations. In the reframed images, the extreme close-up of Liechti's face becomes a two-dimensional field of pixels. The artist, as it were, has dissolved into his work. This motif is also echoed by the intricately processed soundtrack, such as when the sound of falling raindrops segues into a rhythmic electronic beeping.

Liechti's lament lists various horrors that may befall the mountain traveler: the unexpected rainstorm, the cable car that gets stuck in the air, the little boy at the hotel who coughs non-stop. And yet, this film too contains images of undeniable beauty. Lush greenery, a meadow bisected by a river, the bright sunlight against the stark stony mountain peaks. Liechti films his subjective point of view while riding the chairlift, and again captures those dreamlike images of his shadow gliding over the landscape. Here too there are surreal shots of mysterious fish swimming in unlikely landscapes, as well as other two- and four-legged creatures from the Liechti bestiary: the collection of animal shots to which he would return again and again in his work.

Both the laments and the ambivalently fascinating imagery reappeared in his 2003 documentary essay *Hans im Glück*, his monumental confrontation with mountain hiking which he dubbed "a *Heimatfilm* for the *Heimat*-less."[4] But by *Ausflug ins Gebirg* they had already been established as part of his filmic universe, along with his role as the wandering artist with the camera, the participant observer looking in from the outside. They pointed the way for other filmmakers to traverse the landscape, carving a fruitful path to navigate between Alpine kitsch and the dogmatic rejection of natural beauty, linking the landscape with inner states, and thus making the transition from the regional to the universal.

[1] The original film titles and official English title translations are taken from Liechti's official website, www.peterliechti.ch.
[2] For more information on the specifically German *Heimatfilm* tradition, see Alexandra Ludewig, *Screening Nostalgia: 100 Years of German Heimat Film*, Transcript Verlag, Bielefeld 2011. The Swiss *Heimatfilm* of the Second World War period shares certain formal characteristics with the German (and Austrian) traditions, but was designed to resist their proto-fascist overtones.
[3] The full monologue voiceover from *Ausflug ins Gebirg* is printed in a collection of Liecht's texts and occasional writings: Peter Liechti, *Lauftext—ab1985*, Vexer Verlag, St. Gallen 2010, p. 5–12.
[4] The tag line "Ein Heimatfilm für Heimatlose" appears in the promotional texts created by Liechti for the film's release, which can be found on the website www.peterliechti.ch. For more on the film, see Marcy Goldberg, "Geography of a Swiss Body: Peter Liechti's *Hans im Glück*," Robin Curtis, Angelika Fenner (eds.), *The Autobiographical Turn in Germanophone Documentary and Experimental Film*, Camden House, Rochester, New York 2014, p. 70–86.

Peter Liechti, *Tauwetter (Spring Thaw)*, 1987 (Switzerland)
16mm film, 8 minutes

Film Forum, *Supervisuell*, and Ciné Circus: Experimental Filmmaking in Zurich in the Late 1960s
Thomas Schärer

Translated from the German by Steven Lindberg

Poster announcing a screening of HHK Schoenherr's *Autoportrait* and a musical performance by Guru Guru Groove, Luzerner Filminformationstage, Kleintheater Luzern, Lucerne, June 1969

Zurich and Switzerland as the nucleus of an international network of experimental filmmakers? Zurich did indeed experience a brief phase of exponential growth in its film scene in the latter half of the 1960s, which was largely shaped by young men whose forms of cinematic expression were experimental and playful. They received attention and recognition very quickly, in a generational shift for Swiss film. In 1967, for example, the Turnus Film production company complained that the Swiss government preferred "short, experimental, avant-garde, and outsider films."[1] The owner of one of the largest film production companies in Switzerland, Heinrich Fueter, from Condor Films, clearly also felt he was on the defensive in 1970. In an open letter to all state and national councilors and "circles with an interest in film," he wrote that it was a mistake to assert that, "the future of Swiss filmmaking belongs to the so-called underground, avant-garde, or recent film alone."[2]

Even though those involved in "underground, avant-garde, or recent film" were very heterogeneous and in essence not very influential, traditional film producers clearly feared that Swiss film was facing a paradigm shift in favor of "free filmmaking" dominated by avant-garde film.

From 1967 to 1970 a networked community of independent film production and screening practices in Zurich that are described as a discrete field in Pierre Bourdieu's sense in the introduction to this volume,[3] emerged in and around the Film Forum film club with both physical and intellectual meeting places, platforms, leading figures, codes of membership, and mechanisms of inclusion and exclusion. This field, in turn, was part of the subcultures and youth cultures forming at the time, within which these young filmmakers moved and worked. This essay examines this interim phase of Swiss film and attempts to offer a brief overview of the networking of the filmmakers' scene without which New Swiss Film would presumably have evolved differently.

The Nonconformists of Zurich

This subcultural community of high school and university students, painters, musicians, graphic artists, architects, journalists, writers, artisans with an interest in culture, and (budding) cineastes was small and met regularly at places such as the Café Odeon or the Café Select, or in one another's homes.[4] As Urban Gwerder, who in 1967 had been inspired by, among other things, a performance of the Living Theater from New York at the Volkshaus Zürich that year and founded the underground magazine *Hotcha*, recalled, this community grew from the mid-1960s onward and began to network internationally as well.[5] One factor in this evolution was the opening of Club Platte 27 by Jonas C. Haefeli, Herbie Wertli, and Eduard Stöckli in the spring of 1965. Located in a freestanding prewar building at Plattenstrasse 27, the club, which gradually spread from the cellar throughout the entire building, was primarily a meeting place at first, but gradually became more of a cultural club,[6] organizing concerts, readings, art exhibitions, performances, and, from

November 1965, film screenings.[7] This "melting pot of all the arts that anticipated 1968"[8] continued to be well attended after it moved to Limmatquai 28 in September 1968.

Das Film Forum (1966–1970)

The conference "Schweizer Film" (Swiss Film) in Solothurn in 1966 inspired Hans-Jakob Siber to give "young enthusiasts [...] an opportunity to meet one another, to discuss their works and problems with one another [...] to exchange experiences, and to inspire and stimulate one another."[9]

After completing secondary school at the Literargymnasium, Hans-Jakob Siber spent a formative year studying in Montana in the United States. After returning to Switzerland, he ended his studies of German and philosophy at the University of Zurich, and founded the Siber + Siber mineral company in 1964, which is still in business today. Starting that year, he traveled regularly to the United States to purchase minerals and fossils, and on each trip he would stop in New York for a few days to purchase LPs and attend concerts. Probably in 1965 or 1966, he met Jonas Mekas in the circles around Andy Warhol's Factory. Mekas had cofounded the Film-Makers' Cooperative in New York in 1962 and told Siber about similar coops in Vienna and Hamburg.[10] As a regular attendee of concerts at Club Platte 27, in the spring of 1966 he suggested screening films there.[11] It is difficult to reconstruct Film Forum's program, because the surviving documentation is sparse, and memories sometimes vague. Following largely spontaneous film screenings by Film Forum at Platte 27, from the autumn of 1966 onward Film Forum showed films there every other Monday.[12] The programs consisted of contemporary short Swiss films, usually by young authors. Because the offerings were modest at first, Siber supplemented them with short films he could borrow for free—thanks to Giorgio Frapolli, who at the time was the director of the Zürcher Filmclub—from the Czechoslovak and Polish embassies. At first these events were small—"a dozen people and a film projector"[13]—as Fredi M. Murer who, at one of the first evenings presented *Pazifik* (1965), his anarchic portrait of his fellow occupants of the Villa Pazifik at nearby

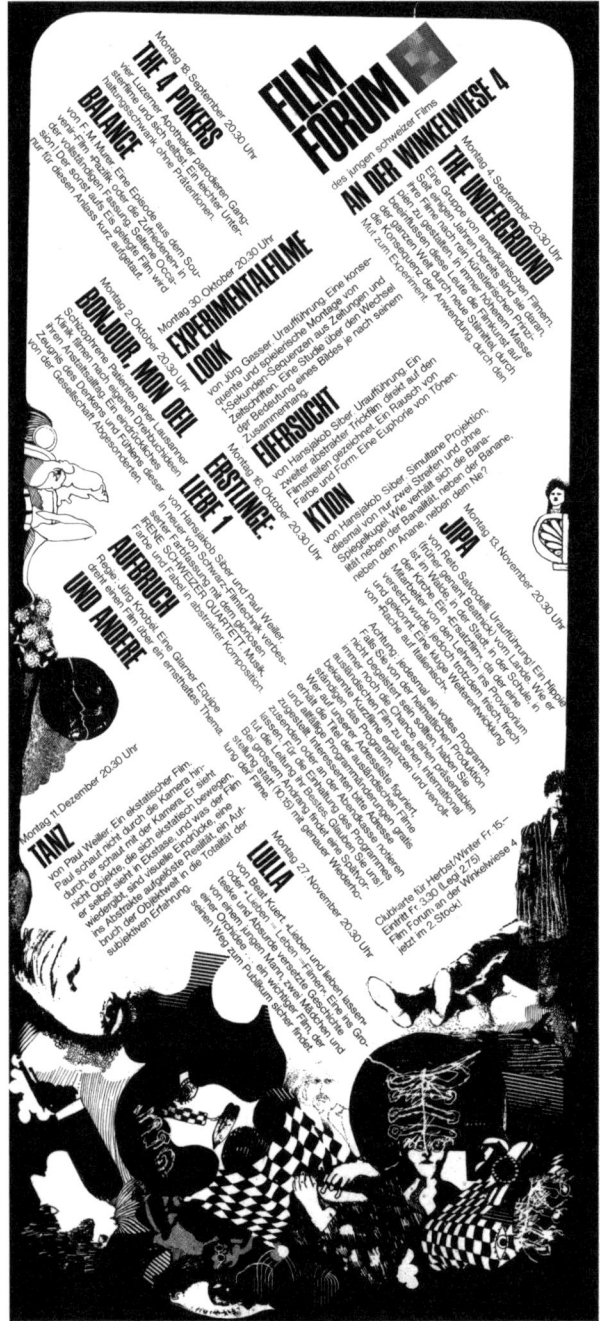

Flip-side of the Film-Forum poster announcing screenings in Zurich, September-December 1967

Plattenstrasse 47, recalled: "People just talked, ate, and drank wine ... Meanwhile the film was running. It was really a mix of wall decoration and a film screening."[14] Siber often announced the screenings by putting up handmade posters in places such as the Café Odeon.

Already after the first season, the space at Platte 27 was too small. From February 20, 1967, Film Forum showed its increasingly well-attended programs at the Theater Winkelwiese, every other Monday, initially in the cellar and then, from the autumn of 1967, on the third floor.[15] This room held 120 viewers. Various participants—Hans-Jakob Siber, Hans Helmut Klaus (HHK) Schoenherr, Beat Kuert— recall that the crowds were so large that sometimes there had to be two screenings. Surviving programs from 1967 onward refer to additional late screenings at 10:15 pm "if the crowd is large." Film Forum, whose official name for a long time was "Film Forum des jungen Schweizer Films" (Film Forum of Recent Swiss Film), was given a logo designed by Emil Steinberger in the autumn of 1967, which was also shown before the credits used to introduce the programs.[16]

As Film Forum itself declared, its most important goal was that of forming a community: "We want to be neither amateurs nor professionals. We are discovering film and discovering ourselves in film. We want film to live off us, not us off film. If we build up something together, we will survive."[17] Siber worked hard to bring different sorts of people into an exchange:

> A monastic school is much more significant than a single monk. And it's like that with everything. A place where you can meet regularly, exchange ideas, where people know one another, where they can help one another ... That is a much stronger organization than if people are plowing their own furrows. That was my conviction. Probably I got that from my stay in America.[18]

Not only were the film enthusiasts who Siber was trying to bring together heterogeneous,[19] but the goals of Film Forum were as well. They consisted of "supporting auteur film, short film, and experimental film."[20] Film Forum's view of film at the beginning of its existence was by no means restricted to experimental films in the strict sense, nor even to Swiss productions. The program notes read: "In case you are not enthusiastic about production from our homeland, you still have the opportunity to see a presentable foreign film. Internationally-known short films supplement and complete our program."[21] The program promised that everyone on the mailing list would receive a list of titles of foreign films.

In the autumn of 1967, however, Film Forum apparently focused its interests on experimental film. In retrospect, Hans-Jakob Siber was very pragmatic about this: "It was too difficult to bring people together. It was easier with experimental films because their authors had no other connections and had no hope that they would soon be discovered and be given 100,000 francs."[22]

A Film Program with Consequences: The New American Cinema Touring Program

Interest in and enthusiasm for experimental films hit its first high point during the *New American Cinema Exposition*, September 4 to 15, 1967, organized by Film Forum and the Zürcher Filmclub together with American critic P. Adams Sitney. Sitney toured with the film program he had cocurated with Jonas Mekas from July 1967 for more than a year "with new art through the old continent."[23] Lasting more than 50 hours in total, the program was shown at the Kantonsschule Zürich auditorium and at the Theater Winkelwiese, as well as at other locations in Switzerland: Lucerne, Solothurn, and Lausanne. Things did not always go smoothly, as Sitney remarked in his report on the trip: "Lucerne, a Catholic Canton, was the first place where censorship has affected our shows so far. A board of three men had to approve all films. After much debate among themselves, they banned [Carl] Linder's *The Devil Is Dead* (1964) and *Overflow* (1966)."[24]

Martin Schaub dedicated an entire page to the cycle in the *Neue Zürcher Zeitung* on September 1, 1967. His text was also reprinted in the extensive documentation of the program. The size of the audiences exceeded all expectations. Sitney reported that films had to be shown more than once: Stan Brakhage's film cycle *The Art of Vision* (1965), which was more than four hours long, was shown three times.[25] *Bardo Follies* (1967) met with the most approval; a group of painters called it the most interesting film they had ever seen. In his regular letters published in the New York journal *Film Culture*, Sitney also mentioned the Film Forum programs. The "filmmakers' cooperative of Switzerland" (i.e. Film Forum) had shown him about three hours of films, and, among these, *Chicorée* by Fredi M. Murer, stood out as "a witty and abstract portrait of Zurich's best poet, a 23 year-old Nerval with about two feet of hair called Urban Gwerder."[26]

Even in retrospect, Sitney was still surprised how committed the Zurich audience's involvement with the films was.[27] He seemed to have stumbled on a genuinely "hungry" audience. Countless film enthusiasts in Switzerland came into contact with experimental films for the first time thanks to this cycle.

Many cinephiles and "young filmmakers" interested in the avant-garde lent essential impetus to the program; for example, Sitney persuaded German painter Hans Helmut Klaus Schoenherr, who had been living in Zurich since 1963, to submit his first film *Thaler's, Meier's, Sadkowsky's Life in the Evening* (1967) to the *EXPRMNTL* festival in the Belgian seaside resort of Knokke-le-Zoute, where it was shown in December 1967.

The attention the media paid to experimental films increased in late 1967. Interviews and portraits (of Fredi M. Murer, Kurt Gloor, Hans-Jakob Siber, and Georg Radanowicz, among others) appeared. One of the high points of this was a two-part series in the large-circulation newspaper *Schweizer Illustrierte* in the spring of 1968, which presented eight "young Swiss cinematic rebels" on its title page and gave them plenty of space to present themselves.[28]

Expanded Cinema

In addition to these conventional screenings, filmmakers such as Siber and HHK Schoenherr experimented with multiple projections, so-called light shows, and presentations of performances and live music. Siber recalled one of these first Expanded Cinema Shows at Platte 27: "We put two people on chairs and completely wrapped them in crumpled paper so that only their necks were visible. They sat in front of the screen and cited some texts or other. Rather absurd ... "[29]

A surviving flyer for one of these, *Ktion* (experiments for two and three projectors, December 1–11, 1966), contained a "personal note to any passersby" that satirically promised medicine or a massage with the following effect: "strengthens immediately, reduces deep-seated pain, contains music, films, recitation, action painting, projection."[30] A later flyer from Film Forum suggests that two or three abstract 8mm films had been projected via a "mirror ball" (disco ball).[31]

Siber constantly refined his "light shows." He appears to have used prism lenses, which he had polished at Siber + Siber, not only for taking photographs—presumably for the first time for *Fahrt durch die Nacht* (Journey Through the Night, 1968)[32]—but also for projections. This is suggested in a Platte 27 program that announced *Electric Jazz* with the Pierre Favre Trio on May 17, 1968.[33] This event, which probably had the largest audience so far, was held in the Kino Le Paris, which accommodated more than four hundred viewers. The spirit of exploring "marginal spheres"[34] influenced both the musical and the visual presentations:

> Recently, the boundaries between jazz and Beat have become fluid [...] At this concert it was not just musicians performing but also projectionists with two swivel film projectors. They used them like musical instruments and, with abstract films that Köbi [Hans-Jakob] Siber painted directly on the film stock (sometimes combined with real footage), conjured up a unique play of light and color in the room and on the walls. A special lens, likewise developed by Köbi Siber, projected each individual film simultaneously two to three times, so that during the performance there were always four to six beams of light producing as many images.[35]

For Hans-Jakob Siber, visual perception was always closely connected to music. Together with his assistant and frequent guest Robert Boner, he dreamed of a new film format, a kind of oversized music video—which Siber realized in 1973 with his film *Die Sage vom Hirten Xeudi und seinem Freund Reiman* (*The Saga of the Herdsman Xeudi and his Friend Reiman*): "I could have imagined that when you go to the cinema—to the Bellevue Kino—you get a joint along with your movie ticket at the box office."[36]

Siber's colleagues HHK Schoenherr, Dieter Meier, and Sebastian Schroeder also experimented with cinematic apparatus, organizing screenings in private homes; showing multiple projections; accompanying silent films with the sounds of a cello (Schoenherr); showing, despite announcements to the contrary, no film at all (Meier); or inviting the audience to participate live in making the soundtracks for films—by reading from a telephone directory if necessary.[37] Sebastian Schroeder showed found-footage amateur films at a Happening at the Lindenhof, and invited the audience to bring their own films.[38]

Experimenting with the apparatus of performance (several projectors, moving projectors, performance, readings, and musical accompaniment) was in vogue in the late 1960s, and not just in artistic and cinematic circles. Clubs began to discover slide and film projections. Georg Radanowicz and Peter Schweri helped make film projections for a nightclub in Milan. Murer remembers that the Dancing Chinchilla on the Limmatquai in Zurich projected experimental films as a precursor to the visuals projected in today's clubs.[39] Films were also found in "high-culture" performances such as readings and ballets. We should mention here the series of readings by Gwerder that were presented in the "multimedia spectacle" *Poëtenz* (Poetency) to audiences in various Swiss and West German cities beginning in May 1965, accompanied by Murer's *Chicorée*, and live music by Jelly Pastorini. In his film series *Mönch* (*Monk*) in May 1968 in the banquet hall of the restaurant Weisser Wind, Siber not only screened his own films, but also read his own texts.[40] In August 1968 Siber produced his film *Fahrt durch die Nacht* for a ballet performance.[41] Jean Deroc's choreography and Siber's photography seem to have been convincing, as they were invited to participate in the Swiss presentation at the World's Fair in Osaka and ten additional venues in Japan.[42]

Their eagerness to experiment, their openness, and their desire to do things together led filmmakers, musicians, dancers, actors and performers, club owners and concert organizers to leap over the boundaries between the arts and media, and between popular and high culture. Very often, the moving image played an important role in these transgressions of boundaries. This development in the direction of an "expanded cinema," as Sheldon Renon was among the first to call it in 1967 and about which Gene Youngblood wrote an eponymous book in 1970,[43] was a phenomenon that could be observed internationally, but that took on different local forms.

Touring Programs: Ciné Circus

The need to improve the network beyond Zurich and show the Film Forum program in the rest of Switzerland led to a traveling program, known as Ciné Circus. From 1967 to 1970, in collaboration with local cinephiles and filmmakers, Film Forum presented programs in Lucerne (November 17–18, 1967), Bern (May 24–25, 1968), Winterthur (December 8, 1968), and Basel (December 23, 1967; November 30–December 1, 1968; and October 23–24, 1970).[44] In Basel, for example, the AKS film group around Clemens Klopfenstein was involved in organizing it.

Greater emphasis was placed on education than in the Film Forum programs. Introductory texts explained the conditions under which the films had been made, and introduced the films and filmmakers.[45] Coorganizer Klopfenstein recalls that, in Basel, Executive Councilor Lukas Burckhardt tried to prevent the controversial evening screening on November 30, 1968, of the film *Blut* (Blood) by Paul Weiller (in which Schoenherr and Siber performed), which showed a naked girl covered in blood.[46]

In Bern, six or seven hundred people watched four screenings.[47] Decidedly different ideas about cinematic quality, as well as about the general production and distribution of films clearly collided. During the screening of *Und Sie?* (*And You?* Germany, 1967) by Wilhelm and Birgit Hein in the block of international avant-garde films curated by Siber, Peter von Gunten and Kurt Gloor allegedly grabbed a spray can to "disinfect the auditorium and screen against bad films."[48]

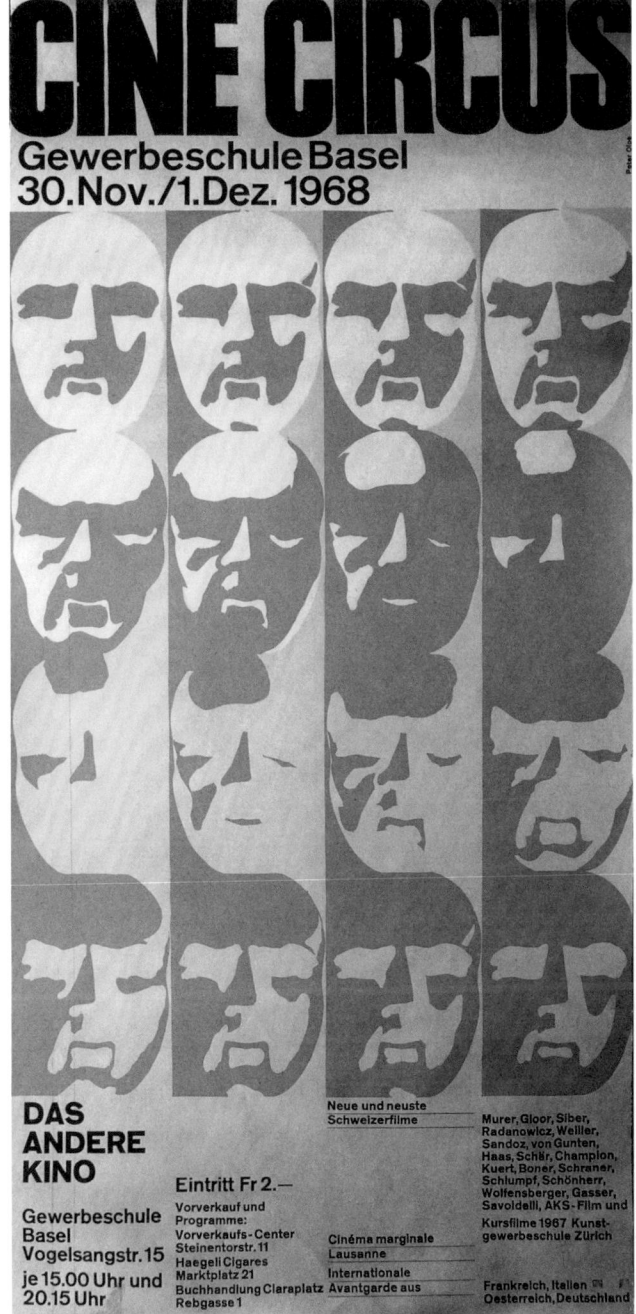

Ciné Circus poster, Gewebeschule Basel, November–December 1969

According to René Codoni, the group of Bern filmmakers, including Peter von Gunten, Guido Haas, Robert Schär, Kurt Gloor, and Leonardo Bezzola who helped organize the program presented at the Kaufmännischer Verein, accused Siber in a leaflet of having unilaterally put together the program with foreign films. Moreover, different ideas about the production and distribution of films clashed. In his three-page "Traktäktchen zur Situation des Filmers in der Schweiz" (Brief Treatise on the Situation of the Filmmaker in Switzerland), Siber warned about a premature commercialization of the films of the young generation, argued for openness and tolerance, and also for showing "difficult, special kinds" of films,[49] whereas von Gunten called for building up and professionalizing Film Forum and Ciné Circus. Von Gunten felt that films should be selected more critically and also distributed internationally.[50]

All kinds of film screenings always meant more than seeing films and meeting like-minded people: they led to networks, were the basis for all sorts of activities, and made it possible in the first place to educate people and to distinguish a separate "experimental film scene."

Production and Distribution

From 1967, Film Forum's scope of activities expanded, explicitly following the model of the Film-Makers' Cooperative in New York, "as self-help [...] by filmmakers for [...] filmmakers,"[51] to include the production and distribution of films. It had great ambitions. Film Forum was supposed to develop into the "fourth estate of film production," alongside "professional film producers, television people, and film amateurs proper" that represented the first three estates.[52]

Informally, by making projectors available,[53] establishing contacts abroad, and offering tips,[54] Siber and his comrades in arms were able to support young filmmakers, but they were unable to build enduring structures for production. Siber's characterization of Film Forum as an "experimental field for new forms for organization film production in Switzerland"[55] was vaguely appropriate, but more a desire than a reality.

Beat Kuert, who made short films himself, took over the administration of the Filmvermittlungsstelle (Film

Education Office) in January 1968,[56] and made the following proposition: "Film clubs, associations, schools, and private parties can borrow films by young Swiss filmmakers from Film Forum for screening."[57] An A4 flyer with Film Forum's logo was presumably created for the Solothurner Filmtage in 1968. In a meeting, Film Forum members also decided to produce a catalogue with a print run of 300 copies.[58]

By 1968, the receipts from the well-attended "propaganda" screenings at the Theater Winkelwiese, which following a general agreement of the filmmakers had been chosen for the Filmvermittlungsstelle, were inadequate to fund Film Forum's activities.[59] The Filmvermittlungsstelle ceased activities in September 1969, but not through lack of demand: 104 films had been distributed, 44 film screenings arranged for authors, and 240 free screenings organized. It could no longer be run on a voluntary basis. The expansion of its activities to the whole of Switzerland also increasingly led to different notions of which films were "worthy of distribution." In 1970, the Film-Pool became the indirect successor organization of the Filmvermittlungsstelle.[60]

A Journal of Its Own: *Supervisuell*

Models such as *Film Culture* from the Film-Makers's Cooperative in New York, and subculture magazines such as *Hotcha*, first published in Zurich in March 1968, led to Film Forum members wanting to form their own journal in the spring of 1968[61]: "Boner, Kuert, Siber, Schoenherr, and Weiller agreed last Friday: anyone who wants to help design the journal pays a cash contribution into a fund."[62] Various proposals for the title were floated; one of Siber's proposals, *Supervisuell*, was chosen.[63] Schoenherr articulated the most specific ideas about its content. He wanted a publication "that shows a very personal view, very direct and well formulated, in its articles." He imagined subjects such as festival reports, film reviews, and "statements from filmmakers about their concepts."[64]

A conflict between Schoenherr and, as well as with Beat Kuert, over Film Forum's guidelines for distribution led to a rift between Siber and Schoenherr even before the first issue appeared in May 1968, and the publication of a film journal, for which Schoenherr had taken primarily responsibility, thus continued separately from Film Forum. Going it alone as publisher Schoenherr convinced his network of filmmaking friends to contribute, and from May 1968 to April 1970 he produced six issues of the journal *Supervisuell*.[65] The "correspondents" listed testify to the ambition to create an international network and practice.[66]

Looking back in 2012, Schoenherr described the journal and recommended that it be imitated: "editorial board, writer, and distributor are one person; a diversity of editorial boards as far as locations and opinions are concerned, and a place of publication (with municipal subsidies); no influence from the place of publication on tendencies."[67] It was not just the financial problems, but also ultimately the fact that there was minimal response that caused the project to come to an end after two years.[68]

The End of Film Forum and the Continuation of Film Screenings at Platte 27

Almost simultaneously with the expansion of Film Forum's activities and the founding of a distribution center and a journal, its screenings began losing audiences. One reason for this is that it had abandoned its popular venue in the Theater Winkelwiese in the spring of 1968. The costs of renting the auditorium were increasing with the larger crowds and increased numbers of screenings,[69] and, ultimately, they seemed too high to Siber, so he sought an alternative.

With the move to the large Auditorium 1 of the Eidgenössische Technische Hochschule (from April to May 1968)[70] and then to the Weisser Wind restaurant banquet hall (from May 1968),[71] crowds declined. The audience never adjusted to "the new location and the new day of the week."[72] Screening locations changed frequently; for example, in November 1968, the Forum was at the Theater am Neumarkt ("Inter-films from 1968 by the AKS collective, Klopfenstein, Aebersold, Schaad").[73] From autumn 1968 to April 1969, its collaboration with Platte 27 appears to have increased. Until the autumn of 1968, alongside its other screenings, Film Forum presented Swiss short films exclusively at Platte 27 on Thursdays. On Tuesdays in 1968 and 1969, independently of Film Forum, Platte 27 presented international film programs under the title "Creative Films."[74]

Club Platte 27, Zurich, ca. 1968

The selection of films for these Platte programs overlapped somewhat with the repertoire of Progressive Art Production (P.A.P.), which was founded by Dieter Meier and Karlheinz Hein in the spring of 1969, following the performance *Underground Explosion*.[75] Meier took over partial responsibility for the program. There was no Thursday screening, which had been organized by the Film Forum, on the programs of Platte 27 from April 1969, and no programs survive after late 1969.

Following the *New American Film Exposition* and extensive programs of films by Robert Nelson (February 1968) and Gregory Markopoulos (May 1968), the Filmclub Zürich no longer showed experimental films, and ceased to exist soon thereafter. The politically oriented film club Der andere Film (DAF, The Other Film) partially stepped into the breech in the autumn of 1968. Its Platte 27 program for February and March 1969 announced *La hora de los hornos* (*The Hour of the Furnaces*) by Fernando E. Solanas and Octavio Getino "together with DAF."

The brief but intense phase of increased interest in experimental film and the film screenings organized with great enthusiasm by volunteers ended in the early 1970s. The reasons for this should be sought in overlapping and, in some cases, opposed developments.[76]

Politicizing Culture

The politicizing of broad circles of society around 1968 increasingly led to viewers and critics demanding social or political relevance, and not just from films. In 1968 Siber responded to French-Swiss film journalist and producer Marcel Leiser's question as to why the films produced by underground cinema were not very explicitly political, but resorted instead primarily to "psychedelia of pure aesthetic effects": "if you express the way you feel, especially in the aesthetic, it is more direct, you immediately express what you are experiencing, not just what you are thinking, but your whole conception of life."[77] At the Solothurner Filmtage, Siber was repeatedly confronted with the accusation that his own films and those of his colleagues were "art for art's sake."[78]

As early as 1967 P. Adams Sitney met with resistance in Zurich to his view that New American Cinema was not "an organ of leftwing political criticism of American society."[79] This clear rejection of political instrumentalization, which Sitney articulated elsewhere as well, was attacked at the experimental film festival in Knokke-le-Zoute at the turn of the year 1967–1968 by representatives of the Sozialistischer Deutscher Studentenbund (SDS, Socialist German Students' Association), including the Berlin film students Harun Farocki and Holger Meins, the latter of whom was later a member of the Rote Armee Fraktion (RAF, Red Army Faction). He branded the "meaningless camera exercises" of the *EXPRMNTL* festival as "American film aggression," and called for "specifically political films."[80] Schoenherr also had reservations about the Kurzfilmfestival Oberhausen: "In Oberhausen the leftists ruled the roost. Or leftist-heavy themes in general [...] They did not appreciate *Supervisuell* at all. That was certainly their right."[81]

Commercializing Art and Culture

The antagonism between those who saw film experiments and short films as exercises for later cinematic challenges (finding an audience, surviving in the market) and those who saw film as a personal, radical-poetic means of expression was manifested in the aforementioned reactions to the Ciné Circus program in Bern in May 1968, as well as in the debate over the Scotoni-Experimentalfilmpreis in 1968. It is not clear what moved cinema owner Eric Scotoni and property developer Attila Scotoni to organize this prize specifically for experimental films for a period of five years.[82] In any case, it was criticized. A group of relatively successful filmmakers, including Murer and Alexander J. Seiler, warned that support for young filmmakers was said to be so limited that a prize only for experimental film was unhelpful. Rather, it was necessary to create "an economic basis for a continuous production with broad public influence."[83]

In the late 1960s the process of negotiation and formation within the film community was more or less complete; neither an experimental film prize limited to five years, nor various attempts to penetrate the art market with films could do much to counter that. Experimental filmmakers in particular were confronted with a decision: make films or make money. Time was on the side of the "commercial" filmmakers, those seeking the "overground," as Siber put it.[84] ("Sterility through excluding oppositional film concepts."[85])

Dieter Meier and Karlheinz Hein attempted in vain, after their openly declared commercial exploitation of the artistic underground with their *Underground Explosion* tour in 1969, to sell experimental films and artist's films in an art context through their label Progressive Art Production (P.A.P.). One of their role models was Paul Sharits, who was able to sell his film stills through galleries.[86]

The programming of the Platte 27 club also reflected this commercialization: from 1968 onward, its film screenings were increasingly replaced by a "discotheque with light show"[87] or "strobo-light shows"[88] with regular hours. In December 1968 the "First Drugstore in Switzerland" opened in the club.[89] Platte 27 continued to exist only into the 1970s, in the end purely as a nightclub under the name Antares.[90]

Film Subsidies, Cultural Policy, and the Formation of "New Swiss Film"

The expansion of film subsidies to feature films when the film law was revised in 1969 opened up the possibility of living not just for films, but also from films. This created not only an opportunity to pursue film as more than a hobby, but also a new competitive situation. The informal hierarchies and associated feelings of defensiveness and envy were unbearable for the community.

At the suggestion of Alex Bänninger, who was working as a film journalist at the time, Murer tested the limits of film subsidy. He applied for a subsidy for quality (Qualitätsprämie) for his film *Chicorée* (1966), which he eventually received after an appeal following the initial negative response.[91] Radanowicz, too, received a subsidy for quality for *Pic-Nic* (1967), which was shown in Knokke, as did Siber for *Jalousie* (1967). And for his final film *Die Sage vom Hirten Xeudi und seinem Freund Reiman* (1973). New Swiss Film began to create structures that still exist today: the Schweizer Filmzentrum (now Swissfilms), the Schweizer

Filmkatalog, diverse societies and associations, and the industry magazine *Cinébulletin*. Filmmakers who operated outside these structures, whether voluntarily or by necessity, had an increasingly difficult time.

It is scarcely a coincidence that with the cautious expansion of the concept of culture after 1968, municipal authorities, the state, associations, and interest groups began to become active in places and contexts that had previously been the realm of private idealist initiatives. It is not the case that these "official" activities prevented individual initiatives; rather, they took up ideas and gestures from the subculture that were floating around, and attempted to integrate their impetus into an emerging cultural policy. Admittedly, this cultural policy was often fragmentary and contradictory. After Mayor Sigmund Widmer visited Plattenstrasse 27 in the summer of 1967, the City of Zurich was willing to support the club and purchased the property.[92] But constant visits from the police, vice squad, and building authorities, and ultimately the termination of their contract, forced the "cultural activists to give up"[93] in February 1968. The building was demolished.

Anticipating support in the form of a "municipal film policy," in 1968 Siber received 2,000 Swiss francs for a new film—petty cash from Widmer's mayoral budget, so to speak—and was thus able to pass on this sum to four other "young filmmakers" of his choice. The task was to screen short films in the spring of 1969 as part of an event organized by the city as a kind of municipal platform. A cultural policy willing to include the film in forums organized by the mayor's department that had previously been reserved for literature and music was evident here, but the criticism that it was creating an alibi was necessarily expressed. When the subsidized films were screened, Martin Schaub condemned the "small-minded, highly paternalistic conception of film subsidy" cultivated by the largest city in German-speaking Switzerland in believing it had "done something for film" with 10,000 Swiss francs.[94]

Other showcase screenings of "young" Swiss filmmakers followed in 1970, sometimes in collaboration with the Arbeitsgemeinschaft Nationales Schweizer Filmzentrum (Working Team of the Swiss National Film Center), today's Swissfilms.[95] Whereas in the program of the spring of 1969 and November 1970 the main focus had been on experimental films, the programming of the municipal platforms shifted to a "overview of Swiss production" in general.[96]

Giorgio Frapolli, the former head of the Zürcher Filmclub, which had already ceased to be active, programmed the films commissioned by the mayor's department for the municipal forum in 1969.[97] Later this turned into a traveling film program shown in various cinemas, and in 1983 it took up its current venue: Studio 4.[98] Bernhard Uhlmann and Rolf Niederer, both of whom had been on the board of the Zürcher Filmclub, were the first codirectors of the stationary Filmpodium.[99] In other cases, too, informal initiatives turned into official posts or institutions: Film Forum's Filmvermittlungsstelle—with some of the same personnel[100]—indirectly became the first film pool that was run by the filmmakers themselves, and was later taken over by the national financed film promotion office Filmzentrum (now Swiss Films). The final Ciné Circus program in October 1970 in Basel was no longer organized by Film Forum either, but rather by the precursor to the Filmzentrum (the Arbeitsgemeinschaft Nationales Filmzentrum) in collaboration with the AKS film collective. In the end it was the national cultural foundation, Pro Helvetia, that financed *Das kaputte Kino* (*Broken Cinema*), a film program of Swiss experimental films curated by Schoenherr that toured various European cities in 1972.[101]

The fact that within a few years independent avant-garde and underground initiatives had evolved into subsidized actions and institutions was a success for those filmmakers who were trying to become established. For those working experimentally—those that Siber had warned against the "overground"—this institutionalization was problematic in the long term. It threatened two central criteria valued by such filmmakers: independence and spontaneity. The will to self-exploitation was, however, flagging on the experimental film scene in Zurich even before filmmaking was structured and formalized. The attitude of breaking out, of being different or doing things differently, which was shared by many, could not be maintained without subsidies. Without them existence was impossible, and with them independence was impossible.

Film Criticism and Film Festivals

Until 1969 interest was focused almost exclusively on the people behind the camera and hardly at all on their films. As part of the presentation of the first works subsidized— by the mayor's department via Siber—the press itself began to engage with experimental films from the spring of 1969 onward. The reviews included praise for individuals, but in some cases were devastating—among other things, the works were criticized for a lack of substance and craft. Alex Bänninger, a reviewer for the *Neue Zürcher Zeitung*, felt substance and intellectual energy were missing in the works of "young avant-gardists" Siber, Weiller, Kurt Kühn, Renzo Schraner, and Kuert: "Precisely because experiment is so necessary, it may be appropriate to expose works as feeble, and accuse them of intellectual arrogance."[102] Bänniger described Siber's *Mönch* series as "fireside cinematography."[103] The vehemence of the criticism must be seen in connection with the emergent New Swiss Film. Many of the more intimate, experimental works did not stand up to the pressure of the expectations in the late 1960s for every debut film, and discussions very quickly turned to the fundamental issue, namely, the future of film in Switzerland. As we have seen, some film critics after 1968 demanded more social relevance.

The defunct *Film-In* festival in Lucerne (1969–1972) dominated prominent program platforms for such films, such as Progressive Art Production, curated by Meier and Hein from 1969 to 1971. In 1972, the festival's final year, however, "progressive" films were lacking.

The Solothurner Filmtage also supported experimental films, which in the early 1970s was programmed on Tuesday mornings. Stephan Portmann, its director for many years, had really encouraged the Basel-based painter and filmmaker Werner von Mutzenbecher to show his films. For von Mutzenbecher, this provided him with an important incentive to shoot a film at least once a year.[104] The program that had been a vibrant program of experimental works quickly thinned to just a few names. The relative importance of experimental short films decreased with the increasing professionalism of filmmaking.

On all levels—festival programming, the attention of audiences and critics, the influence of the "avant-gardists" within the growing community of filmmakers—experimental short films (once again) led to a niche existence, as is evident not least from the programming in Solothurn. The few longer experimental films being made in the early 1970s as part of Deutschschweizer Fernsehen's Aktion Jungfilmer (German-speaking Young Swiss Filmmakers Action) subsidy initiative,[105] such as *Alfred R.* by Radanowicz (1972) and *Stella da Falla* (1971) by Reto Andrea Savoldelli, were either barely noticed or torn apart by the critics, who had previously lavishly praised short films by these same directors, especially *Lydia* (1969) by the "wunderkind" Savoldelli.[106]

Following his medium-length Alpine rock opera, *Die Sage vom Hirten Xeudi und seinem Freund Reiman*, Siber put an end to his personal involvement in filmmaking, in part for financial reasons, during its screening at the prestigious Forum des jungen Films in 1974, even though he had received encouragement from the critics and felt that this film had been accepted by the broader film community as well.[107]

Schoenherr abandoned his role as a mediator with the closure of his journal *Supervisuell* in 1970 and the one-time tour *Kaputtes Kino* in 1972,[108] but he remained faithful to his radically individualistic and conceptual style of filming. He made films in accordance with Robert Walser's maxim that one can "be an artist unsuccessfully" until 1993.[109] His patrons, and then for many years his wife's salary, enabled him to continue this existence.[110]

Counter Culture

The height of alternative film production and reception largely overlapped with the rise of counter culture, whose exponents distanced themselves from conformism in general and from the "dogmatism" of the new left. They were united by common interests, such as American and British underground bands, but also by superficial identifying signs such as long hair, which Siber wore until 1972.[111] Siber characterized the self-image of this community as follows: "We are outsiders! We are against society!"[112] The motivation to form an identity, to violate the conventions of society and of art, developed a cohesive power for a few crucial years, and then eroded as a result of political polarization, the fragmentation of subcultural groups, and also the commercialization of the culture. Gwerder ceased publication of his journal *Hotcha* in 1971, and in retrospect assessed the period from 1967 to 1971 as productive, but also frustrating: "Because it diverged too much, forming ghettos. People could no longer support one another."[113] This fragmentation of the subculture into increasingly specific, separate groups was accompanied by an enduring fascination for an alternative aesthetic, which from the mid-1960s often provoked scandal through violations of taboos such as presenting nudity, for example. After 1968, sexuality, which had previously been taboo, was increasingly common in commercial cinema.

In short, from 1966 to 1969, it was indeed accurate to speak of an "experimental film scene in Zurich." But lively as it was, and despite all the inspiration that the members of this sociotope took from this period, it atomized just as quickly. The feeling or the desire to be part of a close-knit community, combined with a decided individualism, was not limited to Zurich in the late 1960s. In her study of artists in New York's Greenwich Village in 1963, Sally Banes observed: "There was an urge toward extreme individual freedom, yet there was an equally strong desire for the glue of social communication. There was an overriding moral imperative toward equality, but at the same time eccentricity and difference were celebrated."[114]

It is not just Beat Kuert who looks back on it that way: "For me, it was a brief period. But it was the essential period."[115] What remain are (often faded) memories, a few programs and films, though the filmographies of those who continued filming and made a "career" tend to be hidden or not listed at all. Even in this essay they have not been given the attention they deserve. Today they are witnesses of a fascinating flash of imagination, experimentalism, entrepreneurial spirit, nonchalance, and radicalism.

[1] Turnus Film in a letter to the federal government after Karl Suter's James Bond parody *Bonditis* failed to get a subsidy for quality. Quoted in Oliver Moeschler, *Der Schweizer Film: Kulturpolitik im Wandel; Der Staat, die Filmschaffenden, das Publikum*, Schüren, Marburg 2013, p. 71.
[2] Heinrich Fueter cosigned this letter along with a coworker, director Nicolas Gessner. Quoted in *Tages-Anzeiger*, November 28, 1970.
[3] Pierre Bourdieu saw this as constituting a social field, including the field of art. Pierre Bourdieu, *The Rules of Art: The Genesis and Structure of the Literary Field*, trans. Susan Emanuel, Stanford University Press, Stanford, CA 1996.
[4] In the mid-1960s, Georg Radanowicz was studying architecture at the ETH, and his daily life went like this: "We would start at the Café Select in the morning. Then we went to the Odeon. And from the Odeon we might go to the Krug … Then we went back to the Select. That was a wonderful life." Georg Radanowicz interviewed on September 25, 2008, as part of Cinémémoire.ch.
[5] Zürcher Kunstgesellschaft (ed.), *Die wilden Sixties in Zürich*, panel discussion related to the exhibition *Friedrich Kuhn – der Maler als Outlaw*, December 12, 2008–March 1, 2009, Kunsthaus Zürich, Zurich 2011, p. 13.
[6] Platte 27 program, May 1968, Archive Robert (Bob) Fischer. "Herbi Wertli was, basically, not interested in culture at all. He just wanted to establish a club. Edi Stöckli was not so fit in culture either. I was the one who wanted to do a gallery … It was already clear that we wanted culture. But my primary goal was really a rehearsal space, where you could have jam sessions. [Grins] Later there was the gallery and film … " Jonas C. Haefeli, interviewed by Thomas Schärer, June 4, 2014.
[7] It is difficult to date the first film screenings at the Platte 27 under the name Film Forum precisely. The journal *Heim und Leben* read: "November and December 1965: The Filmclub Zürich is settling in at the Platte." See *Heim und Leben*, September 24, 1966. Author B.M. wrote in an undated circular to members, probably in 1967 (Archive Fischer): "We will no longer have to meet exclusively in the catacombs … The plan is for the spaces on the second floor and the attic to be used entirely by our club."
[8] Fritz Billeter, "Performance – Die eigene Haut zu Markte tragen," in Fritz Billeter and Peter Killer, *1968: Zürich steht Kopf. Rebellion, Verweigerung, Utopie*, Scheidegger & Spiess, Zurich 2008, p. 109–116, esp. 110.
[9] Theopil Dänzer, "Ein Forum für den jungen Schweizer Film," *Zürichsee Zeitung*, April 6, 1967.
[10] Hans-Jakob Siber, interviewed by Thomas Schärer and Fred Truniger, part 1, May 10, 2011. The cofounders were, among others, Rudy Burckhardt, who was from Basel but was living in New York; Swiss photographer Robert Frank; and Gregory Markopoulos, who in the late 1960s was living in Switzerland.
[11] "There were still other rooms in the Platte 27 building that were not being used. And that gave me the idea of screening films there." Hans-Jakob Siber, interviewed by Thomas Schärer and Fred Truniger, part 1, May 10, 2011.
[12] Dänzer, "Ein Forum für den jungen Schweizer Film" (see note 9).
[13] Hans-Jakob Siber, interviewed by Thomas Schärer and Fred Truniger, May 10, 2011.
[14] Fredi M. Murer, interviewed by Thomas Schärer and Fred Truniger, December 19, 2012.
[15] Theophil Dänzer, "Ein Forum für den jungen Schweizer Film."
[16] A strip of 16mm film with part of the opening credits has been preserved in the Archive Siber (now in the Lichtspiel Bern).
[17] "Mitteilung an die, die Filme gemacht haben, machen oder machen wollen," leaflet distributed at the Solothurner Filmtage in 1968, Archive Klopfenstein.
[18] Hans-Jakob Siber, interviewed by Thomas Schärer and Fred Truniger, part 2, July 13, 2011.
[19] Speaking to Marcel Leiser, who had founded Cinéma Marginal Distribution in 1968, Siber described the wide diversity of motivations: "At Film Forum there were people who had ideas about cinema that were absolutely opposed. Precisely because some thought that Film Forum was merely the first step on the way to a commercial cinema, while the others wanted to create a cinema separated from commerce, extremely free and personal." *Construire* (August–September 1968).
[20] Film Forum program, February–April [1968], Archive Siber.
[21] *Film Forum des jungen Schweizer Films*, program September–December [1967], Archive Siber.
[22] Hans-Jakob Siber, interviewed by Eric Jeanneret, January 21, 1990. The tapes are available at the Cinémathèque suisse, Penthaz.
[23] Anonymous, "Underground: Ein Fest für die Augen," *Der Spiegel* no. 48 (1967), p. 187.
[24] P. Adams Sitney, "The New American Cinema Exposition," *Film Culture* no. 46 (Fall 1967), p. 26–28, esp. 26.
[25] *Ibid.*, p. 26.
[26] *Ibid.*
[27] Conversation with P. Adams Sitney, Zurich, May 11, 2011.
[28] Urs Aebersold, Clemens Klopfenstein, Philipp Schaad (all three of whom belonged to AKS), Renzo Schraner, Georg Radanowicz, Hans-Jakob Siber, Klaus Zaugg, and Guido Haas, *Schweizer Illustrierte*, no. 19 and no. 20 (May 1968).
[29] Hans-Jakob Siber, interviewed by Thomas Schärer and Fred Truniger, part 2, July 13, 2011.
[30] Original flyer in the Archive Siber. For more detail on Expanded Cinema in Zurich, see Fred Truniger, "Die 'Underground Explosion' und das Expanded Cinema in den 1960er Jahren in Zürich," René Müller et al. (eds.), "Beschränkungen," special issue of *Cinema*, no. 67 (2012), p. 128–141.
[31] "Simultane Projektion diesmal mit nur zwei Streifen und ohne Spiegelkugel," Film Forum des jungen Schweizer Films, September–December program [1967].
[32] The film was a collaboration between composer Leo Nadelmann (who wrote an eponymous score in 1961) and choreographer Jean Deroc, and it was part of a performance of music and ballet first presented in July 1968 at the Parktheater Meilen. On this, see Truniger, "Die 'Underground Explosion' und das Expanded Cinema" (see note 30).
[33] Program, May 1968, Archive Fischer. In addition to Pierre Favre, the trio included Irene Schweizer and Jiri Mraz.
[34] Platte 27 flyer (A4 format), May 1968, Archive Fischer.
[35] *Ibid.*
[36] Hans-Jakob Siber, interviewed by Thomas Schärer and Fred Truniger, part 2, July 13, 2011.
[37] Self-painted posters for Schoenherr's *Autoportrait*, Saturday, June 29, 1968, Langstrasse 14, flyer announcing a screening of *Daydream* at the Cinéma Studio Uto on February 12, 1970. Archive Schoenherr, in Lichtspiel/Kinemathek, Bern. Dieter Meier's screenings of *Echter Diskussionsfilm* (8 min.) at the Solothurner Filmtage in 1968, and of *Papierlign* 1969 at the *Film-In* in Lucerne in 1969, P.A.P. catalogue 1971, unpaginated.
[38] The screening was held on June 23, 1972. Among other things, Schroeder presented *Albuquerque*, a film he had found at a flea market in Albuquerque, his own work. See H. S., "Szenen aus dem wirklichen Leben: Der Filmemacher Sebastian C. Schröder organisiert am 23. Juni

auf dem Lindenhof ein Happening für Amateur-Filmer," *Züri Leu*, June 13, 1972.
[39] Fredi M. Murer: "It was also a dance. They were the first to do psychedelic projections and run experimental films as nightclub decorations." Fredi M. Murer, interviewed by Thomas Schärer and Fred Truniger, December 19, 2012. Murer called this club a precursor of Platte 27. The noise control department of the municipal police of Zurich lists under "Nightclubs" a Chinchilla-Club in operation from 1966 to 1968. Hence this club was in operation at the same time as Platte 27. *Pic-Nic* by Georg Radanowicz (1967) was a film commissioned by an Italian Nightclub–probably in Milan–that wanted an endless-loop projection for a dinette. ("Junger Schweizer Film in Zürich," *Tages-Anzeiger*, September 7, 1968.) Peter Schweri performed *Three Walls with Film- and Slide-Animation* for the Blackout Club in Kloten near Zurich (see the essay by Michael Hiltbrunner in this book).
[40] "Einladung zum ersten bis vierten Mönch. Filme und Texte von Hans-Jakob Siber, Donnerstag, den 9. Mai 20.30 [1968]. *Der erste Mönch, Der blaugründe Mönch, Der schwarze Mönch, Der rote Mönch*, Suite für Siemens-16mm." Program, Archive Fischer.
[41] "It began with a divertimento by Peter Mieg, danced to choreography by Jean Deroc. It was followed by free jazz impressions by Max Keller and a light show by H. J. Siber. Then the "Esquisse de danse" with composer Armin Schibler at the piano (world premiere). Also, for the first time, *Fahrt durch die Nacht* by Leo Nadelmann was heard with a sound-film montage by H. J. Siber." Charles Wunderly to Fred Truniger, e-mail, August 9, 2017. An outdoor serenade at the Parktheater Meilen had been planned, but because of poor weather it was held in the Allmend school building instead.
[42] Hans-Jakob Siber, interviewed by Thomas Schärer and Fred Truniger, part 1, May 10, 2011: "I produced them [the films] and the ballet group danced in these projections. Because there were several projectors, my task was see to it at every performance that I had the right platforms."
[43] Gene Youngblood, *Expanded Cinema*, Dutton, New York 1970; Sheldon Renan, *An Introduction to American Underground Film*, Dutton, New York 1967. The first mention of the term dates back to Stan VanDerBeek, "'Culture: Intercom' and Expanded Cinema: A Proposal and Manifesto," *Film Culture*, vol. 40 (Spring 1966), p. 15–18.
[44] All of the programs except those for the first screenings in Basel have survived; the program for Lucerne is undated. (The date is based on Madleine Dubois, "Steckbrief junge Künster vor: Hans-Jakob Siber," *Tages-Anzeiger der Jungen*, December 27, 1967.) Archives of Siber, Schoenherr, and Klopfenstein.
[45] "These films are different from those that you are familiar with from the cinemas ... No stars and millions spent. We don't have them and can't have them. But we film anyway." Sheet accompanying the first *Ciné Circus* program in Lucerne in October 1967, Archive Klopfenstein.
[46] Program, second *Ciné Circus* Basel, Archive Schlumpf; Clemens Klopfenstein, interviewed by Thomas Schärer and Fred Truniger, Bevagna, June 12, 2012.
[47] René Codoni, "Raus aus dem Getto," *Zürich Woche*, September 13, 1968, p. 11.
[48] *Ibid*. In 2013 Peter von Gunten could no longer recall, but suspected that he and Gloor had been inspired by experiences from audience interventions at the Kurzfilmfestival Oberhausen. Peter von Gunten, interviewed by Thomas Schärer and Fred Truniger, July 5, 2013.
[49] Hans-Jakob Siber, "Traktäktchen zur Situation des Filmers in der Schweiz: Gesammelte Gedanken," June 1968, typescript, CSZ.

[50] René Codoni, "Raus aus dem Getto," p. 11.
[51] Hans-Jakob Siber to HHK Schoenherr, June 20, [1972].
[52] Hans-Jakob Siber, "Das Zürcher Filmforum," *Cinema*, no 56 (1968), p. 838.
[53] "An die Filmmaker: die Zusammenarbeit des Filmforums und der Platte 27 ermöglicht täglich von 21–02 Uhr auf 8 und 16 mm Projektoren eure roh oder Fertigfilme zu Visionieren (Voranmeldung Willkommen)," Platte 27 program, February–March 1969, Archive Fischer.
[54] Prepared in writing as "tip lists," "Mittteilung an die, die Filme gemacht haben, machen oder machen wollen," leaflet distributed at the Solothurner Filmtage, 1968, Archive Klopfenstein.
[55] Hans-Jakob Siber, "Das Zürcher Filmforum," *op. cit.*, p. 838.
[56] Undated flyer, Archive Klopfenstein. The following films were offered: *Balance, Meteorit, Promenade en biver, Umleitung, Wir sterben vor, Liebe 1, Out of this world, Jalousie, Tanz, Look, Rache auf Italienisch, Jipa, Lulla, Sylvia, Spiegelei, Fortschritt*.
[57] Film Forum program, February to April [1968], Archive Siber.
[58] [Film Forum] Bulletin, July 1968. Archive Schlumpf.
[59] Hans-Jakob Siber to HHK Schoenherr, June 30, [1972], Archive Schoenherr in Lichtspiel/Kinemathek Bern.
[60] Solothurner Filmtage, Informationen 1969, 22–22 (Brochure CSZ).
[61] "It was Siber's wish that we do something like that. And unfortunately I have ... It never occurred to me. I thought: 'Sure, if he wants it.' But I had to buy paper, and that sort of thing. And when it was time, I said to Siber that he had to contribute to it. I wouldn't pay for all of it myself. And he refused." HHK Schoenherr, interviewed by Thomas Schärer and Fred Truniger, March 28, 2012.
[62] "Startup capital (to keep the editors going). Siber's proposal: 300 francs. So Kuert, Siber, Schoenherr pay 300 each. Boner and Weiller 50 each, if they can." Film Forum circular, April 2, 1968, Archive Schlumpf.
[63] Film Forum circular, April 2, 1968, Archive Schlumpf.
[64] *Ibid*.
[65] For more detail on *Supervisuell*, see Thomas Schärer & Fred Truniger, "*Supervisuell*, Ciné Zirkus und Kirche der Linken: Alternative Filmkulturen in Zürich," Fernando Ramos Arenas, Ursula von Keitz (eds.), *Cinéphilie*, Augenblick: Konstanzer Hefte zur Medienwissenschaft, Schüren, Marburg 2015, p. 31–44, esp. 38-43.
[66] The first issue lists Birgit Michaelis (later Birgit Hein) as correspondent; the second issue, three months later, lists Ernst Schmidt Jr. (Vienna), Birgit Hein (Cologne), Alfredo Leonardi (Rome), and Jonas Mekas (New York) as autonomous editors. The masthead amends this: "Editors in San Francisco (Robert Nelson) and New York (Jonas Mekas) are being established."
[67] HHK Schoenherr, *Neue Zürcher Zeitung*, December 21, 1990.
[68] Schoenherr himself saw it differently: "I became known for *Supervisuell*. But I wanted to be known for my films. I saw that it was the wrong way. My films were suffering from it." HHK Schoenherr, interviewed by Thomas Schärer and Fred Truniger, March 28, 2012.
[69] Between 50 and 300 Swiss francs; 600 Swiss francs for two screenings.
[70] Circular to members, March 27, 1968. (On April 22, 1968, a selection of underground films from western Switzerland.)
[71] Hans-Jakob Siber to HHK Schoenherr, June 30 [1972], Archive Schoenherr in Lichtspiel/Kinemathek Bern.
[72] *Ibid*.
[73] November 8, 1968, typescript, Film Forum program, handwritten note: "8:30 p.m., Neumarkt. But I warn you: it is rather boring! Best, PH." Archive Schlumpf.
[74] Platte 27 program, March [1969], Archive Fischer.

[75] The multimedia "living" or "monster show" *Underground-Explosion* in the spring of 1969 at the Volkshaus ran under the label "Platte 27." Platte-27-Programmzettel. "Platte 27 in the Volkshaus […] Organizer: Hein München, Supervision: Meier Zürich, Independent Film Center." April 1969, Archive Knauer. For details of this show, see Thomas Schärer and Fred Truniger, "Underground Explosion: A Vaudeville of the Avant-Garde," in this volume, and Truniger, "Die 'Underground Explosion' und das Expanded Cinema."
[76] See Thomas Schärer and Fred Truniger, "Underground Explosion: Le music-hall de l'avant-garde," *Décadrages: Cinéma, à travers champs*, no. 21 (2012), p. 132–145, esp. 142–143.
[77] *Construire*, August/September 1968, Archive of the Cinemathèque Suisse, Zurich; File: "Experimental."
[78] Hans-Jakob Siber, interviewed by Thomas Schärer and Fred Truniger, part 2, July 13, 2011.
[79] "The Italian Radio in Zurich interviewed me, but the head of the station, an orthodox Marxist, refused to broadcast because I contradicted his idea that New American Cinema was essentially an organ of leftwing political criticism of American society." P. Adams Sitney, "The New American Cinema Exposition," *Film Culture*, no. 46 (Autumn 1967), p. 26.
[80] The protesters distributed leaflets: "FIGHT AGAINST OPEN AND UNDERGROUND AMERICAN IMPERIALIST AND CINE-IMPERIALIST AGGRESSION ALL OVER THE WORLD." See Xavier Garcia-Bardon (ed.), "*EXPRMNTL*: Festival hors-normes, Knokke 1963 1967 1974," *Revue belge du cinéma*, no. 43 (December 2002), p. 51.
[81] HHK Schoenherr, interviewed by Thomas Schärer and Fred Truniger, March 28, 2012.
[82] The occasion for the foundation was the 75th anniversary of the Aktiengesellschaft Eugen Scotoni-Gassmann and the Bauunternehmen Eugen Scotoni AG, *Neue Zürcher Zeitung*, November 7, 1968: "Die Kontroverse um die 'Auszeichnung guter Filme': Notwendigkeit privaten Mäzenatentums." There is no evidence that Scotoni was interested in experimental films. Perhaps it was less a decision in favor of experimental films than it was a decision against "auteur films," a decision against a new generation of Swiss filmmakers who wanted to bring works (which were often critical of society) into cinemas.
[83] Kurt Gloor, Fredi M. Murer, Georg Radanowicz, Renzo Schraner, June Kovach, and Alexander J. Seiler, "Zürcher Filmpreis 1968: Ein offener Brief an den Stadtpräsidenten Dr. Sigmund Widmer vom 31.10.1968," *Die Tat*, November 9, 1968. For more detail on this, see Thomas Schärer, *Zwischen Gotthelf und Godard: Erinnerte Schweizer Filmgeschichte*, Limmat, Zurich 2014, p. 277–281.
[84] Hans-Jakob Siber, "Traktäktchen zur Situation des Filmers."
[85] Ibid.
[86] German gallery owner Rolf Ricke represented Paul Sharits in Europe, Rolf-Ricke-Archive, https://archiv.adk.de/bigobjekt/22273 (last accessed March 2020). P.A.P produced lavishly designed catalogues and was represented by a booth at the Art in Basel fair in 1970 and 1971. Dieter Meier, interviewed by Thomas Schärer and Fred Truniger, part 2, July 7, 2011; PAP-Katalog, 1971.
[87] Platte 27 program, January 1969, Archive Fischer.
[88] Platte 27 program, February–March 1969, Archive Fischer.
[89] Platte 27 program, December 1968, Archive Fischer.
[90] Under the names Club Platte 27/Antares Club, the municipal police kept files from 1968 to 1976. Stadtarchiv, V.E. c.68 Lärmbekämpfungstelle der Stadtpolizei Zürich, Akten 1968–76.
[91] Fredi M. Murer interviewed by Thomas Schärer and Fred Truniger, December 19, 2012

[92] Erika Hebeisen, Elisabeth Joris, Angela Zimmermann, *Zürich 68 – Kollektive Aufbrüche ins Ungewisse*, Hier + Jetzt, Baden 2008, p. 215. See also Jonas C. Haefeli, interviewed by Thomas Schärer, June 4, 2014.
[93] Roland Gretler, "Wie Zürich ausser SBG, FDP, BGP, VBZ auch AJZ zu einem Begriff wurde, oder Lose your dreams and you will lose your mind," Billeter & Killer (ed.), *1968: Zürich steht Kopf*, p. 77–84, here p. 78. The same publication mentions the "officially controlled demolition of the building at Plattenstrasse 27," p. 241. The building was to be replaced by a supermarket that was never built. Today it is a parking lot.
[94] Martin Schaub, "Unscharfe Bilder und Vorstellungen," *Tages-Anzeiger*, March 21, 1969.
[95] "Im Zürcher Filmpodium: Junge Schweizer," *Tages-Anzeiger*, March 11, 1970.
[96] Program, Podium, Musik, Literatur, Film, September to November 1970. Archive Schoenherr in Lichtspiel/Kinemathek Bern.
[97] Giorgio Frapolli and Bernhard Uhlmann, interviewed by Thomas Schärer and Fred Truniger, June 6, 2012.
[98] The opening program in the autumn of 1983 included films by HHK Schoenherr. That leading representatives of the city still had a fairly narrow-minded view of culture, despite this reopening, can be seen in statements by Mayor Sigmund Widmer on the occasion of youth riots in 1980, and calls for a broader support of culture. Rock music was not culture, he observed. See https://rotefabrik.ch/de/akteure/ig-rote-fabrik/#/ (last accessed March 2020).
[99] Giorgio Frapolli and Bernhard Uhlmann, interviewed by Thomas Schärer and Fred Truniger, June 6, 2012.
[100] Telephone conversation with Beat Kuert on April 12, 2013.
[101] "By providing a credit line of 12,000 francs, Pro Helvetia enabled Schoenherr to present his extremely avant-garde concept of the *other cinema*, namely, the *broken cinema*." Hans-Peter Manz, *Die Tat*, April 29, 1972.
[102] Alex Bänniger, "Filme junger Avantgardisten im Städtisches Podium," *Neue Zürcher Zeitung*, March 17, 1969. The reproach of a lack of craft was made by, among others, Esther Fischer-Homberger, "Zur 'Werkschau Schweizer Film,'" *Reformatio: Evangelische Zeitschrift für Kultur und Politik*, no. 20 (1971), p. 135–139. "Stephan [Portmann, the then director of the Solothurner Filmtage Festival] said, that is a niche. Swiss film needs you. You have to be in it. And he when he was no longer part of it, things changed quickly." Werner von Mutzenbecher, interviewed by Thomas Schärer and Fred Truniger, March 13, 2013.
[103] Alex Bänniger, "Städtisches Podium: Zürichs Underground-Film," *Neue Zürcher Zeitung*, March 4, 1969.
[104] From 1970 until the late 1980s, Mutzenbecher presented a new work in Solothurn nearly every year.
[105] The director of Schweizer Fernsehen, Guido Frei, announced the Aktion Jungfilmer at the Solothurner Filmtage in 1969 and made 300,000 Swiss francs available for freelance productions. An independent jury of renowned members was established, on which Robert Boner, as a representative of Film Forum, sat, among others. It had to assess numerous proposals from which, after an astonishing decision in 1970, the two most radical projects—*Stella da Falla* by the self-taught filmmaker Reto Savoldelli and *Alfred R.* by Georg Radanowicz—were chosen.
[106] For more detail on this, see Schärer, *Zwischen Gotthelf und Godard*, p. 569–571.
[107] Hans-Jakob Siber, interviewed by Thomas Schärer and Fred Truniger, part 2, July 13, 2011. From then on, Siber dedicated himself to dinosaurs. His excavations and his successful Sauriermuseum in Aathal earned him an honorary doctorate from the University of Zurich.

[108] The often-negative reactions to the film screenings in Munich, Cologne, and elsewhere that came back in 1972 via Swiss ambassadors and cultural attachés were summed up the by *Tagesspiegel* in Berlin in a relatively conciliatory way: "today, where a diversity of possibilities of cinematic expression, from the underground to profitable consumer film coexist in an almost peaceful way, a program with experimental film studies can scarcely shock the eye. It was very different in the days of New American Cinema, and Swiss filmmakers unintentionally present themselves as its late successor here." A.F.S., "Das 'kaputte Kino': Schweizer Kurzfilme im Arsenal," *Der Tagesspiegel*, May 25, 1972. Copies of various letters, Archive Schoenherr in Lichtspiel/Kinemathek Bern.

[109] HHK Schoenherr, interviewed by Thomas Schärer and Fred Truniger, March 28, 2012.

[110] The City of Zurich's Filmpodium presented his films regularly and it was honored in October 1991 by the Film Anthology Archive in New York with a retrospective supported by Pro Helvetia.

[111] Hans-Jakob Siber, interviewed by Thomas Schärer and Fred Truniger, part 2, July 13, 2011.

[112] *Ibid.*

[113] Urban Gwerder, quoted in Marcel Zwingli, "Weltweiter 'Cornegidouillezap!': Kleine Ideotopografie der Unterground-Zeitung 'Hotcha,'" Erika Hebeisen, Elisabeth Joris, Angela Zimmermann, *Zürich 68 – Kollektive Aufbrüche ins Ungewisse*, Baden 2008, p. 135–145, esp. p. 144.

[114] Sally Banes, *Greenwich Village 1963: Avant-Garde Performance and the Effervescent Body*, Duke University Press, Durham, NC 1993, p. 255.

[115] Telephone conversation with Beat Kuert, April 12, 2013.

Notes from *Hors-Champ*: On Experimental Filmmaking in Basel in the 1970s and 1980s
Ute Holl

Translated from the German by Steven Lindberg

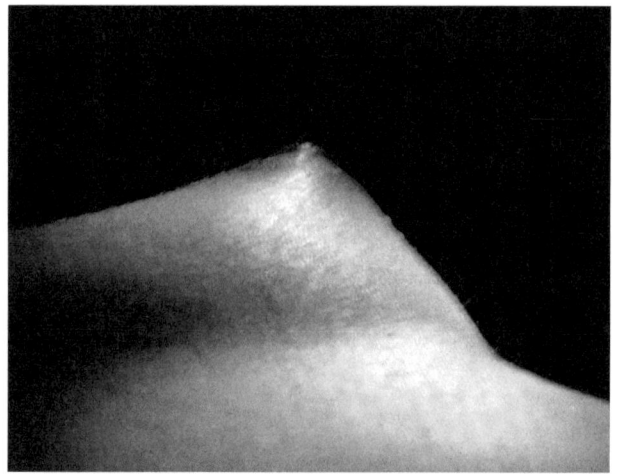

Bernd Fiedler and Balz Raz, *Parallaxe*, 1986 (Switzerland)
16mm film, 90 minutes

Hors d'oeuvre: Sources and Materials, Wine and Hot Dogs

Experimental films are not simply cinematic; rather they are spatial arts, performances, milieus, territorial occupations. Like performances, they negotiate the connection between theatricality and politics.[1] Experimental films are operative films, even if sometimes they have no plan. Texts about experimental films are, in turn, like travel guides—they promise all sorts of things, but also give the feeling there is nothing authentic or essential to be said. They call attention to the fact that experience, whether artistic or political, can only be described with difficulty, and cannot be reproduced. All writing reveals a lack of aesthetic experience, it fails to capture the color of images, the haptic quality of light, the smell of projector lamps, the noise of projecting Super-8 and 16mm films in galleries, back rooms, squatted buildings, at night, toward morning, in smoke-filled rooms in which everyone is talking at once, amateurs and artists, budding talent and tough guys. It is unclear what a criticism of this cinema should focus on—materials, techniques, screenings, or the influence that these films had on cinema in general? The aesthetics of experimental film deals, first of all, with the specific, the artisan, the haptic, and the tactile, not only on every reel, but also on every poster, every printed page, every typed note on the film. This was also true for experimental film in Basel. Page six of *Filmfront* no. 3 reads:

> Film festival at the Litfass-Säule, Bläsiring 19, Basel. Filmmakers from Basel show their films, Saturday, August 26, from 6.30 pm. Free admission. Anyone who wants to take a break from the film marathon can relax in the gallery with wine, beer, and hot dogs. ASSOCIATION FOR INDEPENDENT FILM (VUF).

This reveals another problem with the sources of experimental films: just as films have a particular format, texts about these films are marked by their typography—typewriter and offset printing. The poster of the typed announcement for the film festival was mounted on an advertising column or "Litfass-Säule"—the very name of the venue. It was illustrated with comic-style sketches—1978 was the time of Claire Bretécher and Gerhard Seyfried— and it also called for artists and critics to send in their articles: "Please submit print-ready entries (typed in as dark a print as possible, with a three-centimeter left margin, drawings are most suitable for illustrations)." Pound on the keys, comrade, it said, for "print-ready" did not simply refer to the words, and send it to: "FILMFRONT work group and distribution, Post Office Box 123, CH 4020 Basel." AG Film said hello to Billy Wilder. Work group meant association, network, a public yet closed community, secret society, craft federation, cooperative, "union,"[2] inclusive and exclusive. This also applied to their form of production, which signaled both exclusivity and exhibitionism—*cinéma copain, cinema povera*, art film, underground film, experimental film, independent film, a united front against commercialism, and everything in the first person: "In the beginning was not Adam, in the beginning was me," Christian Meyer wrote in the first issue of *Filmfront*. "My qualities and characteristics are reflected in my films."[3] In the beginning, in Basel as elsewhere, was Narcissus, the man, his optical apparatuses, his water for self-reflection, and the many men who peer into it. The program for the Bläsiring did not contain a single film by a woman, but some are sure to have dropped by to enter the darkness of the film marathon and the light of the gallery, in search of wine and beer, to eat hot dogs and criticize films. I know a few women from Basel. They are bold and sharp and leave nothing without comment. The documents produced by the young men, aged around 20 or 25, as they proudly point out in *Filmfront*, were not, in any case, intended for eternity: while the university library in Basel did have the first issue of the journal properly bound, the page numbers in the margin have been cut off. None of it can be cited in a traditional scholarly fashion. Everything has to be read like material from an unreliable source. From the second issue onward, the page numbers are at the bottom of the page, there is a three-centimeter margin, room for notes by typists, women, and others present. But can one write about experimental film from Basel at all, when one has not been part of the experience, as an outsider, from offscreen, using faded offset sources and faded memories? What would a good document about experimental cinema actually look like?

From what perspective can one write about experimental film at all? Especially when avant-garde film itself aims to avoid central perspectives and practices a nondirectional gaze. In *New American Cinema*, people like Jonas Mekas and Stan Brakhage were carefully read by the *Filmfront* people in Basel. "Imagine an eye, unruled by man-made laws of perspective," Brakhage wrote paradigmatically, "an eye unprejudiced by compositional logic, an eye which does not respond to the name of everything, but which must know each object encountered in life through an adventure of perception."[4] Adventures of the eyes, experiments in perception were made in the 1970s and 1980s, and these films preserve these experiences much as old records hold memories—every time you play them, the sound changes, and after 30 or 40 years you hear everything differently. Old experimental films viewed on DVD have a different effect than when seen on the original material; the soundtrack sounds different through today's headphones than it did at Kleinbasel's music scene by night in the old days—which today also looks different, tidier and cleaned up. How, then, is a non-Adam "I" supposed to write about it, and what is more, on a computer, on which the force of the keystroke does not matter, a computer that is not only capable of simulating all the typographers in the world at once, but which can also invite 500 people to a gallery in one go, that does not need to gather an audience for experimental film because it has networking, a computer that can play the digitized experimental films from Basel whenever it wants to? And to make it authentic, I could always smoke a cigarette while watching. I am writing from far away, both in time and space.

This is not a journey, not a tour, not of Basel, not of its film scenes, nor its crazy ego trips. The "I" of the critic has its doubts as to whether it is even possible to write a scholarly survey about the Basel experimental film scene. Its methodological framework and genealogy are marked by the films themselves, which are clearly in the tradition of Aleksandr Medvedkin, Sergei Eisenstein, and the Dziga Vertov Group. They are also in the tradition of Mekas, Andy Warhol, Jack Smith, and Peter Kubelka, and include films that follow the concept of social movements, in the context of film cooperatives, whose forms, semiotics, and aesthetics of reception have already been accurately reconstructed.[5] In the tradition of the Nouvelle Vague, the Basel filmmakers themselves engaged in writing. With *Filmfront*, the title of which was taken from Ernst Bloch, there was a conceptual approach from the outset. But even if those films point to their own genealogies, appeal to traditions and styles, they are in no way imitative. There is a form of obstinacy, held as a virtue in Basel, which is also difficult to describe. Therefore, this chapter cannot merely talk of a few individuals, two or three post office boxes or addresses. To a certain extent, its task is to reconstruct experimental film in Basel, during the 1970s and 1980s, as seen from the moon, *vista della luna*, from beyond the border, from offscreen.

Hors-Mémoire—The Margins of Memory

On the program of the Videoforum held in Freiburg im Breisgau, in 1988, among the many films on social movements and the aesthetics of resistance that I recall, there was one film that I remember well—*Japsen* (1988) by Muda Mathis and Pipilotti Rist. In the 1980s they were both in René Pulfer's class at the Höhere Schule für Gestaltung in Basel (School of Design), exploring what video was and could be.[6] Everything in their work was unbelievably different—what sort of creatures were these that breathed, stumbled, turned, and buzzed around, with their beautiful moon- and camera eyes? With their crazy jokes on screen that poked fun at God and the world, not to mention their music, every note of which was taken seriously and cracked like a circus whip? Rhythm and Les Reines Prochaines.[7] Only 30 years later do I realize that these were images that send cameras and mixers to the margins, and yet, also belong to the science of cinema, viewed from the perspective of video and its art forms. The Basel videos construct video dances, just as Maya Deren and Yvonne Rainer made filmic dances. At the same time, they negotiate femininity and feminism in the history of film. *Japsen* does so in five chapters: Madness, Hysteria, Flight, Love, and Laughter. First, at its center is the knee, which, of course, has no center, and a red stocking and boot shot in front of a green meadow and woods, and then again in an endless panning shot. Second: images of women are clear references to the images of hysteria produced at the hôpital de la Salpêtrière, standing for hybrid women's bodies, sex controlled through chronophotography. Third: a party for technology girls. Fourth: homage to the baroque, music, and math, and then, fifth, while the old laboratory camera addressed the eye, video filming involves the whole body in shooting and observing. In all cases, boundaries are transgressed in passing, video lines are overwritten, and the memory is made while shooting—a voluntary memory, and feminist.

The forgetful "I" of the critic was able to repeat that in Basel in 2016, at VIA, on Amerbachstrasse, parallel to the Bläsiring, a "random marriage of convenience" where people work on films, show videos, organize events, and establish archives. This is where *Japsen* can be found, along with *Die Tempodrosslerin saust* (*The Speed Throttler Chokes*, 1990), but not currently *Messer im Kompott* (*Knife in the Compote*, 1988) by Muda Mathis and Käthe Walser, as the archive is being remodeled, in cooperation with Bildwechsel, another feminist film center located in Hamburg, founded in the 1980s at Rostockerstrasse 25. Chris Regn is the flying mediator, performer, and artist who brought the network together and who distributes the art. It is easier to remember on an external hard drive what one forgets internally: videos from Basel are feminist, but in unforeseen ways. After all, the center is called VIA and not EVE. What these people like best is rotating the camera, mounted on all sorts of turntables so that it becomes eccentric in the literal sense of the word and not simply centrifugal. André Bazin claimed that film images were centripetal, unlike painting and its tableaux:

> The picture frame polarizes space inward. On the contrary, what the screen shows us seems to be part of something prolonged indefinitely into the universe. A frame is centripetal, the screen centrifugal.[8]

A third space is being created here—neither a mask nor a frame, but a space for rendering visible something that is not really conceived for the eye. These are films with no *hors-champ*,[9] films that create their own immanent, exclusive, stubborn, and cheerful worlds. Nothing here is indebted to a school, even though the audiovisual design class founded by Pulfer and Enrique Fontanilles at the Schule für Gestaltung in Basel did lead to crucial changes, and not only there. Nothing in the videos of that class recalls the works of those young men who founded independent film in the back room of a bar in Basel in the 1970s. Indeed, young as those filmmakers might have been then, they were still ten years older than Les Reines Prochaines and other video princesses. But they once shared a common address. *Filmfront*, the journal of the VUF, or AFI in French (*Association pour le Film Indépendant*), ascetic, manifesto-like, conceptually difficult, and presented in the language of historical materialism, was, from the third issue on also for sale in Germany, in Hamburg, at Rostockerstrasse 25, for 3 Deutsche Marks. At the precise place where the paths of VIA and Bildwechsel cross. The price of the first issue of

Filmfront was, by the way, "4 CHF, 4 DM, 4 F" for Switzerland, Germany, and France. Basel definitely has more borders than Hamburg, and hence also more *hors-champs*.

Hors-Champ and Offscreen: The Blind Spot of the Visible

The offscreen is an invisible power or, more precisely, the power of the invisible. What is visible in cinema, French film theory insists, is merely an imaginary mirror of the field beyond the mask, the *hors-champ*, which is made up of all that has been excluded: "the collection of elements (characters, settings, etc.) that, while not being included in the image itself, are nonetheless connected to that visible space in an imaginary fashion for the spectator."[10] Whatever "I" append to an experimental film with pen or keyboard is also merely the resonance of something imaginary that I see from a distance, with a delay: on the screen, monitor, in films, with an eye to that which is missing because it is offscreen. What of the excluded can be seen here? Where can we perceive the reality of the "not included"? The answer to that question is also a lesson to be learned from Basel filmmakers and their cooperatives.

Clemens Klopfenstein, a student at the Kunstgewerbeschule (School of Applied Arts) in Basel from 1962 to 1965, a precursor of the *Filmfront* people, and hence the avant-garde properly speaking, had also begun filming in a project group, with Urs Aebersold and Philip Schaad. His experiments with light and lighting demonstrate that experimental cinema does not simply film the excluded, but can actually reveal what previously failed to appear in the field of the visible. In 1978, long after he had vanished into the Italian Off, Klopfenstein filmed *Geschichte der Nacht* (*Story of the Night*) with high-speed film stock that was developed in photochemical laboratories. On his journey through European nights, Klopfenstein filmed the margins of cities, of societies, of the continent, and even of perception, without any additional lighting, showing people, things, and actions that were actually supposed to remain invisible. As a tester for the film industry, Klopfenstein was experimenting with the limits of visibility.[11] This experimental quality remained firmly bound to the chemistry lab, not an uncommon occurrence in Basel, where Hans Richter had already experimented with color films for the chemical industry back in the 1920s.

The Allgemeine Gewerbeschule (General Trade School) and its applied arts section, the Zeichen- und Malklasse (Drawing and Painting Department), where Klopfenstein had once been a student, was the most important workshop for *cinema povera* and *film brut* in Basel. Typography played a prominent role here in the 1960s, as is evident from Klopfenstein's early experiments and his fondness for the Umbria font up until the experimental films of the squatters in the 1980s, who carefully chose that lettering for their titles. It is the genealogy of Basel experimental film in the Allgemeine Gewerbeschule that explains this attention to light and color, a close proximity to chiaroscuro drawing, a fondness for blurriness and the effects of movement on the screen, and in general a concentration on the screen, on the image, and its visibility. The drawing and painting students were clearly less worried about the *hors-champ*, the offscreen, the imaginary vanishing lines of the field of vision.[12]

Among the Gewerbeschule painter-filmmakers, Werner von Mutzenbecher, a student in the painting department from 1957 to 1960, occupies a crucial position. He was already an established painter when he discovered, in Paris in 1968, cinematic forms that were poles apart from the cinema that he knew. This led him to experiment with 8mm and 16mm formats. Mutzenbecher's film *Rom* from 1979—he too was *fuori campo* in Italy at the time—is a study of seeing, shot on 8mm film, precisely at the juncture between the camera and the painter's eye. The film feeds on the curiosity with which eyes can scan things and facades in a tactile way, and it exercises a knowledge of draftsmanship with its baroque mathematical foreshortening and compression, vanishing lines, especially montage, and the techniques of the Soviet avant-garde applied to narrative, object-oriented relationships. Mutzenbecher essentially values strong forms with as much improvisation as possible. His works from a painter's studio, which soon encompassed the entire open city, differ from conventional filmmaking in terms of their isolation and a certain "I"-relatedness of their production. At the same time, they blazed a trail for others for a variety of further experiments.

For six years, from 1973 to 1979, Mutzenbecher gave a film class to drawing teachers every Saturday, which gradually brought Basel's *Filmfront* people together. It was intended as an elementary instruction along the lines of Josef Albers' concept of preliminary courses: space, time, movement, light, montage, material, and time-axis-manipulations were explored week after week in short, improvised projects. The impact of these courses can be seen and felt in the famous films of Basel's "angry young men" of the 1970s. In these films, slow is slow, and fast is fast, bright is bright, and darkness structures the images. People work within the frame, only the noises on the soundtrack come from elsewhere. If there is anything structural in these films, it is in their analysis of color and form; there are no nostalgic or emotional motives. A good example can be seen in the films of Ruedi Bind, the author of the *Filmfront*'s founding manifesto, who had summarized the fundamentals of the independent film under the title of "*Frühlingserwachen*, A. standort, B. blick-und bewegungsrichtung, C. die eingeworfenen fenster" (*Spring's awakening*: A. location, B. direction of view and movement, C. the broken windows). In Brechtian lowercase, it evokes a Marxist discourse. Point 14 reads: "rather than dependence on enormous outside capital for production, rather than dependence on dealers and producers for the distribution of works: direct contact and direct collaboration with film viewers, for their part, and at the same time contact, collaboration, union, associations, cooperatives with other filmmakers."[13] This in no way means aligning with others. Bind's film *Fenster A* (*Window A*, 1975) is an uncompromisingly strict composition of walls, windows, and views that first isolates them from the rest of the world and then, shot by shot, allows them to become images in their own right. In *Parallaxe* (1986), a film essay by Bernd Fiedler and Balz Raz, on which Mutzenbecher occasionally helped out as cameraman, the filmmakers worked with layers of images. For example, in one long shot of a bicycle leaning against a red brick wall, pedestrians pass by in the middle ground and traffic with cars and mopeds in the foreground, marking the screen like light and dark, thick and thin brushstrokes. These remain not so much as colors but as mental impressions, layering the image as in a painting. In a later shot in the film this is reflected by a tin clown automaton that mechanically draws a portrait as if programmed, and thus translates three-dimensional realities back into the two-dimensional. This film essay is given a counterpoint in the form of entirely asynchronous sound montages, inversions of magnetic tape for the soundtrack, looped industrial sounds interrupted by the shrill, unpleasant ringing of an alarm clock, which is apparently intended to disturb the film's beautiful state between dream and reality. Thus, the impacts of the offscreen and *hors-champ* are indebted to the film's acoustic quality, and not to the structures of the image as screen.

Off-Beat: Rhythm

Raz, a former student of the Berlin Film Academy and a friend of Mutzenbecher from their common night shifts at the Basel post office, kept a record of his experiences in the form of cinematic diaries. As *Filmfront* confirms, his work followed the approach taken by Jonas Mekas, but was by no means aesthetically dependent on him. Mekas himself was present in the journal as a remedy, as an antidote to the mainstream: "Every break away from conventional, dead, official cinema is a healthy sign."[14] Another great cinematic diarist was Thomas Hungerbühler, also a student at the Kunstgewerbeschule, and a *Filmfront* man. Hungerbühler employed different formats in which he dovetailed private and political experiences, archivist and artist at the same time. Richard Bucher, in his diary of cities, chronicles the destruction of the city, Basel, which in his images casts off its old robe of the baroque and emerges into an unclear modernity. Here too, a passion for typography appears everywhere, if unintentionally, to give the films their own historic dimension, probably clearer in retrospect than at the time of production. It is not easy to explain where the humor in these films comes from and when precisely it is left out. For all the precision of its execution, it is Urs Breitenstein's *Tagesfilm* (*Day Film*, 1992) that shows a brilliant sense of humor: for instance, in the stop-motion sequences in which the routines of the residents and the mailman are demonstrations of the madness of automatism. Indeed, the filmmaker sees himself as one them. The cityscape itself, by contrast, seems as impassive as Buster Keaton's face.

Breitenstein, who had left Basel in 1978 to go to the Cooper Union School of Art and had participated in the Independent Study Program at the Whitney Museum in New York only to later attend the Städelschule, shot his *Zeil-Film* in Frankfurt am Main in 1980. It features another stylistic method that, in various forms, returns in the aesthetics to many experimental films of the Basel group: the pan. Breitenstein took his camera to the Zeil, Frankfurt's main shopping street, while this was under construction, letting it rotate faster and faster across a nearby construction site, with arrhythmic interruptions that seem like the hiccups of the man behind the camera, until the whole image dissolves into a study of the color planes of a 1980s architecture that was out of date before it even began to be built.

André Lehmann's films also clearly deserve a place among the great studies of cities and plazas. In *Westside Highway NY 77* (1977), *Manhattan 8 Standorte* (*Manhattan 8 Locations*, 1977), and his more recent film, *Ber-Lin 99/00* (2003), for example, manipulations of time lines are not merely arrangements of experiences of places and times, but compositions that establish new rhythms. Compared to work by other students at the Kunstgewerbeschule in Basel, Lehmann's films are like pieces by Thelonious Monk, which rely on intervals, pauses, and gaps, and thereby obtain their drive, speed, and intervals, from which no one can escape. The other extreme would probably be Klopfenstein's films, which are more akin to compositions by John Coltrane, and explore materiality qua sensitivity. Many filmmakers followed his lead here, in different ways. Another is the inventive Matthias Bosshart, whose studies of light and faces push the speed of 8mm film to its limits with light and candles. Bosshart also uses found film footage, which he duplicates and further manipulates revealing its own light rhythms. Werner von Mutzenbecher, too, works with similar rhythm-and-material studies when he copies 8mm films onto 16mm stock and reedits them. In other work, he employs Standard 8mm stock, which comes as 16mm film, but is cut down the middle axis in the lab after "double" exposure. Mutzenbecher leaves the 16mm strip as it is, uncut, projects it with a 16mm projector and, through this procedure, generates random correspondences between the parallel 8mm fields (*4 × 8*, 1988). His films use various methods to turn light rhythms into space. In *Untergrund* (*Underground*) in 1985, for example, he steps into the projection beam and his silhouette becomes an avatar in the film's cinematic space. Mutzenbecher had, incidentally, studied philosophy with Karl Jaspers in Basel and, in his seminars, developed the idea of the leap that is necessary to get from thinking to faith, which, in cinematic terms, was conceived of as a jump into on-screen space. "Film was for me always half dream, half reality."[15] Doublings, condensations, folds, and blackouts reveal a Basel scenario that becomes visible only in the context of cinema.

Basel does not fit into any frame, even for people from Hamburg. It is barely Switzerland at all, but rather very much beyond German borders, French but not France; second-generation immigrants from the Balkans go to school here, having had first-hand experience of Germany's new wars. In the Canton of Basel there are 12 mosques, a reminder that our monotheistic culture is composed of three religions. Hardly anything in Europe is more European than Kleinbasel; Italian is spoken on the street; anyone who cares about their appearance goes to an Albanian hair stylist, and the neighborhood magazine, *Mosaic*, is published in four languages, now including English for the benefit of the expats of the pharma-industries. In 1977, filmmaker Urs Berger wrote in the first issue of *Filmfront*: "The Quartierfilmgruppe Kleinbasel [Kleinbasel Neighborhood Film Group] grew out of an initiative group that sought to build a neighborhood and cultural center on the site of the former of Kleinbasel barracks." In June 1977, the Quartierfilmgruppe shot a Super-8 film about evictions and squatting on the lower stretch of Rheinweg and on Florastrasse: "The basic idea behind our barracks project and our film work is this: if we want to entice the citizens or residents of the neighborhood out of their reserve, we must establish an alternative public sphere." People can be reached "on the street, in bars, when shopping. We could consider open-air screenings," and all political life "is important to our filmmaking."[16] Even in films about social movements, attention toward typography meets the eye: the essential aesthetic features for designing information in *Mir bsetze* (*We Squat*) of 1980 are typographic, albeit from the arsenal of the punk flyer: 1. handwritten title on a red background; 2. white Letraset on blue background; 3. typewriting on white paper; 4. typewriting on a blue background.[17] Urs Berger, who had, among other projects, initiated the Quartierfilmgruppe Basel, operated the camera himself. On the one hand, the squatters were filmed with sympathy and, on the other, the police presence was also treated with quasi-ethnological interest. In "Über Experimentalfilme" (On Experimental Film) made in 1976, Werner von Mutzenbecher had written about the tradition of Alexandre Astruc and the *caméra-stylo*:

> anyone who has actually taken up a camera out of interest and pleasure in film, and perhaps also out of disgust with the entrenched position of commercial cinema, has taken a first step. They take their camera along, as once the painter or the traveler took a sketchbook, and use the miniature camera as if it were paper on which they quickly note things.[18]

Mutzenbecher had, until recently, a studio in grounds of the former Kleinbasel barracks. Painters and filmmakers had been meeting on the parade ground since the 1980s. The gap between filmmakers, social movements, and art filmmakers was perhaps not so great in Kleinbasel as it has been elsewhere.

Not only in filming, but also in their writing, the experimental filmmakers of Basel formulated positions, and experimented with conceptual fields combining political and aesthetic positions. Whether as squatters, activists, theorists, as collectives or individual artists, they worked on relationships between the formal and conceptual in a spirit of critical inquiry: "In fact, every artwork, even the hermetic work, reaches beyond its monadological boundaries by its formal language. Each work, if it is to be experienced, requires thought, however rudimentary it may be."[19] For Urs Breitenstein and Lehmann of *Filmfront*, and for painter Marcel Stüssi, who unfortunately is no longer with us, these approaches marked the way out of the backroom of the bar where the filmmakers' group was founded, into contemporary galleries. It is precisely this growing success that makes the protagonists, who are still alive, point out that they have not been a homogenous group, even if—or especially because?—the audience can recognize similarities in their oeuvre from the last 30 years.

Hors-Temps: Outside of Time

In the 1970s and 1980s, generally, generations of experimental filmmakers differed not so much in the forms they used, as in their preferred formats of Super-8 or video. Formats distinguished the different groups as did politics, aesthetics, and, indeed, distribution circuits. This was not the case in the context of independent film in Basel. As early as 1978, *Filmfront* had abandoned the purism of the powerful Super-8, and called on its readers to come to Bärenfelserstrasse, just around the corner from Bläsiring and Amerbach, to discuss the issues of video and its technical and financial aspects. These could scarcely be gauged insofar as future developments were unpredictable. Aesthetic questions were primary: "It seems more important to focus on subject matter than to worry about equipment at the moment."[20] In the same issue, ethnologist Béatrice Götz called on people to experiment with combining Super-8 and video devices and attempt to better coordinate experiments, "which the Algerians have been able to do for some time."[21] Everyone benefited from the broad network of connections in Basel. In January 1979, a program organized by the VUF was shown at the Solothurner Filmtage for the first time. *Filmfront* was triumphant: "Super-8 and video will be accepted as equals in the Solothurner Filmtage program."[22] Reinhard Manz, one of the founders of the Basel film movement, remained one of the most resilient bridges into the 1980s— a bridge toward video culture, and crossovers between art, film, and critical aesthetics. However, in his scornful *Vom Fortschritt (On Progress)*, of 1991, he added his own sardonic commentary on film technology through various generations of video-material: what improvements have all these new features and colors managed to give us? He films himself entangled in cables while the video images become more and more feeble with every copy. Three years earlier, Manz had, in his very lovely 16mm Kodachrome film *Vie Centrale*, created several multiple exposures of street scenes in Paris, in the tradition of Louis-Jacques-Mandé Daguerre's

Reinhard Manz, *Vie Centrale*, 1988 (Switzerland)
16mm Kodachrome film, 5 minutes 18 seconds

Boulevard du Temple, made precisely 150 years earlier, and set them each to a separate soundtrack. He revisited the contrast between volatile movements and the remanence of architecture and everything that does not move. The sensitivity of the film material enabled Manz to develop a sensorium for the past, to produce sensitivity to fleeting shadows, to reveal in the veils of exposure times a distance and foreignness of people, however close they were to the camera and how familiar they might be to us. Nearly 30 years later, the confusion of voices on the soundtrack, on which the voices of the people assert themselves against their ephemeral images, still preserves a dense memory of a lost city soundscape.

Pas de Hors-Scène: Nothing Obscene from Basel

Underground or experimental film—at least in the East or West Coast American context—always stimulates the gaze upon the visible body and the effects of its desire, and much of the success of the films of Stan Brakhage, Jack Smith, and Andy Warhol is due to their thematization of "sex, psyche, et cetera."[23] Yet, the early experimental film scene involving the young men of Basel remained surprisingly abstinent with regard to everything sexual, and followed the Protestant asceticism typical of the town. Klopfenstein, a man from Bern among the once-young men from Basel, is, so it seems, the only person who associated experiments with cinematic sensitivity to stories of obsession and love, albeit not as a Satanic ritual in the spirit of Kenneth Anger, but as a poetic fable. His *Ruf der Sibylla* (*Call of the Sibyl*) of 1984 is at once painting and cinema; it is about the knowledge of traditional drugs, but also about the impossibility of acting in movies insofar as film can always show the moment after the scene, what is off-stage, when the hero crashes into the backdrop. But even this off-screen is not ob-scene—on the contrary. Filmmaking in Basel, with its precise content, well-formulated artistic positions, politically rapid interventions, and very dry humor shows little interest in the excesses of the body or in moral transgression. No one talks about eroticism. The 90th minute or so of *Parallaxe* by Fiedler and Raz shows a pulsing carotid artery, curves of naked bodies, and then a close-up of a woman's bare breast with goose bumps. But as soon as the audience gets ready to hold its breath, a brown briefcase falls onto an armchair. Basel remains sober and busy. Certainly, the framing in Lehmann's *Manhattan* can be described as highly erotic. The transitions between the world above and the world below in his brilliantly chosen details of subway entrances and 42nd Street presumably convey more of a combination of violence and desire than all of Mutzenbecher's *Orpheus* films. As far as mad passion among the *Filmfront* filmmakers is concerned, however, we have to wait for the works by the Dellers brothers in the 1990s. The formal dominates in *Filmfront*; its very name refers to Bloch but not to his complex knowledge of and about relationships. It is therefore hardly surprising that artist-curator Simon Lamunière writes in retrospect: "Although the art scene in Basel at the time was interesting, it seemed somewhat ossified to me. Even the city's museums were not quite up-to-date."[24] The bold men of *Filmfront* would certainly shout out with Brakhage: "Make place for the artist. Do it now. For you, as well as for him, tomorrow is too late!"[25] But they lacked the second part, the ecstatic element that Brakhage, as a young man in 1955, boasted of resolutely: "I am young and I believe in magic. I am learning how to cast spells. My profession is transforming."[26]

In Basel, the transformative, eccentric, and humorous remained a matter of later queens and their videos with a clipped off-screen. No more referring to the space and time beyond the frame. Instead they did the right thing and exposed themselves. Should one appeal to Adorno here?

> No artist knows with certainty whether anything will come of what he does, his happiness and anxiety, which are totally foreign to the contemporary self-understanding of science, subjectively registers something objective: the vulnerability of all art.[27]

The exposure of women artists challenges art. That is true for the Basel video group, too. Knees, teeth, breasts, the body rendered with skin, bones, and spit between the toes, are on the screen. They refuse to be moved off the scene, literally, into the ob-scene. These films keep the message "on." In the three-channel installation, *Was ist mit Deinem*

Haar? (What's Up with Your Hair? 1994), by Muda Mathis, the camera once again rotates with centrifugal force, so that a spinning head speaks to us as Duchamp's anemic cinema once did. "I'm glad," says the spiraling woman's mouth in the twisted woman's face, "that you have such short arms and can't reach very far." Certainly not into the *hors-champ*. In experimental film, especially in Basel, the *hors-champ* remains negotiable.

[1] See Benjamin Wihstutz, "Introduction," Erika Fischer-Lichte, Benjamin Wihstutz (eds.), *Performance and the Politics of Space: Theatre and Topology*, Routledge, New York 2013, p. 1–12.
[2] See *Filmfront*, no. 1 (1978), n. p. The complete series of *Filmfront* can be accessed at blog.zhdk.ch/sfex.
[3] Christian Meyer, "Adam: Meine Art zu sehen," *Filmfront*, no. 1 (1978), n. p.
[4] Stan Brakhage, "Metaphors on Vision," Bruce McPherson (ed.), in Stan Brakhage, *Essential Brakhage: Selected Writings on Filmmaking*, Documentext, New York 2001, p. 11–71, esp. p. 12.
[5] See Julia Zutavern, *Politik des Bewegungsfilm*, Schüren, Marburg 2015; Urs Berger, Ruedi Bind, Julia Zutavern (eds.), *Filmfrontal*, Reinhardt, Basel 2010; Irene Schubiger (ed.), *Schweizer Videokunst der 1970 und 1980er Jahre. Eine Rekonstruktion*, JRP|Ringier, Zurich 2009.
[6] See Irene Schubiger, *Schweizer Videokunst*, p. 161.
[7] Les Reines Prochaines were founded in 1987 and are an all-female Swiss music band and performance group. Pipilotti Rist was a member from 1988 to 1994. Their lyrical songs draw on many different genres and traditions.
[8] André Bazin, "Painting and Cinema," *What Is Cinema?* trans. Hugh Gray, vol. 1, University of California Press, Berkeley 2005, p. 164–169, esp. p. 166.
[9] In English, the French term "hors-champ" can be translated as "offscreen" or "out of frame." However, here the author alludes to the theory of "hors-champ" as developed by André Bazin and later critics writing for the *Cahiers du Cinéma* [editor's note].
[10] Jacques Aumont et al., *Aesthetics of Film*, trans. Richard Neupert, University of Texas Press, Austin 1992, p. 13.
[11] See Clemens Klopfenstein in conversation with Thomas Schärer and Fred Truniger, January 8, 2012.

[12] See *Blast of Silence* (1973–1974); *Der Tag isch vergange (The Day Is Over*, 1975); the photo series *paese sera* (1974), *Roma notte 74* (1974), *Umbria notte 75* (1975); and the chapter by Simon Koenig in this volume.
[13] *Filmfront*, no. 1 (1978), p. 4.
[14] See *Filmfront*, no. 6 (1979), p. 4. Conversation with the author in Mutzenbecher's studio, July 14, 2016.
[15] Studio conversation, July 14, 2016.
[16] *Filmfront*, no. 1 (1978).
[17] See *Filmfront*, no. 8 (1980), p. 43.
[18] Werner von Mutzenbecher, "Über Experimentalfilm (1976)," *Filmfront*, no. 6 (1979), p. 15–17, esp. 17, reprinted in Sabine Schaschl-Cooper, Isabel Zürcher (eds.), *Werner von Mutzenbecher – Im Film sein*, exh. cat., Kunsthaus Basel Land/Modo, Freiburg im Breisgau 2006, p. 75–76.
[19] Theodor W. Adorno, *Aesthetic Theory*, trans. Robert Hullot-Kentor, University of Minnesota Press, Minneapolis 1997, p. 462.
[20] *Filmfront*, no. 3 (1978), p. 29.
[21] *Filmfront*, no. 1 (1978), p. 21.
[22] *Filmfront*, no. 5 (1979), p. 7.
[23] See Parker Tyler, *Sex, Psyche Etcetera in the Film*, Horizon, London 1971; *Underground Film: A Critical History*, Da Capo, New York 1995.
[24] Simon Lamunière, "Erlebnis, Leidenschaft, Freundschaft," Reinhard Manz, René Pulfer (eds.), *Video Rewind: Videowochen im Wenkenpark, 1984/1986/1988*, Merian, Basel 2013, p. 6–76, esp. p. 6.
[25] Stan Brakhage, "Make Place for the artist," *Essential Brakhage*, p. 74–76, esp. p. 74.
[26] *Ibid*.
[27] Adorno, *Aesthetic Theory*, p. 353–354

Filmfront, no. 3, 1978, p. 6

ART SPACES AND EXHIBITIONS

Expanded Kunsthalle: The Role of Cinema at the Kunsthalle Bern under the Curatorship of Harald Szeemann (1961–1969)
Nicolas Brulhart

Translated from the French by Miranda Stewart

View of the *Jesús Rafael Soto: Kinetic Works 1950–1968* exhibition installation, Kunsthalle Bern, Bern, 1968

Historically, film tended to be screened or projected in parallel to exhibitions by institutions that, in the postwar period, were abreast of the latest discourses in contemporary art—first and foremost, modern art museums and Kunsthalles. The growing presence of the moving image closely accompanied the transformation of museums into cultural centers. In the 1960s, institutions that provided cutting-edge art and experimental cinema entertained a complex give-and-take relationship that sought to expand culture and transform its host infrastructure. There was a belief in the artistic potential of the moving image—this underpinned the growing numbers of film screenings within the museum context, and the role model provided by the cultural film industry and its collective imaginary. From the point of cultural history, this mutual influence is hardly surprising. Its resulting chiasmus led to an ideal site described in this article.

Film, cinema, its materiality, and economy, interacted with new arrangements for contemporary art production: exhibitions, archives, curators. Exhibition organization, much like film production, took place within an expanding cultural leisure industry, poised between democratization and consumption.

In order to take stock of the role of film and the film industry's collective imaginary in the transformation of the exhibition apparatus, it is necessary to look outside the history of the artworks themselves. The history of exhibitions must be traced, and, further, include the history of art spaces in a wider sociocultural context, in this instance, the ideas that defined the public space needed to host European culture in the postwar period. In the years after the war, the institutionalization of works enabled a historicization of the avant-gardes, and this produced a discourse that was to provide an historical bedrock for neo-avant-garde practices. This historicization is important—the history of the modernization of the museum and the mediation of the art space by technology effectively goes hand in hand with the discourse training of media historians, a group to whom I belong.

The Kunsthalle Bern offers a particularly fine example of the recurrent presence of film, and cinema's pivotal role in the institutionalization of contemporary art. This process also lay at the root of the emergence of the curatorial role (the exhibition curator as auteur) and archive creation, an activity that allowed exhibition production to be charted. In this sense, the Kunsthalle Bern is a model institution, and the history of the exhibitions held here offers us a genealogy of the curatorial role courtesy of multimedia archives.[1]

This article outlines the presence of film at the Kunsthalle Bern in the 1960s under the curatorship of Harald Szeemann. It relocates his activities within the development of a postwar contemporary art network, and places them within a wider cultural context. My research into institutional infrastructures becomes progressively more psychological in its approach to the author of the exhibition and the cinematic imaginary. Harald Szeemann displayed a very specific interest in the medium of film and the influence of cinema in thinking new forms of exhibition and their media coverage, to such an extent that it could be characterized as a desire for cinema. From 1961 to 1969, when he was curator, film became increasingly central to the institution. In 1974, his brief return to the Kunsthalle Bern as curator of *Les Machines célibataires* (*The Bachelor Machines*) can be seen as allowing him to take a critical look at the 1960s and his desire for expansion. Is an aspiration of this nature compatible with a desire to develop critical thinking about the media? To what point is this curatorial unconscious, of which Szeemann is a prime exponent, subject to critique as a typically modern visual unconscious structured by masculine fantasy?[2] Perhaps the real issue here is the extent to which it is possible to map Szeemann's career onto the gradual breakdown of this modern optical unconscious.

The Contemporary Emerges

Since the postwar period, Bern has been a postwar capital with a select artistic circle revolving around the guardian spirits of surrealist art, including Meret Oppenheim, Otto Tschumi, and Serge Brignoni. Dancer Daniel Spoerri[3] and painter Dieter Roth figure alongside more local treasures such as playwright Claus Bremer, and Bern artist Christian Megert and his gallery Aktuell. In the 1950s, under the management of Arnold Rüdlinger (1946–1955) and subsequently Franz Meyer (1955–1961), the Kunsthalle Bern was the main meeting place for the local and international art scene. Films were rarely screened and, when they were, projections served specific purposes—mainly documentary or educational. They provided the finishing touch to exhibitions and showed workshop practices or artists at work. They were accompanied by anthropological talks, or made reference to other cultures.[4]

During that period, contemporary art was bound up with creating a transnational visual language shared by a tiny circle of insiders. Discourse about the art object revolved around the notion of dynamism, and reflected advances in abstract painting and metal sculpture. There was therefore a quest for all that was new while, at the same time, numerous retrospectives of historical avant-garde artists underpinned modern art's historical canon.[5] A new dialectic began to emerge, with "modern classics" providing the bedrock on

which to build a vocabulary of contemporary art. After the
Second World War it became increasingly common to see
the coproduction of exhibitions between different European
institutions; they were interested in creating networks,
sharing exhibition costs, and reducing catalogue production
costs. This mass-production approach helped to consolidate
certain exhibition formats: retrospectives, local exhibitions,
solo and group exhibitions. In Bern, Arnold Rüdlinger forged
strong links with European partners (galleries, museums,
and collectors), thereby placing the Kunsthalle Bern on the
international map. He presented himself not as a mere
director, but as the patron of a vision and a discourse that
legitimated an entire program. In 1952, *Tendances actuelles
de l'École de Paris I* (*Current Trends in the School of Paris I*) took
stock of the latest advances in art in Paris.[6] The connectivity
at the core of this exhibition created a temporality cadenced
by a growing urge to keep contemporary art at the cutting
edge. This feeling of contemporaneity was experienced
simultaneously by a network of players in the art world.
The modernization of transport and communications
infrastructure impacted on the visual arts and aesthetics.
The internationalization of art was essentially marked by a
gradual transition from Paris, the capital of the avant-garde
and new postwar painting, characterized as l'École de Paris,
to New York and its modernity.

The Infancy of Art—The Exhibition Theater

In the 1960s, people frequently talked of a Bernese scene,
populated by a new generation of artists, Herbert Distel,
Rolf Iseli, Markus Raetz, Roland Werro, and Oscar Wiggli
among them.[7] In the bohemian atmosphere of the old-town
cellars, which had blossomed into bars and theaters,
Bern witnessed the emergence of a modest countercultural
scene.[8] Harald Szeemann, a history of art student at the
University of Bern, mounted one-man shows in a small
auditorium, the Kleintheater at Krammgasse 6. Here he
developed a taste for popular and more experimental kinds
of theater. His first two actions as a curator, which he took
even before he was appointed to this post at the Kunsthalle
Bern, give us some idea of where his reference points
and his centers of interest lay. In 1957 Szeemann was

recommended by the Kunsthalle's current director Franz Meyer, to lead to completion an exhibition on the theme of *Dichtende Maler – Malende Dichter* (*Painters Writing—Poets Painting*) at the Kunstmuseum St. Gallen when the previous candidate pulled out.[9] The same year, in the tiny theater at Krammgasse 6, he brought together a selection of original documents as a tribute to Hugo Ball, an artist who he admired, 30 years after his death.

In 1960 Szeemann was in Paris writing up his doctoral thesis. He was a frequent visitor to the Cinémathèque française and various cine-clubs. Meyer told him that he was about to leave his post as director, and that the Kunsthalle Bern would be looking for a successor. In 1961 Szeemann was chosen by the committee to assume the curatorship of the institution. After he had successfully brought to fruition several exhibitions already planned by his predecessor, he embarked on his first, more personal, project. In 1962, using his knowledge of theater and performance, he proposed *Puppen – Marionetten – Schattenspiele (Asiatica und Experimente)* (*Dolls—Puppets—Shadow Theater [Asia and Experimentation]*), an expanded exhibition based on the use of multimedia, and a style inspired by a theatricality that was used to undermine exhibition conventions.[10] The main Kunsthalle auditorium suddenly became a stage for a variety of performances. The exhibition boasted eight linked events. In addition to the performances staged in the auditorium, there were presentations in the Schulwarte building,[11] film screenings, and talks accompanied by films at a variety of venues, rounded off by a display of puppets from different periods in the exhibition space.[12] In the introduction to the catalogue Szeemann outlined his intentions:

> This exhibition should not be seen as a historical review, but rather as stimulation,[13] the opportunity to explore an interesting topic, and a form of theater art—dolls, puppets, shadow theater—just to see what there is. The idea now was to push the boundaries of the Kunsthalle as an art center, as much as its internal space would allow [...] After several successful experiments in the reading of texts accompanied by screenings of associations of images, the idea now

was to repurpose the main Kunsthalle auditorium and use it to host a full program of performance evenings.[14]

Some participants in the exhibition moved back and forth between the fields of art and performance. This was the case, for example, of Harry Kramer.[15] He was an entertainer, dancer, choreographer, and inventor of kinetic sculptures, which he used as attractions in his experimental films. Kramer was a proponent of a mechanical theater. Jacques Polieri was another artist who moved between the visual arts and performance. He loaned photographs of objects that belonged to the collections of the Centre expérimental du spectacle (Experimental Theatre Center, Paris), which he directed. Polieri was responsible for the Théâtre Ranelagh (Ranelagh Theater) program, and the Festival de l'Art de l'Avant-Garde (Festival of Avant-Garde Art).[16] He was a stage designer and producer and carried out experiments into stage mechanization and electrification.

The events program of the *Puppen – Marionetten – Schattenspiele (Asiatica und Experimente)* exhibition drew directly on the exhibition events organized at the Moderna Museet in Stockholm, particularly *Rörelse i konsten* (*Movement in Art*), the first major institutional kinetic art exhibition in 1961.[17] Szeemann's exhibition was held in a variety of venues close to the Kunsthalle, and sought to open up traditional exhibition space to different types of live performance. This initial curatorial gesture already contained elements that later become part of his signature style. Further, the spontaneous creation of the exhibition cued a primal scene, set within what is effectively a theater, both in the material and the mental sense of the word (with all its attractions and mediations), located in the heart of the institution. This opens up to reveal a structured imaginary of the public space that served Szeemann as a basis upon which to articulate discourses and use devices. The exhibition drew on popular culture as a carnivalesque tool to be used in undermining the classic codes of the conservative museum exhibition. Its rationale sought to include and accumulate, in short, to expand. Szeemann projected, from his curatorial role, a desire for expansion.

The Schulwarte theater, Bern, 1960s

Defense of Experimental Cinema—Screenings at the Kunsthalle Bern

The experimental cinema screened at the Kunsthalle Bern in the 1960s fell outside the traditional circulation network for these objects, such as independent filmmakers' cooperatives. The films were mainly sourced through loan requests to film archives and museum collections. The Moderna Museet in Stockholm, a partner institution in producing exhibitions, was a regular recipient of film loan requests.[18] Since its opening in 1958, this museum had been a pioneer in Europe in defending and legitimating experimental cinema as an art. Its program included screenings and its collections contained films. Its director, Pontus Hultén, even had a background as a filmmaker.[19] Following in the footsteps of curator Willem Sandberg, he viewed film as an essential form of modern aesthetics.

Harald Szeemann, inspired by progressive European museums such as the Moderna Museet, and the Stedelijk Museum in Amsterdam, was clearly determined to include experimental cinema in his early projects, as can be seen in his choice of screenings associated with exhibitions. In 1961, during his first exhibition devoted to the Bernese surrealist painter Otto Tschumi, Szeemann organized a screening of surrealist cinema in partnership with the Cinémathèque suisse and the Cinémathèque française. The screening took place at Schulwarte, normally the venue for the Kunsthalle's performances, projections, and talks as it boasted a theater specially adapted for projection.

In 1962, the Kunsthalle Bern hosted a dual exhibition of international stature: *Vier Amerikaner: Jasper Johns, Alfred Leslie, Robert Rauschenberg, Richard Stankiewicz* (*Four Americans: Jasper Johns, Alfred Leslie, Robert Rauschenberg, Richard Stankiewicz*) and an exhibition on Francis Picabia. The *Vier Amerikaner* exhibition was organized by Hultén at the Moderna Museet, and traveled to the Stedelijk Museum in Amsterdam before reaching the Kunsthalle Bern. It marked the arrival of a new generation of American artists in Europe, and the increasing presence of a network of galleries and institutions producing cutting-edge contemporary art with, as prime exponents, the Castelli Gallery in New York and its partner institution in France, the Sonnabend Gallery. The tensions at the heart of this new international scene were brought to the fore by the proposal for this dual exhibition[20]: on the one hand, leading young American artists with their new market, and on the other, the historicization of the European avant-garde, essentially from Paris. Szeemann wanted to use the selection of experimental films by Jonas Mekas, Albert Leslie, Robert Frank, Shirley Clarke, and John Cassavetes already shown by the Moderna Museet within the *Vier Amerikaner* exhibition.[21] However, with the exception of *Pull My Daisy* (1959) by Robert Frank and Alfred Leslie, they had all been imported through the Swedish consulate and had already been returned to the United States. The screening was proving quite tricky to organize. Szeemann was quick to react and managed to procure, from the Cinémathèque suisse and Freddy Buache, its director, a loan of copies of historical avant-garde films to supplement the exhibition on Picabia. On August 29, 1962, there was a screening, mainly of the classics of French avant-garde cinema,[22] which also included *Pull my Daisy* as an example of New American Cinema.

Film occupied an increasingly central place in the curator's imaginary when it came to designing exhibitions. In 1965 Szeemann organized a new, expansive, and generous group exhibition focusing on kinetic art: *Licht und Bewegung (Light and Movement)*.[23] It was produced by the Kunsthalle Bern, and was supposed to tour Europe. These major exhibitions were to a certain extent "distributed." The only way that curators could cover the costs of a project of this size was to send it on tour. In principle, the exhibition theme—kinetic art—was bound to include film; most kinetic artists have dabbled with film, and the cinema machine is critical in defining the mode of attention that is central to kinetic art.[24] Szeemann mentioned, in the talk he was invited to give at the exhibition opening in Düsseldorf, the direct links that exist between kinetic art and film art:

> Kinetic art? Kinetics, as we know, is the learning of movement. In popular belief, the term conjures up this idea as well as cinema production.[25]

The organization of screenings to accompany the exhibition is proof indeed of the curator's determination to be able to select. However, counter to the myth of selection by an omnipotent curator, the Kunsthalle Bern archives show just how hard it was to get films in the appropriate formats at the right time. The Kunsthalle made a plethora of requests: to TV broadcasters for documentaries (the BBC, the TSR for film documentaries about Jean Tinguely; Hessian broadcasting (RTL) for material about the artists in Zero); directly to certain artists (Henri-Georges Adam, Jésus Rafael Soto); and to the Cinémathèque suisse. However, it was ultimately to prove more challenging to put together a screening from heterogeneous sources than it was to mount an exhibition. Szeemann had to go back to the Cinémathèque suisse for the loan of a selection of avant-garde films, and this provided the basis for a first screening, which only offered the haziest reflection of the contemporary practices of kinetic artists. Szeemann decided to try again. On December 9, 1965, seven films were screened. They all came from the Moderna Museet.[26] The screening took place in the main Kunsthalle auditorium with an operator, a 16mm projector, a sound system, and a screen, all rented for the occasion from the Schulwarte. It was held late, more than three months after *Licht und Bewegung* had closed, so the films were no longer associated with the works in the exhibition. Despite the presence of many works that took the form of problematized vision devices, objects that captured attention or directed where the spectators were to move, the exhibition included no films.

In 1967, Szeemann organized an exhibition that turned out to be the most popular of his time in office. *Science Fiction* picked up on a theme of popular culture that cinema had appropriated for itself. The project is evidence of an expanded view of the exhibition. Anthropological discourse legitimated this particular cultural appropriation. Szeemann invited artists to respond to artifacts, antiques, and contemporary trinkets, pulp fiction, ephemera, posters, toys, gadgets, and rare books, and produce works. In parallel to the exhibition, he programmed classic science-fiction movies at the Cinéma Royal, a city-center commercial cinema. The films were sourced via the Cinémathèque suisse and Jacques Ledoux, the director of the Cinémathèque royale de Belgique in Brussels, as well as from more traditional distributors. Szeemann negotiated the Swiss premiere of *Who Are You, Polly Maggoo?* (William Klein, 1966), and sought to include more radical cinema. On the advice of the artist Erró, he managed to get hold of a film that the artist had made at the Sandoz laboratories (Eric Duvivier, *Concert mécanique pour la folie ou la folle mécamorphose*, 1963 [*Mechanical Concerto for Madness*]), and *La Jetée* (*The Jetty*, 1962) by Chris Marker.

While the films screened at the Kunsthalle Bern were all part of the exhibition, they could also be seen independently. In 1966, specific screenings were devoted to New American Cinema. This marked the Kunsthalle Bern's most stable ongoing relationship with a form of experimental cinema at this time. In 1966, films by Taylor Mead were screened without being specifically associated with an exhibition. In 1967, films by Bruce Conner and Kenneth Anger were screened in the main Kunsthalle auditorium. They were effectively an independent event, but were announced on the exhibition poster. In 1968, an entire program was devoted to filmmaker Robert Nelson. The same year, the Kunsthalle devoted an evening to Gregory Markopoulos. The filmmaker was living in Switzerland at this time; however, the organization of the screening was via the Filmklub Zürich, a distributor, which made the process even more complicated. Finally, during the exhibition *Live in Your Head: When Attitudes Become Form (Works—Concepts—Processes—Situations—Information)* of 1969, Philip Glass, who gave a concert at the Kunsthalle, had brought with him a copy of *Wavelength* (1967), a film by Michael Snow, the recent winner of the Grand Prix at the *EXPRMNTL* festival in Knokkele-Zoute (Belgium, 1968). The film was screened at the Schulwarte on March 21, 1969, in a program that included sound recordings by Steve Reich and a concert by Philip Glass. Szeemann designed several Swiss film programs following the template of the New American Cinema screening, hoping that, by association, he might impose some coherence on a movement that had none at the time.[27] In 1967 the Kunsthalle organized several evening events under the title of New Swiss Cinema, with, for example, screenings devoted to Fredi M. Murer (1967) and Peter Radanowicz (1968).

The Kunsthalle Bern, much like other similar institutions, was involved in building a canon of experimental cinema.[28] In the 1950s, a film might be screened for its documentary or ethnographic virtues. This trend declined in the 1960s, when programming of specifically experimental cinema emerged—classics of the historical avant-garde, kinetic art, artists' films, and different national New Cinemas were now top of the bill. In the case of Bern, and Switzerland, which did not have a well-organized experimental cinema scene, the Kunsthalle took an interventionist and committed approach to legitimizing the subject and its program, and made film its prime medium in the defense of the expanded arts. Szeemann saw experimental cinema as a practice that did not have a place of its own. He was critical of the Bern cinema circuit and its over-commercialization. In an article published in the *Tages-Anzeiger* upon the departure of Szeemann from the Kunsthalle in 1969,[29] one journalist noted that, in addition to international exhibitions, Szeemann had wanted to expand the Kunsthalle and create an auditorium for "independent film" (freier Film) and a space for local artists. This project never came to fruition, although his desire for expansion would appear to have been a constant during his term of office.

An Expanded Kunsthalle Bern and the Cultural Turn in Art

The Kunsthalle Bern modeled its ambitions on the major European museums with which it collaborated, such as the Stedelijk Museum and the Moderna Museet. However, the infrastructure needed to host events of this nature was not available locally. Film programming was a major strategic argument in the call to expand the Kunsthalle's infrastructure. Indeed, the minutes of the committee meeting of the Kunsthalle Bern Association, dated June 13, 1963, read:

> [...] the director (Szeemann) gave an overview of the programming for 1963–1964. In his presentation, he stressed the importance of expanding[30] the Kunsthalle's cultural responsibility, from that of a museum that hosts exhibitions to that of a cultural center, a "living" museum (such as the Louisiana in

Copenhagen or the Stedelijk Museum in Amsterdam).[31] It would involve the construction of a multipurpose hall (designed to host exhibitions, films, theater, concerts, talks) in the "inanimate" grounds behind the Kunsthalle. This would certainly be a reasonable objective for the 50th anniversary of the Kunsthalle in 1968 [...] According to one member attending the assembly, plans to expand the Kunsthalle had been drawn up before the war.[32]

A text dating from March 1965, written by Szeemann, outlines this expansion project. Yet again, this document contrasts the "static" museum with the "dynamic" art centers in terms of design—the Kunsthalle Bern needed to move from being "a space for exhibitions to a place where things happen." The emphasis here is on the performing arts—performance and film; these ephemeral, event-type forms are central to any art center if it is to serve as a bellwether of contemporary practices, and also if it wants to attract a new public.

Since the Second World War, museums have no longer been considered temples to art, but rather convivial spaces where the arts can meet each other. Museums try to deploy what modern art had gained in environmental terms, and include this in their programs, architecture, and the ways in which they present and host exhibitions. Consequently, "the organization of film evenings, poetry readings, plays, and puppet shows increases the number of visits to each exhibition."[33] This expansion project, which was presented to the commission in March 1965, included an important new structure for the Kunsthalle Bern:

> [...] according to architect Klauser's draft plan, on the west side, which corresponds to the garden, there will be the following rooms over two or maybe three floors: a) A large room for exhibitions, film projection, talks, an experimental stage of a minimum of 14 by 28 meters by 6.5 meters high, with natural light from the ceiling, and movable walls.[34]

This expansion was intended to allow the functions of the historic building to be better distributed. It would create workspaces, including four offices instead of the two offices and a cash desk that there were at that time, and a meeting room. The project included other significant modifications. For the first time it mentioned the creation of an archive room (for photographs and catalogues) and a bar. This focus on public hospitality brought the art center closer to the leisure culture.[35] This decision to use modular architecture and create an information base laid the foundations for the new generation of art centers that flourished in the 1970s.[36] The inclusion of the expanded arts, the presentation of events, and the Kunsthalle's new architecture can be understood in light of what Fredric Jameson called the "cultural turn."[37]

In the 1960s Szeemann argued for the opening up of the institution that he directed. However, his rhetoric changed with the winds of the 1968 revolution. In 1969, Szeemann stepped down as the director of the Kunsthalle Bern to become an independent curator. In his contribution to the Art, Technology, and Communication symposium held in Lausanne in 1971, he revisited his 1960s expansionist rhetoric:

> There is no point in repeating the discussions we have had over the last two years. They may have been inspiring initially, but they have since become increasingly tiresome. In short, there were discussions that went on and on about the social role of the artist, the worthlessness of the artist, and the degradation of artworks in terms of mere information. The only thing that people talked about was "information," and the publics and societies that this information was intended to benefit. Ultimately, the man "behind" the art was forgotten—eclipsed by the economic boom in the art market in the late 1960s. The primary objective was to open up museums and make art accessible to as many people as possible. Indeed, we believed that we had met this objective insofar as increasing numbers of visitors appeared to confirm the fulfilment of our hopes and aspirations. However, the rot had already set in. Artists themselves tried to withdraw from this paradise by creating "impossible" works. Yet, objects, and anything included in objects which confirms the famous artistic communication

"triangle," set us right back on the road to the museum. All alternatives exist on paper alone—we must not confuse art with life [...] For too long have we believed, in recent times, that art could serve a useful purpose. We were wrong. The only chance for art to survive is for it to be autonomous—artists only ever have moral or political standing when their works are of quality.[38]

In 1960, the Situationists had given up on their attempts to bring life into museums. Their project *Die Welt als Labyrinth* (*The World as Labyrinth*), which was intended to link the inside of the exhibition space to the town of Amsterdam, was abandoned because of budget and security constraints imposed by Willem Sandberg, the then-director of the Stedelijk Museum. However, he did not hesitate to take inspiration from some of this Situationist project's more radical ideas to transform his museum into a living space where he could offer a manageable experience in the shape of an exhibition. At that time he was in conversation with Bernhard Luginbühl, Jean Tinguely, and Daniel Spoerri about the possibility of transforming an artwork into a total environment, and of making the art exhibition into a "dynamic labyrinth" inspired by the fairground and its attractions.[39] These discussions led Tinguely and Luginbühl to embark on projects and manifestoes advocating the production of Stations Culturelles (Cultural Stations), which created a huge hodgepodge of fairground environments and consumer-consumption appliances. These "cultural station" projects, contemporary versions of Total Artworks, mobilized the same entertainment dynamic that underpinned the redesign of the 1960s museums, merging radical architecture, ecology, counterculture, and modern town planning.[40]

Machine Iconology

Harald Szeemann introduced experimental cinema to the Kunsthalle Bern. However, he never directly explored issues related to film exhibition, and often merely presented films in cinema format. He was much more interested in the imaginary potential of cinema, and this influenced the shape of his exhibitions and the relationship between how they were staged and the multiple ways in which they were mediated. For him, cinema was a machine that embodied the relationship between a certain plasticity of subjectivity and its mediation, whether this was through technological devices or artworks. He used cinema as yet another device in his construction of a curatorial discourse. Cinema became an abstract model that stood for modernity's visual culture.

All of Szeemann's major exhibitions bore the mark of this link, which is one of the constitutive principles of modernity—the harnessing of technology to a constructivist notion of subjectivity. In 1965, at a time when kinetic art exhibitions were legion, a number of curatorial decisions made *Licht und Bewegung* (*Light and Movement*) stand out. In the exhibition catalogue Szeemann appeared to emphasize the size of the exhibition—the catalogue inventory lists 175 exhibited objects. He also included photographs of the exhibition being set up, and works not yet installed strewn on the floor of the institution, ready to be taken in hand by the curator. Szeemann saw his exhibition as a path. He classed works according to movements and related these to a discussion of the history of technologies. The exhibition was manifestly contemporary in nature while, at the same time offering a spatialization of its curator's dialectical and historical thinking. The invitation card included an annotated plan of the Kunsthalle. Arrows indicated a path to be followed, tracing the history of the exhibited works, which were arranged by technology: the entry to the building was reserved for (mechanical) machines; next came kinetic Op art, mobiles and magnets, sound structures, light; finally, the last room was reserved for cybernetics. The kinetic moment was presented as a transition—the shift from the mechanical to the cybernetic.

At the opening of *Licht und Bewegung* at the Kunsthalle Düsseldorf, Szeemann gave an introductory talk to his traveling exhibition. He mentioned *Les Machines célibataires* (1954, *The Bachelor Machines*), a publication by Michel Carrouges (the title of which was drawn from Marcel Duchamp's *Grand Verre*), and contrasted Carrouges' theoretical stance with the type of artwork that, in his view, dominated kinetic art. While bachelor machines attract attention and entrap subjects, kinetic art does not feed off this morbid impulse, but rather furthers the efforts of the historical avant-gardes to place technology at the service of a liberating project.[41] The concept of bachelor machines sees human/machine interaction in terms of self-sufficient and repeated cycles of libidinous consumption, while kinetic art injects this interaction with the potential to open up a universalist vision. Szeemann presented his project as an attempt to reveal technology's utopian potential through the haptic visual reality present in the works. They are described in terms of communication, contact, and emotion. Kinetic works, despite often being no more than illusionist strategies produced by mechanical springs, seek an effect and a mode of attention proper to the age of the cybernetic subject. However, kinetic art seeks a spectacular conquest of a territory in a way that falls largely within a modernist approach to space. *Licht und Bewegung* marked a milestone in a new curatorial discourse on technology. The exhibition foreshadowed Szeemann's desire to organize a major retrospective on the impact of the machine on the aesthetics of the 20th century.

Committee minutes dating back to 1967 mention a project for an exhibition planned for 1968 to celebrate the institution's 50th anniversary: *The Iconology of The Machine*. This title echoed Pontus Hultén's retrospective exhibition held in 1968 at The Museum of Modern Art in New York: *The Machine as Seen at the End of the Mechanical Age*.[42] In December 1967, in a letter to Rolf Wedewer, then director of the Museum Morsbroich in Leverkusen, Szeemann said that Pontus Hultén had mentioned that he intended to mount an exhibition on the iconology of the machine, and had asked Szeemann to give up his own project. From that point on, *The Iconology of the Machine* was transformed into what would later become *12 Environments*. The machine project was abandoned. The advent of new practices and the emergence of a counterculture led Szeemann to remove the historical dimension of the proposal and try to find a more contemporary approach. The particular form of contact sought by kinetic works that often operated through visual touch points became liberated in the environment. Every room at the Kunsthalle Bern was devoted to an immersive artistic intervention. Bazon Brock's introduction to the exhibition catalogue addresses this issue:

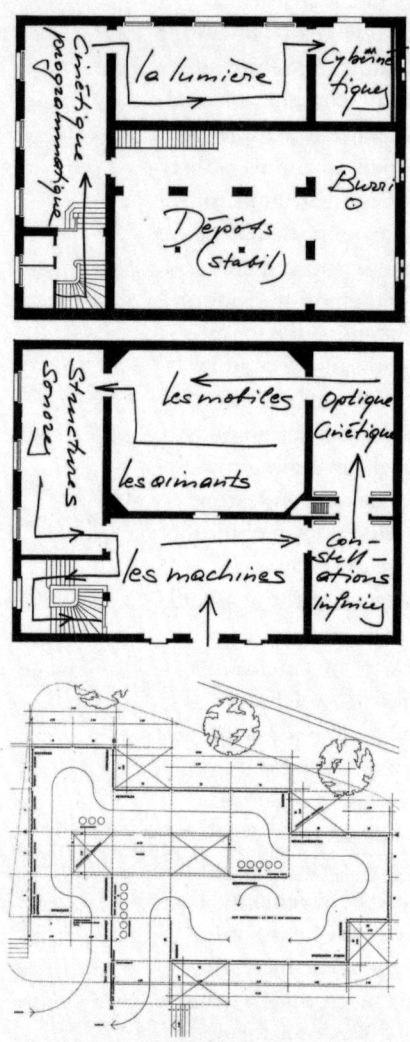

Flyer announcing the *Licht und Bewegung* exhibition, Kunsthalle Bern, Bern, 1965

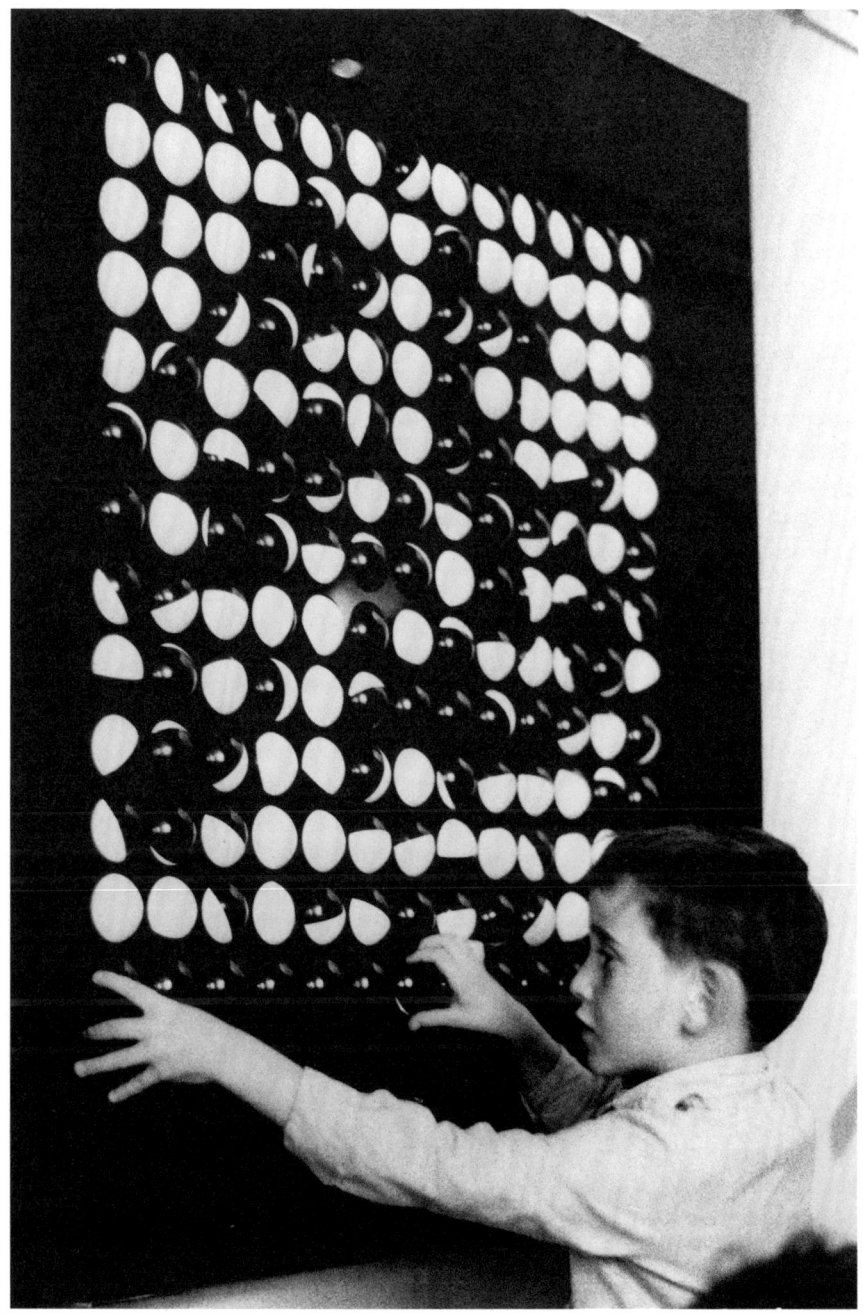

View of the *Licht und Bewegung* exhibition, curated by Harald Szeemann, Kunsthalle Bern, Bern, 1965

To escape this overly closed form of reception, we must build a space where it is possible to create immediate reception. This can be achieved through using the forms offered by the mixed media of light shows.

One type of environment was of capital importance to Szeemann—"environment through film." When Jean-Luc Godard failed to respond to his invitation, the curator turned to Lutz Mommartz, the German experimental filmmaker who had recently won an award at the 1967 *EXPRMNTL* festival in Knokke-le-Zoute. With Szeemann's agreement, he presented his *Zweileinwandkino* environment. *Zweileinwandkino* did not merely comprise a selection of Mommartz' films—it was more in the nature of Open Cinema. The exhibition catalogue contained a note indicating how this film environment should be used:

> This two-screen cinema can be used to screen films specifically made for this device, as well as films that have not been designed to be projected together. If a crowd fills the space between the screens, the absurdity of a particular film becomes patently obvious to this crowd. The spectator occupies the main role in this installation in relation to everything produced in this environment. The emptier the space, the more the projection becomes a kinetic object in its own right. Furthermore, projectors may simply project light and not film [...] *Zweileinwandkino* is a meeting place for people who want to be stimulated in a particular way, without being told what to do. It is not so much particular films that are shown, but rather stimulating material.[43]

Other environments were created by artists affiliated to the Zero group and the Düsseldorf scene, to which Lutz Mommartz belonged. Günther Uecker presented giant nails; Konrad Lueg, a system of luminous flashes and phosphorescent walls that allowed visitors to cast their shadows. These "environments" which, once exhibited, became works, came from a different creation and presentation space. They were taken from the Creamcheese discotheque in Düsseldorf, a meeting place jazzed up with multimedia projects by artists. This was not an insignificant transfer of context. Artists' environments interfered with the expanded multimedia devices that were becoming a new electronic culture: feedback, sampling, control decks, and multiple tracks all combined to create a behaviorist discourse around the multisensory control of an immersed body, whose emotions could be modulated. Typical spectators were no longer transfixed by the screen, but stimulated by electronically coordinated multimedia patterns.

The *12 Environments* exhibition was a collage of fragmentary trends, some taken from Pop art, others from multimedia counterculture, and yet others from reflexive and contextual thinking. It was followed by an exhibition that crowned Szeemann's achievements in seeking to combine (visitor) subjectivity with mediation, thus turning the exhibition into an experiment into modes of attention and the ways that these build up historically and culturally over time. *Live in Your Head: When Attitudes Become Form (Works—Concepts—Processes—Situations—Information)* was the logical conclusion to this trend toward cybernetization and performance in the exhibition. Electric cables powering neon lighting and assorted tape drives were on open view at the Kunsthalle Bern. Electricity was everywhere, from the ringing of the telephone to the ubiquitous presence of sound. The exhibition was akin to a performance, a magnet that required multiple mediations. Szeemann wanted to include Gerry Schum's videos, but his efforts met with no success. Swiss television was intrigued by the spectacle and reported it—American artists were on site and creating in situ. *When Attitudes Become Form* employed a strategy that made the mounting of the exhibition a spectacle in its own right—it invited artists to come and construct their works on site and let their actions be seen. The artists invited included Joseph Beuys, Michael Heizer, and Lawrence Weiner, to mention but a few. The exhibition suggested a network of relationships, although only a third of the artists presented in the catalogue were actually exhibited. It was a supreme communication strategy that drew on multiple forms of mediation. In this sense, it was television, at the center of the long interview with Szeemann, that brought together shapeless works that become dematerialized, and the very real spectacle of the mediatization of the information contained in the works. In his next group exhibition, *Pläne und Projekte als Kunst* (*Plans and Projects as Art*), brought to fruition by his successor, art was reduced to proposals some of which were no more than diagrams, while others were actually implemented in the exhibition space.

Bachelor Machines

Harald Szeemann left the Kunsthalle Bern at the end of 1969. He had spent eight and a half years at the helm of the institution, spearheading his ambition to open it to a wider public, to include new practices, and to modernize its infrastructure. With his friend the gallerist Claude Givaudan, he organized a retrospective of his activities in a Paris venue. It was called *8½*, the title being yet another allusion to cinema, namely Federico Fellini's 1963 film of the same title. In a letter to his friend Paul Lohse, written on his way back from Cuba, Szeemann said that he wanted to make films. Together with his artist friends Balthasar Burkhard and Bernhard Luginbühl, he had a project. His film was to be called *1 × 1 × 1 + 150 feuilles* (*1 × 1 × 1 + 150 Sheets*). The curator, whose latest exhibitions had caught the public eye, responded to press enquiries about his activities. He decided to go independent. Sitting by his window, he thought about the street and what was happening outside.

> My idea with the Agency is to be available for anything that might happen. I would like to film my street over the course of the year, to make an anti-consumer-product film with provocation, occupation, inside, outside, and hospitality as its themes. All and sundry, as an example. I would also like to print flyers and manifestoes. All these activities, when all the Agency can boast is an attic, a table, a telephone, and three stamps.[44]

The curator had used mediation strategies that were no longer available to him; he now presented himself instead as a producer. He was particularly committed to one of the last exhibitions on which he worked. It was a project called *Die Strasse* (*The Street*). His collaborator was Jean Leering, the curator at the Van Abbemuseum. *Die Strasse* seemed to walk all over the contradictions that beset the 1960s. There was now no discussion of the institution or the place and status of art. The exhibition was straightforward, it was about outdoor events, and did not burden itself with links between the outside and the inside of the institution.

In 1974, as an independent exhibition curator, Szeemann sent an exhibition proposal to Johannes Gachnang, then the director of the Kunsthalle Bern. Its title was *Les Machines célibataires*. The interactive and participative dimension that he, as a curator, had advocated for major group exhibitions in the 1960s, was revisited and subtly placed at a critical distance. The objects shown, the various installations, the constructions that, for some people, were born of a literary imagination, distanced the visitor. The autonomy of the works internalized the relationship between the subject and technology. This relationship made interaction no longer one of democratic emancipation, but rather rendered it libidinal, which involved consciously and critically reinscribing it into a logic driven by desire. Szeemann noted, on the back cover of the catalogue: "*Les Machines célibataires* is, in funding terms, an alternative venture potentially similar to cinema production."[45]

As the director of the Kunsthalle Bern in the 1960s, Szeemann's career demonstrated his commitment to an idea of expansion which, I believe, is underpinned by a modernist visual unconscious. While *Les Machines célibataires* offers a rereading of his curatorship at the Kunsthalle Bern, might it not also offer, in its critique of a certain conception of the interaction between humans and technology, a commentary on the construction of masculine subjectivity? It is necessary "to turn one's very conception of space inside out."[46]

[1] See Peter Schneemann et al., *Localizing the Contemporary: The Kunsthalle Bern as a Model*, JRP|Ringier, Zurich 2018.
[2] I refer here to Rosalind Krauss' analysis in *The Optical Unconscious*, MIT Press, Cambridge, Massachusetts 1993, which relates this unconscious to the construction of a neutral spatial imaginary to be conquered ("to turn one's very conception of space all inside out"). See also T. J. Clark, *Farewell to an Idea. Episodes from a History of Modernism*, Yale University Press, New Haven, Connecticut 1999; and Mark Wigley, *The Architecture of Deconstruction. Derrida's Haunt*, MIT Press, Cambridge, Massachusetts 1993.
[3] Daniel Spoerri is perhaps better known as a visual artist, but originally trained as a dancer.
[4] See Arnold Rüdlinger's exhibitions—*Japanische Kunst* (1950), *Kunst der Südsee* (1952), *Kunst der Neger* (1953)—which were accompanied by ethnographic talks and film screenings.
[5] For example, in 1947, after the war, Arnold Rüdlinger co-produced a Fernand Léger exhibition with Willem Sandberg, the director of the Stedelijk Museum in Amsterdam.
[6] *Tendances actuelles de l'École de Paris* was a three-part exhibition that took place at the Kunsthalle Bern in 1952 (part I), 1954 (part II), and 1955 (part III).
[7] For a local history of the Bernese scene in the 1960s, see Harald Szeemann, "Die Berner Kunstszene in den sechziger Jahen," *Bern 66 → 1987*, Kunsthalle Bern, 1987, p. 31–35.
[8] For a description of the nonconformist scene in Bern in the 1960s, see Fredi Lerch, *Müllers Weg ins Paradies. Nonkonformismus im Bern der sechziger Jahre*, Rotpunktverlag, Bern 2001.
[9] Szeemann sums up what he gained from this first curatorial experience in a few words. "Not only did I thus discover my medium, but also an awareness that I could give everything my signature style. And in the exhibition as a medium I saw the same impetus as in theater … " Tobia Bezzola and Roman Kurzmeyer, *Harald Szeemann— with by through because towards despite: Catalogue of all Exhibitions 1957–2005*, Springer, Zurich/Vienna/New York 2007, p. 36.)
[10] Just as was the case with happenings, for example, theatrical form and the notion of theatricality underpinned the economy of non-absorbing attention and the art of copresence offered by the neo-avant-gardes. See, for example, Michael Kirby, "The New Theater," *Tulane Drama Review*, vol. 10, no. 2, Winter 1965.
[11] The building constructed symmetrically opposite the Kunsthalle Bern on the Helvetiaplatz bridgehead is in keeping with the Kunsthalle Bern's architecture. The Schulwarte serves as a multipurpose theater in the museum district and a media library for schools in Bern.
[12] The exhibition hosted performances of mechanical theater by Harry Kramer, a puppet cabaret by Fred Schneckenburg, and a reading accompanied by films by Max Bührmann. Ulrich Baumgartner mounted a performance of shadow theater, Yves Joly a puppet show, *Die Klappe*, and Harry Kramer several films.
[13] It is difficult to pinpoint Szeemann's references precisely; when he invokes a lexicon of the shocking, he is drawing on German aesthetic thought, and modernist theories of theater. The notion of stimulation is central to the conception of modern aesthetics.
[14] Harald Szeemann, "Introduction," *Puppen—Marionetten—Schattenspiele (Asiatica und Experimente)*, exh. cat., Kunsthalle Bern, Bern 1962, n.p.
[15] A few months later, Szeemann organized the exhibition *Harry Kramer. Sculptures Automobiles—Marionnettes—Films* (Harry Kramer. Kinetic Sculptures—Puppets—Films) at the City Art Gallery in Biel/Bienne.
[16] The Festival de l'Art de l'Avant-Garde was held in Marseille between 1956 and 1960. It included an interdisciplinary international avant-garde covering cinema, theater, music, and dance.
[17] *Rörelse i konsten* was a remake of the *Bewogen Beweging* (Moving Movement) exhibition held in 1961 in the Stedelijk Museum in Amsterdam, which then toured from Stockholm to the Louisiana Museum in Copenhagen. The exhibition included performance, contemporary work, and a varied program of films of different kinds—by the historical avant-gardes, animation artists (Len Lye), kinetic artists (Alexander Calder, Robert Breer), as well as films by Harry Kramer, and Stan VanDerBeek's *New American Cinema*.
[18] On the history of experimental cinema at the Moderna Museet, and in Sweden more generally, see John Sundholm, "Chance and Play, or Marvellous Machines; A Forgotten Swedish Film Avant-Garde," Tania O/rum, Jesper Olsen (eds.), *A Cultural History of the Avant-Garde in the Nordic Countries 1950–1975*, BRILL, Leiden 2016, p. 349–358. For a history of film departments in modern art museums similar to The Museum of Modern Art, see Haidee Wasson, *Museum Movies: The Museum of Modern Art and the Birth of Art Cinema*, University of California Press, Berkley/Los Angeles 2005.
[19] Pontus Hultén participated in an animation film by Robert Breer, *Un miracle* (1954), and with Robert Breer made the kinetic film *Le Mouvement* (1955), based on its homonymous exhibition at the Denise René Gallery in 1955. In 1949, in collaboration with Hans Nordenstöm, he shot *Det tryckta ordet 500 dr* (500 Years of Printed Words); in 1955, with Nordenstöm and Gösta Winberg he shot *En Dag i Satden* (A Day in the Town); he shot his last film in 1957, *X*. In building up his network, the central role played by Billy Klüver in negotiating transatlantic links should be mentioned. Relations between the Moderna Museet and the Kunsthalle Bern became even closer in the 1960s with the friendship between Pontus Hultén and Swiss artists Jean Tinguely and Daniel Spoerri.
[20] Szeemann's initial intention was merely to mount a Francis Picabia retrospective by repeating the exhibition hosted by the Musée Cantini in Marseille (1962). Franz Meyer had set up the contacts for this. However, problems with the collector in Marseille responsible for the loan of most of the exhibition meant that he had to come up with a backup solution.
[21] The Moderna Museet *Four Americans* catalogue contains the program of events that accompanied the exhibition. Apart from an evening devoted to John Cage's music and another to the Beat Generation poets, there were three sessions of New American Cinema with films by Jonas Mekas, Alfred Leslie, Robert Frank, Shirley Clarke, and John Cassavetes. See *Four Americans*, exh. cat., Moderna Museet, Stockholm 1962.
[22] The precise list of films screened appeared on the projection contract with the Schulwarte. 16mm: Hans Richter, *30 Jahre Experimente*; Man Ray, *Retour à la Raison* (Return to Reason); Man Ray, Robert Desnos, *L'Etoile de Mer* (The Starfish); Man Ray, *Mystère du Château de dé* (The Mysteries of the Château of Dice); Antonin Artaud, Germaine Dulac, *La Coquille et Clergyman* (The Seashell and the Clergyman); Henry Chomette, *5 minutes de cinéma pur* (Five Minutes of Pure Cinema) 1926; René Clair, Francis Picabia, *Entr'acte*; Robert Frank, *Pull my Daisy*.
[23] The exhibition title is taken from a section of documenta III (1964) curated by Arnold Bode. The selection included works by Harry Kramer, Nicolas Schöffer, Jesús Rafael Soto, Jean Tinguely, Heinz Mack, Otto Piene, Günther Uecker, ZERO, and GRAV.
[24] See, for example, Victor Vasarely, "Notes pour un Manifeste," *Le Mouvement*, Galerie Denise René, Paris 1955; Groupe de recherche d'art visuel [GRAV], *Propositions sur le Mouvement*, Paris 1961.

[25] *Licht und Bewegung kinetische Kunst: 2 Februar bis 13 März 1966*, Kunsthalle Düsseldorf.
[26] The list of the films screened included: Viking Eggeling, *Diagonalsymphonie* 1924; Len Lye, *Rhythm*; Stan VanDerBeek, *Science Friction*; Per Olov Ultvedt, *Nära ögat*; Carlos Cruz Diez, *Fisicromia*; Robert Breer, *Homage to Jean Tinguely's Homage to New York*.
[27] See François Bovier, Balthazar Lovay, Sylvain Menétrey, Dan Solbach (eds.), *Film Implosion! Experimental Cinema in Switzerland*, Fri Art/Revolver Publishing, Fribourg/Berlin 2017.
[28] On the construction of an experimental cinema canon, see Kristen Alfaro, "The Case of Anthology Film Archives and the Formation of a Canonical Avant-Garde," François Bovier (ed.), *Early Video Art and Experimental Film Networks. French-Speaking Switzerland in 1974: A Case for "Minor History,"* ECAL/Les presses du réel, Lausanne/Dijon 2017, p. 245–252. It is difficult to discern any systematic choice of screening venue other than the fact that Szeemann liked to distribute events to a number of venues in addition to the Kunsthalle Bern. The Schulwarte was frequently unavailable, and this is most probably the reason why more screenings were held at the Kunsthalle Bern.
[29] See Toni Lienhard, *Tages-Anzeiger*, Zurich, June 5, 1969, reprinted in Harald Szeemann, Jean-Christophe Ammann (eds.), *Von Hodler zur Antiform. Geschichte der Kunsthalle Bern*, Benteli, Bern 1970, p. 23.
[30] The term he used, "Erweiterung," was taken from the notion of Expanded Cinema and the Expanded Arts.
[31] On the inherent clash between the modernity of the museum as a mausoleum, see, for example, Theodor W. Adorno, "Valéry Proust Museum," *Prismes*, Nevil Spearman, London, 1967. The notion of a living museum can be found in most modern museums. It is at the heart of works by Alexander Dorner, Frederik Kiesler, and Sigfried Giedion, present in the construction of the Museum of Modern Art, and promoted by El Lissitzky.
[32] "Vom Ausstellungsort zum Ort des Geschehens," Kunsthalle Bern Archives, author's translation.
[33] *Ibid*. This leitmotiv for dynamism turned up later in the slogan for the documenta held in 1972, which was designed as 100 days of activities, and not as an exhibition.
[34] "Vom Ausstellungsort zum Ort des Geschehens."
[35] The Sandberg model saw museums as cultural centers. Culture was seen as the combination of all modern and performing arts. This emphasis on performance was a step toward a biopolitical paradigm.
[36] See Kim West, *The Exhibitionary Complex: Exhibition, Apparatus, and Media from Kulturhuset to the Centre Pompidou, 1963–1977*, Huddinge, Stockholm 2017.

[37] The term "cultural" is used here in the sense defined by Fredric Jameson in *The Cultural Turn: Selected Writings on the Postmodern, 1983–1998*, Verso, Brooklyn 1998.
[38] "Art, Technology, and Communication," International Symposium organized by the École cantonale des Beaux-Arts et d'Art appliqué de Lausanne, Institut d'Etude et de Recherche en Information visuelle, Lausanne 1972.
[39] In 1959, Tinguely, along with Claus Bremer and Daniel Spoerri, was the joint author of "Beispiele für das dynamische Theater," *Das neue Forum*, no. 7, 1958/1959, p. 109. Tinguely defined, in the following terms, the mode of attention that he sought to arouse in visitors by Dylaby: "Visitors who see a funfair are struck by an exciting mix of extreme, visual, physical, and mental sensations." (Ad Peterson, "Dylaby, ein dynamisches Labyrinth im Stedelijk Museum 1962," Bernd Klüser, Katharina Hegewisch (eds.), *Die Kunst der Ausstellung. Eine Dokumentation dreissig exemplarischer Kunstausstellungen dieses Jahrhunderts*, Insel Verlag, Berlin 1991, p. 160.)
[40] Machine art was a project whose internal logic was wedded to socialism. Tatlin's project for a monument, much like the towers created by Schöffer and Tinguely, or Constant's New Babylon, are all part of the shift from a working space to a leisure space—they bear witness to a type of changing emotions that drive consumption. Many people have noted this *Nachträglichkeit* (backwardness) of the neo-avant-gardes which can be found, for example, in the constructivist inspiration for American minimalist sculpture, which emerged at a time when The Museum of Modern Art started to historicize these movements by making objects autonomous.
[41] "The precise call for an artwork did not take place for the first time until the 20th century. It was part of a spirit of renewal which included theater, architecture, music, movie-going, technology, industry, and science."
[42] Pontus Hultén, the curator, had initially been commissioned to mount an exhibition on kinetic art. The MoMA exhibition catalogue starts with a quote from Michel Carrouges' work, *Les Machines célibataires*.
[43] *12 Environments: 50 Jahre Kunsthalle Bern*, Kunsthalle Bern, Bern, 1968.
[44] "L'Agence H. Szeemann, interview exclusive," in *Chroniques de l'Art Vivant*, no. 10 (April 1970), p. 19.
[45] *Jungesellenmaschinen/Les Machines célibataires*, exh. cat., Alfieri, Venice 1975.
[46] Rosalind Krauss, *The Optical Unconscious*, p. 51.

Underground Explosion: A Vaudeville of the Avant-Garde
Thomas Schärer and Fred Truniger

Translated from the German by Ben Letzler
A first version of this essay was published in French: Thomas Schärer, Fred Truniger, "*Underground Explosion*: le music-hall de l'avant-garde," *Décadrages. Cinéma, à travers champs*, no. 21–22 (2012), p. 132–145.

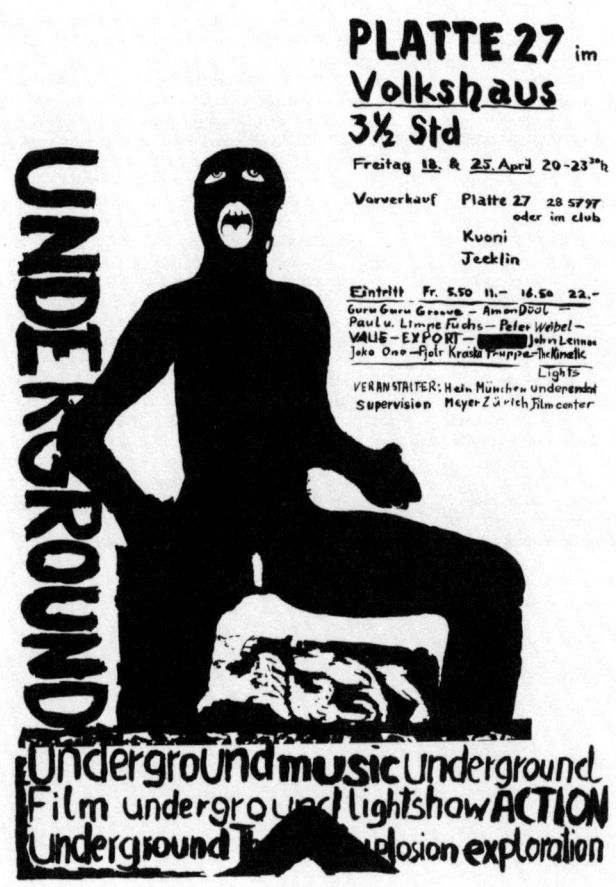

Flyer for the *Underground Explosion* festival, Zurich, April 1969

On September 9, 1970, American artist and filmmaker Carolee Schneemann wrote to David Curtis, who that year had organized the *International Underground Film Festival* at the National Film Theatre in London together with Simon Field. In her letter Schneemann described a sense of the world that had gripped artists from the early 1960s onward: "We had to break it up rake it up shake it up rattle roll movement went to emotion for me physicality 'sensory bombardment.'"[1]

The happenings of the mid-1960s represented a convergence of very different art forms. There were new forms of expression anchored in the historical moment, driving forward the fusion of art and body, art production and lived experience. These new artistic practices were based on the logic of transgression and contributed to the general political climate characterized as "underground" by artists and the media. The notion of "expanded cinema" which is used to define these practices remains today "a flexible term that designates a large spectrum of events which include film or projection,"[2] and which retains only a distant link with traditional cinema.

These experiments around the techniques of cinema and its contextualization were at the center of the *Underground Explosion* tour in 1969, which combined music, performance, theater, and light with film projections. This essay seeks to examine the works shown in the context of Expanded Cinema, and the ephemeral nature of these shortlived avant-garde events.

A Brief Boom: Experimental Films with a Mass Audience

At the end of the 1960s the number of visitors potentially interested in participating in countercultural events increased. Ever expanding audiences filled performance spaces, enticing organizers to engage in a growing commercialization that reached its peak between 1967 and 1969. Expanded Cinema programs were a particularly suitable format for this kind of event, since they incorporated the audience both physically and spatially. Even pure presentations of experimental film enjoyed exceptional public interest. In the Swiss context, for example, Hans-Jakob Siber founded the Film Forum at the Theater Winkelwiese in Zurich in the spring of 1966. By the autumn of 1967 he was screening experimental film programs, some of which he had to show to audiences of up to 200 spectators twice in an evening to meet the demand.[3] Alongside the second Cologne art fair in 1968, the group of independent filmmakers that made up XSCREEN presented "international experimental films, experimental beat music, and poetry readings" on two successive evenings to audiences of about 1,000 spectators in the newly finished Neumarkt subway station in Cologne.[4]

The fourth edition of the *EXPRMNTL* festival, which took place over the New Year of 1967–1968 in the Belgian seaside resort of Knokke-le-Zoute, was an inspiration to the independent European film scene, giving it an explosive new impetus. In Germany, at the beginning of 1968, no less than three initiatives sprang up in just a few weeks: the Hamburger Filmcoop, XSCREEN in Cologne, and the

Undependent Filmcenter in Munich began to produce, distribute, and project independent films.[5]

A year later, in cooperation with the young Zurich artist and bohemian Dieter Meier, Karlheinz Hein[6] and his Undependent Filmcenter mounted a series of events that was the culmination of mixed-media events, both in terms of audience numbers, and commercial organization. Between April 15 and May 6, 1969, the huge multimedia exhibition *Underground Explosion* toured the cities of Munich, Zurich, Essen, and Cologne, attended by between 1,500 and 3,000 paying audience members per show. The series was of a piece with major events that had already become legendary in the United States, such as Andy Warhol's multi-media live performance event *Exploding Plastic Inevitable* (1966), and *9 Evenings: Theatre and Engineering*, a series of performances by Experiments in Art and Technology, a collective of artists and engineers founded by Billy Klüver and Robert Rauschenberg in 1966.

Underground Explosion: The Dream of the Gesamtkunstwerk

Unlike the model of the complete work of art as it was conceived in late Romanticism, the mixed-media and light shows of the 1960s drew on many different media (music, theater, set design, architecture) not to evoke or construct a myth, but rather to abolish physical and spatial boundaries with a view to the active participation of spectators. The uninhibited expression of desire was an integral part of the spirit of the times, as was drug use, which was valued as an effective and legitimate means to expand consciousness. Timothy Leary's psychedelic prayers celebrated "post-bourgeois anti-art." In these gatherings, the movement of bodies and colored lights were meant to facilitate the transmission of "individual pleasure through a collective narcissistic ecstasy."[7]

The *Underground Explosion* tour brought together rock bands like The Guru Guru Groove fronted by the Munich drummer Mani Neumeier (who also composed music for films by Siber and HHK Schoenherr) and Amon Düül II from Munich, Bavarian musicians Limpe and Paul Fuchs, Pjotr Kraska's theater group Wath-Toll from Zurich, the kinetic group The Kinetic Lights, and the Vienna action artists and filmmakers Peter Weibel and Valie Export. The event was part of the still-young tradition of mixed-media events, and transcended the limits of a pure film happening. The filmic repertoire, usually shown without sound alongside other presentations, included works by Schoenherr and Weibel, actions by Otto Muehl idiosyncratically filmed by Viennese artist Kurt Kren,[8] and a "famous and much criticized SS film on the Warsaw Ghetto."[9]

The organizers commissioned Kren to document the tour. The result, *23/69 Underground Explosion*, has very little in common with a conventional documentary, instead taking its place in Kren's body of experimental film work. Kren ran his material through "the shredder of extreme time lapse."[10] The ceaseless camera movement, sudden cuts, the techniques of under- and overexposure of the image and of backlighting, as well as single frame shooting cause light flashes and streaks to flare up stroboscopically from the darkness. Abstract and representational audiovisual fragments of the performances come together, causing the celluloid to amalgamate into a psychedelic whole that, in its vitality, intensity, and unity, approaches the experience of an intensification of life (characterized by Meier in the flyer for the event as "Big Living").

Looking at the film image by image, it does fulfill the expectations linked to its status as a document. Some faces are discernible: light from projectors outlines the naked figure of Limpe Fuchs against a bluish-black background, Mani Neumeier is at work behind his drums, and the Wath-Toll group crawl like sleepwalkers across the stage. There are dancing points of light, oozes of colored liquids, film images that lose themselves in an ephemeral blur, photographers pulling out their cameras. The Kinetic Lights use a rotating mirror to project "bilious green light onto the walls, and color bubbles from slide projectors create an abundance of fields of other colors."[11] Export's *Tapp- und Tastkino* (Tap and Touch Cinema, 1968) appears, as does Weibel, naked, and being given oral sex by Export (*Hommage à Greta Garbo*), before reading a text from a manuscript. Later in the performance letters are cut from a frame formed by a piece of fabric.[12] A sort of water cannon extends threateningly into the auditorium of the Volkshaus in Zurich. What Export and Weibel called their *Kriegskunstfeldzug* (War Art Campaign,

1969) culminated in whipping and soaking the audience, which is not shown in the film.[13] Kren's film shows it was not easy to get the audience, the majority of whom were neatly dressed, to let down its guard.

The *Underground Explosion* was probably named in reference to The Living Theater, as "an intensification of life [Big Living] that would uncover new forms of expression through the coming together of a wide variety of media […]"[14] What was intended as a synthesis of music, theater, performance, light show, and film presentations was only partially achieved judging by the reactions of contemporary reports. For example, journalist Matthias Knauer, at the time also a teaching assistant in the musicology department of the University of Zurich, reported on the event in the *Volksrecht*, writing:

> Only the first part of the three-hour program bore any relation to what had been advertised; afterward the excellent Beat group Amon Düül started playing alone on the stage, with films projected on two screens simultaneously. To end the show the light-show group The Kinetic Lights—unfortunately with limited means—expanded the optical dimension to the entire space. The transition from this performance to the Wath Toll's theater was a disaster. Later in the evening the continuity of the sequence of events that seemed to be forthcoming at the beginning of the performance came to naught.[15]

A reporter for the *Süddeutsche Zeitung* was similarly skeptical about the Munich event at the Circus Krone tent:

> When the Munich pop music group Amon Düül II began to play at deafening volume in the arena's darkness, the notions of time and space seemed to dissolve; this was what artists from the American underground in particular rave about, namely the total mystification of the audience—albeit only for a short time.[16]

It was not only the absence of preparation, the lack of time for rehearsals, and unexpected technical and organizational issues that led to the event being more of a "circus program of the avant-garde" (Dieter Meier) or "a series of revue numbers"[17] than the intensified experience of life that had been the objective. Rivalries and inadequate cooperation onstage led to an explosive atmosphere that countered the hope for synthesis. Mathias Knauer summed this up:

> The intended "total-art-in" was not achieved. Instead of totality, the evening provided a juxtaposition of successive performances and actions. Instead of expansion, ecstasy, and explosion there were breaks and disjunctions. Beat music, films, lightshows, actions, theater—all remained separate; the different groups barely stayed together and were not in harmony.[18]

Certainly, the report of each different manifestation of event reflected something different; but is seems that in general improvisation increasingly took over. Hope of a spontaneous alliance across the disciplines did not correspond to the reality of what happened on stage. According to gossip among journalists, Amon Düül II, an "eleven-people-strong Free Beat commune from Lake Ammer," distanced itself from the rest of the event.[19] Karlheinz Hein recalled that "the members of the Amon Düül group didn't get Weibel's fiction. They saw it as reality [...] which made for absurd conflicts." The provocations by Weibel and Export, who threw balls of barbed wire into the audience, took on very real consequences in Essen, where both a policeman and Export herself were injured.[20]

    The dream of the collective dissolution of boundaries in a total art thus constituted a failure for the performers, who brought opposing ideas of artistic action; out of pride, each sought to defend the uniqueness of their own project. Weibel, for example, spoke only of his use of art as a tool of war.[21] Although the "underground supershow," as it was called on the flyer for the Zurich event, was organized by a film distribution company, the films became a fringe event, and were not properly projected, due, in the most part, to technical problems linked to the insufficient power of the lights, the focal distance of the 16mm projectors, and a lack of screens.[22] At the Circus Krone in Munich Kren's films were projected on four sides of a screen hung in the form of a cube; this installation was reduced successively during the tour to a single screen, and installed so badly that it was hardly noticed. The artists of The Kinetic Lights who had conceived a light show that was supposed to create an all-enveloping perceptive experience, unfortunately only appeared at the edge of the stage, and so were not very successful, as was noticed by a reporter at the event at the Sporthalle in Cologne.[23]

Playing with Status: Underground

The reasons for the public's astonishing enthusiasm for this event (it attracted almost 3,000 spectators) are certainly not the result of a single factor. However, the event's status as part of the counterculture certainly played a central part, as expressed in the prominent use of the term "underground." From the mid-1960s onward, "underground" was used as a general term for youth counterculture, and instrumentalized in virtuoso fashion by the *Underground Explosion*.

Market logic demanded that an event of this size operate within established structures. Thus, tickets could be purchased by major commercial distributors such as the Jelmoli group or the Jecklin music store. In addition, the public was willing to invest a considerable sum, which in Zurich ranged from 5.50 to 22 Swiss francs.

Karlheinz Hein recalled that the advertising for *Underground Explosion* was aggressive. "In Munich we were the first to stick ads on construction sites and vitrines without permission." In Zurich, an unsupervised group of billboard posters recruited by Dieter Meier went too far. They not only glued their posters, which boasted the purported involvement of John Lennon and Yoko Ono—who indeed landed the same day at Zurich airport, in order to travel on to Montreux—on construction fences, but also on jewelers' shop windows on the Bahnhofstrasse in Zurich. After complaints by horrified shopkeepers, co-organizer Meier was obliged by the police to personally "scrape off the posters […] with razor blade-like devices while subject to public ridicule."[24]

The incriminating poster showed a stylized, seated black silhouette with mouth wide open, an unambiguous

Performance by the Wath-Toll theater company, performed at the Volkshaus in Zurich on April 18, 1969, in the context of the *Underground Explosion* event

Valie Export, *Tapp und Tast-Kino* (1968), performed at the Volkshaus in Zurich on April 18, 1969, in the context of the *Underground Explosion* event

Audience at the Volkshaus in Zurich on April 18, 1969, in the context of the *Underground Explosion* event reference to the performance of singer Limpe Fuchs, who was naked and painted black. The bone of contention was a narrow white opening drawn on her crotch that was not difficult to read as a vagina. The press contributed to the sense of scandal for the Zurich event. The newspaper *Blick* printed the following on April 11 under the headline: "Sex Shock Show: Protest Against Dumbing Down!":

> A girl, stark naked and painted black as sin, sits on a brightly lit stage; she fidgets. Next, an infrared camera films the carnal act of an artist couple while the stage remains plunged in darkness. These and other scenes meant to shock the bourgeoisie can be seen onstage at the Volkshaus in Zurich on April 18 and 25.

On April 17, the newspaper carried another report of the event—a probable ban by the authorities that could be prevented only by introducing a minimum audience age of 18. As a consequence, the performance that involved the sexual act was cautiously canceled for "technical reasons."

The presence of the police was a calculated and desired component of mixed-media counterculture events: provocation through violence and sex, and their intentional use to orchestrate a scandal, guaranteed the necessary level of publicity, and thus a mass audience. At the same time, the commotion made possible at least a remnant of the authentic underground feeling that was under dire threat from commercialization through advance ticket sales and numbered seats.[25] The Essen show ended when Weibel/Export not only sprayed the audience with water, but also hurled "balls of barbed wire fresh from the factory" at them.[26] This was too much for the authorities in Stuttgart who banned *Underground Explosion*, and the police stopped the protest by the countercultural scene. In the eyes of some, this was more fitting than an event without the presence of the authorities. Or as Fred Viehbahn concluded in the *Kölner Stadtanzeiger* on May 5, 1969: "The police will not intervene in Otto Muehl's film screenings [...] A member of the public said with regret that this really was as if the soup had not been seasoned." On the other hand, the cancellation of the second date planned in Zurich (April 25) was apparently the result of a business decision, since it was not expected that the Volkshaus could be filled a second time.[27]

The aggression of the police, the bans and accusations of scandal made less impact on the reception of the event than did the often dramatized recollections of extraordinary audience numbers and the war-like atmosphere of the venues.[28]

Despite the efforts of the artists to create an authentic explosion of the underground, there is no overlooking the fact that *Underground Explosion* was in fact underground *exploitation*. Even if the individual acts were presented by artists who could properly term themselves "underground," the staging as a product for mass consumption drained the essence from the concept of the counterculture, which became suspect to many. This can be seen clearly in Dieter Meier's announcement on the flyers for the event, the fuzzy meaninglessness of which obscured the already hazy outlines of the concept by discrediting it and trying to use it to elevate the event at the same time:

> The expression "underground artist" is either inappropriate or tautological, one or the other. *Underground Explosion* uses this sensationalist term and gives it its meaning back. Artists who are not looking for commercial success have been confronted by an audience that understands underground as a label like "pop" and "beat" and "wine" and "beer." Of course nearly every artist wants to sell their work; but if they produce independently and solely with sales in mind, then they will be insultingly called an "underground" artist.[29]

After the Explosion: Visiting the Ruins

The *Underground Explosion* program and its success in terms of audience numbers make it clear that for a short time Expanded Cinema was able to establish itself as a live art form alongside music, theater, and artistic performance. The hallucinatory effects of stroboscopes, still new at the time, and the flicker of experimental films were inducive to breaking down the barriers between mind and body and created a feeling of immediacy and contemporaneity.

The projection of film and light make the spatial and mental immersion in images, colors, tones, possible, thus satisfying the public's taste for new sensorial experiences. This encounter between music, moving images, light, and performances was meant to provoke an intensified experience of life—the "big living." As a *live* event, Expanded Cinema was able to take elite, essentially minority forms of underground film, and market them as "live events" to an extent that seems astonishing today.

The "total-art-in" was situated between two opposing positions: the contradiction between an underground status, and a commercial mass phenomenon, and between radical individualism and resistance to social structures, on the one hand, and the longing for the dissolution of the self in the collective experience of presentation and perception, on the other. According to the influential credo of the hippie generation, everyone should be able to do what they want, when and where they want. This position also characterized the *Underground Explosion*: "The Düül group introduced anarchy to music: each plays what they want to play at that moment, for themselves."[30] These anarchic intentions, however, are not really compatible with the contemporary idea of breaking down boundaries, whether this is in terms of the disappearance of the individual into the mass, or the suppression of distinctions between the arts.

The explosion did take place in terms of attendance numbers, but left a stale aftertaste. Through its commercialization, the underground had lost its hold on youth counterculture. *Underground Explosion* marked the beginning of the end of a short window during which openness, curiosity, aspirations and the uniting momentum of the rising of the youth movement in the years around 1968 allowed an experimental and ephemeral coalition of different radical forms and forces that were to fan out very soon thereafter into different formats and groups with specific orientations, whether political, aesthetic, psychedelic, psychological, or environmental.

The ideal of an intensification of life was not attained. The fragmented presentation of individual contributions underlined the failure of the original undertaking of *Underground Explosion*: the variety show brought together a mosaic of musical, acrobatic, and performative attractions with no overarching dramaturgy. The impresario brought individual performances together without thinking much about their cohesion. The irony of history is that the counterculture and its legendary attractions reached their audience in a format that was doomed to disappear.[31]

Retrospectively, *Underground Explosion* should be understood as a singular speculative event around a value—fascination with the underground—that was gaining ground, but which in fact participated in the destabilization of the youth counterculture of which it was supposed to be a part. The tour marked both the peak and the onset of the decline of the idea of the commercialization of experimental (film) forms.

One of the defining factors that would explain the interest in experimental film is linked to expectations around the transgression of taboos, as well as in scenes with explicit sexual content. This theme, soon in competition with far more explicit scenes found in the emerging pornographic film industry, helped to generate interest in the more multifarious society of post-1968. With the decline in the shock factor of pornography, experimental cinema lost one of the subjects that had contributed to its popularity among such a wide audience. Beyond this, an important change can also be found in its critical reception. From 1968 on, professional critics predominantly praised films that depicted, reflected on, and criticized social conditions. Film students from Berlin, Ulm, and Brussels, including future activist Holger Meins, were already protesting at the *EXPRMNTL* festival in Knokke-le-Zoute in 1967/1968 against experimental films as escapist formal games that did not address pressing social questions.[32] Film production changed alongside film reception: narrative films began to concentrate thematically on specific social conditions and politically motivated stories, and socially critical documentaries increased in importance. Thus experimental film's engagement with the medium's aesthetic and formal aspects lost its appeal to the audience. Taking Swiss film history as an example, one can see the convergence in time between the rise of politically conscious films and the almost complete disappearance of experimental films roughly between 1970 and 1973—but that would be another story.

Finally, the fascination with novelty and difference declined, and formal experiments became a pleasure for a marginal, art-educated audience. The underground was once again a niche, and underground artists returned to their isolation and to marginal events that asserted their own legacy.

A Short-Lived Legacy: Progressive Art Production

Soon after *Underground Explosion*, Hein and Meier founded a label together, Progressive Art Production (P.A.P.),[33] which they used to run a market-driven approach to experimental film than the conventional film cooperatives that mostly operated on a more local level. The business model of P.A.P. ran into trouble, however, with the evaporation of the audience numbers that had made presentations of experimental films possible in the first place. New channels for distribution had to be found.

P.A.P. had already expanded its areas of activity geographically in 1969. For example, it had curated experimental film programs at the Festival d'Avignon in 1969, at the 1969 and 1970 *Film-In* festivals in Lucerne, and in Cannes in 1970 and 1971. P.A.P. participated in a seminar on underground film at the Venice Film Festival in 1970. That same year Hein and Meier made another attempt to get experimental film out of its niche position. Perhaps inspired by Meier's initial success as a visual artist (taking part in exhibitions and performances at the Institute of Contemporary Arts London, the Kunstmuseum Luzern, the New York Cultural Center, and in the Aktionsraum 1 at Goetheplatz in Munich), P.A.P. sought to establish film on the art scene. At Art Basel in 1970 and 1971 they rented a booth in which they showed works by associated artists and offered them for sale as Super-8 copies.[34] However, they soon gave up their renewed efforts to gain a foothold in the art world as distributors and film gallerists for experimental films. Although there seemed to be growing interest in film production in the art world and the booth enjoyed some esteem among visitors, sales were far less than expected.

Meier gained the recognition as an author and artist that P.A.P. was not able to achieve as an intermediary structure. After enjoying international successes with his pop band Yello in the 1980s and 1990s—not least due to his innovative music videos—his experimental short films from the 1960s and 1970s have now been appreciated for some years at art exhibitions as an important part of his oeuvre.

As we have sought to show, the *Underground Explosion* tour was situated at at the end of modernism: established cultural forms were in crisis, while cultural politics—to the extent they existed—strengthened, in their rigidity, the desire for cultural renewal and the creation of a counterculture. This aspiration was at the center of the variety show of the avant-garde, *Underground Explosion*.

At the same time, the Progressive Art Production label and in particular the *Underground Explosion* tour can be seen as precursors to the postmodernism of the 1970s and 1980s—a period in which many artists no longer regarded the avant-garde and commercialization as mutually exclusive. But this is also a period in which the boundaries between different fields of artistic activity started to blur, and in which cultural tolerance made it far more difficult to orchestrate scandals and explosions.

[1] Carolee Schneemann, "Expanded Cinema. Free Form Recollections of New York" [1970], David Curtis, A. L. Rees, Duncan White (eds.), *Expanded Cinema. Art Performance Film*, Tate Publishing, London 2011, p. 92.
[2] A. L. Rees, "Expanded Cinema and Narrative: A Troubled History," David Curtis, A. L. Rees, Duncan White (eds.), *Expanded Cinema. Art Performance Film*, p. 12.
[3] Interview with Hans-Jakob Siber on July 13, 2011.
[4] Wilhelm & Birgit Hein (eds.), *XSCREEN: Materialien über den Underground-Film*, Phaidon, Cologne 1971, p. 116. The event on October 15, 1968, was presented with the title *Underground Explosion*. Another performance of the *Underground Explosion* tour, with the same name but under different sponsorship, took place on May 6, 1969, in Cologne, and is described in detail below.
[5] These newly founded groups emerged from the discussions that took place at the festival spanning the New Year in Knokke-le-Zoute. Representatives came together from a wide variety of existing and incipient "coops" from New York, London, Naples, Turin, Rome, Frankfurt, Hamburg, Berlin, and also Zurich, where Hans-Jakob Siber had founded the Film Forum in 1966, which met to discuss P. Adams Sitney's initiative to found an organization of European distribution cooperatives for independent film; see Nicole Brenez, "Un monde où il ne faudrait plus choisir entre le bonheur et la félicité," Xavier Garcia Bardon (ed.), *EXPRMNTL – Festival hors normes, Knokke 1963, 1967, 1974*," *Revue Belge du Cinéma*, no. 43 (December 2002), p. 47. Such a union came about neither in Knokke-le-Zoute nor at the First European Meeting of Independent Filmmakers held in Munich from November 12 to 17, 1968. The meeting in Knokke-le-Zoute nonetheless influenced the founding of cooperatives in Germany in the spring of 1968.
[6] Karlheinz Hein, the brother of XSCREEN cofounder Wilhelm Hein, was musically active as a student and earned money organizing concerts with jazz musicians and "independent rock groups." This work gave him good contacts both in the music scene and in the independent film milieu.
[7] Dieter Baacke, "Untergrund. Einblick und Ausblick," *Merkur*, no. 266 (1970), p. 533.
[8] Karlheinz Hein, P.A.P. Progressive Art Production. *Filmgalerie, Filmverleih, Lagerkatalog 1972*, PAP, Munich 1972, n. p.
[9] "JvM," "Knall ohne Wirkung. 'Underground Explosion' im Zirkus Krone," *Süddeutsche Zeitung*, April 17, 1969.
[10] Michael Palm, "Which way? Drei Pfade durchs Bild-Gebüsch von Kurt Kren," Hans Scheugl (ed.), *Ex Underground Kurt Kren: seine Filme*, PVS, Vienna 1996, p. 117.
[11] *Tages-Anzeiger*, "Extrablatt der Jungen," April 23, 1969, p. 15.
[12] This was probably *Cutting* (1967–1968). See Danièle Roussel, *Der Wiener Aktionismus und die Österreicher, Gespräche*, Ritter Klagenfurt 1995, p. 122.
[13] Danièle Roussel, *Der Wiener Aktionismus und die Österreicher*, p. 122.
[14] It is in these terms that Dieter Meier described the event on the flyer.
[15] Mathias Knauer, "Underground Explosion. Anmerkungen zu einem 'total-art-in' im Volkshaus," *Volksrecht*, April 24, 1969.
[16] JvM, "Knall ohne Wirkung. 'Underground Explosion' im Zirkus Krone," *Süddeutsche Zeitung*, April 17, 1969.
[17] Fred Viehbahn, "'Underground Explosion' wurde fast zur Nummernrevue," *Kölner Stadtanzeiger*, no. 103, May 5, 1969, p. 12.
[18] Mathias Knauer, "Underground Explosion. Anmerkungen zu einem 'total-art-in' im Volkshaus."
[19] Fred Viehbahn, "'Underground Explosion' wurde fast zur Nummernrevue," *op. cit.*
[20] Danièle Roussel, *Der Wiener Aktionismus und die Österreicher*, p. 122.
[21] *Ibid.*, p. 134.
[22] Weibel and Export considered their actions—abusing the audience, *Tap and Touch Cinema*, and the homages to Greta Garbo and McLuhan—as replacements for film (parafilmic events).
[23] Fred Viehbahn, "'Underground Explosion' wurde fast zur Nummernrevue," *op. cit.*
[24] Interview with Dieter Meier, July 7, 2011.
[25] In hindsight, Dieter Meier explained this strategy with regard to Weibel/Export's performances as follows: "We wanted to give the 'Underground' a superficial aggression to protect its identity, so to speak" (Dieter Meier interviewed by the authors). See also, Michael Michalka, "'Schiessen sie doch auf das Publikum!' Projektion und Partizipation um 1968," Michael Michalka (ed.), *X-Screen: Filmische Installationen und Aktionen der Sechziger- und Siebzigerjahre*, Walther Koenig, Cologne 2004, p.103.
[26] Winfried Heinen, "Stacheldraht ins Publikum geworfen," *Neue Ruhr Zeitung*, May 8, 1969.
[27] Interview with Karlheinz Hein, May 23, 2012.
[28] See in particular Christoph Wagner, "Der Krieg findet im Saal statt," *WOZ – Die Wochenzeitung*, April 23, 2009.
[29] Platte 27 flyer for *Underground Explosion*.
[30] Winfried Heinen, "Die Underground-Show ist erst ab 18 zugelassen," *Neue Ruhr Zeitung*, May 3, 1969.
[31] The Varieté Klara in Basel, the last establishment of its kind in Switzerland, closed its doors in 1968.
[32] Xavier Garcia Bardon (ed.), "EXPRMNTL – Festival hors normes, Knokke 1963, 1967, 1974," *Revue Belge du Cinéma*, no. 43, Bruxelles, 2002, p. 51.
[33] Whereas Hein and Meier, when organizing *Underground Explosion*, had still used the company names of Independent Filmcenter and Dieter Meier Filmproduktion, the programs that they curated a month later at the Film-In film festival in Lucerne were already distributed under the P.A.P. label. Meier said that he initially took part mostly as a financial backer, but then joined Hein for many P.A.P. events.
[34] Karlheinz Hein (ed.), *P.A.P. Progressive Art Production. Filmgalerie, Filmverleih, Lagerkatalog 1972*, Munich 1972.

P.A.P. (Progressive Art Production): A "Film Gallery" for "Political and Pornographic" Cinema
François Bovier

Translated from the French by Miranda Stewart
A first version of this article was published in French and German in François Bovier, Balthazar Lovay, Sylvain Menétrey, Dan Solbach (eds.), *Film Implosion! Experimental Cinema in Switzerland*, Fri Art/Revolver Publishing, Fribourg/Berlin 2017, p. 21–33.

P.A.P. stand at Art Basel, Basel, 1970
Published in *P.A.P. Filme*, exhibition catalogue, P.A.P., Munich 1972

Film distribution is not just a matter for the commercial cinema network or cine-clubs and independent cinemas, or even the "general-interest" or "specialist" festivals they engender. The institutional structure of the black box is just one cinematic configuration among many. Film has been used for many other purposes—industry, science, the military, family entertainment, education, etc. Film can convey information and contribute to a performance or a festive event, to mention but a few of its potential uses, and occupies a whole variety of spaces in the private, public, and semi-public domains.

In recent decades we have witnessed the gradual absorption of film into the field of contemporary art—what some have termed a "cinematographic turn" in contemporary art—occupying both major museum institutions and independent exhibition spaces.[1] This phenomenon, which was described by Jean-Christophe Royoux in the 1990s as "exhibition cinema,"[2] presupposes that film is relocated to the ideological space of the white cube and integrated within the art market. Expanded Cinema events—ranging from *Movie-Drome* (1963) by Stan VanDerBeek,[3] to Andy Warhol's performances of *Exploding Plastic Inevitable* (1966–1967),[4] to Charles and Ray Eames' contributions to the world exhibitions in Moscow (1959), Seattle (1962), and New York (1964–1965),[5] and Ferdinand Kriwet's multimedia events in the 1960s,[6] to mention but a few examples from the spectrum that runs from countercultural spaces to commercial performances—have now been displaced and relocated to the economic context of galleries and museums, institutions designed to legitimate contemporary art. This crossover or, in a sense, assimilation, dates back to the 1930s. We can take, for example, the Julien Gallery in New York, where Joseph Cornell presented his films,[7] and The Museum of Modern Art, where, it has to be said, interaction with experimental cinema remains marginal. Maya Deren tried to infiltrate MoMA, asking for help from Iris Barry, who founded their film department in the early 1930s. However, the museum had already thrown in its lot with Hollywood—and Abstract Expressionism—and only very gradually started to include avant-garde, independent cinema in its collections.[8] In the 1970s, galleries and museums began to take an interest in film,[9] including, for example, Claude Givaudan and Christiane Aubry in Paris, René Block in Berlin, Rolf Ricke and Art Intermedia in Cologne, Konrad Fischer in Düsseldorf, Heiner Friedrich in Munich and Cologne, Gimpel Fils in London, and Castelli/Sonnabend in New York.[10] Film was now exhibited in galleries and offered for sale and distribution, just like any work of art—despite the technical difficulties inherent in displaying it, which minimized its presence and potential development. Some exhibitions, notably *Projected Images* at the Walker Art Center in Minneapolis in 1974,[11] and art fairs such as *Prospect 71—Projection*, in Düsseldorf,[12] also played a crucial role in this shift in type of venue used to screen independent cinema and artists' films.

Using the descriptive categories proposed by Jay David Bolter and Richard Grusin,[13] we could argue that, in this instance, film is "remediated" through the exhibition medium: it is reformatted via conventions for hanging works and the use of environments constrained by museum walls. Nevertheless, in principle, nothing stands in the way of other configurations, possibly of a more hybrid nature, or those that maintain the specificity of the film apparatus. This is what happened in Germany at the end of the 1960s. On the one hand, Gerry Schum's *Fernsehgalerie* (Television Gallery, 1969–1970) used television to reconfigure the exhibition—the context was arguably that of video art, albeit a type of art still not yet clearly distinguishable from that of artists' films. At the same time, Progressive Art Production [P.A.P.], a setup explicitly designed as a film gallery [Filmgalerie] by Karlheinz Hein, kept the black box as the context of the exhibition and film did not dissolve into the field of environments—or installations, as they are more commonly known today.

The relatively brief period occupied by Schum's TV and then Video Gallery (1969–1970), where he sold video copies of works by Joseph Beuys, Jan Dibbets, and Mario Merz up until his suicide in 1973, is now famous.[14] No longer did the public have to come to see works that were deemed to be the most difficult and experimental of their time; the television set would now take art to the public or, better still, into viewers' homes. At the same time as selling and producing videos, Gerry Schum made two broadcasts that revolutionized the exhibition medium, "remediated" by the TV set (but actually shot on 16mm): *Land Art* (1969), produced by Sender Freies Berlin/SFB, with films on Barry Flanagan, Dennis Oppenheim, Jan Dibbets, Marinus Boezem, Richard Long, Robert Smithson, Michael Heizer, and Walter De Maria, and *Identifications* (1970), produced by Südwestfunk Baden-Baden/SWF, with contributions by 25 artists from Germany, the USA, the UK, the Netherlands, France, and Italy. The exhibition was no longer limited by time or space as it was broadcast live.[15]

However, little has been written about the activities of P.A.P. (1969–1972), which sold and distributed artists' films, along with photographs and para-cinematic objects by Otto Muehl, Wilhelm and Birgit Hein, and Takahiko Iimura.[16] This text aims to outline the film gallery's main activities, drawing on the two film catalogues published in 1969 and in 1972 by P.A.P., and on its actual programming.[17]

Karlheinz Hein founded P.A.P. in 1969 and was soon joined by Dieter Meier. Its headquarters was located in Munich (where Heinz lived), with Zurich (where Meier lived) as a second address.[18] Meier was thus able to offer his Expanded Cinema films and performances. The latter included *Letterfilm* (1969) with a script based on the iteration of the words *Kopf* and *Baum*; *Paperfilm* (1969), with an instruction to hold a sheet of paper in front of one's eyes; *Eye Film* (1969), with instructions to keep a transparent film in front of one's eyes; *Selbstportrait*, with instructions to enter and leave a room on four occasions; and finally *Raum-Zeit-Test* (1969), with instructions to remain immobile in a room for a set period of time. It should be remembered that Meier was, at that time, actively involved in the independent cinema scene, culminating with his feature film *81,000 Units*, produced between 1968 and 1970, and exhibited at the *EXPRMNTL* International Festival in Knokke-le-Zoute in 1974.[19] Hein assumed the duties of distributor, curator and programmer, and indeed producer, alongside Meier. The P.A.P. film gallery took over from the Undependent Film Center, founded by Hein in Munich, in 1968, to show underground films. The *Underground Explosion*[20] tour of musical, theatrical, physical, and film performances, organized by the Undependent Film Center in 1969, laid the foundations for P.A.P.: several of the films shown in *Underground Explosion* appeared in its catalogue—for example, those of Otto Muehl, a Vienna actionist, Kurt Kren, an Austrian filmmaker who documented actionist performances, and HHK Schoenherr, a German filmmaker who moved to Switzerland in 1963 for a film project on Robert Walser, which he finally completed in 1978.[21] Of particular importance was the performative and *provocative* dimension of this event, which was hugely successful, attracting between 1,500 and 4,000 viewers in Munich, Zurich, Essen, Cologne, and Stuttgart. It created the best possible publicity, and Hein and Meier went on to reproduce it with a greater or lesser degree of boldness depending on the context, which ranged from countercultural venues such as the alternative XSCREEN theater, to the institutionalized milieu of art fairs, such as Art Basel. *Underground Explosion*'s strategy was to whip up scandal and controversy through performances of Expanded Cinema such as those by Valie Export and Peter

Weibel—in *Tap and Touch Cinema* (1968), for example, Export invited the public to touch her chest through a cardboard screen, thus shifting the voyeurism inherent in cinema to tactile communication. In Zurich their performance, which included fellatio on stage prior to spraying the public with a water cannon and hurling diatribes at them invoking the Vietnam War, led to police intervention.[22]

In the first catalogue, in 1969, P.A.P. was presented as a film gallery and a film distribution company (the catalogue was published by *P.A.P. Filmgalerie Filmverleih* [film gallery and film distribution]). As Birgit Hein wrote to Alfredo Leonardi on June 17, 1969, P.A.P., "the new registered company owned by Karlheinz Hein and Dieter Meier," specialized in the sales and distribution of films: "They buy films and sign individual contracts with filmmakers for distribution and sales on a 50:50 basis, which is the only realistic figure possible if you want professional management."[23]

The 1972 catalogue, entitled *P.A.P. Filme 1972*, focused on the films themselves, and their rental price featured at the end of the catalogue (3 DM per minute). P.A.P. soon refocused its activities on film distribution rather than sales; this did not prevent it from producing films such as *Political Portraits* (1969) by Gregory Markopoulos, a series of film portraits financed by Meier and screened for the first time at the Avignon Festival in 1969. The film, however, suffered poor circulation due to a dispute over copyright between Markopoulos and Meier. In any case, the film gallery had a very diverse range of activities and used programming as one way of occupying public space.

Indeed, P.A.P. did not only offer artists' films for sale and rental, but also organized film programs and performances of Expanded Cinema at a range of venues (cinema and theater festivals, art fairs and museums, and even countercultural spaces). In this sense, P.A.P. operated more like a collective of artists and filmmakers. From August 10–14, 1969, at the 23rd Avignon Festival,[24] P.A.P. offered a wide program of international films, starting each evening at midnight. *Scenes from Under Childhood* (1967–1969) by Stan Brakhage was screened next to *Twice a Man* (1963) by Markopoulos on the first evening; the second screening was devoted to a tribute to Kurt Kren; the third brought together films by Schoenherr, Birgit and Wilhelm Hein, Otto Muehl and Meier; the fourth compared *Political Portraits* by Markopoulos with a film portrait of Schoenherr; and the last brought together films by Meier, Carolee Schneemann, and Paul Sharits. It was a vast selection with varied screenings—alternating between a hyper-subjective film by Brakhage, film portraits by Markopoulos and Schoenherr, performances by Viennese actionists, Sharits' flicker films, and even Schneemann's feminist perspective on performance. As mentioned in the brochure published for the event, all of these films were available to rent. Here P.A.P. assumed the duties of programmer in the context of a highly reputed avant-garde theater festival, and thereby combined its film distribution and sales activities—although *Fuses* (1965) and Carolee Schneemann's Expanded Cinema works never in fact made it into the P.A.P. catalogue.

As one might expect, P.A.P. had a presence at cinema festivals. In 1969, 1970, and 1971, it participated in the Lucerne *Film-In* Festival as a programmer. In 1969, P.A.P. proposed a performance evening and three screenings that offered more than just the works featured in its catalogue[25]: a Kurt Kren retrospective; a screening with films by Markopoulos, Brakhage, Schoenherr, the Heins, Sharits, and in addition Lutz Mommartz; another screening, focusing on the German and Austrian scenes, with Schoenherr, Muehl, Meier, the Heins, with another outsider, Werner Nekes. The performance evening, on this occasion, consisted simply of offering films with live sound, with the Guru Guru Groove band for *Autoportait*, (1967–1968), by Schoenherr, and a contribution by Meier to accompany his own film *Unterbrochene Flugverbindungen* (1969).

In 1970, P.A.P. offered an Expanded Cinema performance by Malcolm Le Grice, and two programs focusing on the exploration of the body and performance.[26] The first, examining the body as an art medium, with films by Iimura, Hans Peter Kochenrath, Muehl, Schoenherr, and Sharits; the second, more formal in nature, with films by Brakhage, Markopoulos, Fritz André Kracht, Meier, and Kren. In 1971, the programming rationale, which involved a degree of independence from the films distributed by P.A.P., was finally fulfilled, and the organization selected "progressive

Swiss films" that did not feature in its catalogue.[27] The first program brought together Peter von Gunten and Kurt Gloor; the second, Hans-Ulrich Schlumpf, Rolf Lyssy, and the theater group Alternative; and the third, Bernhard Luginbühl and Jacques Thévoz. P.A.P. also had a presence at the Cannes film Festival, in two consecutive years, 1970 and 1971, in the Directors' Fortnight section.[28] In 1970, Karlheinz Hein, Wilhelm and Birgit Hein, Kren, and Kochenrath attended (with a series of screenings that started in the evening and did not finish till dawn); in 1971 those present included Karlheinz Hein, Wilhelm Hein, Kren, Kracht, and Vlado Kristl who designed the "Jamais avec vous" ("Never with you") poster (which clearly did not mince its words!) announcing the programs. Finally, a P.A.P. program was screened at the 20th Mannheim Cinema Festival, from October 4–9, 1971.[29] As can be seen in the brochure published by P.A.P. on this occasion, films by Iimura, Markopoulos, Kracht, and Kristl were screened; here again, films of physical performances were shown side by side with more formal approaches.

P.A.P. also participated in art fairs, as befitted its status as a film gallery; it was present at Art Basel, when the fair was founded in 1970, and in the following two years.[30] The P.A.P. stand gave pride of place to Muehl's actions and "material films"—at the 1971 and 1972 festivals, a full-page photograph of an action by Muehl appeared in the catalogue for the Basel event.[31] As can be seen from the photographs in the 1972 catalogue published by P.A.P., in 1970, the organization presented the works in its repertoire at its stand at Art Basel, using a device that cut across the conventions of both exhibitions and film screenings. Frames from films were screened as slides, while the films were projected in 16mm inside the same space (Meier can be seen sitting at a desk littered with paper). While the film gallery probably did not garner the commercial success it had banked on, it is undoubtedly true that P.A.P., at least within the context of Art Basel, did manage to find an effective interrelationship between the white cube and the black box. Slides were used to document films and provide a "fixed," "determined" quotation; the act of screening films at the stand made it into a kind of art environment and gave P.A.P. representatives the opportunity to receive the public and promote their catalogue. It was clearly an exhibition of films in various states—fixed images, film "environments," printed catalogue—and the stand was similar to a film gallery where the public are free to walk around and create their own mental "edit" from works that heighten the material dimension of the celluloid and the physical presence of the body as a performance medium. Finally, it should also be noted that P.A.P. participated in talks at contemporary art events: in May 1970, it was invited to an international symposium on underground cinema held at the Venice Biennale, clearly showing that P.A.P. belonged both to the fields of contemporary art and of independent cinema.

It is not easy to reconstruct P.A.P.'s public activities accurately. It would appear to have been a fully-fledged cultural actor whose strategy was to "market" artists' films and publicize Expanded Cinema. It is, however, easy to refer to the catalogues published by P.A.P. and identify the works available for distribution or sale. Artists were chosen depending on who Hein and Meier chanced to meet, and an informal network of principally European, independent filmmakers emerged. This network partly overlapped with correspondents for *Supervisuell* (1968–1970), an underground fanzine founded by Schoenherr; such people included Robert Nelson, Birgit Hein, and clearly Schoenherr himself, as well as his brother, Paul Schoenherr. P.A.P. was undoubtedly also involved in the endeavors of XSCREEN, an independent cinema founded in Cologne in 1968 by Birgit and Wilhelm Hein. It distributed pornographic films to keep it on a financially sound footing, while at the same time becoming one of the main rallying points for German and Austrian independent filmmakers[32]; the Hein couple, who were jointly responsible for numerous films, regularly presented the work of the Viennese Actionists, creating a bridge between underground cinema and performance.

Markopoulos, who was only tangentially involved in this network, also appears in the catalogue. He was a former advocate for New American Cinema, and his work systematically exploited the tension between isolated frames and shots held for longer periods of time. He took part, alongside Meier, in the 1969 Cannes Film Festival, where they organized a joint press conference for their films, to which hardly anybody turned up.[33] The film gallery also forged contacts with the British "structuralist-materialist" scene, and Peter Gidal and Malcolm Le Grice both featured in the catalogue, as did Stephen Dwoskin, an American involved in the founding of the London Film-Makers' Cooperative[34] who, nonetheless, took a back seat when it came to the controversial debates initiated by Peter Gidal over the American "structural" scene. In addition to Nelson, Sharits and Brakhage (with a single film, *Scenes from Under Childhood* 1967–1970) represented experimental American cinema. There was also Iimura, a Japanese filmmaker working out of New York whose films were regularly screened in the United States and Europe; *Ai (Love)* (1962), appeared in the 1972 P.A.P. catalogue, referred to in glowing terms by Jonas Mekas. The desire to include artists' films within the lineage of the historical avant-garde was also evident—the 1972 catalogue offered films by Charles Dekeukeleire, an independent Belgian filmmaker who had used abrupt, discontinuous editing in the 1920s. In particular, the Viennese Actionist scene was extremely well represented—in addition to Kurt Kren's extremely elaborately edited films documenting performances, the catalogue offered works by Otmar Bauer, Günter Brus, Hans Peter Kochenrath, and Muehl. Films by Kracht and Kristl also had much in common with the raw, violent, physical performances of this art scene. The ubiquity of this performance model, which was, in a way, an outrageous, dystopian version of physical art, was the main defining feature of P.A.P. compared with other galleries that sold films (Givaudan, Block, Gimpel, Sonnabend/Castelli, etc.). It was probably this appetite for exhibiting the body through extreme actions that led Hein and Meier, to describe the works by Kren, Markopoulos, Warhol, and Robert Nelson as "provocative political and pornographic films"[35] when they were screened at the initiative of XSCREEN in a metro station under construction in Munich in August 1968 on the occasion of the art fair, in parallel with actions by Muehl and concerts by Amon Düül II, Guru Guru Groove, and CAN—predictably the police turned up, confiscated the films, and recorded the identities of the viewers.[36]

"Political and pornographic films": these two terms, taken together, appear to sum up the strategy of the P.A.P. film gallery, which espoused the avant-garde tradition of giving public taste a slap in the face, a tradition that was reenergized by the "provocative" and scandalous performances of the Viennese Actionists with, for example, films signed by their protagonists or filmed and edited by Kren, who asserted the independence of his point of view. XSCREEN, as we have already said, also employed this strategy of combining the avant-garde and the pornographic, which, with hindsight, might appear rather astonishing. This is perhaps why the line taken by P.A.P. is also, on the face of it, paradoxical—a predictable failure, yet a one that is still relevant today. The organization sought to be part of the contemporary art market and yet the works it offered were essentially anti-institutional, underground, and transgressive. The "product" offered for sale undermined the very foundations of "commodity fetishism" in that it embraced excess and obscenity. It is closer to the spirit of *potlatch* than it is to that of exchange value. Market forces and "autonomous art" institutions come up hard against physical performance and the concreteness of the film medium—in this instance, essentially the *Materialaktionen* (material actions) of Muehl and Guenter Brus, and the materiality of film as practiced by Kren. There is therefore no discernible trace of "modernism" or "formalism" in the films distributed by P.A.P. There is rather a series of operations, actions, events, and performances inextricably linked to the materiality of the body and celluloid, both of which are subjected to transgression, to *profanation*.

---

[1] See François Bovier & Adeena Mey (eds.), *Exhibiting the Moving Image. History Revisited*, JRP|Ringier, Zurich 2015.
[2] See Jean-Christophe Royoux, "Pour un cinéma d'exposition. Retour sur quelques jalons historiques," *Omnibus*, no. 20 (April 1997), p. 11–15.
[3] See Gloria Sutton, *The Experience Machine. Stan VanDerBeek's Movie-Drome and Expanded Cinema*, MIT Press, Cambridge, Massachusetts 2015.
[4] See, in particular, Branden W. Joseph, "'My Mind Split Open': Andy Warhol's Exploding Plastic Inevitable," *Grey Room*, no. 8 (Summer 2002), p. 80–107.

[5] See Eric Schuldenfrei, *The Films of Charles and Ray Eames: A Universal Sense of Expectation*, Routledge, London/New York 2015.
[6] See Gregor Jansen and Ferdinand Kriwet, *Kriwet. yester 'n' today: Kunsthalle Düsseldorf Galerie im Taxispalais*, Dumont, Cologne 2011.
[7] See Julien Levy, *Memoir of An Art Gallery*, Putman, New York 1977.
[8] See Alain-Alcide Sudre, *Dialogues théoriques avec Maya Deren. Du cinéma expérimental au cinéma éthnographique*, L'Harmattan, Paris 1996; Peter Decherney, *Hollywood and the Culture Elite:*

How the Movies Became Americans, Columbia University Press, Columbia 2005; Haidee Wasson, *Museum Movies: The Museum of Modern Art and the Birth of Art Cinema*, University of California Press, Berkeley/Los Angeles 2005. It should also be noted that Maya Deren's films, much like the animation cinema produced by artists and independent filmmakers during the 1930s, have now been clearly accepted into the field of contemporary art (this is the case at the new rooms housing the Whitney Museum's collection, which, in 2015, showed films by Maya Deren and Mary Ellen Bute side by side).

[9] It should, however, be noted that, at that time, artists' films were regularly shown at Kunsthallen and major art exhibitions such as documenta. Furthermore, the EXPRMNTL festival in Knokke-le-Zoute was the main rallying point for independent filmmakers in Europe.

[10] On the inclusion of films in the market economy of galleries, see Erika Balsom, *After Uniqueness: A History of Film and Video Art in Circulation*, Columbia University Press, New York 2017.

[11] See *Projected Images: Peter Campus, Rockne Krebs, Paul Sharits, Ted Victoria, Robert Whitman*, exh. cat., Walker Art Center, Minneapolis 1974.

[12] See *Prospekt '71: Projection*, exh. cat., Städtische Kunsthalle, Düsseldorf 1971.

[13] See Jay David Bolter and Richard Grusin, *Remediation: Understanding New Media*, MIT Press, Cambridge, Massachusetts 1999.

[14] In this respect, see Ulrike Groos, Barbara Hess, Ursula Wevers (eds.), *Ready to Shoot: Fernsehgalerie Gerry Schum*, Snoeck, Cologne 2004.

[15] *Land Art* was broadcast on the German public broadcasting channel Erstes Programm (ARD) on April 15, 1969, at 10.40pm, to an estimated 100,000 viewers, and SWF broadcast *Identifications* on November 30, 1970, at 10.50pm.

[16] See the advertisement at the end of the P.A.P. publication, *XXe Filmwoche Mannheim*, Mannheim 1971, n. p. A number of works documenting performances by Muehl (*Zock, Psychomotorik, Aktionsfotos, Mama und Papa, Der Geile Wotan* and *O Sensibility*), a book by Wilhelm and Birgit Hein (*Porno Riffle Book*), and a film on paper by Iimura (*Taka Iimura's Image Bag*) were offered for sale.

[17] See Progressive Art Production Filmgalerie Filmverleih, *Lagerkatalog 1969*, P.A.P., Munich 1969; Progressive Art Production, *PAP Filme*, P.A.P., Munich 1972. I also draw on the interview by Fred Truniger and Thomas Schärer of Karlheinz Hein, in July 2012. I curated an exhibition on P.A.P. with Baltazar Lovay, the director of Fri Art Kunsthalle Fribourg, at Artgenève, in January 2017 (see the catalogue republished on this occasion: *Film Implosion! Experiments in Swiss Cinema and Moving Images*.)

[18] See the first pages of the 1969 P.A.P. catalogue, and the section about this organization in the 1970 Art Basel catalogue; it should be noted that in 1971 and 1972, Karlheinz Hein alone represented P.A.P. in the Art Basel catalogues.

[19] *81,000 Units*, lasting approximately one hour—the first version, lasting 70 minutes, was called *100,800 Units*—exploited the discontinuity between frames, the "units" referred to in the title, essentially fine editing modules. Anthony Moore's sound track (this composer was also working with Schoenherr and Nekes at the time) contributed to the hypnotic quality of the film. Meier later put his name to video clips for his band, Yello, and generally chose not to use 16mm film as his medium.

[20] See Thomas Schärer and Fred Truniger, "*Underground Explosion*: le music-hall de l'avant-garde," *Décadrages*, no. 21–22 (2012), p. 132–145, in English in this volume.

[21] See Ulrich Gregor (ed.), *HHK Schoenherr: cinéma expérimental*, Pro Helvetia/L'Âge d'Homme, Zurich/Lausanne 1985.

[22] See "Cry for Fame: Raus aus der Kunst – Rein in die Kunst. Dieter Meier im Gespräch mit Peter Weibel. ZKM Karlsruhe, 8 April 2011," Stefan Zweifel (ed.), *Dieter Meier. Works 1968–2011 and the Yello Years*, Walther König, Cologne 2011, p. 19.

[23] See *Kinematograph*, no. 3 ["W+B Hein: Dokumente 1967-1985. Fotos, Briefe, Texte"], 1985, p. 33. It should be noted that this issue of *Kinematograph* was edited by Birgit Hein.

[24] See P.A.P., *XXIIIe Festival d'Avignon*.

[25] See *Film-in*, exh. cat., Lucerne 1969.

[26] See *Film-in*, exh. cat, Lucerne 1970.

[27] See *Film-in*, exh. cat., Lucerne 1971.

[28] See *Festival de Cannes*, exh. cat, Cannes, 1970 and 1971.

[29] See P.A.P., *XXe Filmwoche Mannheim*. In 1969, P.A.P. also screened films in Weimar (see the P.A.P. catalogue, [untitled, undated], Weimar, 1969).

[30] See *Internationale Kunstmesse Basel*, Basel, 1970; 1971; 1972, n. p.

[31] It should be noted that the 1971 catalogue shows that a selection of films by the artists represented by the P.A.P. Gallery was exhibited, as was documentation about Muehl's material actions [*Materialaktionen*]. The 1972 catalogue was more explicit: in addition to films by represented artists, the exhibition also included documentation of Muehl's material actions, a book by Iimura, and a box by Kren, a poster about the creation of Schoenherr's *Das Kaputte Kino 5*, and some Super-8 reductions of films about the Actionists by Kren.

[32] See Wilhelm and Birgit Hein, Christian Michelis, Rolf Wiest (eds.), *XSCREEN. Materialien über den Underground-Film*, Phaidon, Cologne 1971. See also Nicolas Brulhart, "W+B Hein, XSCREEN et la réception impossible du cinéma élargi en Allemagne," *Décadrages*, no. 21–22 (2012), p. 61–80.

[33] See "Cry for Fame: Raus aus der Kunst – Rein in die Kunst. Dieter Meier im Gespräch mit Peter Weibel. ZKM Karlsruhe, 8 April 2011," p. 20.

[34] See Stephen Dwoskin, *Film Is ... International Free Cinema*, The Overlook Press, Woodstock 1975.

[35] *P.A.P. Filme*, n. p. This allegiance to radical "pornographic" practices was diametrically opposed to the neoclassical aesthetics of films by Markopoulos, just to take the most obvious example.

[36] See *Kinematagraph*, no. 3, p. 22. Following these events, Rolf Wiest, a member of XSCREEN, published a circular denouncing the dissymmetry between the status of artists' films in art institutions and in alternative circles, and, to put it more simply, between galleries and the street: "What is art in a Kunsthalle, as it is marketable, is criminal in a metro station." Enno Stahl, "'Kulturkampf' in Köln, Die XSCREEN-Affäre 1968," *Geschichte im Westen*, no. 22, Klartext Verlag, Essen 2007, p. 188, quoted by Nicolas Brulhart, *op. cit.*, p. 70.

P.A.P.: A "FILM GALLERY" FOR "POLITICAL AND PORNOGRAPHIC" CINEMA

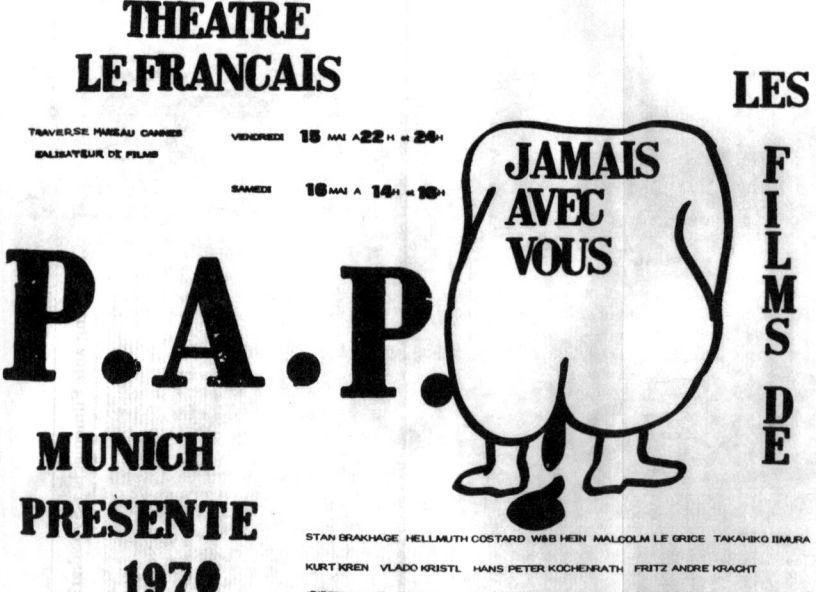

Poster announcing *Jamais avec vous* screenings at the Cannes Film Festival, 1971
Published in *P.A.P. Filme*, exhibition catalogue, P.A.P., Munich 1972

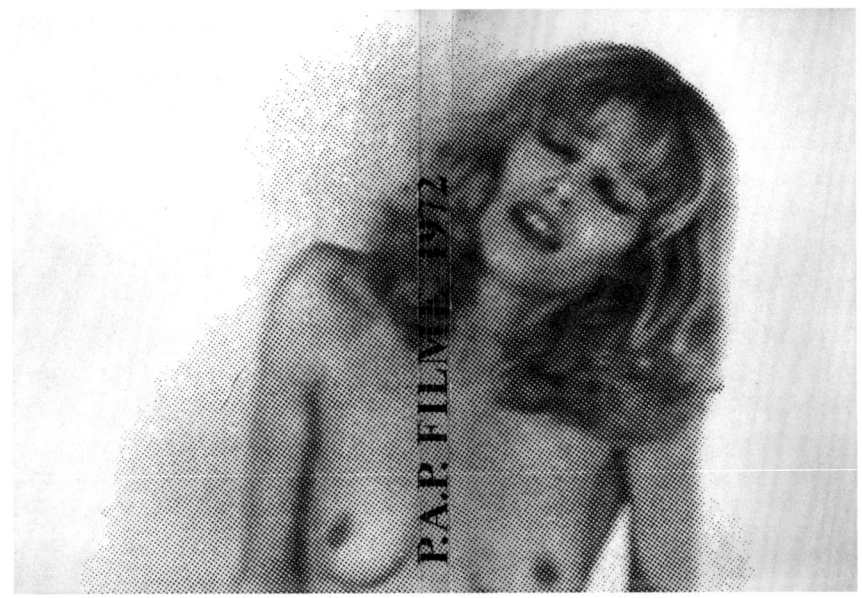

Cover of *P.A.P. Filme*, exhibition catalogue, P.A.P., Munich 1972

Exhibiting Structural Film?
Annette Michelson, Between
Criticism and Curating
Adeena Mey

Cover of *New Forms in Film*, exhibition catalogue, Montreux 1974

In his critical account of *New Forms in Film*, an exhibition devoted to the most current research of American independent cinema, and organized by Annette Michelson in 1974 in Montreux, Switzerland, Dominique Noguez, one of France's foremost theoreticians and promoters of experimental film, criticized the retrospective for being too structured.[1] For Noguez, if *New Forms in Film* acted both as an assessment and a manifesto of New American Cinema, offering one of the first "readings" of "American filmic modernity," the plurality of works that could be included under the umbrella term of New American Cinema[2] was cut off from everything produced on the West Coast—a production distinguished, according to him, by more exuberance and irrationality than its New York counterpart—to favor films characterized by rigor and austerity. Yet, as partial as it might have been, Noguez nevertheless acknowledged Michelson's selection for being coherent and intelligent, a choice able to show the newest and most remarkable directions of what henceforth could appear, as he wrote, as a "New New American Cinema."[3]

Widely known as an early editor of *Artforum* before going on to found the journal *October* together with Rosalind Krauss in 1976, in parallel to her main activities as a critic, editor, translator, and professor, Annette Michelson also participated—if we allow ourselves to reframe it in contemporary terms—in the constellation of curatorial practices. In the wake of the so-called "cinematic turn" in contemporary art, *New Forms in Film*, as well as other "exhibitions" or film programs in which Michelson was involved as organizer, could shed light on the increasing interest surrounding the status of film and the moving image in the field of contemporary art, and more specifically on the integration of experimental cinema into museum and gallery contexts, as these events represent specific historical examples of attempts to present structural cinema within the context of art spaces. As Noguez remarked in the same passage, Michelson's *New Forms in Film* differed from the previous, usual, modes of showing experimental film as "furtive presentations at the Cinémathèque" or in "muddled white nights."

Montreux, 1974

New Forms in Film took place from August 3–24, 1974, in the town of Montreux on the shores of Lake Geneva in Switzerland. Advertised in the press release as "weeks of American avant-garde cinema in Montreux," *New Forms in Film* consisted of a survey that brought together the work of Bruce Baillie, Stan Brakhage, Robert Breer, Hollis Frampton, Barry Gerson, Ernie Gehr, Ken Jacobs, Peter Kubelka, George Landow, Jonas Mekas, Yvonne Rainer, Paul Sharits, Harry Smith, Michael Snow, and Joyce Wieland, and took the form of a series of screenings, each presenting the production of one of the 15 filmmakers and artists individually. According to the catalogue, Annette Michelson was invited to Switzerland to curate *New Forms in Film* by curator and art critic René Berger, who was at the time director of the Musée cantonal des Beaux-Arts in Lausanne, and by Galerie Impact, also in Lausanne. Berger had early on championed video art through his theoretical writings, and the integration of the medium into exhibition spaces in Switzerland.⁴ Financial support was provided by the local tourist board, which also loaned its newly built Convention Centre for the event. Over the course of three weeks, the audience could engage in sustained viewings of, for instance, choreographer Yvonne Rainer's *Lives of Performers* (1972), a film associated with minimalist and postmodern dance; Michael Snow's *Wavelength* (1967), which at that point had become a landmark in experimental filmmaking and pivotal for the formation of Michelson's discursive apparatus; or, as on the evening of August 8, attend a joint screening and roundtable discussion of works by Michael Snow, Jonas Mekas, and Robert Breer, with all three filmmakers present.⁵ There were two daily screenings, starting at 5pm and 9pm, each introduced by Michelson, and concluding with a public discussion. Five of the filmmakers (Michael Snow, Jonas Mekas, Robert Breer, Peter Kubelka, and Ernie Gehr) were present to talk about their work. Kubelka gave two lectures in addition to screenings of his complete works: the first was entitled "Metric Cinema" (the name he gave to his theory of montage based on principles of seriality and permutation in music), while in the second he addressed the question of "Articulation in Cinema."⁶

This presence of filmmakers and the inclusion of theoretical debates and talks in *New Forms in Film* were part of Michelson's agenda to define a specific mode of presenting and experiencing films made under the label of New American Cinema, a vague term designating the range of films made outside the studio system, and combining a reduced economy of means with a quest for alternative regimes of visual representation. Indeed, as Michelson wrote in the press release:

> *New Forms in Film* has been planned as more than merely a series of screenings. It is designed as an occasion for intensive contact between a new audience and a contemporary art form. For this reason we have invited five filmmakers to be present for several days of conversations, talks, and

demonstrations. It is our hope that contact will be both formal and intensive.[7]

Even though this passage is obviously aligned with the marketing dimension any press release is intended to fulfill, Michelson's insistence on the event as being more than just "a series of screenings" is worth looking at critically. *New Forms in Film* did not take place in a film theater, nor in an informal venue where the "muddled white nights" of underground cinema mentioned by Noguez were usually organized. It was not a clear example of an attempt to integrate the moving image into museum or gallery spaces, as was the case with the exhibition *Prospect 71—Projection* (1971) for instance; nor was it intended to situate experimental cinema in large-scale art exhibitions, as in *Sonsbeek 71* (1971) and documenta 5 (1972).[8] Rather, the films were presented according to the spectatorial conventions of the "traditional" film apparatus, a projector and chairs being arranged in one room of the Montreux Convention Centre. Helene Kaplan, who worked as Michelson's assistant on the show, projected some of the films, while filmmakers present in Switzerland, such as Ernie Gehr, projected their work themselves. In this respect, *New Forms in Film* is similar to other surveys of avant-garde film, including P. Adams Sitney's *New American Cinema Exposition* that toured Europe in 1964 and 1967, as well as *EXPRMNTL*, the Experimental Film Festival of Knokke-le-Zoute in Belgium (1947–1974).

Reviews of *New Forms in Film* refered to it as either "weeks of American Avant-Garde Cinema," as a "festival," or as an "exhibition"; yet, as Michelson pointed out in the catalogue, the project was "conceived more on the lines of an exhibition than a festival."[9] This insistence on her survey as an exhibition rather than a festival was briefly thematized by Michelson in an article written by French film critic Louis Marcorelles in *Le Monde*:

> [she] insisted that the event be called an "exhibition," no pun intended or snobbery, but to emphasize a qualitative difference. Films are not spectacles to be consumed, but must be looked at as in a painting exhibition, and one should be able to dwell upon

particular details, as well as, accordingly, analyze a work.[10]

Further on in his critical review, Marcorelles reported that this analogy between film and painting was recalled by Michelson after each screening by way of the notion of "materiality," a term that refers to the politics of modernist film practice in the way it "is considered to be a refutation of the transparency of conventional film technique through the full exploration of the material properties of cinematic expression," and, unlike and contrary to dominant cinema, in the way it operates an "anti-illusionist" critique.[11] Even if only briefly touched upon, it can be understood that, if *New Forms in Film* proposed a conceptualization of spectatorship and of the modes of exhibiting films (as art exhibition), it did so by applying a model of viewership borrowed from the visual arts to film. Hence, by the same token, it suggested their closeness in phenomenological terms to the extent that both participate in the same regimes of visuality.

If, at the time of this exhibition in Switzerland Michelson was already mostly known as a theorist of avant-garde cinema, her interpretative frame of structural film having become the dominant analytical mode of this body of work, before a more marked transition into writing about cinematic arts, her previous published work had mostly dealt with the practice of visual artists. In his study of the modes of film analysis, historian David Bordwell acknowledges Michelson's writing on film as having integrated avant-garde cinema into the canons of modernist art history and criticism, and as having constructed a frame for film analysis he termed "interpretative," in which the work of artist-filmmakers becomes a model for knowledge and cognition.[12] If Michelson established a critical canon for writing about experimental cinema, to understand how her works on the moving image and on the visual arts informed each other, and what this interaction might tell us about the relationship between criticism and modes of exhibition in turn, it is necessary to look at the ways in which her discursive strategies and concepts have circulated, as well as how they have been translated between her work on different art practices.

Art and Film (Criticism) as Epistemologies

In her seminal essay of 1969 on sculptor Robert Morris, Michelson identified a crisis in art criticism ushered in by emerging artistic practices, notably those presented in the exhibition *10×10* at the Dwan Gallery in 1967, which included works by Robert Morris and other future major minimalist artists, whose "new attitude" and "new sensibility" created a situation in which art became, according to her, "apodictic,"[13] of absolute certainty. This gave shape to a new aesthetic landscape that revealed the insufficiencies of the art criticism of the time, founded, wrote Michelson, on a form of "idealism." Hence, what Morris undertook was a critique of traditional sculptural conventions, and of the virtual space it both produces and rests upon to generate, following Michelson's reading of *Untitled (Corner Piece)* (1964), "a space common to object and beholder."[14] This conception of sculpture as an exploration of concrete space, of its sensible parameters, and of the laying bare of the structures of the sculptural object prompted Michelson to bring it close to philosophical activity, most specifically to phenomenological inquiry:

> It is the commitment to the exact particularity of experience, to the experience of the sculptural object as inextricably involved with the sense of the self and of that space which is their common dwelling, which characterizes these strategies as radical.[15]

Further on in the essay, making analogies between Morris' sculptures and postmodern dance, as well as with the French *Nouveau roman* of Alain Robbe-Grillet, the explorations of objects and bodies in their spatial settings initiated in these three fields constitute, she wrote, "a central focus for modern epistemological inquiry."[16] If, in the context of minimal art, Michelson grounds her argument in Maurice Merleau-Ponty's phenomenology, her defense of an epistemology (rather than an aesthetics or history, for instance) of modernism can be seen as a generic epistemic stance that traverses her critical work. In a lecture delivered at the Solomon R. Guggenheim Museum in 1970 on "Art and the Structuralist Perspective," Michelson mentioned, as Krauss later reminded us, "the disappointment of Structuralism's hostility to abstract art, a philistinism unworthy of the movement's extraordinarily formal thinkers,"[17] and rightly raised the question of their similarities: "How can a scientific methodology so closely analogous to that of modern aesthetics reject contemporary aesthetic form?"[18]; it is henceforth with and against them (in this specific instance, Claude Lévi-Strauss' *Anthropologie Structurale*, 1958) that she staged her own encounter between structuralist thought and modernist art, both, she wrote, inhabited by the same "crisis of the real." The "Great Divide"—between world and representation; object and subject; thing and sign—which defines modernity has triggered conceptual and aesthetic proposals which try to bring these poles back together or inhabit the gap between them; yet, they have fostered the chiasmus between a linguistic apprehension of the world and the movement toward the concreteness of modern art. Michelson noted, however, "there is an epistemology of modernism that questions the object as it questions the word, thereby questioning the sign."[19]

If many practitioners and writers have relativized or even rejected the association between film practice and structuralism as understood in philosophy and the social sciences, there is no doubt that, in the case of Michelson, her interest in minimal art, postmodern dance, avant-garde film and modernist culture in general, is part of a wider interest in a rewriting of modernity largely supported by her exposure to structuralism and French thought.[20] In the "Foreword in Three Letters" to a special issue of *Artforum* devoted to film that she edited in 1971, replying to British filmmaker and theorist Peter Gidal's criticism addressed to her essay on Michael Snow,[21] in which he raised the issue of "structuralist film terms," Michelson came up with the following answer:

> To my own limited mind, perhaps by formation in the Paris of the 1960s, "structuralist terms" simply cannot suggest themselves with any clarity or relevance in the context of our particular discussion [...] I now invite you to consider how it is that writers of such obvious temperamental differences as yourself and myself should care so passionately for the same film [...]

> It is true that my conviction as to the nature and importance of that transcendence and its redefining function is grounded in an interest in critical traditions richer than that of film—in the history and criticism of art and music, in certain methodological options offered by contemporary philosophy.[22]

Film scholar Malcolm Turvey has rightly noted that Michelson's work escapes disciplinary boundaries, and that the heterogeneity of the theoretical sources she employs in her writing makes it barely possible to find any strict allegiance to a single school of thought or to a single thinker for, he asserts, "she is instinctively a *critic*, not a theorist."[23] If I tend to agree with this reading, by reconstructing Michelson's articulation of structuralist ideas with structural film, my intention is certainly not to imply that she conceives of the latter as a formalization, a literalization, or an embodiment of the former. Yet, if her critical enterprise is marked by such a theoretical "agnosticism" it is so to the extent that it enabled her to interpret a situation marked by the convergence of "epistemological inquiry and cinematic experience [...] in reciprocal mimesis."[24] This is a move we could read as an attempt to affirm the subversive value of New American Cinema and of minimalism in its renegotiation of the avant-garde/traditional dialectics, and to eschew the autonomy of the art work by integrating politics into what Gregory Taylor has called her "reflexive phenomenology."[25] Already in the concluding paragraphs of her essay on Robert Morris, the strategy of the minimalist artist producing a sculptural form expanding into the actual space of human action is brought close to the "revolutionary tradition of constructivism," in particular Alexander Rodchenko and Vladimir Tatlin. Morris' work, she writes, "moves into the real space of the functional while preserving the aesthetic non-functional character of sculpture."[26] It creates a relation between form and function that draws a homology between the artist and the engineer, and on the respective modes of production of the artistic and industrial spheres, suggesting the labor dimension of the artist's work.
In addition, she draws a parallel between the reception of Tatlin's *Monument to the Third International* (1919–1920) and the hostile tone of the discussions that welcomed Morris' early

work,[27] concluding that it is "the conception of a structural order, grounded in the 'culture of materials' as the condition of a fundamentally, radically transgressive movement, which Morris inherits from a revolution and its aesthetic innovations."[28] Here, the core ideas of the critical agenda of *October*, as the editorial of the first issue would put it, are already recognizable, named "in celebration of that moment in our century when revolutionary practice, theoretical inquiry, and artistic innovation were joined in a manner exemplary and unique."[29]

"Radical Aspiration" in the Museum

By developing a critical apparatus enabling the interpretation of minimalism and structural film (as well as dance and even blockbuster films such as Stanley Kubrick's *2001: A Space Odyssey*, 1968) as mimetic, reflexive models of human cognition and perception (sculpture about space as such; film about the act of seeing itself; dance that dissects movement per se, etc.), as illustrated in her writing about Morris, the move away from the object and its analysis opened it to its apprehension both on the levels of its contexts of production and reception.[30] In the case of film, this positioning of the political alongside the attack on illusionism operated by structural film was formulated in an essay published on four occasions, entitled "Film and the Radical Aspiration."[31] In a movement analogous to her treatment of Morris in which she established a trans-historical link between minimalism and constructivism, with film Michelson also turned to the Russian historical avant-gardes, most specifically to the "intellectual cinema" of Sergei Eisenstein. As film scholar Gregory Taylor has shown, the connection she built between Stan Brakhage's cinema—which she herself described as "hypnagogic," and as having moved from "Abstract Expressionism, severing every tie to that space of action which Eisenstein's montage had transformed into the space of dialectical consciousness"—and that of the Russian filmmaker and theorist enabled her to inscribe him as part of the group of filmmakers she turned to in order to champion "the assault upon the space of representation,"[32] the idea defended throughout "Film and the Radical Aspiration." More precisely she wrote:

> The New American Cinema must therefore be seen as
> a powerfully explicit critique of the existing economic
> and social order upon which Hollywood, like Detroit,
> is founded. The formal radicalism of these artists
> is to be understood as grounded in the economic
> and social radicalization of the filmmaking process
> itself.[33]

Gregory Taylor has shown that this theoretical politicization of the New York filmic underground into Marxist and utopian traditions—a political stance previously more familiar to European streams of film criticism—enabled her to "assume a privileged position in the American avant-garde's progression, this time (in accordance with the European model) away from art production and criticism altogether, and into the realm of cultural/political theory."[34] As for D. N. Rodowick, he has pointed to the way Michelson's formulation of anti-illusionism conflated "ontological and epistemological arguments" in the context of film theory and "political modernism."[35]

If both arguments certainly underline some of the complexities regarding specific instances of the articulation of art, theory, and politics in the protean work of Michelson, a look at concrete situations—to go back to *New Forms in Film*— namely modes of film exhibitions, might illuminate the way some of her discursive constructions, as well as their underlying aesthetic and political agenda, were practically unfolded and renegotiated. Indeed, as she commented herself in the second version of "Film and the Radical Aspiration":

> The discomfort and hostility of many, indeed most,
> film critics to those aspects of contemporary cinema
> which bypass, contradict, or transcend the modes
> and values of psycho-social observation is familiar;
> *they provide, in fact, both context and target for this series of
> occasions known as a "festival."*[36]

As an exhibition apparatus, *New Forms in Film* raised a few questions. As stressed by Michelson herself, the Montreux exhibition was really intended to create and sustain a

European audience for the New American Cinema. If articles in the local press encouraged people to see some of the films, they nevertheless expressed misunderstandings and the public's sometimes shocked reactions, and betrayed the fact that, apart from actors from the European film and art scenes, very few people attended.[37] Nevertheless, in a discussion between P. Adams Sitney and Michelson published in *Artforum* in 1975, Sitney acknowledged that *New Forms in Film*—along with the Hamburg Film weeks and the expansion of distribution networks—was one of the factors that enabled access to the American underground in Europe.[38] And in fact, the movement toward public forms of presentation and discussion—complementary as well as expanding the format of the written essay—can be traced back further. Throughout the 1960s the way experimental cinema was engaged with and presented was most often associated with the creation of counter-public spheres, whose existence was often ephemeral but allowed for moments of intense and alternative sensorial experiences or gatherings related to radical politics. Looking both backward and forward, the history of radical politics includes the occupation of film theaters by workers' movements in France in the 1910s, Expanded Cinema events in the 1960s, and the "film discos" in Vienna in the 1990s.[39] If *New Forms in Film* unfolded in the form of a hybrid apparatus (a projector and chairs mimicking a cinema within a room of a convention center at a slick lakeside resort in Switzerland), it can be seen as a reterritorialization of structural film into the field of art, for it represented both the continuation of former events as well as their expansion into European territory.

As a matter of fact, in 1974 *New Forms in Film* was a Swiss iteration as well as the extension of a former film program organized by Michelson in 1972 at the Guggenheim Museum as part of its Summer Arts Festival. Taking place from August 2–13, the series aimed to present "recent tendencies in advanced filmmaking and to show major, large-scale works not often seen in public." If critic Bill Simon wrote in the pages of *Artforum* that "most of the films shown can be categorized as structural films […] this group of films, more than ever, invites a reconsideration of the conditions and characteristics of the structural film,"[40]

Michelson's intention was to present these filmmakers and their work "as a group [...] for the rigor and innovative energy with which they have questioned the convention of cinematic illusionism, thereby attaining, in the late 1960s and 1970s, a maturity which is now that of the New American Cinema."[41] Yet, regardless of the question of the cohesion of this "group" and the multiple labels by which it was identified, what the event contributed was, according to art historian Philip Glahn, "identifying a break in the history of film and bringing about a shift in the critical debate."[42]

If her writing gained recognition to the point it defined the standard approach in writing about experimental film, this was possible through the double dynamic of reappropriating it into the sphere of the museum, as well as by consolidating (with all the exclusions this entailed) the categories of structural film and of New American Cinema.[43] However, this integration of film into art spaces did not result in attempts at spatializing film—as contemporary debates emphasize, referring to the question of site or of apparatus (schematically the white cube and the black box)—but as another gallery show involving the expertise of Michelson suggests, it revolved around issues of the specificity of film, the authorial status of filmmakers and artists, as well as around their institutional inscription. In 1973 the exhibition *Options and Alternatives: Some Directions in Recent Art* presented to the audience of the Yale University Art Gallery current research in painting, sculpture, performance, and film, this last section being organized by Michelson. In an accompanying text written by curator Klaus Kertess, the problem of exhibiting film and performance was explicitly raised. Entitled "Notes on the Anatomy of an Exhibition," Kertess discussed the place of non-object-based art such as film and performance over several paragraphs. Regarding the status of film in the exhibition, he wrote that:

> The weight given to filmmakers, beyond the individual merits of the works, and their inclusion in the painting and sculpture section of the exhibition, is to underline their role as artists. Until quite recently, filmmakers were seldom dealt with on the "art-scene" [...] The efforts of critics like Annette Michelson, as well as the increasing number of painters and

sculptors now involved with film and video, have gone a long way in breaking down useless barriers. Perhaps this exhibition is another step in that direction.[44]

The solution for including these non-object-based works was as follows: the performance part—that is a concert of Philip Glass' *Music in Twelve Parts* and Yvonne Rainer's film *Lives of Performers*—took place in the sculpture hall, while Rainer's work, along with the body of work Michelson called, following Eisenstein, "intellectual cinema," was shown inside the gallery, but in a traditional film-screening setting, with a fixed schedule.

Today, as contemporary art seems to be increasingly reshaped, in a process of "becoming-cinema," and as the renewed interest in forms such as Expanded Cinema, paracinema,[45] and "cinema by other means"[46] complicate the landscape and the objects that present themselves to critics, theorists, and historians, raising questions as to the ontological status of the cinematic, Annette Michelson's relentless defense of structural cinema, and her trajectory between writing, editing, translating, teaching, and, as we have seen, curating, is exemplary. The "radical aspiration of film" and what we might be tempted to call the "Michelsonian apparatus," i.e. the system of relationships between art and film, the spectator or audience, the critical frames, as well as the institutional contexts through which they become intelligible and unfold, represent a singular object, both from a contemporary and a historical perspective. Indeed, experimental cinema, once an autonomous sphere punctually intersecting with the fields of art and film, is now more and more shown in the context of art museums and galleries and reinscribed in the "attention economy" of exhibitions saturated by multiple temporalities and audio-visual fluxes, which turn museums into sites of permanent cognitive labor. Michelson's insistence on a sustained if not conventional spectatorial activity of avant-garde film, and on its aesthetic-political underpinnings might thus serve as a case to historicize our contemporary moment. Also, while working at the intersections of diverse media such as film, sculpture, dance, and painting, the Michelsonian apparatus seems at odds with contemporary paradigms such as systems or information art, the broad nexus of practices falling under the general term of art and technology, or even Expanded Cinema (which she criticized for its technophilia and proximity to commerce), which might constitute another point in a genealogy of exhibited moving image work. As a matter of fact, they anticipate the same real-time economy that shapes contemporary art in the post-digital era, and indeed, our lives today. It is with these two prospects in mind, at least, that one might contemplate anew the relevance to the present of Annette Michelson's radical aspiration.

[1] Dominique Noguez, *Éloge du cinéma expérimental* [1978], Paris Expérimental, Paris 2010, p. 114–115.
[2] See for instance Gregory Battcock, *The New American Cinema: A Critical Anthology*, E.P. Dutton, New York 1967.
[3] Dominique Noguez, *Éloge du cinéma experimental*, p. 114–115.
[4] See François Bovier, Adeena Mey (eds.), *René Berger. L'Art vidéo*, JRP|Ringier, Zurich 2014.
[5] Montreux Tourist Office, *New Form in Film*, program leaflet, Montreux, 1974. While the catalogue edited by Annette Michelson is entitled *New Forms in Film*, the promotional material published by the Montreux Tourist Board kept "form" in the singular. I am following the spellings as they are printed.
[6] Montreux Tourist Office, *New Form in Film*, program leaflet, Montreux 1974.
[7] Annette Michelson, *New Form in Film. Press Release*, Montreux 1974.
[8] The exhibition *Prospect 71—Projection*, curated by Konrad Fischer and Hans Strelow at the Kunsthalle Düsseldorf, which included films by artists associated with minimal, postminimal, conceptual, and land art, as well as works by experimental filmmakers, constituted, according to film scholar Maxa Zoller, "film projection-based exhibitions," and exposed the film apparatus itself for a lack of appropriate ways of exhibiting films in museums. See Maxa Zoller, *Places of Projection. Recontextualizing the European Film Canon*, PhD Thesis, London, Birkbeck College, University of London, School of History of Art, Film and Visual Media, 2007, p. 131–164. Conceived as a site of "activity" rather than a traditional exhibition, and curated by Wim Beeren, *Sonsbeek '71* presented works by conceptual, minimal, and land artists, outdoors, across Holland. It included an inflatable pavilion designed by the British artists' collective Event Research Structure Group, in which films such as Robert Smithson and Nancy Holt's *Swamp* (1969), Michael Snow's <—> *(Back and Forth)* (1969), and Robert Morris' *Gas Station* (1969) were screened. As part of Harald Szeemann's documenta 5, a film cycle entitled *Documenta Filmschau* was included at the Kino Royal. It presented seven sections devoted to "New American Cinema," with films by Barry Gearson, Larry Gottheim, Andrew Noren, Paul Sharits, Joyce Wieland, Stan Brakhage, Michael Snow, David Rimmer, George Landow, Ken Jacobs, Tony Conrad, Hollis Frampton; three sections of "New European Cinema" with films by Werner Nekes and Dore O., Klaus Wyborny, Birgit and Willem Hein; a section devoted to Russ Meyer and "Erotic Cinema" with films by Stephen Dwoskin and Irm and Ed Sommer; two sections of "Sozialistischer Realismus" with films from China; and additional showings of political films and "Trivialpornographie." See *Documenta Filmschau: vom 1. 7. bis 5. 7. '72 im Kino Royal*, program poster, documenta 5, Kassel 1972.
[9] Annette Michelson (ed.), *New Forms in Film*, Corbaz, Montreux 1974.
[10] Louis Marcorelles, "Le nouveau cinéma américain. Une 'exposition' du septième art," *Le Monde*, August 27, 1974, p. 1. Author's translation.
[11] David N. Rodowick, *The Crisis of Political Modernism. Criticism and Ideology in Contemporary Film Theory*, University of California Press, Berkeley/Los Angeles/London 1994, p. 4–5. Here Rodowick explicitly draws on Michelson to identify this specific feature of political modernism in the field of film and film theory.
[12] David Bordwell, *Making Meaning. Inference and Rhetoric in the Interpretation of Cinema*, Harvard University Press, Cambridge/London 1989, p. 57–64.
[13] Annette Michelson, "Robert Morris—An Aesthetics of Transgression," Julia Bryon-Wilson (ed.), *Robert Morris*, October Files 15, MIT Press, Cambridge, Massachusetts 2013, p. 7–49, originally published in *Robert Morris*, exh. cat., Corcoran Gallery of Art, Washington, DC 1969.
[14] Ibid., p. 22.
[15] Ibid., p. 24–25. In the paragraph following this sentence, Michelson supports her argument referring to her notes from Maurice Merleau-Ponty's lectures at the Collège de France which, as the footnote suggests, she attended, and which were subsequently edited as Claude Lefort (ed.), *Le Visible et l'invisible, suivi de Notes de Travail*, Gallimard, Paris 1964.
[16] Annette Michelson, "Robert Morris—An Aesthetics of Transgression," p. 37.
[17] Rosalind Krauss, "Preface," Richard Allen, Malcolm Turvey (eds.), *Camera Obscura Camera Lucida. Essays in Honor of Annette Michelson*, Amsterdam University Press, Amsterdam 2003, p. 9.
[18] Annette Michelson, "Art and the Structuralist Perspective," *On the Future of Art*, Solomon R. Guggenheim Museum, A Viking Compass Book, New York 1970, p. 51.
[19] Ibid., p. 52.
[20] The relationship between structural film and structuralism deserves further and more careful attention. In fact, there exists very little consistent literature on this specific issue, which is more complex than a simple attitude of differentiation toward theory on the part of filmmakers. P. Adams Sitney who first coined the term "structural film" mentions the emergence of "academic critics under the influence of Foucault, Derrida, and Lacan" without singling out structuralism in *Visionary Film. The American Avant-Garde 1943–2000* (Third Edition, Oxford University Press, Oxford/New York 2002, p. 410). His own take on the notion is indeed more indebted to Greenberg. Filmmaker and writer Malcolm Le Grice who is associated with the British structural/materialist film theorized by Peter Gidal, wrote the following on the relationship between structuralism and structural films: "The development of experience depends on developments of structuring. I see the movement from Cezanne to Analytical Cubism as the historical basis of visual structural art. Structuralism in art would seem to imply a broadly representational, or more accurately, homological, condition. This 'homology' is defined by Lévi-Strauss as an analogy of functions rather than of substance. In *The Structuralist Activity*, Roland Barthes talks of a process whereby the structuralist decomposes the real and then recomposes it. The reconstructed 'object,' which I take to imply mainly the structuralist art object, is described as a simulacrum of the 'natural object' and is seen as 'intellect added to object' [...] It is perhaps this concentration on structure as process or activity which most recommends the project to the time-based film medium at the present time. However inadequate it might be later, I would like for now to confine the use of the term 'structuralism' in film to situations where the space/time relations of a filmed situation are reformed or transformed through a definable structuring strategy into a new 'experiential' (as opposed to didactically conceptual) homology." Malcom Le Grice, "Kurt Kren's Films," Peter Gidal (ed.) *Structural Film Anthology*, BFI, London 1978, p. 60–61.
[21] Annette Michelson, "Toward Snow (part I)," *Artforum*, IX (June 1971), p. 30–37.
[22] Annette Michelson, "Foreword in Three Letters," *Artforum*, X, (September 1971), p. 9.
[23] Malcolm Turvey, "Introduction," Malcolm Turvey, Richard Allen (eds.), *Camera Obscura Camera Lucida. Essays in Honor of Annette Michelson*, p. 24. Original italics.
[24] Annette Michelson, "Toward Snow (part I)," p. 30. Michelson's insistence on avant-garde film as epistemology

is also articulated in an article devoted to Dziga Vertov, published at a later date than both her essays on Snow and Morris, in which she applies this model to Vertov. As she puts it: "If the filmmaker is like the magician, a manufacturer of illusions, he can, unlike the prestidigitator and in the interest of instruction of a heightening of consciousness, destroy illusion by that other transcendentally magical procedure, the reversal of time by the inversion of action. He can develop, as it were, 'the negative of time' for 'the Communist decoding of reality.' This thematic interplay of magic, illusion, labor, filmic techniques, and strategy, articulating a theory of film as epistemological inquiry, is the complex central core around which Vertov's greatest work [*Kino Glaz*] develops." Annette Michelson, "From Magician to Epistemologist. Vertov's *The Man with a Movie Camera*," P. Adams Sitney (ed.), *The Essential Cinema*, New York University Press, New York 1975, p. 95–111.

[25] Gregory T. Taylor, "'The Cognitive Instrument in the Service of Revolutionary Change': Sergei Eisenstein, Annette Michelson, and the Avant-Garde's Scholarly Aspiration," *Cinema Journal*, vol. 31, no. 4 (Summer 1992), p. 52.

[26] Annette Michelson, "Robert Morris—An Aesthetics of Transgression," *op. cit.*, p. 43.

[27] "For Trotsky, it is a nonfunctional intrusion, a luxury in the devastated city of the postrevolutionary period. The *Monument* provoked a discussion, which in fact recalls those who greeted the appearance of Morris' early work. It was a kind of 'primary structure' for its contemporaries." *Ibid.*, p. 45.

[28] *Ibid.*, p. 46.

[29] "About October," *October*, no. 1 (Spring 1976), p. 3.

[30] Hence, as Branden Joseph puts it, following Maurice Berger's and Hal Foster's readings, Morris' "anti-formalist dynamic will become the foundation on which the anti-institutional of the later work of Morris, Smithson, and others is built." Branden W. Joseph, "Robert Morris and John Cage: Reconstructing a Dialogue," *October*, vol. 81 (Summer 1997), p. 64–65.

[31] Annette Michelson, "Film and the Radical Aspiration," *Film Culture*, no. 42, Fall 1966, p. 34–42. Reprinted in Gregory Battcock (ed.), *The New American Cinema. A Critical Anthology*, E.P. Dutton, New York 1967, p. 83–102; P. Adams Sitney, *Film Culture Reader*, Praeger, New York 1970; reprinted Cooper Square Press, New York 2000, p. 404–422. A subsequent, revised version was published as the introduction to the catalogue of *New Forms in Film*: Annette Michelson (ed.), *New Forms in Film*, Montreux 1974, p. 9–16. Engaging with film as a revolutionary practice, a medium in this regard taken she says between "convergence and dissociation," Michelson devotes her essay to Truffaut, Godard, and Resnais. In the 1974 revised version, the section she devotes to the French New Wave Filmmakers is replaced by reflections on Deren's poetics and her role in a genealogy of the American avant-garde that has shifted toward "the epistemological mode of discourse," which allows her to write a few concluding remarks on some of the filmmakers presented in Switzerland (Jacobs, Sharits, Frampton, Gehr, Landow, Wieland, Snow).

[32] See her edited volume, "Eisenstein/Brakhage. Special Film Issue," *Artforum*, XI, no. 5 (January 1973).

[33] Annette Michelson, "Film and the Radical Aspiration: An Introduction," *New Forms in Film*, p. 11.

[34] Gregory T. Taylor, "'The Cognitive Instrument in the Service of Revolutionary Change': Sergei Eisenstein, Annette Michelson, and the Avant-Garde's Scholarly Aspiration," p. 56.

[35] David N. Rodowick, *The Crisis of Political Modernism*, p. 154.

[36] Annette Michelson, "Film and the Radical Aspiration," in Gregory Battcock (ed.), *The New American Cinema. A Critical Anthology*, E.P. Dutton, New York 1967, p. 89. My italics.

[37] Interview with Annette Michelson, September 8, 2011, New York. If the aim of building an audience for the New American Cinema gave average results, Annette Michelson had managed to finance new prints of each film presented, which filmmakers were able to keep after the exhibition. As for the reception of *New Forms in Film*, the local paper *L'est vaudois* covered the event throughout August 1974.

[38] Annette Michelson, P. Adams Sitney, "A Conversation on Knokke and the Independent Film Maker," *Artforum*, vol. XXIII (9– May 1975), p. 63–66.

[39] See for instance Anna Schober, "Political Squats: Cinema and City as Movers of the Real," in Christian Emden, Catherine Keen, David Midgley (eds.), *Imagining the City, Vol. 1: The Art of Urban Living*, Peter Lang, Oxford 2006, p. 249–271.

[40] Bill Simon "New Forms in Film," *Artforum*, vol. XI, no. 2 (1972), p. 78.

[41] "Summer Arts Festival '72 at the Guggenheim Museum," press release, Solomon R. Guggenheim Museum Archive, 1972. The filmmakers and artists presented at *New Forms in Film* 1972 were: Jonas Mekas, Hollis Frampton, Stan Brakhage, Michael Snow, Harry Smith, Joyce Wieland, Ernie Gehr, Paul Sharits, Barry Gerson, Yvonne Rainer, and Ken Jacobs.

[42] Philip Glahn, "Brechtian Journeys: Yvonne Rainer's Film as Counterpublic Art," *Art Journal*, vol. 68, no. 2 (Summer 2009), p. 80. In this regard, Glahn's reading aligns with Bordwell's.

[43] This break was summed up the same year by Michelson herself in the catalogue of a Vancouver exhibition called *Form and Structure in Recent Film* which she helped organize, through a rhetorical line she repeated on numerous occasions, asserting that the common feature of the exhibited artists (here Frampton, Gehr, Jacobs, Landow, Sharits, Snow, and Wieland) was their "assault on the space of representation" which suggests a shift toward "an epistemological concern with the nature of filmic process and experience, which will require another space, another time, those of a new cinematic discourse." See Annette Michelson, "An Introduction to Form and Structure in Recent Film," Dennis Wheeler (ed.), *Form and Structure in Recent Film*, Vancouver Art Gallery, Vancouver, 1972. This coincides with Branden Joseph's analysis of Tony Conrad's *Yellow Movies* (1973), produced after his return from Europe where he encountered Wilhelm and Birgit Hein, Otto Muehl, and the Viennese actionists. According to Joseph, the *Yellow Movies* represent Conrad's enterprise of subverting the category of structural film as Sitney had defined it in *Visionnary Film*. Thus, 1972 marks a moment of crisis of the notion of structural film, and Michelson's and Conrad's takes, and reworkings of it might be read as representing two divergent branches in a genealogy of the notion. See Branden W. Joseph, *The Roh and the Cooked: Tony Conrad and Beverly Grant in Europe*, August Verlag, Berlin 2012.

[44] Klaus Kertess, "Notes on the Anatomy of an Exhibition," *Options and Alternatives: Some Directions in Recent Art*, exh. cat., Yale University Art Gallery, New Haven, Connecticut 1973, p. 9–10.

[45] See, for instance, Jonathan Walley, "The Material of Film and the Idea of Cinema: Contrasting Practices in Sixties and Seventies Avant-Garde Film," *October*, no. 103 (Winter 2003), p. 15-30.

[46] Pavle Levi, *Cinema by Other Means*, Oxford University Press, Oxford/New York 2012.

Video Art—Under- and Over-Exposure/Exhibition: Early Exhibitions in French-Speaking Switzerland
Geneviève Loup

Translated from the French by Miranda Stewart

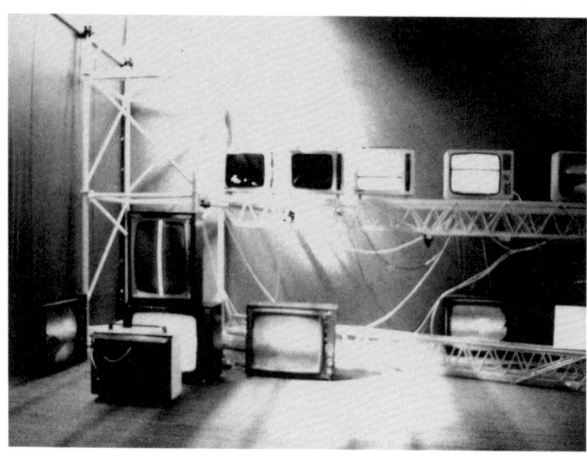

Jean Otth, *Abécédaire télévisuel I*, 1972
Exhibition view, *Implosion*, Musée cantonal des Beaux-Arts de Lausanne, Lausanne, 1972

Jean Otth, *Abécédaire télévisuel II*, 1973
Exhibition view, *Regarder ailleurs*, Palais de la Bourse, Bordeaux, 1973

The video art practices that emerged in French-speaking Switzerland at the end of the 1960s rapidly made inroads into galleries and museums. Some years previously, artists in the United States had already placed their video practices within a broader context. In this article I shall explore the permeability of and differences between artistic and aesthetic uses of video and communication strategies, which both demand social involvement and employ different distribution channels. I shall examine the dominant history of video art as a production largely centered in the United States and set it against a more minor, local history. I shall focus on two essential questions. How did video art emerge in French-speaking Switzerland, a distinct cultural and geographical area, and to what extent did it displace what had been created in the United States, and to a lesser extent in Europe, in the late 1960s? To what extent do video practices

tend to define and rearticulate the conditions of the
aesthetic experience in the course of their development?

Video Art—A New Field of Artistic Experimentation?

When artists from various fields of activity first became
interested in video, they did not initially focus on practices
specific to the electronic image. It was not until the 1970s
that video art became a field in its own right. It was an
aesthetic field which largely defined itself by what it was not,
and sought institutionalization by setting itself apart from
the structures of television broadcasting, the narrative
schemas and technical requirements of cinema, the immediacy of performance, and the picture-object of painting.
While artists explored the medium's production and
reception conditions, the legitimizing bodies evaluated
video art's aesthetic properties against a backdrop of
traditional artistic disciplines, failing to place it within any
particular social or political context.

Rosalind Krauss' essay, "Video: The Aesthetics of
Narcissism"[1] clearly exemplifies this trend. The art historian
criticizes a lack of externality in the works produced with
a closed-circuit device at the beginning of the 1970s, but
takes no account whatsoever of their political context.
For example, she construes Vito Acconci's *Centers* (1971) as
a parodic gesture of self-reflective withdrawal typical of
modern art. Indeed, her metaphorical interpretation of the
artist's outstretched arm pointing in the direction of the
screen as a narcissistic representation of the artist's double
does not capture the wider picture. Acconci used this
approach to question the mechanisms that underpin the
involvement of the audience in the television image.
Acconci's pointing gesture is not one of identification,
but rather evokes the iconography of propaganda posters
recruiting for the American army and the threat of the
pointed gun. This act of intimidation prompts viewers to
turn away from the image and focus their gaze on the
monitor frame. This tension between a point that focuses
attention and its deflection onto the broadcast medium
demonstrates in itself an openness toward the medium.

The modernist approach to video as a medium would
arguably appear to reject all consideration of cultural

references external to the field of art. Greenberg's focus on technical processes and the different sensory systems involved prevails—video is defined as a new territory to be explored via formal experimentation with the electronic image. Early historians of these practices saw the quest for unexpected aesthetic qualities in terms of their experience with other more familiar techniques. Dany Bloch,[2] who was, at that time, in charge of the video department of the musée d'Art moderne de la Ville de Paris, inscribed this territory of discovery within a very traditional lineage:

> Video art, a 1970s research art, must essentially be defined through research. The artist becomes a researcher—camera and video recorder replace tubes of paint and brushes, and the electronic apparatus, through the creative imagination stimulated by technology, acquires the potential to become painting or sculpture.[3]

Yet, this model of artist/researcher harnessing new technical resources comes from an earlier, more inventive species. Initial approaches to video were based on a particularly productive cross-fertilization between disparate cultural practices. Effectively, even before Nam June Paik used one of the first "portable" video cameras that began to appear on the market in 1965,[4] he reconfigured television circuits, drawing on his research at the Electronic Studio of the Westdeutscher Rundfunk (WDR). His approach sought to question indeterminacy and variability as parameters of musical composition,[5] and yet this perspective took on a whole new meaning when his "prepared" television sets were exhibited at Galerie Parnass, in Wuppertal in 1963. The notion of a "prepared" instrument, borrowed from John Cage, refers to a different way of using ordinary objects to alter tones and their intensity and resonance. This changes the function of the instrument and generates unusual sound effects. It is an approach which, when adapted to the television set, distorts how television programs are broadcast, by connecting the device to signals from frequency generators, radios, and recording devices. These interferences degrade the images and sounds that are broadcast, and result in dilated, duplicated, or diffracted patterns on the screen. At a different level, the exhibition visit is designed to take place in an acoustic environment with multiple entrances. By placing electronic circuits and the flow of the body through space in parallel, *Exposition of Music—Electronic Television* (1963) encouraged the audience to become aware of their active role in moving through space and time.

This interdisciplinary approach to experimentation was the result of attempts to decompartmentalize aesthetic fields at Black Mountain College, where John Cage, one of Paik's leading influences, had taught on an occasional basis from 1948. Courses at Black Mountain, following philosopher John Dewey's theory of experience, sought less to remove the constraints inherent to each practice than to reorganize the relationships between them. As Joëlle Zask succinctly observes:

> according to Dewey, any theory aiming to set individuals apart from their body of knowledge [...] is [...] contrary to modern scientific thinking. Experience, on the contrary, refers to a phase when knowledge is constituted by an individual in a cognitive process unrelated to representation, contemplation, or recognition of an idea supposedly already in existence [...] Experience is something that we do, not something that is done to us. Dewey explains that it consists of establishing a relationship between experiencing something and the fact of then going on to engage in an action. Without the guidance and channeling provided by both being affected and reacting to it, action is no more than agitation [...] Experience therefore develops in a space introduced by the intermittent discontinuity between means and ends, between a receptive state and an action, between a stimulus and a response.[6]

Consequently, according to Dewey, it is under "conditions of resistance and conflict"[7] proper to an open environment that "a continuity with the very process of living"[8] is brought into play.

This idea of a confrontation between different fields of knowledge is also at the center of the collaboration between engineers Billy Klüver[9] and Fred Waldhauer, and artists Robert Rauschenberg and Robert Whitman, which, in 1966, gave rise to Experiments in Art and Technology [E.A.T.], an organization dedicated to the interaction between art and technology. This organization emerged from the *9 Evenings: Theater and Engineering* (1966) festival, during which some 30 engineers specializing in new technology worked on projects by ten artists without interfering in the aesthetics of their work. This bringing together of different strands of knowledge created hitherto unknown technological instruments such as sound sensors and a modular system linked to theater production devices which adapted sound and light effects to the performers' movements.[10]

For believers in autonomous art, the adverse effects of technology were grounds enough for segregating aesthetic and scientific objects. Billy Klüver criticized this compartmentalization, which led to a loss of a sense of reality, as much in engineering as in art. In his view, interactions between art and technology demystified, in a practical way, those theories of communication that conferred on technology the power to extend the body by dilating it in space, thereby generating global awareness.[11]

Furthermore, the *9 Evenings* performances questioned the aims of industrial inventions. In Rauschenberg's *Open Score*, the lighting at the 69th Regiment Armory dimmed each time a tennis racquet hit the ball, until the room was plunged into darkness, and a crowd on the stage was filmed with infrared cameras. This technique had been used by the American army during the Vietnam War. In this instance, it did not serve to locate the enemy, but rather maintain a visual link between the performers' bodies and the audience. Other interventions used the moving image to question the economics of spectacle and the media and their physiological imperatives. In *Kisses Sweeter Than Wine* by Öyvind Fahlström,[12] the performers' actions were reproduced by a closed-circuit camera and set against intermittent projections of scenes taken from TV broadcasts, advertising, sci-fi films, and educational documentaries. All these different visual and auditory appeals, including the testimony of a soldier from the Korean War who had become a drug addict, reflected the background of political conflict and the military history of the Armory building. *Grass Field* by Alex Hay, produced in collaboration with engineers Herb Schneider and Robert Kieronski, used sine waves and other electronic noises to convey the apparently inaudible sounds of the artist's bodily organs including brainwaves, muscle activity, and eye movements. Fluctuations were captured and stimulated by electrodes and then amplified by loudspeakers. When his body became still, the imperceptible movements of his face were amplified by a video projection onto a large screen.[13]

While the video images produced for *9 Evenings: Theater and Engineering* amplify the performers' actions with a view to rendering specific physical processes perceptible, the technical experiments developed in the research laboratories at television channels targeted communications systems. For example, WGBH Educational Foundation in Boston, supported by the Rockefeller Foundation, hosted artists in residence. In 1969, program producer and director Fred Barzyk invited Allan Kaprow, Nam June Paik, Otto Piene, James Seawright, Thomas Tadlock, and Aldo Tambellini to produce works to be presented in a 30-minute broadcast. *The Medium is the Medium* (1969) was the name of one program and alluded to McLuhan's well-known proclamation "The Medium is the Message"[14] with a down-to-earth tautology.

For this communications theorist, the medium shapes and controls the scale and form of human association and action. The contents and uses of such media are as diverse as they are ineffectual in shaping the form of human association. Indeed, it is only too typical that the "content" of any medium blinds us to the character of the medium.[15]

Of all electrical technologies, television plays an educational role as it requires the viewer's active participation. Effectively, the electrical circuit's configuration logic replaces the fragmentation and linear links of mechanical technologies. This transition from the sequential to the simultaneous affects modes of perception: specialized segments of attention have shifted to total field, and we can now say, "the medium is the message" quite naturally.[16] This sensory switch calls on artists to sensitize the audience so that it is in the appropriate conditions to receive the media.

In response to this, artists began to question the utopian vision of a community brought together by television by highlighting various types of disconnection. *The Medium is the Medium* presented, among others, *Black* by Tambellini, *Hello* by Kaprow, *Electronic Light Ballet* by Piene, and *Electronic Opera 1* by Paik. While Paik transformed images of a dancer in the studio and TV footage into graphic compositions, Kaprow connected four locations via video input. Two cameras were placed in the WGBH channel studios, with two more in a school and in MIT. All sites were linked via a closed-circuit television network, which allowed them to transmit and receive the broadcast through a device similar to one used for telephone conferencing. To connect, passersby had to introduce themselves with the following words: "Hello, I see you." The technicians in the control room randomly filtered the sounds and images from all four sites, broadcasting partial sequences, in a form of crosstalk that emphasized the falseness of exchanges based on phatic communication.

Following the success of this broadcast, between 1969 and 1970 Paik enjoyed a residency at this very channel. The artist used part of his grant to go to Tokyo and create a video synthesizer with engineer Shuya Abe. The Paik-Abe Synthesizer was designed to edit several live sources taken from television broadcasts, colorize them, and then alter relationships between contrasts and brightness. This research not only sought to trigger optical effects by manipulating sound, but also to push the boundaries of the technical equipment used by the television studios. Unlike the aesthetics of cinema editing which proceeds by shots, the electronic image is worked on from a scan line. This technical characteristic makes it possible to cut elements from a shot as well as to edit and overlay them to allow disparate spaces and times to coexist. Paik went on to deploy the different potential effects generated by this synthesizer in *Global Groove* (1973), a videotape produced and broadcast by the New York channel, WNET-TV.

In certain countries such as Germany, the cultural remit of television channels encouraged the production of artistic projects in response to individual initiatives. Gerry Schum's *Fernsehgalerie*, for example, was designed as a specific exhibition format intended for television. *Land Art*, which launched the gallery's program in 1969, presented, on the Sender Freies Berlin public station, a series of artists' films shot on film. Although the use of film was a first experience for some of these artists, the transition from situated three-dimensional interventions to their optical transmission problematized the issue of moving works outside of their artistic context, and the impermanence of the exhibition itself. Television mediation also involves placing artistic projects in a particular slot in a TV schedule. This delocalization of production sites is problematized in terms of the migration of works toward what Robert Smithson referred to as "dissolving terrain."[17]

While, as Philippe Dubois has said, video was "a way of thinking television with its own forms," these attempts did not bring about the expected cultural transformation.[18] In "Video Art: Old Wine, New Bottle," Allan Kaprow concluded that the use of television as an art medium had not displaced traditional conceptual frameworks or aesthetic attitudes.[19] Indeed, the impact of any changes in artistic paradigms generated by taped art performances and video installations has been of lesser importance than the cultural and social transformations brought about by militant video. The art market has encouraged artists to adopt a particular frame of reference, and this has led to videotapes of artistic performances being presented as "if in a pocket movie theater."[20] Nevertheless, closed-circuit video installations have drawn attention to the circumstantial factors that encourage audiences to observe their own performances both as actors and viewers of a situation. This relationship with a particular environment seeks to regulate the ecology of what Gilbert Simondon has called an "associated" milieu that acts as a connective force between internal and external realities.[21] However, according to Kaprow, the use of hardware and linkage does not actually involve the participation of the audience unless the exhibition context is stratified and multifaceted. Consequently, the viewer's body cannot be directed by predetermined surroundings. The production of a changing space in which viewers can act allows individuals to develop relationships selectively, and organize simultaneous events with particular receptiveness. This local experience of attention is vastly more intense than the myth of a global awareness automatically stimulated by electronic media.[22]

Influenced by John Cage's classes on the composition of experimental music at the New School for Social Research in New York, in 1959, Kaprow called into question the aesthetic underpinnings of the categories established by the open forms of happenings and environments. He had participated in a WGBH research program in 1969 and also produced several videos and documented his happenings. His first tape, *Then*, dates from 1974. In this work, presented, among others, at the *Impact Art Video Art 74* exhibition in Lausanne, to which we shall return, the artist encouraged the audience to exercise its observation skills and put to the test its preconceived notions. In the first part, a close-up of a man's face draws attention to the main action—an ice cube is melting in his mouth. The voice of a woman offscreen asks, "How much longer?" In response, he silently shakes his head. He finally swallows the melted ice once it has changed from solid to liquid. In response to the spectator's potential impression of slowness, he questions our perception of time by repeating the same question over and over again. Then the man says, "Now," and this present moment stands in a counterpoint to the past evoked by the title of the tape.

In the next part, a hand holds a glowing object and its rays penetrate the skin. A woman's voice asks, "Is it light enough?"[23] A man's voice replies, "Not yet." Again, the situation is repeated until the heat of the light becomes intolerable and the bulb is dropped. When the woman asks the question again, the response is in the affirmative. The lightbulb swings from an electrical cord placed above a plate on which there is an ice cube melting under the effects of the heat. The woman's voice asks about the cube and its wetness.

By questioning the audience's recognition reflexes in this way, viewers are led to reconsider the various ways in which a same situation can be defined. Experimentation is now seen as the "testing or trial of a principle."[24] While the use of a video camera by Kaprow allowed him to measure the extent of local actions over a period of time and to contrast the cold light of the photons of the electronic image with incandescence, the real point of this technique was to enable the artist to carefully examine the apparent evidence of banal situations.

The definition of experimentation offered by Elie During, Laurent Jeanpierre, Christophe Kihm, and Dork Zabunyan sums up this approach:

> Experimental art is a technique of questions rather than answers [...] Experimentation, understood as the pivot between artistic activity and ignorance, is a strategy whereby incompetence contains within it the potential for a new regime of competence.[25]

Consequently, artists who experiment are not acting as experts or as guarantors of a particular aesthetic genre, nor are they guided in their approach by the innovation offered by new technologies. In the words of Laurent Jeanpierre, "to experiment, simply using a new material, transferring a unique gesture from one medium to another, or even producing new creative rules or new constraints, is not enough in itself."[26] Artistic practices produce astonishment when they resist a preprogrammed transformation process and trigger the unforeseen in a particular set of circumstances—"Experimentation becomes a critical operator for art once the decision has been taken to make 'local use' of it."[27]

A Circumscribed Topos—The Early Days of Video Art in French-Speaking Switzerland

What effectively happens when these issues are framed within a local geographical area? What happens to research that first emerged in the United States and Germany when it migrates toward artistic practices that do not flourish under the same technological conditions? In our case, French-speaking Switzerland lacked any substantial industrial economy comparatively speaking. In America artists benefited from the technical infrastructure of television channels mainly funded by foundations of entrepreneurs, yet no such resources existed in Switzerland. However, its art and gallery markets were extremely active, as can be seen from the International Salon of Pilot Galleries. Three such salons had been organized by René Berger at the Musée cantonal des Beaux-Arts de Lausanne in 1963, 1966, and 1970, when he was director (until 1981). At the last of the salons, exhibitors included the Howard Wise Gallery. In 1969, this New York gallery had produced one of the first video art exhibitions, entitled *TV as a Creative Medium*. The gallery owner declared in the exhibition catalogue that television had the power to transform education, and be the stepping-stone to a communications utopia.[28] Paik offered *Participation TV* as one of the works, an installation comprising several color television monitors with a feedback effect that offered the audience a multiplied image with blurred edges.

In French-speaking Switzerland *ACTION/FILM/VIDEO*, an early exhibition of video art and films, was held at the Impact Group Gallery and the Galerie de l'Académie in 1972.[29] This group, founded in 1968 by Jean Scheurer, Pierre Guberan, Henri Barbier, Jean-Claude Schauenberg, Jacques Dominique Rouiller, and Kurt von Ballmoos, with Bertrand Caspar, Archibald Ganslmayr, Mick Müller, and Jean-Pierre Tzaud, brought together painters and sculptors to work on a project designed to display contemporary art.[30] This exhibition, which jointly presented film and video, was organized by Barbier, Schauenberg, Scheurer, Janos Urban, and Claude Vallon.[31] Nevertheless, ultimately, interest in video was for the most part driven by Jean Otth, the main organizer of the *Impact Art Video Art 74* exhibition. By that time he had finished his studies in history of art at Lausanne University and subsequently at the Ecole des Beaux-Arts de Lausanne, and had also attended classes given by René Berger at the University since 1969: "Aesthetics and Mass Media: Television." In this course, Berger examined works by contemporary artists including Otth, Gérald Minkoff, and Fred Forest. Furthermore, Berger had been the expert consulted by cultural journalist Claude Vallon when he wrote "René Berger, Director-Curator of the Musée cantonal des Beaux-Arts, Lausanne. The era of the video recorder" for the *ACTION/FILM/VIDEO* exhibition catalogue.

As noted by François Bovier in his article "The Medium Is the Network,"[32] the artists participating in the *ACTION/FILM/VIDEO* exhibition were recruited by means of a registration form sent to local and international artists and to organizations such as the Yellow Now Gallery. In his opening remarks to the catalogue, Claude Vallon declared that this event was designed to question "communication, image, and image content" through cinema. Nevertheless, the economy of cinema was challenged by the more independent economy of video:

> Artists are now explorers, scientists, whose inventiveness (and this is the critical word) is needed by others and lays the ground for yet more works. We are now engaged in a research process, where we will, nonetheless, need to be careful not to fuel a new art market.

This familiar rhetoric around innovation was played out socially, where the video recorder was used in different ways to observe behaviors, and even became an instrument to bring people together in community interactions. As Berger declared in his interview with Vallon, this interweaving of relationships was the result of a technical metaphor for the continuous motion of the videotape and its simultaneous viewing:

> There is a difference between the nature of cinema and that of video. The former involves editing while the latter abhors editing. It is a wild instrument that enables immediate confrontation, and that ultimately has its own particular character. Cinema is a spectacle that is repeated.[33]

Jacques Monnier, in his contribution to the catalogue, distinguishes between the artistic practices of video and the professional practices of filmmakers and camera operators for television. He also refers to the precarious nature of the exhibition, which has more in common with a workplace and transit area than the planned layout of gallery space:

> some perforated crates which served interchangeably as seats or pedestals for the devices, wires trailing freely from electric plugs to projectors, video recorders, and monitors, three or four cathode-ray screens, the walls themselves serving as receptacles for images which, for brief moments, transformed their rough edges into lunar craters. Generally

speaking, the equipment rejected any value as a fixed asset and any monumental status which might have undermined the desire of visitors, who were free to enter and leave as they wish, to attend the simultaneous screenings standing up, sitting down, or even lying on the ground.[34]

In this early exhibition, the Impact Group related the concept of action to film and video production processes and also to the stealthy way in which an audience, invited to walk about in an unstable environment, views images. Unlike the optical absorption in a picture as advocated by Greenberg, here the viewer's body is brought into play by the exhibition's installation apparatus. While walls are no longer designed to be homogenous surfaces, the discontinuous space takes the display principle underlying the exhibition even further by applying a sequential logic; indeed, François Bovier notes that while "silver and magnetic tapes shared the space [they] were not screened simultaneously: from 6.30pm to 11pm, depending on the day, either videotapes or films were screened on the ground floor (in the Impact Gallery) and on the first floor (in the Galerie de l'Académie)."[35]

The artistic bent of video becomes even clearer in the second event, *Impact Art Video Art 74*, organized by the Impact Group two years later. There has been further research into historical significance of these two events in "Exhibited Cinema," a research project directed by François Bovier at the École cantonale d'art de Lausanne. Furthermore, a selection of videos from these two exhibitions was set up (rather than reconstructed) at the Circuit art space in Lausanne, from April 17 to May 23, 2015.[36] In the original *ACTION/FILM/VIDEO* catalogue, there was no indication of how the videos and 16mm and 8mm films were arranged in space. Artists including Jochen Gerz, Eric Andersen, and Jacques Louis Nyst participated, along with others who are less well known. There was a good representation of the first artists from French-speaking Switzerland whose practices included video: Minkoff (who also showed several Super-8 films), Otth, Urban, and René Bauermeister, who, on this occasion, only showed Super-8 and 16mm films. Filmmakers such as Erwin Huppert and Eva Lurati also took part in the exhibition.

The exhibition catalogue included texts by Minkoff and Otth—these were documents provided by the artists for the exhibition. While Minkoff used video as a medium to create a tautological mise en abyme, for Otth, "[the] televisual and videotape space is a pictorial space."[37] These words were used when talking about *Ombre A* (*Shadow A*) (1972), Otth's very first video work produced in collaboration with Jean Scheurer, which was shown in this exhibition, and is described in these terms in a monographic catalogue produced by the Centre d'Art Contemporain in Geneva:

> In the first part, this tape is an attempt to capture a shadow graphically. To visualize a duration I used a spray of black paint to mark a shadow in the present, and an anticipated one in the future. The chosen topic was that of a menhir. In the second part, there is the formal destruction of my own shadow, first with black paint, and then with synthetic "sand." In terms of televisual language, this work primarily uses the pictorial possibilities offered by values (video's range from black to white).[38]

As part of the *Limites* series, this work contrasts a video recording with a primary gesture of inscription. The outline used to mark out the contours of a silhouette created by a light projection is constantly redefined by the instability of the shadow. This bringing together of two, arguably anachronistic, techniques, questions the historical and anthropological motivations for creating films through capturing images. To identify what is happening in the field of vision, the viewer must distinguish between different levels of reality, and yet any such demarcation is blurred by the way in which video images constantly reconfigure the situation.

This work, grounded in the anachronistic gap between the gesture, which is at the origin of the drawing, and video, which is the means of reproduction, was invested with new meaning at an exhibition curated by Michel Thévoz, and presented from November 3 to December 10 of that year at the Musée cantonal des Beaux-Arts de Lausanne: *Implosion, Musée expérimental 3* (*Implosion, Experimental Museum 3*).[39] This particular Otth video is associated with different types of perturbation streamed over 12 monitors. Half of these images are captured on a video recorder and then manipulated for light and contrast: *Perturbation X, Perturbation I, Perturbation II, Perturbation III, TV—Autoportrait, Ombre A* (1972). These disruptions allow the artist to reveal the visual nature of "the very structure of televised material." He also gives visibility to "underlying aesthetics" and forges a relationship between the instability of the TV picture and the luminescence of the electronic image in resonance with the variations in texture and light found in an Impressionist painting.

In *TV—Autoportrait*, the artist intermittently displays the "de-structuring" of the image by partially concealing the readability of his portrait. The use of scratches and stripes of different depths disrupts the distinction between the surfaces and the underlying strata of the image, which are swapped around by effects of over- and under-exposure to light. The video has no sound recording and yet the metamorphoses of the pictures created by technical interference are dynamic, in counterpoint to the relatively static position of the artist. These technical manipulations were created by an engineer and then selected by the artist: "In this experiment there has been no alteration of the image other than by electronic means."[40] Its random, rhythmical noise is reminiscent of the flicker effect and the flapping of the frames at the heart of the very notion of cinema. This unstable electronic signal tests both the viewer's concentration and the persistence of the image.

The artist covered the screens of the remaining monitors of *Découpages-Perturbations* (*Cuttings-Perturbations*) with cut up pieces of black plastic. By obliterating part of the image in this way, he reframes the reception of programs by partially restricting the field of vision and increasing the importance of sound. This focuses attention on random details; it also, paradoxically, intensifies observation by limiting the field of vision. The fourth exercise in this series, *Abécédaire télévisuel* (*Television Alphabet Book*) involves the television set, as described by the artist, as a "minimalist sculpture."[41] Later called *Menhir TV*, this upturned monitor broadcast a white line in an analog orientation. But unlike the immobile axis of *Zen For TV* that was presented by Paik at the *Exposition of Music—Electronic Television* in 1963, the white line across the screen of *Menhir TV* subdivides as it oscillates from right to left. This movement then accentuates the fragmentary nature of the electronic signal, evoking the pulses of an oscilloscope measuring amplitude variation.

This particular Otth collection of videotapes and monitors is associated with slides, to which the artist refers as "proofs." In photographic documents of the exhibition which can be viewed on the *Autour du Concile de Nicée* (*On the Council of Nicea*) DVD,[42] monitors of different sizes are lined up on a shelf, others are placed underneath at different heights, set back against the wall. *TV—Autoportrait* is projected on the wall, as befits a permeable approach to video and film formats. This installation adopted a different configuration when it was shown again the following year in Bordeaux as part of *Regarder ailleurs* (*Look Elsewhere*),[43] the first contemporary art exhibition organized at the CAPC-musée d'Art contemporain de Bordeaux by Jean-Louis Froment, in which the television sets were arranged on scaffolding reminiscent of a building site.

The principle of accumulation, dislocation, and reassembling, which underlies this installation, along with the manipulation of television programs, reflects descriptions of the *Implosion* exhibition, namely "the brutal disintegration of the TV receivers, the central tube of which is a vacuum."[44] The exhibition curator evoked economic, social, and ecological disturbances, and referred to McLuhan to encourage artists to do something to offset the paralysis caused by technology by offering other relationships with the environment. Any "individual consciousness" elicited by a short-circuit to the nervous system was indeed threatened, under the twin pressures of information saturation and media processing. While this metaphor for a state of mind was potentially employed to refer to techniques other than electronics, the exhibition, which brought together different artistic practices, showcased video works that experimented with changes in sensory perception. In it, the media were no longer viewed as an extension of the body, but rather as a physiological constraint to be re-sensitized. The installations presented disorganized the principle of visibility appropriate to the museum as institution, and caused its premises to implode through entropic circulation.

Vilém Flusser, Professor of Communications Theory at the University of São Paulo, introduced the issue of the exteriority of the field of art by offering a rereading of the closed-circuit device in "Minkoff's Mirrors":

> Currently art is art about art and knowledge has started to become concerned with the possibility of knowing knowledge [...] We are beginning to feel dizzy, because the reflecting mirror opens to show an abyss, a reduction "ad infinitum," which threatens to swallow us up [...] If we want an idea of what this abyss means, we should describe Minkoff's experience in down-to-earth terms. Three mirrors reflect each other, namely a television screen, a camera, and a video recorder, and all three are linked to each other in a circle. The camera films the screen, the screen absorbs the camera, the video recorder records this process, the screen absorbs the videotape, the camera absorbs the tape on the screen and so on ad infinitum. But this is not, it should be said, a closed circuit [...] The circuit that I am describing is open, we can intervene between and within the reflecting mirrors, we can become an integral part thereof, we can act and suffer therein, in terms of the hierarchy of the abyss, because the abyss of one mirror is none other than the surface of another and, at a second level, the abyss of a third, etc. [...] surfaces are constantly being pushed back. We should consider two things: 1) chronology has changed perspective, what was once anteriority is now depth. 2) Minkoff is not only the viewer's object as in traditional mirrors, but he is his own object in a hierarchy that extends to the abyss, and in every level of this hierarchy.[45]

Otth, further questioning the duplication of the roles of actor and viewer, launched *Impact Art Video Art 74* to delve further into the disparate practices of video. This exhibition lasted for eight days, similar in length to a festival format. It was presented at the Musée des Arts décoratifs de la Ville de Lausanne, and organized with two other artists, Henri Barbier and Jean-Claude Schauenberg, along with the engineer Serge Marendaz. It sought to "portray video as an artistic medium, without necessarily emphasizing this feature over all others, e.g. sociological, political, or educational video."[46] Works by 90 artists were presented, including videos by Vito Acconci, Trisha Brown, Valie Export, Luciano Fabro, Fred Forest, Simone Forti, Jochen Gerz, Luciano Giaccari, Frank Gillette, Dan Graham, Joan Jonas, Allan Kaprow, Jannis Kounellis, Shigeko Kubota, Les Levine, Urs Lüthi, Mario Merz, Gérald Minkoff, Antoni Muntadas, Maurizio Nannucci, Muriel Olesen, Dennis Oppenheim, Jean Otth, Nam June Paik, Charlemagne Palestine, Yvonne Rainer, Martha Rosler, Sarkis, Allan Sekula, Janos Urban, Woody & Steina Vasulka, Bill Viola, Wolf Vostell, and Peter Weibel.

The catalogue included an extract from a thesis by Luciano Giaccari, at the time the artistic director of Studio 970/2 in Varese, a center for video-related studies and activities. The author distinguishes between practices by format and viewing practice: videotapes, recordings of performances, and video environments. These artistic practices are separate from the mediating role of documentation, reporting, and educational and critical video. However, while different purposes can indeed be identified, individual fields are, unfortunately, viewed here as closed entities governed by predetermined categories.

Further academic support was provided by René Berger, who played an important role in giving this exhibition international importance. In "L'Art vidéo: défis et paradoxes"[47] (Video Art: Challenges and Paradoxes), video is seen as a specific art separate from television insofar as it reconfigures the latter's modes of broadcasting and reception. Compared with traditional techniques, video art permits a reflexive experience in observation: "Painting stops at the portrait. Video captures the movement both of what is outside and what is within."[48] Furthermore, by exposing the very structure of the image, it serves to demystify new technologies. By escaping the "economic imperative" of market value, "it is clear that under these conditions any judgments we may make about video art cannot simply be modeled on our habitual practice."[49] He criticizes Allan Kaprow for framing the challenges of video art as issues of legitimacy. For him, its disparate uses open the doors to new fields of research related, among other things, to the introduction of a temporal dimension into the exhibition space. However, his objection is based on a misunderstanding of the American artist, whose criticism was directed more at the difficulty experienced by the art world in shedding its dominant conceptual framework.

The temporal dimension introduced by video questions the unified character of the exhibition. Otth, in *Anatomie de l'éternité* (*Anatomy of Eternity*) (1974), makes simultaneous use of a live closed-circuit recording, and prerecorded video and sound tracks. The camera, set on a tripod, captures a bunch of dried flowers, and the image is conveyed live to a monitor. It alternately broadcasts previous recordings, in such a way as to disturb the temporal anchoring of the visible image. When viewers stand in front of the camera, they can verify its actual nature. At the same time, a soundtrack of a reading of *A Universal History of Infamy. A History of Eternity* by Jorge Luis Borges accompanies the image. In one of the photographs of the exhibition, the machines are placed at random on a worktable that would be more at home in a workshop than in the framed spaces of a museum.

Otth exhibited three more videotapes. *Hommage à Mondrian* (*Homage to Mondrian*) (1972), which is part of the *TV-Perturbations* series, and comprises a still shot of a painting by the modern artist. The frame shows a picture hung on the wall of a museum, and this lets the viewer see details of the architecture of the exhibition space and the neon lighting system. The geometric lines of the pictorial composition have been reconfigured by the lines of the technical interference found in video, and then obscured by distortions of the image, which create depth beneath the surface of the screen. The obliterations render the geometric pattern of the painting unreadable as the independence of the abstraction is overlaid by the infrastructure used to mediate it, namely the exhibition and the documentary shot. Video reproduction of the canvas highlights, by framing the shot in a particular way, the paradoxical visibility of the exhibition device, and redirects attention toward the environment outside the monitor screen. As Walter Benjamin has indeed noted, architecture attracts less rapt attention, with the viewer "noticing the object in an incidental fashion."[50] This approach, which differs from the contemplation of the expert eye, raises the issue of the habituation produced by visual devices that occupy the social space.

Working at the limits of perception, the artist describes this as "an extremely simple operation where the primary action is to separate two forms" and create a rift between "two surfaces," thereby questioning the ambiguous spatiality of the video image. The limit is part of the dialectic between a dark contour line that isolates, and a passage that "opens" and is in itself a fascinating problem that has been overlooked because of its ostensibly trivial nature.[51]

Limite B (le lac) (*Limit B [The Lake]*) (1973) marks the gap that is needed to bring nuanced distinctions into play. The image of a sunset over Lake Geneva reveals the silhouette of a mountain range, and reflections of sunlight on water accompanied by the murmur of the waves. The sun's rays reflected in the water make the horizon stand out. Superimposed on this recording is an electronic horizontal white line that moves up and down in counterpoint to the limits of the field of vision. *Limite E* (1973) handles the coexistence of different levels of reality differently; the artist attempts to mark the outline of his shadow against a wall, and then his image on a slide in which he appears, seen from the back, drawing on a wall, and finally, superimposed on the traced outline, his image is projected in Super-8. The limit does not signify confinement, but rather the possibility of redefining the parameters of an aesthetic experience.

The Testing of Institutional Topos

Otth's *Limite E* was the first video purchased by Lausanne's Musée cantonal des Beaux-Arts, in 1973. The artist's studio, essentially a confined area for experimentation, can be contrasted with the permanence of institutional collections, which are designed to preserve our heritage. In "Les mousquetaires de l'invisible: la vidéo-art en Suisse"[52] (The Musketeers of the Invisible: Video Art in Switzerland), an article published in 1977, Berger presented the first Swiss artists to work in video: Bauermeister, Minkoff, Muriel Olesen, Otth, Urban, Urs Lüthi, Jacques Guyonnet, and Geneviève Calame. These people may well have "started working later than Paik, Gillette, Ira Schneider, Peter Campus, Beryl Korot, and many others,"[53] but genealogy is no longer a principle that applies in this context; "this is perhaps the first time in the history of art that an explanation by influence fails."[54] Nevertheless, prior to this generation, Paik recognized Cage's contribution in *A Tribute to John Cage* (1973/1976)—the composer's modus operandi influenced his own approach to experimentation. To what extent was Switzerland really a "peripheral place for video"[55] to use Berger's term? Why should it be seen as immune to historical and geographical relationships, when the overriding feature of the 1972 and 1974 Impact Group exhibitions was precisely its inclusion in an international context, thereby affording Swiss artists the opportunity to meet much wider challenges?

In the United States and certain countries in Europe, artists had used television as an additional venue for technical experimentation and a means of broadcasting and making works more publicly accessible. Why, then, would a move to an exhibition format have curbed ambitions such as these? For René Berger, experimentation had now been relocated in the break with the forms and patterns of television communication, and attention had now been focused on clearly defined spaces, in counterpoint to the dominant structures of what he called "techno-communication." In 1981, Berger referred to the relationships of scale involved in moving from a place of exhibition to its exteriority: "In that case, installations are, if I may say so, relocation models with the corollary that 'places' other than those that we are accustomed to in our everyday practice are not only possible, but already exist latently."[56]

Nevertheless, the relationship between a work and a particular political, social, or economic environment is governed by symbolic agency: "Topographic determination comes with a symbolic determination, which regulates and institutionalizes a particular type of social relationship (this explains my use of the term 'topos')."[57]

While these institutions set up partitions that restrict the movement of viewers, video installations, by encouraging the body to position itself in space, highlight this cultural segmentation. In addition to this topographic representation, authors such as Kurt Lewin have highlighted the psychological impact of topology, which does not derive from metaphorical relationships, but rather from behavioral effects produced by the positioning of an individual in a particular environment.[58]

Although the structures of this social and cultural environment are unlikely to have been reconfigured, which suggests, as does Jean Otth, that we would be better to stop "wasting our time justifying this medium,"[59] people like Berger have nonetheless helped to embed new artistic practices into a local landscape still steeped in cultural traditions.[60] The definition of a field specific to video later led to the creation of spaces specifically designed for these purposes. In French-speaking Switzerland, the International Video Week founded by André Iten in 1985 became the main video event; it was significantly renamed the Biennial of Moving Images in 1999 and was held at the Centre pour l'image contemporaine Saint-Gervais (CIC), in Geneva until 2005.[61] The CIC closed down in 2008, and the Biennial was taken over by the Centre d'Art Contemporain in Geneva in 2014. It is fairly safe to assume that greater independence is to be found in exhibition areas outside institutions that allow experimentation with current issues in video art.[62]

The aesthetic experience of video works is determined by the particular geographical and historical circumstances of the locality in which they are produced and disseminated; in return, video art offers insights at a local level into the production and reception conditions of different artistic practices. The traditional exhibition format marked the beginnings of video art in French-speaking Switzerland, and this has led art historians to reproduce familiar conceptual categories. In this regional context, the fact that artists have stepped outside museum institutions can be seen less in current social and political realities than in the transformations in perception brought about by new forms of communication.

Jean Otth, *Abécédaire télévisuel I*, 1972
Exhibition view, *Implosion*, Musée cantonal des Beaux-Arts de Lausanne, Lausanne, 1972

[1] Rosalind Krauss, "Video: The Aesthetics of Narcissism," *October*, vol. 1 (Spring 1976), p. 50–64.
[2] Dany Bloch, who was born in 1925 and died in 1988, was a video art specialist in France. She published her thesis on video art in 1982: Dany Bloch, *Art et vidéo 1960–1980/82*, Editions Flaviana, Locarno 1982.
[3] Dany Bloch, "L'art-vidéo," *Traverses* ("Circuits/courts circuits") (16 September 1979), Centre National d'Art et de Culture Georges-Pompidou/Éditions de Minuit, p. 72–80.
[4] The quotation marks are perfectly justified—the Portapak was neither portable nor light in 1965 and required an electrical socket.
[5] Susanne Neuburger, "Terrific Exhibit. 'Time Art' alias Music in the Exhibition Genre," Susanne Neuburger (ed.), *Nam June Paik. Exposition of Music, Electronic Television, Revisited*, Walther König, Vienna/Cologne 2009, p. 31–43.
[6] Joëlle Zask, "Le courage de l'expérience," Jean-Pierre Cometti, Éric Giraud (eds.), *Black Mountain College. Art, démocratie, utopie*, Centre International de Poésie/Presses universitaires de Rennes, coll. "Arts contemporains," Marseille/Rennes 2014, p. 20.
[7] John Dewey, *Art as Experience*, Perigee Books, New York 1934, p. 35.
[8] *Ibid.*, p. 68.
[9] Billy Klüver had a PhD in electrical engineering and, from 1958, was employed by Bell Telephone Laboratories where he carried out research into lasers.
[10] Sylvie Lacerte, "*9 Evenings* and Experiments in Art and Technology: A Gap to Fill in Art History's Recent Chronicles," Dieter Daniels, Barbara U. Schmidt (eds.), *Artists As Inventors. Inventors as Artists*, Hatje Cantz, Ostfildern 2008, p. 160.
[11] Billy Klüver about *9 Evenings*, quoted by S. Lacerte, p. 163–164: "It wanted to achieve very specific practical and social goals. Its development was coincident in time with the spreading mysticism about technology, the McLuhan concept that the communication means were the extensions of the body, the psychedelic experience as an element of art!" Harriet De Long, *9 Evenings: Theatre and Engineering* [manuscript]; Series I. Project files; box 2, "9 Evenings," 1966; Experiments in Art and Technology; Records, 1966–1993; Getty Research Institute, Research Library, Accession no. 940003.
[12] Descriptions of the performance found on The Daniel Langlois Foundation website, which contains all the records of *9 Evenings*: http://www.fondation-langlois.org/html/e/page.php?NumPage=1792, last accessed March 2020.
[13] Information from Catherine Morris, "9 Evenings: Theatre & Engineering," Sabine Breitwieser (ed.), *EAT Experiments in Art and Technology*, Walther König/Museum der Moderne, Cologne/Salzburg 2015, p. 84, 85, 89.
[14] Marshall McLuhan, *Understanding Media: The Extensions of Man*, McGraw-Hill Company, New York 1964. It should be remembered that the first chapter of the book is entitled "The Medium is the Message."
[15] *Ibid.*, p. 27.
[16] *Ibid.*, p. 31.
[17] "The Land Art films shot by Gerry Schum of the *Fernsehgalerie* in Berlin leave something to be desired; nevertheless, they do indicate an attempt to deal with art in the landscape. Television has the power to dilate the 'great outdoors' into sordid frontiers full of grayness and electrical static. Vast geographies are contracted into dim borders and incalculable sites. Schum's 'Television gallery' proliferates the results of Long, Flanagan, Oppenheim, Beuys, Dibbets, De Maria, Heizer, and myself over unknown channels which bifurcate into dissolving terrains." Robert Smithson, "Art Through the Camera's Eye," 1971, a text that remained unpublished during the artist's lifetime, Jack Flam (ed.), *Robert Smithson: The Collected Writings*, University of California Press, Los Angeles 1996, p. 374. Smithson mentions Beuys, who went on to participate in a later project called *Identifications*.
[18] Philippe Dubois, "L'état-vidéo: une forme qui pense. Une histoire en deux mouvements," Christophe Boutin (ed.), *Vidéo Topiques. Tours et retours de l'art vidéo*, Musée d'art moderne et contemporain, Strasbourg 2002, p. 49.
[19] Allan Kaprow, "Video Art: Old Wine, New Bottle," *Artforum*, vol. 12, no 10 (1974), p. 46–49.
[20] "It is worth mentioning in the context of video art tapes, because this is the way the tapes are presented to the audience: as if in a pocket movie theater." *Ibid.*, p. 46.
[21] See Gilbert Simondon, *L'Individuation à la lumière des notions de forme et d'information*, Éditions Jérôme Millon, Grenoble 2005.
[22] "This hardware linkage proposes to positively alter the behavior of human and nonhuman participants alike, as if it were some infinitely readjustable ecology." Allan Kaprow, "Video Art: Old Wine, New Bottle," p. 47.
[23] The phrase "Is it light enough?" plays on the polysemy of the word light, which is used both in terms of brightness and weight.
[24] Allan Kaprow, "Experimental Art" [1966], *Essays on the Blurring of Art and Life: Expanded Edition* (articles compiled by Jeff Kelley), University of California Press, Berkeley/Los Angeles/London 2003, p. 72.
[25] Elie During, Laurent Jeanpierre, Christophe Kihm, Dork Zabunyan, "Introduction," *In actu. De l'expérimental dans l'art*, Les presses du réel, Dijon 2009, p. 18.
[26] Laurent Jeanpierre, "Introduction aux conditions de l'art experimental," *In actu. De l'expérimental dans l'art*, p. 312.
[27] *Ibid.*, p. 15.
[28] See *TV as a Creative Medium*, exh. cat., Howard Wise Gallery, New York 1969.
[29] In addition to information from original exhibition catalogues, further historical details can be found in François Bovier, "'The Medium Is the Network'—the Impact Group and the Emergence of Video Art in French-speaking Switzerland," translated from the French by Miranda Stewart, in François Bovier (ed.), *Early Video Art and Experimental Film Networks. French-speaking Switzerland in 1974: a Case for "Minor History"*, ECAL/Les presses du réel, Lausanne/Dijon 2017, p. 57–72.
[30] The name of Christiane Cornuz appears in the introduction to the catalogue. List supplemented by research from François Bovier.
[31] See *Impact*, *ACTION/FILM/VIDEO*, Lausanne, Galerie Impact, 1972, n. p. It should be noted that Janos Urban, an artist close to Fluxus, was a pioneer of video art in French-speaking Switzerland, and that Claude Vallon was a cultural journalist. This catalogue has been reproduced in part in François Bovier and Tristan Lavoyer (eds.), *Black White Box Cube*, ECAL/Circuit, Lausanne 2015.
[32] François Bovier, "'The Medium Is the Network'—the Impact Group and the Emergence of Video Art in French-speaking Switzerland."
[33] Claude Vallon, "Nouvelles aventures", *ACTION/FILM/VIDEO*, n. p.
[34] Jacques Monnier, "Videonomad", *ACTION/FILM/VIDEO*, n. p.
[35] François Bovier, "'The Medium Is the Network'—the Impact Group and the Emergence of Video Art in French-speaking Switzerland."
[36] See François Bovier, Tristan Lavoyer (eds.), *Black White Box Cube*.
[37] These words have been reproduced in "Espace TV" (May 1972), in *Jean Otth. Travaux vidéo 1970–1980*, exh. cat., Centre d'art contemporain, Geneva 1980, p. 1.

[38] Jean Otth, introductory text to *Ombre A* (1972), in *Jean Otth, Travaux vidéo 1970–1980*, p. 59.
[39] *Implosion, Musée expérimental 3: Otth, Grob, Huber, Urban, Zaugg, Bertin, Camesi, Gramse, Minkoff, Villalba, Olivotto, Kalkmann, Ducimetiere, Brocklehurst*, Musée cantonal des Beaux-Arts, Lausanne 1972.
[40] Jean Otth, introductory text to *Autoportrait I* (1972), *Jean Otth. Travaux vidéo 1970–1980*, p. 19.
[41] "Exercice IV de l'abécédaire televisual," Irene Schubiger (ed.), *Reconstructing Swiss Video Art from the 1970s and 1980s*, JRP|Ringier, Zurich 2009, p. 92.
[42] *Jean Otth, Autour du Concile de Nicée, Anarchive 4* (DVD edited by Anne-Marie Duguet), 2007.
[43] *Regarder ailleurs: Jean Otth, Gina Pane, Gérard Titus-Carmel, Claude Viallat*, Palais de la Bourse, Bordeaux 1973.
[44] Michel Thévoz, "Implosion," *Implosion, Musée expérimental 3*, p. 1.
[45] Vilém Flusser, "Les Miroirs de Minkoff," *Implosion, Musée expérimental 3*, p. 41.
[46] *Impact Art Video Art 74*, Galerie Impact, Lausanne 1974, n. p.
[47] This text was initially published in the *Impact Art Video Art 74* catalogue, and was later reproduced in the volume edited by François Bovier and Adeena Mey, *René Berger, L'Art vidéo et autres essais (1971–1997)*, JRP|Ringier/Les Presses du réel, Zurich/Dijon 2014, p. 28–54.
[48] *Ibid.*, p. 41.
[49] *Ibid.*, p. 35.
[50] Walter Benjamin, "The Work of Art in the Age of Mechanical Reproduction," Hannah Arendt (ed.) *Illuminations: Essays and Reflections*, trans. by Harry Zohn, Schocken/Random House, New York 1969, p. 240.
[51] Jean Otth, "Les Limites (Interrogation sur les "réalités" de l'image" (1973), *Jean Otth, Travaux vidéo 1970–1980*, p. 49.
[52] René Berger, "Les mousquetaires de l'invisible: la vidéo-art en Suisse," *Cinéma, Lausanne*, no. 4 (1977) (special issue "Vidéo & Cie"), p. 39–43. This text has been reproduced in the volume edited by François Bovier, Adeena Mey: *René Berger, L'Art vidéo et autres essais (1971–1997)*, p. 84–88.
[53] *Ibid.*, p. 85.
[54] *Ibid.*, p. 86.
[55] *Ibid.*
[56] René Berger, "Les installations vidéo: au carrefour des topiques," *L'Art vidéo et autres essais (1971–1997)*, p. 100–108, here p. 107.
[57] *Ibid.*
[58] Kurt Lewin, *Principles of Topological Psychology* [1936], Martino Publishing, Eastford, Connecticut 2015.
[59] "Quelques réponses aux questions de Maria-Gloria Biccochi" (February 1980), *Jean Otth. Travaux vidéo 1970–1980*, p. 3.
[60] In 1981, René Berger founded the International Association for Video in Arts and Culture (AIVAC) and launched a series of talks at the Locarno VideoArt Festival.
[61] See Jean-Michel Baconnier's history in "BIM 2014: Des anciennes à la 'nouvelle' Biennale de l'Image en Mouvement," *Décadrages. Cinéma, à travers champs*, no. 29–30 (Spring 2015), p. 225–238.
[62] Since 2007, Association Trafic's Home Cinéma, founded by artist Jean-Michel Baconnier in Lausanne, has designed its programs to redefine the inheritance of this history, and test out new screening formats such as websites thus exploring the connections between the arts and digital technology. See H. C. 2.0: http://www.trafic.li/home-cinema-2-0.php (last accessed March 2020).

Beyond Frontiers: The Singularity of René Bauermeister's "Moving" Work
Jean-Michel Baconnier

Translated from the French by Miranda Stewart

René Bauermeister (Switzerland)
Hommage à Duchamp, 1976
Video, 6 minutes 22 seconds

Visual Connection, 1972
16mm film, 7 minutes

Aléatoire I, 1978
Video, 4 minutes 10 seconds

René Bauermeister is, along with Gérald Minkoff, Muriel Olesen, Jean Otth, and Janos Urban, a leading pioneer of video art in Switzerland.[1] Yet his work has received very little attention either from art historians or from video specialists. René Berger is one of the few video art theoreticians to have mentioned Bauermeister's work in his seminal text, "Les mousquetaires de l'invisible: la vidéo-art en Suisse" (The Musketeers of the Invisible: Video Art in Switzerland), as well as in a tribute following the artist's premature death in 1985.[2] This neglect also applies to the presence of his works in museum collections. For example, while the André Iten Collection (which now belongs to the Médiathèque du Fonds d'art contemporain de la Ville de Genève) holds eleven of his videos, purchased in 1997 after his death (excluding one donation), the Fonds des arts plastiques collection de Lausanne does not hold a single work. Indeed, the leaflet presenting the René Bauermeister Foundation, which was set up and entered into the Lausanne Commercial Register on March 30 1988,[3] reads, "during the artist's lifetime, his work remained confined to a circle of specialists, both in Switzerland and abroad."[4] Nevertheless, the Foundation has wisely placed a significant corpus of documents and works in the La Chaux-de-Fonds Fine Arts Museum to "raise awareness of the work and research carried out by the video maker from La Chaux-de-Fonds."

The inventory of this collection comprises two lists, one typewritten and the other handwritten with 16 pages of appendices. Photographs of various kinds (reproductions of paintings, photographs, installations, sculptures and drawings, performance documentation, private photographs) and written matter (letters, press articles, descriptions of video installations, screenplays, synopses, etc.) are all housed in three boxes, four filing cabinets, and a variety of document holders (sleeves, envelopes, document cases), and are all itemized. The original works (videotapes, photographs, installations, paintings, etc.) are stored in drawers, and the museum collections held in storage have never, to my knowledge, been shown at a retrospective exhibition.

My aim in this text is to offer some thoughts about Bauermeister's oeuvre in relation to the moving image, to show the relevance today of his singular work which is of importance in the hybridization of different media, as well as in the multiple artistic references that it evokes. It is clear that it is necessary to examine the artist's archives in some depth in order to rescue him from the amnesia that surrounds his artistic work, which justifies the expression that "no one is a prophet in their own land." Indeed, a journalist introduced him in the following terms, "Nowadays, René Bauermeister enjoys a considerable reputation, and yet our country knows very little about what he does."[5]

As I have already said, there is precious little specialist literature about Bauermeister's work, with the exception of Berger's work. When I consulted the artist's archives, I found a short interview by Marcel Schüpbach,[6] an article by Jacques Monnier-Raball entitled "La vidéo entre art et communication" (Video between Art and Communication),[7] another by Jacques Dominique Rouiller, "L'aventure des signes et de la signification" (The Adventure of Signs and Meaning),[8] along with various press cuttings about his exhibitions, mainly taken from French- and German-language Swiss newspapers. These included, for example, a brief report by Pierre-Henri Liardon in *24 Heures*[9] on the occasion of Bauermeister's exhibition at the Impact Gallery, and a few lines by Martine Lanini in the *Tribune de Lausanne* covering the same event.[10] While the artist's exhibitions were indeed covered by the national press, documents from this source offer very little substantive information about his work, not because of any lack of interest, but because they were so short that there was no space for analysis. It is unfortunate then that Bauermeister's work did not benefit from art criticism; however, the artist himself wrote about his own practice and that of other artists, producing accounts of exhibitions and festivals. These reports are not without interest if I want to pinpoint the originality of his work and his status as a "researcher." His writings and extensive readings are central to an endeavor to gauge his undoubted expertise in a variety of (cultural, artistic, and technical) areas of video art and experimental cinema in Switzerland and France.[11] They also offer a window into his interest in certain contemporaneous artistic movements which fed into his own work, including conceptual art, some of whose leading artists he met on trips to the United States. His archives reveal that he made at least two trips to California on the West Coast. The first took place in 1972; it was covered by a brief two-and-a-half-page account typewritten by Bauermeister himself, under the title of "Art Shopping in Los Angeles."[12] He lists some of the galleries that he visited on La Cienega Boulevard of the City of the Angels, including Irving Blum, Nick Wilder, Eugenia Butler, and Riko Mizano, and his discovery of the Pasadena Museum. There he came across the works of artists such as Larry Bell, John McCracken, Tony DeLap, Craig Kauffman and De Wain Valentine, and he met art critic Seth Siegelaub when he visited the California Institute of the Arts. At these meetings he got a sense of the rivalry at that time between Californian art and the powerful New York scene, which had a market that set it apart. Some of the artists of *The Pictures Generation* managed to get around this, such as Jack Goldstein, who Bauermeister was later to meet, and with whom he exchanged anecdotal letters that can be found in his archives. Bauermeister ends his account by noting that he had been invited to take up a residency the following year, in 1973, in the Arts Research Department of the California Institute of Technology. This second visit would probably not have taken place were it not for an invitation to Bauermeister from artist and theoretician Ken Friedman to take part in a symposium on "The Public Imagination." On this occasion, he presented his work at the De Benneville Pines Camp and Conference Center on the hills outside Los Angeles in April. This new trip was described in an article entitled "Art, jet et mass média" (Art, Jet, and Mass Media)[13] published in *La Gazette littéraire* of Saturday May 26, and Sunday 27, 1973. He added a few more details in this article about his meetings with protagonists of the conceptual art scene (artists, critics, institution directors), such as Lynda Benglis, John Baldessari, Paul Brasch, George Neubert, Lydia Vitale, and James Welling, and the importance of video in museums and art schools in the US.

Bauermeister crossed borders, and not just those offered by these cultural events that were quite exotic for the times; he also crossed disciplinary borders, and his diverse references became the hallmark of the approach he took to tackling the challenges of his artistic work. This cross-fertilization merits further research, particularly his links with the Fluxus movement. He makes very little mention of these in his writings, although clearly his meeting with Ken Friedman, who, in 1966 was a leading light in setting up *Fluxus West*, must have influenced his artistic thinking, as indeed must have been the case for his meeting with Allan Kaprow. All this notwithstanding, the main focus of this text is to examine the contribution of conceptual art to his work.

At the Crossroads between Conceptual Art and the Intellectual Legacy of Duchamp

Bauermeister took his references both from American and European art, two strands that came into contact in the second half of the 1960s through exhibitions, such as Harald Szeemann's landmark *When Attitudes Become Form*. As art critic Jack Burnham noted, these exhibitions served to bring together "artists involved with objects, arrangements, outdoor situations, and conceptual ideas."[14] In his view, this miscegenation of influences from the conceptual art of the New World, and movements such as the New Realism of the old continent, could be said to have originated in "Duchamp's post-Cubist output [which] is conceptually oriented, while a few of the proposals in his book, *Marchand du sel*, are purely conceptual works."[15] It is true that some conceptual artists admit to being, to a greater or lesser extent, part of the Duchamp tradition. Joseph Kosuth, in his famous article "Art after Philosophy" published in 1969,[16] notes that:

> The "value" of particular artists after Duchamp can be weighed according to how much they questioned the nature of art; which is another way of saying "what they added to the conception of art" or what wasn't there before they started. Artists question the nature of art by presenting new propositions as to art's nature. And to do this one cannot concern oneself with the handed-down "language" of traditional art, as this activity is based on the assumption that there is only one way of framing art propositions. But the very stuff of art is greatly related to "creating" new propositions.[17]

Marcel Duchamp gave a similar reply to Pierre Cabanne who asked him in an interview, "What is the cerebral genesis of *The Large Glass*?":

> I really didn't want to worry about visual language …
> (PC) *Retinal*
> Consequently retinal. Consequently, retinal. Everything was becoming conceptual, that is, it depended on things other than the retina.[18]

Like Kosuth and Robert Morris,[19] Bauermeister showed an interest in the work of the inventor of the readymade with a video entitled *Hommage à Duchamp* (*Homage to Duchamp*, 1976, video, 6'22"). He wrote that he had

> tried to break with the geometric continuity of a space. This experiment in space "levitation" was to some extent a challenge to Euclidean geometry.

> By making this frame, I felt as if I was playing a very close game of chess—what was at stake was an irreversible pendulum movement over time.[20]

Indeed, this video is less a homage to Duchamp's entire oeuvre and more a kind of intellectual and referential musing about *The Bride Stripped By Her Bachelors, Even (The Large Glass)* (1915–1923), using a technological device to produce a mise en abyme on different screens. It should be noted that the tautological dimension of this homage itself alludes to the self-reflexiveness of many conceptual artists (I will return to this point). *Hommage à Duchamp* (1976) opens with a fixed shot that presents a monitor placed at an angle on the screen; it does not face the viewer, but is inclined away. The first sequence broadcast on this monitor is an aerial shot of the surface of a table to the right of the screen. The camera lens is aimed vertically downward to film this horizontal shot. This device serves to mediatize a performative event—a piece of glass is placed on the table top and is broken with a hammer by an off-screen performer. We see, at one and the same time, the piece of glass, which is broken "live" on the table, and the recording of this action mediatized by the monitor screen, which, itself, is virtually broken. The performer then sticks the fragments of the glass plate onto the monitor screen; as they are identical in format, the image of the broken glass gradually materializes on the screen as it is stuck on. When the glass is completely pieced back together on the monitor, this screen is switched off, and the loss of back lighting shows up all the cracks. The superimposition of shots, in space and time, gives the illusion that the screen is no longer virtually broken, but is "actually" so, and this disturbs its viewers who start to wonder about the truth of the information they have been shown through this mediatization. For Bauermeister, these concerns are central to his work as a video maker:

> There is always that imperceptible slippage, mismatch, subtle shift, which makes it difficult to compose. Seen from within, and trapped in the dizzy whirl of the feedback from my electronic fantasies, it is very risky to judge distances or the extent to which something is actually real.[21]

Thus, *Hommage à Duchamp* not only alludes to an anecdote about *The Large Glass*, which was broken during transportation in 1926,[22] it also references the two artists' common desire to break away from canonical codes of representation by configuring time and space in such a way as to bring into question our perception of our environment.

In reference to this issue, Bauermeister said that another of his films, *Processus* (*Process*, 1972), constitutes

> [a] reflection on the complex notions of the perception of reality and the definition of space. The 14 sequences that make up this film are based on interferences, mismatches, and points of alignment between images and what they convey. This visual deconditioning is structured around uncertain factors such as the ambiguity of appearances of reality, and the particular forms used to represent reality. The aim of this research is to show the extent to which all information is relative.[23]

In this series of sequences, Bauermeister films different physical actions and body positions. This gives the effect of oscillating between familiar situations and moments of rupture, and provokes feelings of "disturbing strangeness" in the viewer. One of the sequences, for instance, shows the face of a man with his eyes closed, who seems to be resting peacefully. Nevertheless, his image is upside down on the screen. This indexical reversal raises doubts about the information conveyed by the image. Our suspicions are confirmed when we gradually discover that the man is hanging by his feet. We feel tension and a certain uneasiness when he starts to go red in the face, as this shift starts to evoke torture. In a matter of seconds, these images take us from a state of comfort to one of questioning the status of what we see in front of us, and our role as observers. Variations in the scopic field in the course of these sequences draw attention to both the context of production and the truthfulness of the information that they provide, and offer different levels of awareness by drawing on psychological mechanisms. For Bauermeister, this psychological dimension is central, and justifies his decision to produce moving images as opposed to concentrating on other media such as drawing or sculpture:

> I have worked in two dimensions (painting), and later in three dimensions (sculpture); however, after a certain time, I became aware of the limitations even of sculpture. It was then that I discovered that cinematographic images offered a new, psychological, dimension. A three-dimensional object ultimately only refers to the evidence that it provides, while an image can have overlapping meanings, indefinite echoes that can cause viewers to reflect in multiple ways and access hitherto unexplored territories. Cinema offers movement and psychological context, both of which are totally absent from the purely visual arts, as they merely offer up inert matter for viewing and interpretation.[24]

Bauermeister's ability to move beyond the visual fixity of an art object by using a psychological approach in relation to bodily movement and events, is, in some ways, akin to the concerns of conceptual artist Victor Burgin. Indeed, Burgin has discussed

> the way in which "objects" in "psychological space," the objects of memory and imagination, may be appreciated in a manner based on our experience of our bodily movement through the physical world; the way in which orientation and markers in real space become superimposed on directions in time and imaginary markers in psychological space, all of these configurations being in some physical way "internalized" in the form of muscular and nervous states that correspond to the structure under consideration.[25]

Victor Burgin notes his dual interest in "the *proprioceptive* level of experience, and the *informational* nature of art."[26] This is a way of thinking the "art-object," in his terms, as not simply being a sub-class of objects, but rather a "sub-class of *information*" and a particular "language." "The context of art is a complex of information and we should take account of the generative and transformational aspect of the experience in real time."[27] Bauermeister invokes temporality in the process of transmitting information, by creating a disjunction between sound sources and visual environments in his films, *Point Zéro* (*Point Zero*, 1971) probably being the best known. In his own words, in this short film he "tried to render perceptible certain concepts of duration"[28] by confronting the viewer with the death throes of a fly projected life-size in space. The scale tends to objectify the moment and "free [the image] from any dramatic potential likely to destroy clear headedness"; this approach is amplified by a desire to show "this last biological change" through "clinical observation." The soundtrack edited together an ambulance siren, the buzzing of the fly, and voices recounting tragic events that have taken place all over the world. The fly lies on its back in the silence of a death foretold in the background. This visual and sound time and space configuration triggers an awareness of the different possible readings of information, of how it may become distorted during the time of its dissemination and its contextual relativity, borrowing from various mediation systems.

More generally, the issue of how information is understood or acts on its components has been widely investigated by conceptual artists such as Dan Graham, Robert Smithson, and Robert Morris. These concerns are part and parcel of cybernetics theory as it developed from the early 1950s onward, after the publication of Norbert Weiner's famous research.

These issues, which were current in the 1960s, clearly did not escape Bauermeister, and are intrinsic to his approach, as can be seen in the final remark of his interview with Schüpbach:

> Information is never permanent; it depends on the observer's point of view; observers can change their stances; and events and things observed can also change. In this way, all variables can alter simultaneously with the relationships between them never remaining constant. All information is consequently relative, as are reality, objectivity, and space.[29]

In Bauermeister's work, the processes of conceptual and formal reflexiveness, which explore the capacity of the media to distort information, are yet another facet of his artistic practice that edges him closer to conceptual art. Indeed, this potential mise en abyme using work created

by folding and unfolding information in boxes inside boxes
was exploited in different ways by this movement to the
extent that one of Robert Morris' seminal works in 1961
(which was officially presented two years later, on March 24,
1963, at the Gordon Gallery in New York[30]), was a simple
wooden box containing the sound of its own making.
Box with the Sound of its Own Making, as the artist explains,

> [c]omprises six pieces of walnut assembled into a
> closed cube. I made the box with hand tools: hammer,
> saw, etc. It took me three hours. As I made it, I used
> a recorder to record the sounds of it being made.
> Before I completely closed the box, I put a small
> loudspeaker inside it. I created a space on one of its
> sides so that a tape recorder could be plugged into
> the loudspeaker. This allowed me to play back the
> sounds I had recorded.[31]

This self-presentation was then pushed to its limits by
Morris through language when, a year later, he produced
Card File (1962). This file contains 48 cards classified in
alphabetical order,[32] which describe in writing "comments
and information about its making."[33] Nevertheless, art critic
Benjamin H. D. Buchloh goes back to self-reflexiveness
in conceptual art as a tautological form, in "Conceptual Art
1962–1969: From the Aesthetic of Administration to the
Critique of Institutions."[34] He identifies an "aggressive
dimension"[35] in this tautology which he links to the statement that a "proposition is true for all the truth-possibilities
of the elementary propositions,"[36] which cuts it off from
reality. This distinction leads to the rejection of any social
function of art, which would lead to a resurgence of the elitist
ambiguity of the "art for art's sake" doctrines for modernists,
which Joseph Kosuth reaffirmed, to argue that conceptual
art aims to free art from the shackles of aesthetics.[37]
Buchloh chose not to use the artist's preferred references,
Wittgenstein and A. J. Ayer, but rather grounded his criticism
of Kosuth's work in a particular view of the ways in which
Roland Barthes and Guy Debord identify tautology as an
ideological symptom of capitalist society that serves to
institutionalize and legitimize economic and cultural factors.
Nevertheless, Buchloh does not direct this criticism at all

conceptual artists, some of who work on exhibition contexts and ways of making art publicly available, such as Dan Graham, Marcel Broodthaers, and Daniel Buren. He further notes that the wide range of approaches adopted within this movement makes it impossible to identify homogenous styles when it comes to writing an historical account. Consequently, he argues that the practices of these artists "demonstrate a deeper and more mature self-reflexiveness than do analytical approaches such as Kosuth's, precisely because they take account of the (social and political) contextualization of art, and do not merely define it by a simple statement of intent."[38] In a comparative study of Buchloh's article and Kosuth, Patrice Loubier observes that:

> Conceptual art marks a precarious tipping point, where artists can, at one and the same time, continue with a "religious veneration of self-referential plastic form,"[39] as in the case of Kosuth, or take the reflexiveness beyond the picture, by analyzing the devices used for the exhibition, legitimation, and dissemination of art, be they walls, picture rails, architecture, or museum policy (Buren and Hans Haacke, among others).[40]

It could further be argued that Bauermeister's work avoids the pitfalls of tautological alienation by its very questioning of the media and information dissemination systems. We should note that while he was aware of Kosuth's article because it was cited by Jack Burnham, he never actually read Buchloh's criticism, as it was written after he had died. Consequently, the feedback effects of the self-reflexive processes deployed by Bauermeister were generated, as we have already seen, by mismatches, interferences, and shifts, thus sidestepping the problem of a repeat reference setting up a fixed loop. He favored spiraling feedback that probes deeply into our relationship with information, the context of its transmission, and its modes of dissemination via a variety of different media. The "meta" version of this approach is particularly eloquent in the video installation *Aléatoire I* (*Aleatory I*, 1978) and *Aléatoire II* (*Aleatory II*, 1978) much as it had been in his film *Visual Connection* (1972). This film is an "attempt to analyze certain codes of visual communication" by editing a succession of alternative images and sounds to different rhythms. Sequences showing a man and a woman facing each other reconstitute an out-of-sync dialogue in English as if in a game of ping-pong. In this video installation, reflexive issues are centered, both literally and figuratively, on the asymmetry of a face informing itself meta-analytically in a soliloquy and via a technical device. The work *Aléatoire I* and *II* was created for the *Espaces 78/1* event, *Video Corpus. Manifestation-enquête sur la vidéographie et corps humain* (*Video Corpus. Event-Enquiry into Videography and the Human Body*) held from February 6 to 13, 1978, at Porte de la Suisse in Paris. Transcribed below, notwithstanding its length, Bauermeister's description of this event, which clearly indicates the process of the shift in the in-formalization of reflexiveness:

> Two cameras are placed side by side and film a face in close-up. They are set to a short focal length. They are set to an identical focal length. The subject sees his or her face reproduced on a monitor screen placed in front of him or her. The experiment can be broken down into two stages. The first is the recording of the image of the face by one of the two cameras for one minute, for example. Then the tape is wound back to the start.
>
> The second stage allows the volunteers to see the left-hand side of his or her face again in playback by playing the tape (an effects generator divides the monitor screen into two equal parts according to the axis of symmetry of the face) while the right-hand half is simultaneously reproduced by the other camera. The two halves thus juxtaposed on the screen recompose the entire face.
>
> This approach causes an asymmetry in its expressive movements and in facial mobility. This quite disturbing mismatch generated by contrasting, in the same image, two distinct time patterns, is even more ambiguous insofar as the arbitrary division of the screen coincides with the "natural" symmetry of the face.
>
> The sound recording allows the two variants, either an individual sound recording of the first or second stage, or, on the contrary, a mixing of both sources.

The way the device works is not unambiguous, as the result is always subordinate to a reciprocal effect.[41]

Bauermeister produced two versions of this performance by Jacques Monnier-Raball, at the time the director of the École cantonale d'art de Lausanne. These are the two recordings that we have today.

Further evidence of the logic of movement in Bauermeister's work, which contributes to its originality as it is not bound by any artistic movement or aesthetic fashion, can be seen in the notion of "event" to which he alludes in this quote. Here it is helpful to return to the contribution of the rather nebulous Fluxus to his work, precisely through the notion of event along with his own critical comments about the mass media like television.[42] Bauermeister's six-part film, *Layla in Camp: Majnun Lying Without* (1975)[43] made in collaboration with the Kulturtäter, the Laïla Group, Olivier Blanchard of the "Théâtre de poche," and artist Herbert Distel,[44] is particularly relevant, as is his "urban experience of video communication," in 1975, in the streets of La Chaux-de-Fonds.[45] This second project consisted of organizing an unexpected and surprising event in a public space—a band of musicians playing at a time and in a place other than those in which they would normally play (concert, festival, parade, etc.). This experiment offered the opportunity to reflect on ways of communicating the improbability of an event of this nature. This explains why they recorded it with a video camera in TV documentary fashion. The point behind this urban disturbance was to cast a critical eye on the modes of communication of a mass medium such as television, and the way in which they relay information deemed to be "exceptional."

The singularity of René Bauermeister's work can be found in the hybrid nature of his aesthetic references, cultural sources, and artistic media, which feed into his ever-changing status as an artist-researcher. Bauermeister's artistic approach is a model of rigor. He is a true *outsider* to the art world, a place too often reserved, by commentators, to works and artists that resist classification, when in fact it is their very originality that makes them pioneers in their field.

[1] See François Bovier, Adeena Mey (eds.), *René Berger, L'Art vidéo*, JRP|Ringier/Les presses du réel, Zurich/Dijon 2014, p. 86.
[2] See R. Berger, "Les mousquetaires de l'invisible," *Cinéma*, no. 4 (1977), and "Ici, René Bauermeister," *René Bauermeister: photographie, travaux vidéo*, Fondation René Bauermeister, Lausanne 1988, reprinted in *René Berger, L'Art vidéo*, p. 84–88 and p. 96–99. René Bauermeister was born in 1930 and died at the age of 55.
[3] On March 8, 1999, the Foundation's headquarters moved to La Chaux-de-Fonds, rue des Musées 33, c/Musée des Beaux-Arts (cf. FOSC: 054 18.03/ of.1999, p. 1797).
[4] Presentation leaflet for the Fondation René Bauermeister, p. 8.
[5] Introductory paragraph, written by a journalist and signed with the initials JdR, prior to the publication in *La Gazette littéraire (Gazette de Lausanne)* of Saturday and Sunday, May 26 and 27, 1973, of Bauermeister's report entitled "Art, jet et mass media," in which he gives an overview of his travels in the United States, artist's archives, shelf mark 5.1.152 (box 1)
[6] Published in *La Gazette littéraire* (*La Gazette de Lausanne*), no. 229, Saturday September 30, and Sunday, October 1, 1972, shelf mark 1.37 (box 1).
[7] Published in the catalogue of the *Espaces* program, which included *Art vidéo: recherches et expériences*, a group show with René Bauermeister, Gérald Minkoff, Muriel Olesen, Jean Otth, and Janos Urban, from March 10 to 13, 1976, at Porte de la Suisse in Paris managed by Pro Helvetia (cf. copy of the file in the artist's archives, shelf mark 2.1.113, [box 1]). This venue, at 11 bis rue Scribe (in the 9th arrondissement), led to the establishment, as Pro Helvetia's first overseas branch, of the Centre culturel suisse (CCS, Swiss Cultural Centre) following the purchase, in 1982, of the Hôtel Poussepin in the Marais district. The CCS then opened in 1985 and is still at same address, 32 and 38, Rue des Franc-Bourgeois.
[8] Published in 1973 in issue 20 of the *Revue suisse de photographie*.
[9] Published in the edition of Friday March 30, 1973, article mounted on card, shelf mark 1.52 (box 1).
[10] Published in the edition of Thursday March 29, 1973, article mounted on card, shelf mark 1.48 (box 1).
[11] See, for example, his extremely enlightening historical essay on the situation of experimental cinema in Switzerland: "Un cinéma inscrit dans la mouvance d'un courant international," *CinémAction*, nos. 10–11 (Spring-Summer 1980), reprinted in François Bovier, Balthazar Lovay, Sylvain Menétrey, Dan Solbach (eds.), *Film Implosion! Experimental Cinema in Switzerland*, Fri Art/Revolver Publishing, Fribourg/Berlin 2017, p. 25–34.
[12] Document containing three typewritten pages in the artist's archives, shelf mark 11.5 A. 336 (filing cabinet 1).
[13] Published in *La Gazette littéraire* (*La Gazette de Lausanne*), Saturday and Sunday May 26 and 27,1973, shelf mark 5.1.152 (box 1).
[14] "La Tête d'Alice. Réflexion sur l'art conceptuel," a type-written copy of which appears in French in René Bauermeister's archives, the original version of which is Jack Burnham, "Alice's Head: Reflections on Conceptual Art," *Artforum*, vol. 8, no. 6 (February 1970), p. 37–43, reprinted in Jack Burnham, *Great Western Salt Works: Essays on the Meaning of Post-Formalist Art*, George Braziller, New York 1974, p. 47–61: 48. It would appear that it had been translated by Bauermeister himself, artist's archive, shelf mark 2.3.126 (box 1).
[15] Jack Burnham, "Alice's Head," p. 48
[16] Joseph Kosuth, "Art after Philosophy," *Studio International*, London, no. 915 (October 1969), p. 134–137.
[17] *Ibid.*, reprinted in Joseph Kosuth, *Art after Philosophy and after. Collected Writings, 1966–1990*, MIT Press, Cambridge, Massachusetts 1991, p. 18–19.
[18] Pierre Cabanne, *Dialogues with Marcel Duchamp*, trans. Ron Padgett, Da Capo Press, Boston 1971 (first published in 1967), p. 39–40.
[19] See Robert Morris, *Ecouter par les yeux. Objets et environnement sonores*, catalogue for the exhibition at the Musée d'art moderne de la Ville de Paris, 1980, p. 106; Robert Morris, "Statement," May 15, 1970 (letter to the Whitney Museum of Art demanding, in response to the US bombing of Cambodia, the immediate closure of its personal exhibition), quoted in Julia Bryan-Wilson, *Art Workers. Radical Practice in the Vietnam War Era*, University of California Press, Berkeley/Los Angeles/London 2011, p. 103.
[20] René Bauermeister, description of the *Hommage à Duchamp* video, typewritten mock-up for the Porte de la Suisse, Espace 76 file, in the artist's archives, shelf mark 2.1.113.
[21] René Bauermeister, untitled, February 1978, artist's archive, shelf mark 5.1.146 (box 1).
[22] Interview by James Johnson Sweeney of Marcel Duchamp, in Marcel Duchamp, *Duchamp du signe*, Champs Flammarion, Paris 1975, p.176.
[23] René Bauermeister, description of the film *Processus*, a typewritten text in the artist's archives, shelf mark 6.1.192 (box 1).
[24] Marcel Schüpbach, "René Bauermeister: Le mécanisme de la perfection," interview published in *La Gazette littéraire* (*Gazette de Lausanne*), no. 229, Saturday September 30–Sunday October 1, 1972, artist's archives, shelf mark 1.37 (box 1).
[25] Victor Burgin, "Response to Three Statements," in David Lamelas (ed.), *Publication*, Nigel Greenwood, London 1970, p. 9–12: 11.
[26] *Ibid.*, p. 11.
[27] René Bauermeister, interviewed by Marcel Schüpbach.
[28] René Bauermeister, description of the film *Point Zéro*, typewritten text in the artist's archives, shelf mark 6.1.193 (box 1).
[29] René Bauermeister, interview with Marcel Schüpbach.
[30] See Gauthier Herrmann, Fabrice Reymond, Fabien Vallos (ed.), *Art conceptuel, une entologie*, Éditions MIX, Paris 2008, p. 9.
[31] Robert Morris, cited in *Ecouter par les yeux. Objets et environnement sonores*, p. 106.
[32] See Caroline Cros' description on the Centre Georges-Pompidou's website available at: https://www.centrepompidou.fr/cpv/resource/cXbkeg6/rGGAR5 (last accessed March 2020).
[33] Gauthier Herrmann, Fabrice Reymond, Fabien Vallos (eds.), *Art conceptuel, une entologie*, p. 9
[34] Benjamin Buchloh, "Conceptual Art 1962–1969: From the Aesthetic of Administration to the Critique of Institutions," *October*, vol. 55, no. 102 (Winter 1990), p. 105–143.
[35] *Ibid.*, p. 130.
[36] Ludwig Wittgenstein, *Tractatus logico-philosophicus*, trans. C. K. Ogden, Dover Publications, New York 1999 (first published 1921), p. 68 (4.46 and 4.462).
[37] See Joseph Kosuth, "Art after Philosophy."
[38] Benjamin Buchloh, "De l'esthétique d'administration à la critique institutionnelle (aspect de l'art conceptuel), 1962–1969," Paul Gintz (ed.), *L'art conceptuel: une perspective*, Musée d'art moderne de la Ville de Paris, Paris 1989, p. 66 [the author cites the first version of Buchloch's essay in French, which was revised in the English version published in *October*].
[39] Benjamin Buchloh, "De l'esthétique d'administration à la critique institutionnelle," p. 128, cited by Patrice Loubier, *Figures de la tautologie dans l'art et le discours critique des années*

1960, doctoral thesis, Université de Montréal, Montreal 2008, p. 70.

[40] Patrice Loubier, *Figures de la tautologie dans l'art et le discours critique des années 1960*.

[41] René Bauermeister, description of the film *Aléatoire I et II*, typewritten text in the artist's archives, shelf mark 6.1.199 (box 1).

[42] See René Bauermeister's article entitled "Vidéo/Télévision, Deux réalités confondues dans l'image électronique," in *Musique/art/spectacle*, no. 4 (April 1975), three photocopies, artist's archives, shelf mark 5.2.153 (box 1).

[43] "*Layla in Camp: Majnun Lying Without* is the title of a Persian Miniature displayed in the British Museum. The film refers throughout to the contents of this miniature and expands this account into a tale recounted in six tableaux. We understand the story in an essentially visual way which calls more directly on the viewer's imagination." Synopsis of *Layla in Camp: Majnun Lying Without*, artist's archives, shelf mark 6.1.225 (box 1). See also the *Kulturtäter Biel-Bienne* press kit, January 14, 1976, shelf mark 6.1.226 (box 1). I have not seen this film, and do not know if any copies of it still exist.

[44] See "Un tournant dans l'activité des Kulturtäter? *Layla in Camp*," an article published in *Journal du Jura*, February 21, 1976, unsigned, René Bauermeister's archives, shelf mark 2.1.86 (box 1).

[45] See "La vidéo entre art et communication," by Jacques Monnier-Raball, three pages with photographs, artist's archives, shelf mark 2.1.108 (box 1).

Structure and Participation in the Films of Tony Morgan
Renate Buschmann

Translated from the German by Benjamin Letzler

Tony Morgan, *Color Suspension*, 1969
View of a performance on the occasion of the *between 1* exhibition, Düsseldorf, 1969

From the start, artist Tony Morgan (1938–2004) never bound himself to a genre. Unlike many artists of his generation, he was not interested in occupying a particular artistic niche nor in creating recognition value on the art market. Morgan shifted between sculpture, painting, performance, and film because he found it essential to investigate the specific characteristics of these different media in his artistic practice, and to interrogate them in the context of related debates. From 1968 until around 1973, Morgan produced numerous experimental films and influenced the art scene in Düsseldorf, where film was given intense attention as a form of artistic expression.[1]

In the late 1960s, Morgan became increasingly involved as a sculptor, with the process culminating in the creation of a sculpture, something he sought to make visible and comprehensible to the observer. This consideration was the impetus for the *between* exhibition series, which Morgan encouraged the Kunsthalle Düsseldorf to mount in 1968.[2] He proposed that the Kunsthalle Düsseldorf use the remodelling periods between established exhibitions for a curatorial experiment in which to try a more direct relationship between artist and observer, or rather between artwork and visitor. The Kunsthalle Düsseldorf eagerly adopted his proposal, and organized short-term *between* exhibitions until 1973, pursuing the principle embodied in the title. On the one hand, attempts were made to create an immediate relationship with visitors through bodily experience, participation, and discussion; on the other, innovative areas of visual art were presented that no longer fit into traditional genres, but were instead situated "in-between." One of these interstitial fields of art was artists' film. Even before the contemporary art significance of media technologies and the moving image was highlighted with the exhibition *Prospect 71—Projection*, experimental films were shown at the *between* exhibitions as a matter of course.

The specific occasion for Morgan's first film in Düsseldorf was an encounter with Daniel Spoerri. When Morgan moved to Düsseldorf in 1968, Spoerri was just opening his legendary restaurant in the city. The two artists were excited about the concept of filming the life cycle of a steak. Morgan remembered the idea for the film as having been born years earlier in a discussion between the two in Paris, when they were debating the "aesthetics of cleanliness" in English sculpture at the time, and the "esthétique de la merde" (aesthetics of shit) in French sculpture.[3] For his part, Spoerri wrote in his *Gastronomic Diary* that the thinking for the film had come to him during a stay on the Greek island of Symi.[4] In dialogue with Spoerri, Morgan ultimately made the film *Resurrection* (1968), deploying the technique of running film images backward to humorously trace the process of the steak's production, and thus to visualize the natural food cycle.[5] Spoerri understood the film's contents as part of his *Eat Art* actions, through which he exposed the cultural conventions of cooking and eating. For Morgan, by contrast, *Resurrection* marked his entry into the conditions and conceptions of filmmaking, the narrative aspect of which he would further pursue in later films.

A consequence of Morgan's process-oriented visual thought was that, at *between 1* in February 1969, he presented the genesis of a sculpture with the action *Colour Suspensions*,[6] but immediately thereafter devoted himself intensely to the time-based medium of film for several years. The results were films that, on the one hand, can be placed in the category of structural film, and on the other hand films in which participation with the audience played a decisive role.[7]

In his minimalist short films, to be projected in loops, and often three minutes in length, Morgan realized reflections on painting and sculpture, and linked the two-dimensional surface of projection to the optional dimension of space. The film *Floor Drip* (1969), in which paint is sprayed onto a neutral substrate, references both Jackson Pollock's "drip painting" and Richard Serra's then-contemporary "splash pieces," as well as the infectious simplicity of events celebrated in the Fluxus movement by such artists as George Brecht in his *DRIP MUSIC (Drip Event)*.[8] Likewise, the film *Paper Drop* (1969) was the purist beginning of a filmic contemplation of sculpture directly tied to Morgan's *Colour Suspensions* action. Whereas Morgan had used the action to transform fiberglass banners and polyester paint into a heavy, hanging, stalactite-like sculpture, in his film he presented the lightness of a crumpled-up paper tissue falling to earth as a sculptural shape. Despite this analytical approach, Morgan sought to attain an illusionistic effect with the films by having their actual projection reflected, via mirror mechanisms, onto the floor. In his 1969 experimental presentations at the Munich space Aktionsraum 1, and with his film *Black Corner* the same year, Morgan examined light as the foundational element of film, and as an image-generating process in the black box of the cinema. Morgan set up a film projector outside Aktionsraum 1 that ran without any film. It was a logical continuation of Nam June Paik's *Zen for Film* (1962–1964), in which a reel of unexposed 16mm film was shown in an interior space. At Morgan's exhibition in Munich, a film projector cast a small rectangle of light onto a courtyard wall in front of which was a patch of grass. This image in light, created solely out of the beam of light from the projector, appeared with varying intensity depending on the changing light conditions during the day and night. Here the pure illumination of a small patch of reality supplanted the fiction of film.

The black-and-white film *Black Corner* (1969), shown at *between 4* and later at *Prospect 71—Projection*, likewise addresses the essential components of film—light and dark—and the appearance and disappearance of images. The film's conception calls for the projection to be directed at the corner of a room, thereby expanding the classical two-dimensionality of film into a three-dimensional arrangement of surfaces, as determined by the collision of walls and floor. The film begins with a "white" film image and shows how this initial image is steadily covered over by an ever-expanding black surface, then transformed back into white in a diametrical process: "The projector must be directed into a corner of a room where the light is 'painted out' with black paint (darkness)."[9] Morgan thus translates the motif of overpainting from the repertoire of painting into the dimension of film. In this way the film image gradually disappears in the dark surroundings of its projection, only to reappear in radiant white.

Morgan was represented by a second film, illustrating his growing interest in audience participation, at the *between 4* exhibition. Looking back, he summarized the situation around 1970 by saying, "At the time it was always about how you could create a relationship with the audience."[10] He made the film *Munich People* (1969) at his exhibition at the Aktionsraum 1 in Munich. Morgan asked the attendees to come in front of the camera one by one and to state their names, the date of filming, and the time of day. The 20-minute film is assembled out of these juxtaposed portraits. This serial method suspended the film's narrative character and ruptured the conventional connection between filmmaker, performer, and spectators:

> The first film, *Munich People*, was engaged with the audience that came in. It was also about the empty space I was in, alone with my camera. My sole desire was to document the people who came to see what I was doing. This is how the audience became my work.[11]

In *between 4*, Morgan once again asked exhibition attendees to permit him to film them and to become part of a filmic

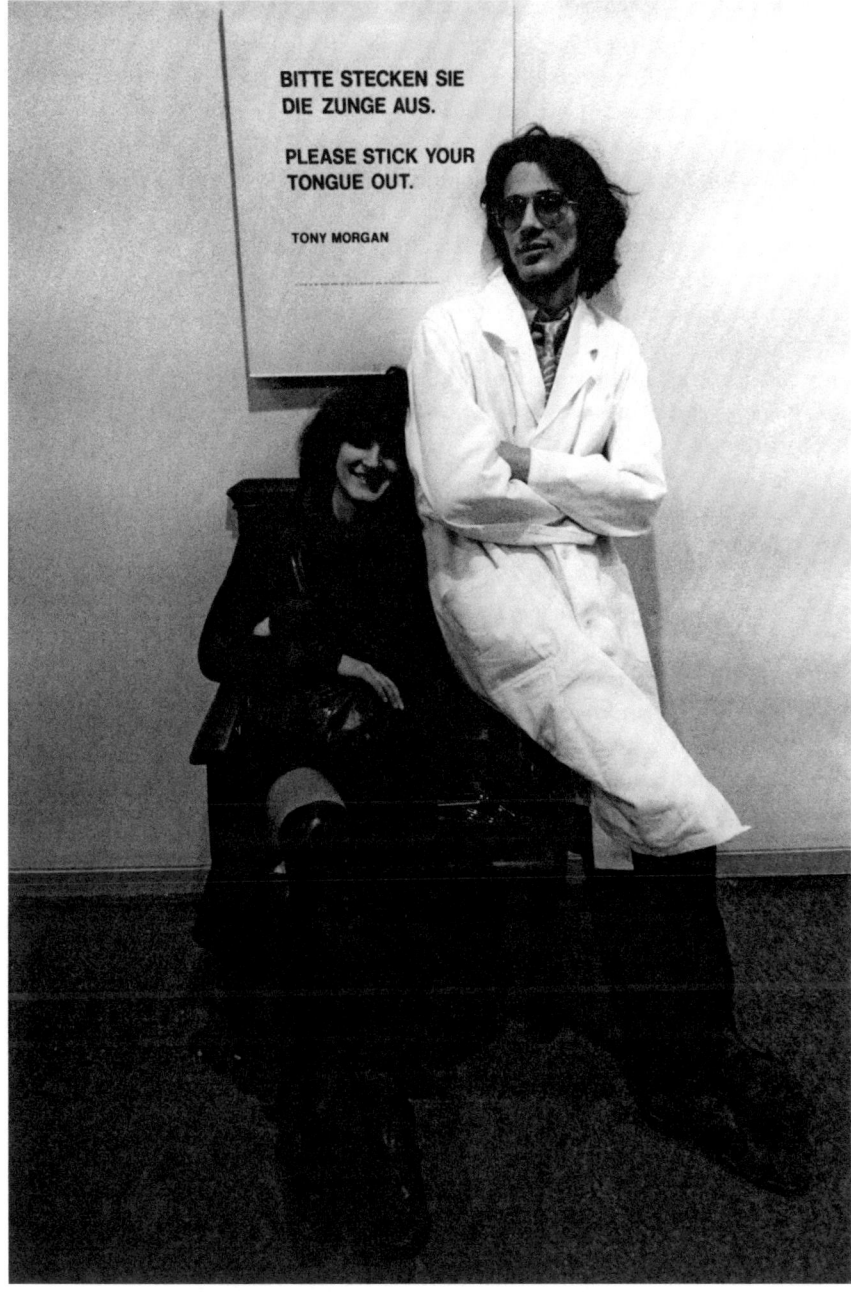

Tony Morgan, *Please Stick Out Your Tongue! Düsseldorf Tongues*, 1970
Exhibition view, *between 4*, Düsseldorf, 1970

performance. Again Morgan selected a stereotyped filming situation, this time that the attendees should follow the instruction, "Please stick out your tongue!" Morgan combined this footage in the film *Bitte strecken Sie die Zunge aus! Düsseldorf Tongues (Please Stick Out Your Tongue! Düsseldorf Tongues*, 1970). Yet, unlike the Munich film in which the performers carried out a neutral self-depiction, this enactment added an element of embarrassment. The participating attendees had to overcome a certain self-consciousness before they could make such a gesture for no reason in front of someone else—even if, in the moment of filming, it was only the camera. On the other hand, some attendees took advantage of the request to have fun with their self-staging, as Morgan recalled:

> The "tongue" film was also about contact between people; I was interested in this organ that you normally don't see. But the film can get somewhat boring and also somewhat unappealing. Some people had really immense equipment in their mouths! Unfortunately, everyone wanted to amuse themselves in this film, and naturally that got somewhat unrewarding for me. The children enjoyed themselves much more than the grown-ups, for whom the request was really embarrassing.[12]

In its repetitive structure and its revealing of a usually hidden part of the body, Morgan's 20-minute silent film *Bitte strecken Sie die Zunge aus! Düsseldorf Tongues* can be compared to Yoko Ono's famous 1966–1967 film *No. 4 (Bottoms)*, presenting the spectator with a succession of close-ups of naked human rear ends, which becomes at once comic and unpleasant. Morgan continued with audience involvement and the serial concept in his films *People's Presence* (1970), *Vis-à-Vis* (1970), and *Description* (1970).

There was an atmosphere of change among artists living in Düsseldorf in the late 1960s who were committed to trying out film as a medium in the visual arts. The exhibition *Strategy: Get Arts*, with which the Düsseldorf art scene made a successful showing at the Edinburgh International Festival in 1970, took this development into account. Film booths were installed for multiple artists, and Morgan showed the film *Description*, which he had conceived for this occasion.[13] The first film class at the Kunstakademie Düsseldorf was inaugurated shortly thereafter, and many film artists, including Robert Filliou, Tony Morgan, and Lutz Mommartz, came together to form the "Filmgruppe Düsseldorf" group. The members were active in advocating a strong public presence for experimental film, supporting each other in their film productions, and conducting vehement debates within the group as to whether artistic film must bear social and political responsibility. Thus, the Filmgruppe Düsseldorf responded to the *Prospect 71—Projection* exhibition with a three-day counter-event, *Film kritisch*, deliberately incorporating local filmmakers, and insisting on the social relevance of films.[14]

Tony Morgan was involved in all these debates and activities. From 1970 on, he also ran a cinema for artistic productions out of his studio, providing a space for film experiments and for the discussions that they prompted. His multifaceted engagement profoundly enriched the Düsseldorf art scene of the time. His films attest to his early efforts to transcend genre boundaries and to think and act intermedially. Morgan continued to pursue process-based concepts and direct exchange with the audience when, from 1972 into the 1980s, he devoted himself almost exclusively to performance. As the embodiment of "Herman," the double he had created, he took the risk of using his performances to call into question the conventions of the museum business and the established roles of artists, curators, and audience. In 1974 Morgan had already taken part as his alter ego Herman in the legendary exhibition *Transformer. Aspekte der Travestie*, curated by Jean-Christophe Ammann for the Kunstmuseum Luzern. In lieu of film, Morgan had connected the specificity of video technology, namely its mirror-like function that made it possible to play back an event on a monitor in real time, to his awakened interest in performance and the forging of identity:

> When I started working with video in New York, it was because I had suddenly discovered Herman, my alter ego, or rather the person on the other side of the mirror, the person who was also the person beyond the little pane of glass on the video monitor.[15]

Morgan lived in Amsterdam from 1984 until 1988, when an artist-in-residence program took him to Geneva.[16] It was quite typical of Morgan that he took on the experiment of another artistic reorientation and worked with painting and printmaking in the 1990s. Morgan founded the Laboratoire d'Impression, a printing workshop combined with an artist-run space, through which he worked to bring renewed attention to contemporary printmaking. Another important project for the artist during his years in Switzerland was taking stock of his films and performance works from the 1960s and 1970s. These works received their first comprehensive showing and appreciation in the exhibition *The Birth of Herman* at the MAMCO (Musée d'Art Moderne et Contemporain de Genève) in 2003.[17]

[1] See Renate Buschmann, "Die Erforschung eines Mediums. Filmbegeisterung in der Düsseldorfer Kunstszene der frühen siebziger Jahre," Renate Buschmann et al. (eds.), *Dazwischen. Die Vermittlung von Kunst*, Dietrich Reimer, Berlin 2005, p. 143–152.

[2] Renate Buschmann, *Chronik einer Nicht-Ausstellung. 'between' 1969–73 in der Kunsthalle Düsseldorf*, PhD dissertation, Cologne University (Dietrich Reimer, Berlin 2006); Renate Buschmann (ed.), *Chronik einer Nicht-Ausstellung. 'between' 1969–73 in der Kunsthalle Düsseldorf*, exh. cat., Kunsthalle Düsseldorf, Cologne 2007.

[3] See Tony Morgan, "Fluxus und Fillious persönlicher Einfluss auf meine Arbeit," Hans-Werner Schmidt (ed.), *Robert Filliou 1926–1987. Zum Gedächtnis*, exh. cat., Städtische Kunsthalle Düsseldorf, Düsseldorf 1988, p. 21–22: 21. Tony Morgan repeated something similar in conversation with the author on February 14, 1999, printed in "Es lohnte sich, darüber nachzudenken, was 'dazwischen' war. Tony Morgan im Gespräch mit Renate Buschmann," *Chronik einer Nicht-Ausstellung*, p. 17–21.

[4] Entry dated May 26, 1967: "During this coprophilic discussion [with a Greek man about emptying the latrine pit] I recalled my film that still has not been made, beginning with a close-up of a fresh turd, then returning through the intestines (X-ray) to the stomach, where the chewed pieces of meat accumulate, which come out of the mouth as steak, which then goes in reverse back to the butcher, who reattaches the steak to the ox in the abattoir, and at the close of the film the ox, revived to a new life, grazes in a sunny and blooming field and, naturally, drops a great big cowpat." Daniel Spoerri, *Gastronomisches Tagebuch*, Edition Nautilus, Hamburg 1995.

[5] *Resurrection* was produced with the assistance of Achim Reinert and premiered at Creamcheese, his Düsseldorf artists' bar, in 1968.

[6] See Renate Buschmann, "Formen der Farbe: Tony Morgans 'Colour Suspensions,'" *Chronik einer Nicht-Ausstellung*, p. 66–72.

[7] A compilation of Morgan's films can be found in the exhibition catalogue *Who the Hell is Herman, Anyway? Tony Morgan 1960–1977*, Musée d'Art Moderne et Contemporain, Geneva 2003. A valuable article written by the artist himself is Tony Morgan, "The Media Explosive Years 1960–1980. Autobiographical Research into the Meaning of Media/Medium," *mediamatic. Dutch Magazine on Media Art and Hartware Design*, no. 1 (1986), p. 23–33, available online at http://www.mediamatic.net/14212/en/the-media-explosive-years-1960-1980 (last accessed March 2020).

[8] Tony Morgan was on friendly terms with Fluxus artists and made films with some of them, for example *Some Events* (1969, with George Brecht), *Double Happening* (1970, with Robert Filliou and Emmett Williams), and *Düsseldorf ist ein guter Platz zum Schlafen* (1972, with Robert Filliou).

[9] Tony Morgan, "The Media Explosive Years 1960–1980."

[10] "Es lohnte sich, darüber nachzudenken, was 'dazwischen' war. Tony Morgan im Gespräch mit Renate Buschmann," p. 21.

[11] *Ibid.*, p. 20.

[12] *Ibid.*

[13] The film *Description* is a group portrait of the artists and organizers participating in the exhibition. Each of the participants—all male—appear full face, while a female partner, shown in profile to one side, describes qualities of her male partner's external appearance and inner character.

[14] The *Film kritisch* event took place at the Kunsthalle Düsseldorf from December 1 through December 3, 1971. See Renate Buschmann, "Die Erforschung eines Mediums."

[15] "Es lohnte sich, darüber nachzudenken, was 'dazwischen' war. Tony Morgan im Gespräch mit Renate Buschmann," p. 20.

[16] Tony Morgan lived with his family in Geneva until his death in 2004.

[17] An accompanying publication was published, *Who the Hell is Herman, anyway? Tony Morgan 1960–1977*.

ART SCHOOLS

Serge Stauffer and the *Film de Recherche*: Traces of a Friendship
Michael Hiltbrunner

Translated from the German by Steven Lindberg

Fredi M. Murer shooting *Vision of a Blind Man*, June 21, 1968

Around 1960, future filmmakers Georg Radanowicz and Fredi M. Murer were attending the photography program at what was then known as the Kunstgewerbeschule Zürich (now the Zürcher Hochschule der Künste, Zurich University of the Arts). Both of them became friends with Serge Stauffer, who was teaching on the program, and both started an exchange with Stauffer that left surprising traces in various films and texts.[1] That was also true after 1965, when Stauffer cofounded the "Form und Farbe" (Form and Color) program for free design, and even after 1971, when the program was continued independently as the F+F Schule für experimentelle Gestaltung (now the F+F School for Art and Design). The contact was not only about experimental film but, at least for a brief time around 1968, there was obviously mutual interest in "research film," film that focuses on its research function.

Kunstgewerbeschule Zürich

Stauffer attended the photography program at the Kunstgewerbeschule in Zurich and taught on that program from 1957 onward.[2] Stauffer had shown an interest in avant-garde art already as a teenager and, along with artist André Thomkins, in Surrealism, and especially in Marcel Duchamp. The study of film was important to Stauffer; apparently, he had assumed the name Serge because he had praised Sergei Eisenstein during a stay at a health spa around 1949 in the town of Leysin in western Switzerland, and from that time on had replaced his own given name, Werner. Later he wrote that Eisenstein was considered the "great master of the art of film," and his theory of montage had "no imitators."[3] In Basel in 1954, Stauffer met and portrayed Lotte H. Eisner, the head curator of the Cinémathèque française and author of *The Haunted Screen* (1952),[4] an important study of film in Germany during the Weimar Republic.

As a teacher on the photography program, Stauffer encouraged any of his students who happened to be interested in film. There were several who attended his course because there was no film program. The *Der Film* exhibition, which ran from January 9 to April 30, 1960, was an important event for them and for other cineastes. The novelty for Zurich of what amounted to a film festival lasting several months was immense; daily film screenings ensured a large audience. Thomas Schärer wrote: "The true heart of the exhibition is a film cycle with more than one hundred key works from the history of film, selected by Mario Gerteis and Hanspeter Manz."[5]

Stauffer curated one section of the exhibition, was involved, under the direction of Hans Fischli and Willy Rotzler, in the preparations for and practical implementation of the exhibition, and codesigned the catalogue with Jörg Hamburger. Georg Radanowicz stated in an interview that Stauffer was "responsible for much of the exhibition material and for the catalogue," and to that end ordered "countless films from the Cinémathèque and from various archives."[6]

The section organized by Stauffer was entitled "Film Directors and Cinematic Styles," with elaborate documentation of 42 feature, documentary, and animated films from 1912 to 1957 featuring screenshots he selected and produced himself. He was assisted by students from the photography program: "One task set by Serge was to present the subject of a film using around twelve screenshots," said Murer, who attended the Kunstgewerbeschule Zürich from 1959, and was a student on the photography program from 1960 to 1962.[7] The decision not to use set photographs, but instead to produce all of the images themselves by photographing a projection of the film meant that all of the films had to be watched several times: "In the lecture hall, we climbed a ladder and photographed the films with a Leica all the way through two or three times," which for Murer was "like film school."[8] Thanks to this experience, he decided to become a filmmaker: "Previously I was not interested in the cinema and film. Later, as a student, I saw many films. During a film by [Robert J.] Flaherty [...] I said to myself: 'Film is my calling.'"[9]

Murer's first films testify to his study of formalism. His short film *Marcel* (1962), for example, for which fellow student Robert Müller operated the camera, featured cuts, perspectives, and contrasts based on the visual language of Sergei Eisenstein; the music of Edgar Varèse, in turn, was well suited to Stauffer's experimental repertoire.[10] In a silent short film produced that same year, *Carrara – Der gefallene Turm von Pisa* (*Carrara—The Fallen Tower of Pisa*, 1962), about the photography program's excursion to Italy, Murer brought play with the materials and with the medium into interaction with the filmed group, which recalled the Nouvelle Vague and hence very current cinema.

Experimental films—such as those of Oskar Fischinger and Hans Richter—did not play a central role in the exhibition of 1960, apart from several experimental feature films such as *Un chien andalou* (1929) by Luis Buñuel. Stauffer's selection testifies to an artistic eye in, for example, the choice of French directors such as Georges Méliès, Louis Feuillade, René Clair, and Jean Vigo. The documents in the publication show his conceptual care in this section of the exhibition. Outside of an exhibition on film that decidedly emphasized the artistic, it probably would not have been understood. Here, however, this presentation joined in its conceptuality a series of others to which Stauffer contributed at the Kunstgewerbemuseum Zürich (today the

Museum für Gestaltung Zürich), for example, *Werner Bischof: Das fotografische Werk* (1957), *Dokumentation über Marcel Duchamp* (1960), and *Georges Méliès – Beginn der Filmkunst* (1964).

Radanowicz, who was a student on the photography program from 1958 to 1960, was able to make his first film for this exhibition: the short film *Elemente des Films* (Elements of Cinema, 1960).[11] Stauffer probably assigned him the task, as Fischli wrote that they had assigned to the *teachers* of the photography program the task of "writing scripts for short films."[12] Initially sounding like a didactic film, because of the informative off-camera voice, *Elemente des Films* turns to the absurd in a series of film tricks. The movements of an anonymous fencer (played by François Billeter) are accelerated, slowed down, interrupted, and played backward, according to the motto: "In film it is possible to create through movement in space not only traditionally formal design but also a new, moving reality that does better justice to our powers of imagination."[13]

The Surrealist subversion of perception that plays out before us presumably seemed like a provocation as well. In any case, it resulted in a conflict with the main teacher of the photography program, Walter Binder-Kempf, who had also produced a film for the exhibition. Radanowicz left the school without receiving a degree.

Luckily, he was able to work for Austrian avant-garde filmmaker Ferry Radax, who he met through Stauffer, on the film *Am Rand* (*On the Edge*, 1961–1963) as an assistant from 1960 to 1961.[14] Future artist Ida Szigethy assisted alongside Radanowicz and experimental poet Konrad Bayer, who had already appeared as a protagonist in Radax's film *Sonne halt!* (*Sun Stop!*, 1962), was one of the actors. The experimental film *Am Rand*, filmed at several locations in Europe, was commissioned by Victor N. Cohen, the founder of the Advico advertising firm in Gockhausen near Zurich, as a gift for his son,[15] and was screened under the title *Um zwanzig* (*Around Twenty*) at the *EXPRMNTL* festival in the Belgian spa town of Knokke-le-Zoute in 1963.[16] These films by Radax were based on slapstick and Surrealistic film tricks, which would also become important in Radanowicz's later films.

Stauffer also expanded his study of film: after a copy of Duchamp's film *Anemic Cinema* (1926) had been acquired, possibly for the Duchamp exhibition at the

Kunstgewerbemuseum Zürich in 1960, Stauffer made screenshots of his own copy of it, which he then sent to the artist for approval in 1961, who recommended cutting out one sequence as "unknown."[17] Stauffer also traveled with the head of the preliminary course, Hansjörg Mattmüller, and (former) students to the *EXPRMNTL 3* film festival in late 1963.[18] Murer in particular was impressed by the trip: "Serge Stauffer took us along to Knokke-le-Zoute [...] It was about film as a possibility for expressing oneself artistically. That was my homeland."[19]

The film scene's enthusiasm for artistic experimental film, which was already widespread in the 1960s, testifies to a powerful division of cultures. On the one hand, there was the cinema whose experimental forms were demonstrated in the films of Jean-Luc Godard, for example; on the other hand, fine art, in which films were perceived as paintings, so to speak. Like museums, cinemas were also struggling to provide an adequate platform for experimental cinematic works. As a result, in the 1960s experimental film evolved into an autonomous subculture and became a point of intersection between artistic genres.

In 1971 Birgit Hein described the composition of this "countermovement," the genre itself, and its component parts in detail. She subdivided experimental film into the "formal film" of Kurt Kren or herself, for example; the "Expanded Cinema" of Peter Weibel or Valie Export; the "narrative film" of Rosa von Praunheim; the "Actionist film" of Otto Muehl; the "political film" of Erika Runge, as well as of Hellmuth Costard; "computer film art"; and "video."[20] As Hein wrote for documenta 6 in Kassel in 1977, such films were no longer about symbolically representing a reality outside the film, but rather about "grappling with the reality of the film and its process of reproduction" and, in the process, "the examination of the illusion of reality took place precisely in the destruction of the real image. What are produced are the individual elements from which this illusion of reality is constructed."[21]

Film de Recherche

From the mid-1960s onward, Zurich also had an experimental film scene, with Film Forum and Platte 27 in particular offering platforms. Truniger described it thus: "The general sense of a new era that dominated Swiss film in the late 1960s also provided impetus for experimental filmmaking."[22]

Filmmaker HHK Schoenherr, who also edited the journal *Supervisuell*, was considered an important exponent in Switzerland.

In the Form und Farbe (F+F) program in free design founded by Stauffer and Mattmüller in 1965, which quickly established itself as a course for free art, film did not play a particular role, perhaps in part because "film work courses" were offered at the Kunstgewerbeschule from 1967 to 1969.[23] In the F+F class, Pop art set the style at first. By the time of the "Teamwork" course taught by Stauffer's wife, artist Doris Stauffer, Happening and Political Action art had gained acceptance at least from 1969 onward. As a teacher on this program, Serge Stauffer continued to be interested in ideas of art as research. In 1968, in a lecture on "design research" at a Swiss Werkbund conference on reforming design education in Baden, near Zurich, he showed, along with other examples from art, the short film *Melinda im Baum* (*Melinda in the Tree*, 1968) by Peter Schweri as an "absolutely unedited film sketch." He concluded that, "artists today have become aware of their activity as researchers," as "researchers of unknown possibilities in the realm of sensitivity."[24] Following this idea Stauffer also presented a "multimedia slide show" called *the nine sense show* at the Kleintheater Luzern in 1968, with the participation of Doris Stauffer, Murer, Markus Raetz, Radanowicz, Anton Bruhin, Renzo Schraner, Schweri, and Schweri's dog.

Schweri attended the preliminary course under Mattmüller in around 1960 and began studying graphic art before deciding instead to work as an artist. Around 1968 he made several films, one of which was about the Stauffer family; it combined absurd happenings and camera pans through their house and garden, and Radanowicz also appeared in it.[25] Another one was for IBM, and again another film-and-slide animation was to be projected on three walls in the Club Blackout in Kloten, near Zurich. Sadly, all of Schweri's films, apart from a digital viewing copy of the Stauffer family film, have been lost. Radanowicz, in turn, invited Serge Stauffer to take part in a group photograph by Peter Gaechter for *Schweizer Illustrierte*, in which Iwan Schumacher, Barbara Davatz, Schweri, Lizzy Schapper, Radanowicz, Pamela Ammann, Klaus Zaugg, Robert Müller, HR Giger, and guest star Robert Nelson appeared with the caption "Junge Schweizer Film-Rebellen" (Young Swiss Film Rebels). At Radanowicz's suggestion, the Zürcher Filmklub in Platte 27 had invited American experimental filmmaker Robert Nelson to show his films in February 1968.[26] According to the program for the excursion to Düsseldorf in 1968, the F+F class visited film artist Lutz Mommartz, who at the time was experimenting with hallucinogenic short films and had won a prize in Knokke-le-Zoute for the "Urselfie" *Selbstschüsse* (*Self-Shots*, 1967).[27]

From 1965 onward, Murer created an oeuvre of experimental short films, two of which portray proponents of Zurich art and counter culture: in *Chicorée* (1966), poet and journalist Urban Gwerder, and, in *Sad-is-Fiction* (1969), Alex Sadkowsky.[28] *Chicorée* was made for Gwerder's *Poëtenz* art performances. In these films by Murer, the medium is knocked out of joint, so to speak, intertwined with art performances, the canvas spattered with paint, and the legibility of the narrative is challenged but not entirely dissolved. Radanowicz made similarly informal short films during this period, such as *Glump* (1967), a "parody commercial" with Schweri and musician Mani Neumeier, commissioned by the GGK advertising agency in Basel, and *Pic-Nic* (1967), the "documentation of a bizarre meal by Zurich artist Friedrich Kuhn" for an Italian nightclub.[29] In the short film *13 Berner Museen* (*13 Bern Museums*, 1968, with Balthasar Burkhard), which Harald Szeemann commissioned for the museums of Bern, and especially in *22 Fragen an Max Bill* (*22 Questions for Max Bill*, 1969), which Radanowicz produced himself with H. Peter Walker, the cinematic narrative was challenged by a critical insistence.[30] The off-camera voice (Claus Bremer) not only repeats statements by Bill, but also openly criticizes them, which at the end of the film leads to a criticism of the film itself.

A change in cinematic language can also be found in the work of Renzo Schraner (1946–1969) who, after attending the Kunstgewerbeschule Zürich around 1960, made animated science films at the Zoological Museum of the University of Zurich, as well as experimental film collages.³¹ The short film *Allah* (1967) provokes with associative Pop art language, and recalls the Monty Python films that would later become famous. A later film loop, just nine seconds long, by Schraner (*Untitled*, ca. 1968–1969), by contrast, is minimal and conceptual.³² We see, from a car, shots of sequences from a drive through the countryside of the Swiss Plateau, with various colors in the background, which loops back to the beginning in a rapid sequence. The Pop stimulus is gone; before us lies only the cliché of the local landscape, captured in a circular sequence that can only really be grasped after extended watching.

Vision of a Blind Man (1968) by Murer was conceived entirely as an experimental situation:

> *Vision of a Blind Man* was an experimental film in the best sense of the word, a kind of research project [...] I was thinking about what would happen if [...] I were to put the camera on my shoulders and film with my eyes covered, letting myself be guided by all my other senses.³³

So on June 21, 1968, the longest day of the year, from dawn to dusk, he was taken by his colleagues Schraner and Christian Kurz to various places in and around Zurich, with his eyes bound and a loaded camera in hand. One scene takes place in Seebach at the Stauffer family's home, with other friends. Serge Stauffer appears in front of the camera with his eyes covered and says to Murer that he has done so out of sympathy for Murer. The film was described as a prototypical "film de recherche" in a Swiss Werkbund interview with Murer, Radanowicz, and Alexander J. Seiler, and was first screened in the spring of 1969. The review in the *Neue Zürcher Zeitung* that accompanied the interview read: "the contradiction between what his camera sees is often amazing; Murer's sometimes helpless, but more often poetically precise reflections show how differently the acoustic reality of the environment revealed itself to him."³⁴

This idea of a "film de recherche" is revealed, at least in this interview, as a possible alternative to the avant-gardes of experimental film and to political film. Political film—as advocated around 1970 by the journals *Filmkritik* in

Germany and *Cinéthique* in France, for example—rejected artistic avant-garde film, which is "defined solely and alone by researching the specific characteristic of an artistic practice" in order to prove that "this art is on a par with others," and hence is "tied to a very idealistic search for essence," as Jean-Paul Fargier wrote in 1972.[35] At that moment, research film presumably was a way out of the already predetermined fields of experimental and political film. The name "film de recherche," as part of science film, referred to recordings on film that document facts for research itself. To that end, the International Scientific Film Association formed a research film committee in 1950 that, from 1952 onward, published the journal *Research Film/ Le film de recherche/Forschungsfilm*. Artistic subjects played no role in it, although technical ones certainly did. In an issue from 1967, for example, new films from biology, ethnology, folklore, and the technical sciences were presented.[36]

There were very few filmmakers in the area of research film who were interested in artistic issues. One of them was certainly Jean Painlevé, who was active as a documentary filmmaker, a scientific filmmaker, and an experimental filmmaker. In 1930 he founded the Institut de cinématographie scientifique (Institute of Scientific Cinematography) in France for research for cinema and research through cinema, and that same year was a cofounder of the international Association pour la documentation photographique et cinématographique dans les sciences (Association for Photographic and Cinematographic Documentation in Sciences) and remained active in this area after the Second World War.[37] Artistic perspective played an important role in all of Painlevé's works, but research film with an interest in the arts was no more able to establish itself as an autonomous branch during this period than was the case for research art in general. Nevertheless, there were such efforts in experimental film, as is demonstrated by *La Région centrale* (*The Central Region*, 1971) by Michael Snow, a radical experiment in which he filmed a barren Canadian landscape with a robotically controlled camera that panned uninterruptedly throughout the space, but never repeated the same shot.

Hansjörg Mattmüller and Serge Stauffer, *Untitled (Volano)*, 1969 (Switzerland)
Parallel projection with two 8mm films, 9 minutes 22 seconds

Georg Radanowicz, *Untitled (F+F Schule, Samstagskurs)*, 1973 (Switzerland)
Super-8 film, 12 minutes 27 seconds

Film at the F+F

No films were made at the F+F program at the Kunstgewerbeschule Zürich before 1969. In late 1968, however, the activity report for the program includes on its list of needs, among other things, instructions to "acquire a film camera" and get a "better projection system."[38] In the autumn of 1969, on an excursion to Volano, Italy, with the class, Stauffer and Mattmüller made two films of the same length for a double projection.[39] The atmosphere was tense: in seeking to curtail the program, the school administration fired Doris Stauffer and Bendicht Fivian from the course. Perhaps for that very reason, the program organized a number of happenings in the courtyard of the residence and on the surrounding sea, which Mattmüller and Serge Stauffer filmed. Bendicht Fivian appears with a performance that recalls a satanic ceremony. As Murer had done a year earlier, Serge Stauffer filmed blindfolded. The film has a floating quality, constantly in motion, but at the same time a documentary calm. The visual language is hippie-esque, and recalls the films of Alejandro Jodorowsky, though without a narrative plot. The two parallel short silent films document a playful and at times surreal activity from two points of view.

Following the excursion, the program made a number of presentations in its defense in which slide and film projections were central. They showed what they called a "minimal" presentation with slides and "a number of films" to the school administration, other programs, students' parents, and the teachers' convention.[40] When the school administration nevertheless stuck to its punitive measures even thereafter, the class and its teachers formed an open protest, decided to quit together in early 1970, and thus triggered a scandal in the national media. The teachers mounted a slide and film show of the F+F program at the "Club Bel Etage" in Zurich in the spring of 1970.[41] Following additional performances and an exhibition at the Kunsthalle Bern in the summer of 1970, in January 1971, Hansjörg Mattmüller, Peter Jenny, Doris Stauffer, and Serge Stauffer founded the F+F Schule für experimentelle Gestaltung.

In 1971 Radanowicz also joined the F+F as a teacher, and offered several film courses. He and artist Urs Lüthi offered a special "Foto-Film" course from June to September 1971. Lüthi led the section on staged photography, with collages of existing photographic material, picture series, and photo novels, and Radanowicz the section with practical film work and the possibilities of cinematic expression, "without reference to film history, professional technique, or Hollywood, Nouvelle Vague, and New German Cinema."[42] In 1972 Radanowicz offered the courses "Neinsager gesucht" (Naysayers Sought) and "Die Filmkamera als Skizzenblock" (The Film Camera as Sketchpad). On one of these courses, the Super-8 film *F+F* (ca. 1971–1972) was produced: a cinematic portrait of the participants as a group.[43] One person after the other is filmed, but only incompletely, so that we cannot perceive the people as a whole, but instead all of them fuse into a single image of lived hedonism at the F+F: calm, confident poses, relaxed and laughing, a naturally individual lifestyle, an amusing coolness of jeans and sunglasses. By leaving some things out and stringing others together, Radanowicz managed to achieve a fascinating look at a scene, using neither narration nor explanation.

The "Die Filmkamera als Skizzenblock" course was also offered by Sebastian C. Schroeder at this time.[44] In short films such as *Collage Nr. 1* (1969) and *Unterschätzen Sie Amerika nicht* (*Do Not Underestimate America*, 1971), he created reflective research or essay films in his own way. By his own account, however, he did not take the role of F+F or his own work there very seriously: "So F+F. With Stauffer. I don't know. He paid us something. Perhaps 120 francs per course or something. We were there and just said some nonsense."[45]

These words express how the F+F was perceived by many: as an institution that was not to be taken seriously. Nevertheless, Schroeder clearly appreciated this platform, and in 1977 in several classes again offered a course, "Film und Video," based on Super-8 films.[46]

In Serge Stauffer's teaching, film played a role as well, one otherwise familiar from video art, for example in the "information-kommunikation" course of June 14, 1973:

> everyone who wants to participate has a certain length of film stock available; the task is to shoot three different shots that when shown in sequence have an *associative* connection. In order to distinguish the

sequences of individual participants, everyone will first shoot a neutral surface for three seconds.

This was followed by another task on the theme of "syntheses": "inspiration for a one-minute film: shoot a brief 'eccentric portrait' of a fellow student that seems out of the ordinary, odd, unusual, abnormal, crazy."[47]

The cinema format and film as genre played no role here. Film became one of various media that the experimental art of the period was using. With his ideas of art as research, from 1976 onward Stauffer developed a comprehensive theory in which art should be reformed "into a specialized profession" that served "social research": it should represent "an extended anthropology" that "deals with the entire human being."[48]

At that time, Stauffer spoke about the film scene in a rather distanced way. For example, looking back in 1974, he said of the excursion to Knokke-le-Zoute in 1963 that it only "supposedly had an influence" on "the evolution of Swiss film."[49] This expressed his disappointment that many of the young filmmakers in the 1970s were trying to make conventional films, and that experimental film could not find a market. Dieter Meier in turn lamented: "Very much in contrast to all the Murers and Radanowiczs of this world, these young filmmakers marched up to these pots everywhere and received subsidies, but this kind of film was never supported."[50]

Nevertheless, the personal friendships remained, and in 1976 Stauffer wrote to Radanowicz: "I enjoyed your short films incredibly, precisely because they are not Warhol films, not Schoenherr films, but have an atmosphere from the 1970s."

At the same time, in this letter Stauffer also expressed his disappointment about the evolution of the film scene in Switzerland: "measured against what I call 'art,' I see little research in film and photography."[51] This quotation shows that Stauffer did not find any particular potential for research art in the experimental film of this period, but rather in the comparatively conventional films by Radanowicz, such as *22 Fragen an Max Bill*.

Film no longer played a particular role in Stauffer's research art. In his teaching materials for 1977, he described "the *video camera* as for us the newest and least-known *sensitive device* for perception, which, properly understood, permits the most feedback and information about the current state of our perception." Because:

> the *camera* (with its points of view) is a kind of directional ray of defined volumes; a "spatial cone" within which certain events can happen [...] an "event space" that is more or less grasped and experienced, but that provides information about our state of mind, and it cannot, in my view, be replaced by any other medium known to us today. Anyone who understands this is in a position to experience and document his own "*event capability.*"[52]

A Brief Episode

In the 1960s, an experimental film scene evolved that was open to ideas of research. The tightrope that these research films walked was neither just to refer to themselves nor to something else, but rather to activate the "research function" as a true enrichment for the film as art form. As Hartmut Bitomsky said in 1971: "Such films explain by exploring themselves as a condition for clarification; they reveal themselves as not untouched by that which they touch. The productivity of these films lies in directing people who write and read "to a true poetics of research."[53] This corresponds to an important spirit of the time, at least in fine art, as Karin Thomas wrote in 1972:

> The fundamental progress of fine art in the 20th century is therefore increasingly articulated conceptually as dispensing with craft virtuosity in depicting naturalistic phenomenality and adapting to the problem-researching methodology of science.[54]

Various artists, such as Ferdinand Kriwet, organized their work around such principles, as Marc Matter wrote:

> He demanded from contemporary literature to abandon "inventions" and reflect instead on its

inherent material, namely language. Found material would likewise determine the composition of his films: Kriwet collected "texts" from the mass media—television images, newspaper articles, and press photographs—dissected and remounted them with the purpose of creating something new.[55]

The films mentioned from Stauffer's circle, such as the loop by Schraner of 1968–1969, the parallel projection by Hansjörg Mattmüller and Serge Stauffer of 1969, the F+F-Film by Radanowicz of 1971–1972, and especially *Vision of a Blind Man* by Murer of 1968 were trying to leave the cinema format behind and activate a "research function" via the medium of film in an artistic way. This phase was only very brief, merely an episode, and was soon, at least at the F+F, replaced by the new medium of video.

[1] Most of the films focused on here were shown in the *Serge Stauffer: Kunst als Forschung* (2013) exhibition that I curated at the Helmhaus Zürich, and the connections described here first became evident in preparing the show. At the time I conducted numerous interviews with, among others, Robert Cohen (son of Victor Cohen), Fredi M. Murer, Jürg Nutz, Georg Radanowicz, Peter Schweri, Doris Stauffer, and Veit Stauffer. For this chapter, I am again grateful for assistance from Murer, Radanowicz, Thomas Schärer, and Fred Truniger in the form of both advice and action. I am grateful to Doris Stauffer, the Graphische Sammlung of the Schweizerische Nationalbibliothek in Bern, and the Zürcher Hochschule der Künste for the opportunity to view their archives, and to the Cinémathèque suisse in Lausanne for information.

[2] Under my direction, the archive of Serge Stauffer in the Graphische Sammlung of the Schweizerische Nationalbibliothek in Bern was made accessible in 2013–2014.

[3] Serge Stauffer, "Filmregisseure und Filmstile," Hans Fischli, Willy Rotzler (eds.), *Der Film: Geschichte, Technik, Gestaltungsmittel, Bedeutung*, exh. cat., Kunstgewerbemuseum, Zurich 1960, p. 49–135, esp. 102–103.

[4] Lotte H. Eisner, *The Haunted Screen: Expressionism in the German Cinema and the Influence of Max Reinhardt*, trans. Roger Greaves, University of California Press, Berkeley 1969.

[5] Thomas Schärer, *Zwischen Gotthelf und Godard: Erinnerte Schweizer Filmgeschichte, 1958–1979*, Limmat, Zurich 2014, p. 53.

[6] Thomas Schärer, interview with Georg Radanowicz, September 25, 2008 (notes), Cinémémoire.ch project, p. 7.

[7] Fredi M. Murer, email to the author, September 1, 2014.

[8] Fredi M. Murer, excerpt from an interview, Thomas Schärer, *Zwischen Gotthelf und Godard*, p. 52.

[9] Bice Curiger, Dieter Meier, Fredi M. Murer, Sissi Zöbeli, "Zweite Gesprächsrunde," *Die wilden Sixties in Zürich: Im Rahmen der Ausstellung "Friedrich Kuhn: Der Maler als Outlaw" im Kunsthaus Zürich*, Zürcher Kunsthaus Kunstgesellschaft, Zurich 2011, p. 22–31, esp. 22–23.

[10] See Fredi M. Murer, "Marcel" (1962), archives of the artist; Fredi M. Murer, "Carrara: Der gefallene Turm von Pisa" (1962), Archive Zürcher Hochschule der Künste, EAA-2005-E01-130.

[11] See Georg Radanowicz, "Elemente des Films" (1960), Archive Zürcher Hochschule der Künste, EAA-2005-E01-119.

[12] Hans Fischli, Willy Rotzler, *Der Film* (see note 3), p. 11.
[13] Georg Radanowicz, "Elemente des Films," p. 41.
[14] See Schärer, interview with Georg Radanowicz (see note 5), p. 10.
[15] See Ferry Radax, "Am Rand / En marge," Cinémathèque suisse, Lausanne, Fonds Topic Film, shelf mark 1982 0930 00–04 (several versions).
[16] See *EXPRMNTL: Third International Experimental Film Competition, Knokke-le-Zoute, December 25th, 1963, to January 2nd, 1964 (Catalog)*, Cinémathèque royale de Belgique, Brussels 1964, n. p.
[17] See Marcel Duchamp, *Die Schriften: Zu Lebzeiten veröffentlichte Texte*, ed. and trans. Serge Stauffer, Regenbogen Verlag Theo Ruff, Zurich 1981, p. 267; Rrose Sélavy [Marcel Duchamp], *Anémic Cinéma* (1926), Archive Serge und Doris Stauffer, GS-STAUFFER-A-06-c-01–02.
[18] F+F teachers, "Pappelmann-Report," Hans-Rudolf Lutz et al. (eds.), *Experiment F+F, 1965–1970*, H. R. Lutz, Zurich 1970, p. 121–152, esp. 123. It names the teacher of the photography program, Walter Binder-Kempf, as having been on the trip; according to Fredi M. Murer's recollection, however, he was not on the trip; see Fredi M. Murer, e-mail to the author, December 22, 2014.
[19] Fredi M. Murer, excerpt from an interview, p. 286.
[20] See Birgit Hein, *Film im Underground: Von seinen Anfängen bis zum Unabhängigen Kino*, Ullstein, Frankfurt am Main 1971.
[21] Birgit Hein, "Film über Film," documenta GmbH (ed.), *documenta 6*, exh. cat., 3 vols., Paul Dierichs, Kassel 1977, vol. 2, p. 255–57, esp. 255.
[22] Fred Truniger, Julia Zutavern, "In der Arbeit künstlerisch, in der Öffentlichkeit politisch: Der Kampf der internationalen Experimentalfilmbewegung um Anerkennung," Urs Berger et al. (eds.), *Filmfrontal: Das unabhängige Film- und Videoschaffen der 1970er- und 1980er-Jahre in Basel*, exh. cat., Friedrich Reinhardt, Basel 2010, p. 19–25, esp. 22.
[23] See Thomas Schärer, *"Wir wollten den Film neu erfinden!": Die Filmarbeitskurse an der Kunstgewerbeschule Zürich, 1967–1969* (with DVD), Limmat, Zurich 2005.
[24] Serge Stauffer, "Beitrag zu weiteren Konzeptionen" (1968), lecture on "design research," Serge Stauffer, Michael Hiltbrunner (eds.), *Kunst als Forschung: Essays, Gespräche, Übersetzungen, Studien*, Scheidegger & Spiess, Zurich 2013, p. 47–51, esp. 50.
[25] Peter Schweri, *Untitled* (Stauffer family film, digitalization), 1968, Archive Serge und Doris Stauffer, GS-STAUFFER-D-01-SCHWERI.
[26] Thomas Schärer, *Zwischen Gotthelf und Godard*, p. 285–86.
[27] Anonymous, "Klasse F+F, Exkursions-Programm, Reise Kassel-Düsseldorf-Essen," September 21–30, 1968 (teaching material), Archive Serge und Doris Stauffer, GS-Stauffer-A-05-a-01, p. 2.
[28] Fredi M. Murer, *Chicorée* (1966); *Sad-is-Fiction* (1969), both: Fredi M. Murer archives.
[29] Thomas Schärer, *Zwischen Gotthelf und Godard* (see note 4), p. 288.
[30] Georg Radanowicz, Balthasar Burkhard, *13 Berner Museen* (1968); Georg Radanowicz, *22 Fragen an Max Bill* (1969), both: Lichtspiel, Kinemathek Bern.
[31] See Fredi M. Murer, e-mail to the author (see note 6).
[32] Renzo Schraner, Untitled (ca. 1968–1969), film loop, Archive Serge und Doris Stauffer, GS-STAUFFER-D-01-SCHRANER.
[33] Fredi M. Murer, excerpt from an interview, Thomas Schärer, *Zwischen Gotthelf und Godard*, p. 292. See also Fredi M. Murer, *Vision of a Blind Man* (1968), archives of the artist.
[34] Anon. ["ju"], "Film: Hohlspiegel unserer Umwelt?: Podiumsgespräch des Werkbundes," *Neue Zürcher Zeitung*, no. 195 (March 28, 1969), p. 11.

[35] Jean-Paul Fargier, "Wachablösung," trans. Beatrix Schumacher, Beatrix Schumacher et al. (eds.), *Filmische Avantgarde und politische Praxis: Gruppe Cinéthique*, Rowohlt Taschenbuch Verlag, Reinbek bei Hamburg 1973, p. 129–162, esp. 132–133.
[36] *Research Film* 6, no. 1 (1967), index.
[37] See Jean Painlevé, "Cinéma et recherche," ca. 1955, manuscript of a lecture at the Palais de la découverte, Paris, Archives Jean Painlevé, Les Documents Cinématographiques, Paris.
[38] F+F teachers, "Pappelmann-Report" (see note 18), p. 133.
[39] Hansjörg Mattmüller, Serge Stauffer, *Untitled* (Volano, "Hansjörg links," "Serge rechts"), two films, Archive Serge und Doris Stauffer, GS-STAUFFER-A-05-d-01 und -02.
[40] F+F teachers, "Pappelmann-Report," p. 137.
[41] Anonymous, "Club Bel Etage, Zürich: 16. März 1970, Lehrer der Klasse Farbe + Form (sic!) (F+F) der Kunstgewerbeschule, Dia- und Filmshow" (invitation), Archive Serge und Doris Stauffer, GS-Stauffer-A-05-a-01, p. 1.
[42] "F+F-Kurse für experimentelle Gestaltung, Zürich, Juni–September 71, Programm 2" (course sheet), Archive Kunsthalle Bern, files on the F+F exhibition in 1970.
[43] Georg Radanowicz, "F+F" (ca. 1971–1972), Archive Serge und Doris Stauffer, GS-STAUFFER-A-05-d-04.
[44] "F+F-Kurse für experimentelle Gestaltung Zürich, 4. Programm, 20. Januar–29. März 1972" (course sheet), Archive Kunsthalle Bern, files on the F+F exhibition in 1970; anonymous, "F+F Schule für experimentelle Gestaltung Zürich" (ca. 1973), promotional brochure, Archive Serge und Doris Stauffer, GS-Stauffer-A-11-d.
[45] Thomas Schärer and Fred Truniger, interview with Sebastian C. Schroeder (transcript), *Schweizer Filmexperimente*, 2011, p. 33.
[46] F+F Schule, "F+F Tagesklasse Freyastrasse, 3. Okt.–23. Dez. 1977" (course sheet), Archive Serge und Doris Stauffer, Bestand Doris Stauffer; F+F Schule, "F+F Tagesklasse Drahtschmidli, 3.10–24.12.1977" (course sheet), Archive Serge und Doris Stauffer, GS-Stauffer-A-11-e.
[47] Serge Stauffer, "information-kommunikation" (June 14, 1973), course sheet, Archive Serge und Doris Stauffer, GS-Stauffer-A-11-d, p. 1.
[48] Serge Stauffer, "kunst als forschung," Serge Stauffer, Michael Hiltbrunner (eds.), *Kunst als Forschung*, p. 179–231, esp. 179.
[49] Serge Stauffer, "Selbstdarstellung. Vergangenheit. 24.11.74" (manuscript), Archive Serge und Doris Stauffer, GS-Stauffer-A-11-d, p. 2.
[50] Dieter Meier, excerpt from an interview, Thomas Schärer, *Zwischen Gotthelf und Godard*, p. 294.
[51] Serge Stauffer, "brief an georg radanowicz, 1976," Serge Stauffer, Michael Hiltbrunner (eds.), *Kunst als Forschung* (see note 24), p. 177–178, esp. 178.
[52] Serge Stauffer, "f+f-tagesschule – herbst 1977, wahrnehmung 2" (November 6, 1977), teaching sheet, Archive Serge und Doris Stauffer, GS-Stauffer-A-11-e.
[53] Hartmut Bitomsky, *Die Röte des Rots von Technicolor: Kinorealität und Produktionswirklichkeit*, Hermann Luchterhand, Neuwied 1972, p. 144.
[54] Karin Thomas, *Bis heute: Stilgeschichte der bildenden Kunst im 20. Jahrhundert*, M. DuMont Schauberg, Cologne 1971, p. 347.
[55] Marc Matter, "The Writer as Filmmaker: On the *Text-Filme* by Ferdinant Kriwet," Gregor Jansen (ed.), *Kriwet: Yester 'n' Today*, trans. Michael Wolfson, exh. cat., Kunsthalle Düsseldorf/Galerie im Taxispalais/DuMont, Düsseldorf/Innsbruck/Cologne 2011, p. 119–121, esp. 119.

Experiences of the Experimental in French-Speaking Switzerland: Ciné-Clubs, Critics, Schools of Art
Interview with François Albera by François Bovier

Transcription by Nicolas Brulhart; translated from the French by Miranda Stewart

FRANÇOIS BOVIER   How would you describe your involvement in experimental cinema in French-speaking Switzerland?

FRANÇOIS ALBERA   I lived through a particular period of time—from the 1960s to the present. I would point to a number of determining factors which broadly include:
1) ciné-clubs, including cinemathèques and occasional special events; 2) cinema festivals;
3) opportunities to meet cinema directors. There is also my own personal contribution to these three areas—my practice, or rather my practices, namely as ciné-club organizer, cinema critic, lecturer in cinema at an art school, from time to time at several other similar institutions, and at universities, as a contributor to festivals, as a publisher, etc.

This is what has made me who I am and this has shaped my practices—having lived through these periods, taken part in these events, and participated in all these activities. My career has been punctuated by breakdowns, readjustments, and turning points of all kinds. I have been a member of particular schools of thought, held particular opinions, met very specific people (organizers of ciné-clubs and festivals, filmmakers), and discharged a variety of duties (press, ciné-clubs, festivals, education).

A key event in my film culture life was my meeting with P. Adams Sitney when he passed through Lausanne, in September 1967, to attend the Congrès international du cinéma indépendant (CICI, International Congress of Independent Cinema) held under the aegis of the Cinémathèque suisse (with its usual partners, *Premier plan*, a Lyon-based journal, and the cinémathèques in Toulouse, Luxembourg, and maybe Munich and Brussels, I can't exactly remember). Sitney mentioned the two visits he made to Switzerland in close succession—Zurich, Lucerne, Solothurn, and Lausanne—in *Film Culture*.[1] It was during his second visit that he came to Lausanne and I met him here.

Sitney arrived with two hours of New American Cinema (NAC) films to show in what was an eclectic program, a bit like all CICI programs, which were designed to screen found, unknown, or forgotten (silent and sound) films. I remember some memorable films by people like Bruce Conner, Stan Brakhage, Robert Breer, and Peter Kubelka. I was blown away. I met Sitney on that occasion and talked with him for ages. I managed to write almost an entire page on that meeting and event for *Le Peuple La Sentinelle*, a journal for which I wrote from time to time.[2]

He was an incredibly fascinating man with a very long beard—I remember that it was red and he smoothed it with his hands when speaking. He spoke very softly and had, what I thought, an unusual take on things. For example, he contrasted how Anne Wiazemsky is portrayed in both Robert Bresson and Jean-Luc Godard, and said that as Godard had discovered Wiazemsky through seeing *Au hazard Balthazar* (Bresson, 1966) Godard was now looking for what Bresson had accessed. This was, however, a pointless exercise. He had also wanted to film the actress Anna Karina in just the same way that Carl Theodor Dreyer had filmed Renee Maria Falconetti in *The Passion of Joan of Arc* (1928), but all he managed to do, in *Vivre sa vie* (*My Life to Live*, 1962), was merely to juxtapose the two images, thus demonstrating the impossibility of the task.

As I was a diehard Godard supporter at that time I found this all rather disconcerting, but also quite true (his comments could be read in light of the Benjaminian distinction between aura and reproduction). Herein also probably lies the difference between Jean-Marie Straub and Godard: Godard "quotes." At the same time, this allegory about Anne Wiazemsky has a strong sexual subtext (virginity, for Bresson). The curious thing is that, at that time, I had applied the Foucauldian analysis of Cervantes' *Don Quixote* in *The Order of Things* to *Band à part* (*Band of Outsiders*, 1964,) in which the characters play at being gangsters; much in the same way as Godard quoted Samuel Fuller and other filmmakers of that ilk in a presentation for the Interjeunesse Ciné-Club.

When Sitney came to Lausanne, he shook up my ideas about what I really liked in cinema at that time, essentially Godard, Glauber Rocha, the "new national cinemas" that emerged in the 1960s and were discussed at length in *Cahiers du Cinéma*, which I read and followed avidly; people like Miklós Jancso, Jerzy Skolimowski, and Carmelo Bene. After that I subscribed (not without difficulty) to *Film Culture*, and devoured lots of American books on the "underground" and New American Cinema. At that time you could easily find these books in London in the bookshops along Charing Cross Road. A trip to London in those days was in fact something of a pilgrimage for cinema lovers—you would come across all kinds of American films which were not distributed elsewhere in Europe, including B and Z movies, available because of the double bills screened in local cinemas.

Sitney's program did not really sit comfortably with the CICI. Freddy Buache, who clearly represented the traditional historic avant-garde (Luis Buñuel, Hans Richter, Fernand Léger, Marcel Duchamp, for example, always featured in his programs, as did Len Lye, Norman McLaren, Oskar Fischinger), and had a feeling for the visual arts (he had worked as an art critic and had connections with a number of contemporary abstract painters, particularly local ones, such as Charles Rollier from Geneva and Pietro Sarto from Ticino and Vaud, and Jean Lecoultre), was overtly hostile to anything experimental or, in any case, American (he did show films linked to the Cobra group, and a few by Robert Lapoujade, and, as an exception to his rule on American films, we also managed to see *David Holzman's Diary* (1967) by James McBride at the Cinémathèque suisse, translated live by Georges Goldfayn, a close friend of Buache, and, in a totally different genre, Raymond Borde's film about Pierre Molinier). This was probably because he didn't have personal relationships with any of the leading lights of the New American Cinema scene, and his circle of interest was still bound up with Surrealism and its offshoots (particularly Belgians such as Luc de Heusch). We can nonetheless see, in the minutes of a progress report from the Assembly of the Committee of the Cinémathèque suisse of September 29, 1967, that "in early September, as part of the CICI, a long session was devoted to New American Cinema in the presence of Mr. Adams Sitney of the New York *Film Culture* magazine [...]"

After this discovery, I developed a lasting interest in this kind of cinema through *Film Culture*, as well as through a number of American paperbacks—for example Gregory Battcock's anthology, *The New American Cinema*[3]; Sheldon Renan, *An Introduction to the American Underground Film*,[4] which I bought in 1968, and, two years later, *Underground Film. A Critical History* by Parker Tyler[5]—and especially by jumping at any opportunity to see these films. Eventually Robert Nelson was invited to the Solothurn Film Festival in January 1968 with several of his films. In the context of their exhibition on new American figurative painting, the Musée d'Art et d'Histoire in Geneva screened a selection of "experimental" films (*Thanatopsis* (1962) by Ed Emshwiller, *Grateful Dead* by Robert Nelson (1967), *See, Saw, Seams* (1965) by Stan VanDerBeek, *Castro Street* (1966) by Bruce Baillie, and *OffOn* (1968) by Scott Bartlett) from July 12 to September 14, 1969, which gave me the opportunity to use the columns of *Le Peuple La Sentinelle* (August 1 and 2, 1969) to contrast the "old and new" American cinemas. I raved enthusiastically about these films as they showed me "a new relationship between mankind and the world" emerging through Brakhage's lyricism and VanDerBeek's reflections on the divorce between technological progress and our emotional and social understanding thereof.

There could have been a second high point in my encounters with experimental film, namely *New Forms in Film* that was held in Montreux's congress hall in August 1974. Leaving aside the fact that I did not attend all the screenings, the conditions surrounding the event (which Louis Marcorelles reported on the front page of *Le Monde* on August 27, 1974) were hardly conducive to this, as the cinema was virtually empty, as was the exhibition. At the time I was making my way back from the Locarno Festival where we had seen *A Bigger Splash* (1974) by Jack Hazan, *Sweet Movie* (1974) by Dušan Makavejev, and *Pink Flamingos* (1972) by John Waters, along with films by Jacques Rivette, Bresson, Werner Schroeter, Rainer Werner Fassbinder, Alain Tanner, Maurice Pialat, and many others. The meetings, discussions, and, dare I say it, the political and historical issues we debated there were a million miles from the stuffy atmosphere of the Convention Center in Montreux. Indeed, if I remember correctly, this was the moment when Annette Michelson, who was connected at that time to the American contemporary art magazine *Artforum*, was ushering in the transition from a cinema for "cinema lovers," to a gallery and museum cinema, with the emergence of the curator as the "director" of the artists' work. These were things that all developed in ways that could not have been foreseen at the time, and that unfortunately tended to overshadow all else. I became uncomfortable in terms of my position as an "intermediary" between experimental or independent filmmakers, and their audiences, particularly students. This position meant that my role was to serve their interests, get them known, give them a platform from which to speak, but be careful not to force them to march to my tune.

What really spearheaded this development was the second American experimental cinema, referred to by Sitney as "structural" cinema. It was no longer underground in the political sense as understood by Stephen Dwoskin (transgression of social taboos, police confiscation of films, bans on screenings, etc.). If we go back to the debate with Gideon Bachmann, Parker Tyler, Amos Vogel, Lewis Jacobs, and Ian Hugo published by *Film Culture* in November 1957,[6] we can see the gap that had opened up between the subversive qualities of this cinema in its early days, and its later institutionalization.

Montreux turned out to be less of a revelation to me than Sitney's two hours of programs. Nevertheless, I owe to the Montreux program my discovery of Michael Snow, which, admittedly, was fairly major. After this opportunity to see *Wavelength* (1967), I made every effort to see other films by Snow and meet him, to introduce him to the public (I screened *La Région centrale* [1971] at the Ecole supérieure des beaux–arts in Geneva with the help of Georges Rey from Lyon), and to invite him as a guest. When Daniel Soutif curated *Le Temps, vite!* at the Centre Georges-Pompidou, he asked me to chair a meeting between Snow and Johan van der Keuken, who each chose one of their own films to "show" to the other. However, the exchange between these two poles of cinema never actually took place, apart from an informal meeting in the café in the company of Hubert Damisch. A much more memorable experience was the talk that Snow gave at Lausanne University thanks to Cinema Spoutnik, the Saint-Gervais Center for the Moving Image in Geneva, and François Bovier in 2000.

These two memories offer a hint of my particular take on experimental cinema. I didn't reject it, quite the contrary, but I wasn't a diehard supporter either. I refused to join a purely experimental closed circle such as the one Sitney set up or tried to set up later. This was in 1976, when Pontus Hultén introduced cinema to Beaubourg shortly after Montreux. He placed it within a particular artistic lineage in an event entitled *A History of Cinema* devoted to what Kubelka, in his contribution to the catalogue, called "true cinema," and Sitney called "independent cinema."

It is interesting to look at why experimental American cinema was called "New American Cinema" for years. This expression emerged at a time when "new" cinema existed all around the world at the intersection of three issues: decolonization; de-Stalinization; and the advent of a new generation of filmmakers and aspiring filmmakers in wealthy countries. This gave rise to a fairly exceptional state of affairs, obviously with differences, but also with similarities, in the three different "worlds" that existed at the time—the West (the dominant countries whose societies were witnessing the emergence of generations of intellectualized middle classes who were trying to forge a place for themselves in the world), the socialist world (with hopes of renewal and increased democratization), and the Third World (which was becoming an economic and political actor, and whose revolutionary movements had been quickly stamped out with the help of the former colonial powers). At that time we talked of a "New Wave," and also of Polish, Soviet, Italian, Brazilian, Algerian, Japanese "new cinemas," to mention a few, to such an extent that, for a number of years, *Cinéma 59* (*60*, *61*, *62*, etc.) even carried a column about these cinemas entitled "Small Planet," which featured all these countries (for example, Bulgaria, Denmark, Bolivia, Canada, Sweden, Greece, Yugoslavia) with the exception, perhaps, of Albania. These movements still fell within the commercial-industrial sector, but sought to disrupt its entire rationale if not to actually reconstruct it ex nihilo (as in the case of countries recently liberated from their colonial shackles).

It cannot be denied that, within these movements, there was considerable formal, narrative, dramaturgical, plastic, political, etc., experimentation. *Film Culture*, just to take that particular journal, had, since the 1950s, followed the renewal of the Italian cinema (neorealism), French cinema (before the New Wave with Robert Bresson and René Clément, and also thereafter), and British cinema ("Free Cinema"). It had discussed the place of the documentary and the contribution of the documentary to fictional works, taken the pulse of the changes wrought by television, taken an interest in films about art, and, naturally enough, covered independent American filmmakers. The general feeling at the time was to encourage the renewal of cinema rather than to define any autonomous space. This was similar to the 1920s, when Germaine Dulac, Marcel L'Herbier, and Jean Epstein sought, with the aid of confrontational critique (Louis Delluc, Léon Moussinac, Jean Tedesco), to engage with popular cinema and not simply focus on sessions for the "happy few" at Ricciotto Canudo's CASA (Club des amis du septième art) film club. They did however promote this kind of session through screenings at the Palais Galliera, the Salon d'Automne, and specialist cinemas such as Le Vieux Colombier and Studio 28, which organized talks and exhibitions, as well as through ciné-clubs.

What is more, the New American Cinema Group's manifesto of September 28, 1960, placed itself explicitly within this New World cinema movement, and held that "official" cinema was running out of breath, partly because it was thematically superficial, generally corrupt, and lacked style and sensitivity. This statement was signed by Lionel Rogosin, Peter Bogdanovich, Alfred Leslie, Emile de Antonio, and not just the Mekas brothers, Shirley Clarke, and Robert Frank.[7] The aim was to offer an alternative to dominant cinema and, if possible, to supplant it. It has to be said, however, that more than one signatory finally ended up moving over to commercial cinema.

The situation in Europe, and indeed in the rest of the world, did not necessarily mirror what was happening in America. No doubt Parker Tyler's article "For *Shadows* against *Pull My Daisy*" in a sense marked a tipping point, at a particular moment in time, between a desire to renew American cinema and a withdrawal to a separate world, which Sitney would later theorize in almost mystical terms— *Visionary Film*—before the gallery- and museum-cinema model set itself up as the norm. Rightly or wrongly, I took a position on this in the catalogue for *Independent American Cinema*, an event organized by Catia Riccaboni, a student from one of my workshops at the Ecole supérieure des beaux–arts in Geneva in 1989 entitled: "'Experimental cinema' in the History of the Cinema." In it, I tried to redefine the meaning of "experimentation." At that time I took this notion to include a broad or expanded view, building on the ideas of experience and experiment in all their senses—the viewer's lived experience of the film, and not merely a "laboratory" experiment on the part of the filmmaker. Experience in the sense of social experience, a shared experience that encompasses both the film and the viewer, and sees them in the light of the reality intended, tackled, captured by the film. That is the "game" [jeu], in the most serious sense of the word, that Michael Snow puts at the center of each of his films, based on the Shklovskyan belief in "art as process"—through the systematic exploitation of the technical characteristics of the camera, for example its ability to swivel from right to left, or to zoom in and restrict the space filmed, the film *experiments*. I prefer the word "stake" [*enjeu*] which underpinned the films of

Jean-Marie Straub and Danièle Huillet, who added to this kind of procedure (360° panoramic shots, for instance), a historical, social, or political reference point, a text, and bodies.

There is no doubt that May 1968 was a defining event for me and played a decisive role in my interest in filmmakers whose practices were in opposition to dominant (commercial) norms. It led to a way of thinking about images and sounds and a use of social and political angles that could get films squeezed out of distribution channels, whereupon they would have to fight to get back in under their own terms (partnerships with independent cinemas, parallel circuits, alternative venues). This struggle was waged both on this terrain and in criticism (magazines, journals). Until 1968, I had vaguely thought about "making cinema," much as many other cinema lovers and active ciné-club members frequently did, and had thought about following classes at the Cinema Conservatory, if that is what it was called, a kind of ultra-modern course set up by Noël Burch and Jean-André Fieschi, the opposite of the Paris-based Institut des hautes études cinématographiques (IDHEC, Institute for Advanced Cinematographic Studies, active from 1943 to 1986).

Before 1968, my framework for "modern" cinema had undoubtedly come from a series of articles by Burch in *Cahiers du Cinéma*. But May 1968 redefined everything, as everything was now politicized. Fortunately, I was at high school in Annemasse at that time (I had been there for two years) and I took part in the social and political movement (challenging teachers, classroom strikes, street demonstrations). As soon as I had finished my final exams, I headed off to Paris to take an active role in what I had been hearing on the radio at the height of the "events." Then I went to Avignon where the Living Theatre (which I had already seen in Geneva—*Small Pieces* at the Théâtre de Carouge and *Antigone* at La Comédie) defied the festival founded by Jean Vilar by refusing to play in the Cour des Papes, and preferring to take their show to the streets.

This led me to start showing film-tracts at the ciné-club in Annemasse to which I belonged brought to us by students from Grenoble. I also took part in political discussions after the films. I even went off to Locarno to meet Godard and heard him say that it was stupid to want to make cinema because that was simply another way of replacing the people you film—what you should do was distribute Super-8 cameras to peasants and workers and allow them to make their own films.

I should now take a step backward chronologically and look at the contribution made by ciné-clubs and magazines in the 1960s, during the time I was at high school, essentially my formative years.

There were at least three important ciné-clubs in Geneva: the Interjeunesse Cine-Club aimed at senior high school students; the CCU, the University of Geneva Ciné-Club; and the Groupe cinématographique des organisations internationales (with a cinema inside the Palace of Nations in Geneva). There were also ciné-clubs run by organizations—in my case the Institut Florimont, where I spent a few "confrontational" years. It was chaired by Michel Dami (who was paid to supervise senior high school students, and who was, at that time, a psychology student with Jean Piaget and had started a thesis in film theory in Paris with the title "Does Cinema Offer a Model for Knowledge?") along with another student supervisor, Jacques Poux, also a member of the university Ciné-Club. Henri and Geneviève Agel regularly held film sessions in this establishment where there were lively discussions between teachers (mainly priests, it was a Catholic school), moderators, and pupils about controversial films such as Buñuel's *Nazarín* (1959) and different versions of *Joan of Arc* (the Agels were clever at playing up their own differences to get the debate going). It was here—with fellow student Kirk Tougas, who later became a Canadian experimental filmmaker—that I started to write for *Le Bateau ivre*, a cyclostyled publication; I also translated Tougas and wrote an article on his poetry. This led to my expulsion from the establishment on a variety of grounds ("atheism, existentialism, and Marxism," although this was, bar the atheism, rather over-exaggerated). In addition to the three ciné-clubs in Geneva, I should add UFOLEIS (Ligue de l'enseignement) at the FJEP (Foyer des jeunes et d'éducation populaire) in Annemasse (where I became a high school pupil after I had been expelled). I should also include the Maison de la Culture in Thonon (which hosted the "Semaine des Cahiers"—that is where I discovered *Not Reconciled* [1965] by Straub and was totally blowed over) and the Annecy Ciné-Club where we would occasionally go when we could get hold of a car (to see, for example, Buñuel's *L'Âge d'Or* (1930) which couldn't be seen anywhere else at that time). And, of course, the Cinémathèque suisse, which organized a screening every fortnight in a school classroom, alternating with the University of Lausanne Ciné-Club. One day Henri Langlois turned up with a film that he had just saved or found during a move. I remember a memorable screening where he presented David Wark Griffith's *The White Rose* (1923), and ended up in floods of tears at the end.

The UN ciné-club, in particular, was run by a man called Garcia, who had lots of overseas connections and could get films from Eastern Europe, Latin America, and Africa that the Swiss Customs would have blocked at the border if anyone else had dared pull such a stunt—films had to be supplied by the two non-commercial Swiss film distribution companies (plus a few other rather more marginal ones) or they had to be distributed through normal channels. *Travelling* documented much of this activity.[8]

Did I see any "experimental" films in these places? In the Knokke-le-Zoute sense of the word I think probably not, although there were echoes of experimental cinema in *Travelling*. I had already heard of this journal before I met Sitney. Marcel Leiser, who had founded and edited it (with a very diverse range of people: the two Dumonts, François Pasche, Marcel Schüpbach, Sylvie Rudhardt, with graphic design by André Chevailler), was himself an independent filmmaker and positioned himself on the "margins." His distribution structure at that time was called "Cinéma-Marginal Distribution." He saw himself as part of the French-speaking Swiss "underground," as Alain Tanner once disparagingly remarked in *Cahiers du Cinéma* in an interview he gave after the Paris release of *Charles mort ou vif* (*Charles Dead or Alive*) in 1969.[9]

The third series of determining factors include writing and, more precisely, cinema criticism.

Participation in ciné-clubs often prompted a desire to prolong these debates and discussions through writing. Presenting films, speaking in public, and preparing film descriptions and articles of various lengths in the ciné-club bulletin, if indeed there was one, or on cyclostyled stylesheets if not, all steered me in the direction of critical writing. We should not underestimate the importance of the role played by ciné-clubs in the intellectual and artistic education of generations of people who have ended up in cultural and educational institutions. Or the role played by those who "supervised" or chaired these learning experiences. In my case, Renato Missaggia, an Italian assembly worker from Terraillon who ran the FJEP ciné-club as a volunteer, was an extremely important influence, and quick to involve me in programming and giving presentations.

The importance of film magazines was a major incentive (*Cahiers du Cinéma*, *Positif*, *Image et son*, *Cinéma 60*, and many more)—as indeed was the fact, amazing when you look back at it, that cinema at that time played a relatively important role in cultural and general journals, and even in the daily papers. In French-speaking Switzerland there was *Travelling*, which I have already mentioned. This was a magazine put together by volunteers and left for sale at the cash desk of any cinema that was prepared to take it. I came to it through friends from ciné-clubs, specifically Jean-François Rohrbasser whom I had known at Interjeunesse. Several other people from Geneva came along at the same time as me—Maurice Rey, Laurent Vonwiller, Sylvie Rudhardt. The first became a psychiatrist, the second an agronomist, and the third a journalist (writing as Sylvie Arsever). Writing makes you want to see more films and read film books. There is also the opportunity to gain accreditation to film festivals. One thing leads to another. Indeed, you could aspire to a column in a newspaper as a stringer, a job that might even be paid (not a lot). Leiser was the critic for *La Nouvelle Revue de Lausanne*. Criticism in major newspapers, in Switzerland as elsewhere, was the prerogative of experienced writers, some of whom had built up considerable reputations. These included Georges Bratschi at *La Tribune de Genève*, Buache at *La Tribune de Lausanne*, Pierre Biner at *Le Journal de Genève* (and later Christian Zeender when Biner had to move to the theater column under pressure from the cinema owners). These people developed a "way of thinking about cinema" in their criticism of film releases. Divisions and positions were marked and fueled by bitter debates in the French press. Weeklies (broadsheets) such as *Les Lettres françaises*, *Arts*, *L'Express*, *Le Nouvel Observateur*, *Les Nouvelles littéraires*, *Le Figaro littéraire* devoted entire pages to cinema, as did, to a lesser extent, the monthlies (NRF, *Lettres nouvelles*, *Les Temps modernes*, *Esprit*). Things were very different then.

I managed to get into *Le Peuple* through a socialist cousin (André Donneur) who had founded the MDE (Mouvement démocratique des étudiants) with Jean-Claude Buhrer (who later managed to get into *Le Monde*). Then, after 1968, when my political views hardly made me a friend of social democracy (*Le Peuple* was awash with editorials by Jules Humbert-Droz and Jeanne Hersch seeking to quash international "leftism" by doing their utmost to discredit it), I joined *La voix ouvrière* (*V.O.*), in 1971, and worked there for the six to ten years when it was still a daily, and continued to work there when it moved to being a weekly with some unfortunate name changes (from 1980 as *VO-Hebdo*; 1986–1995 *VO-Réalités*; and then from 1995 *Gauchebdo*). My writing activities varied over time—they depended on who I met, what caught my attention, and, later on, the rather more academic discussions in the university world (*Synchronos kinimatografos*, *Cahiers du Cinéma*, *Art Press*, *Dialectiques*, *France nouvelle*, *Révolution*, *Tout va bien*, *Skrien*, *Cinémathèque*, *Positif*, prior to today's magazines such as *Vertigo*, *1895 revue d'histoire du cinéma*, *Décadrages*, *Cinémas*, etc.). I even contributed, when I was at the university in Lyon, to the French Communist Party's regional weekly, *La Voix du Lyonnais*, and later to its daily paper *Le Point du Jour*.

Festivals were the fourth determining factor. My passion for films through my experience of ciné-clubs and my critical writing put me on this path. First in Locarno (with "Cinema e Gioventù" which was an offshoot of the ciné-clubs), and then as a critic. If you wanted to go to Cannes or Venice, you had to be accredited by a newspaper and *V. O.* was my ticket.

The great thing about going to festivals is that they let you appreciate the diversity of cinema throughout the world, a diversity that commercial distribution, in a single country, can never provide. A festival is an exhibition in the sense that there is a hierarchy of works designed to showcase the right people. However, there is nothing to prevent a

CINEMA : Festival de Cannes

« Apocalypse Now » : l'Amérique au Vietnam

De notre envoyé spécial
François ALBERA

Présenté in extremis parmi les films en compétition du Festival de Cannes, *Apocalypse Now*, de Francis Coppola, fut un des films marquants de cette manifestation. C'est aussi un événement politique — mais cela, l'industrie, la presse et, peut-être bien, Coppola lui-même, vont tout faire pour lui faire oublier.

Le projet de ce film remonte à 1968. Coppola a mis dix ans pour le réaliser, réunir les 30 millions de dollars qu'il a coûté, le tourner, malgré l'opposition des autorités US, et le « monter » depuis presque trois ans. C'est dire que ce film est tout le contraire de l'ignoble *Voyage au bout de l'Enfer* de Cimino, réalisé contre *Apocalypse Now* et couvert d'oscars et de fausses gloires pour lui barrer la route.

Le contraire, car le film de Coppola n'exalte pas l'Amérique en caricaturant les Vietnamiens, en jouant des ressorts immondes du patriotisme et du racisme pour l'unité de la Nation américaine : le film de Coppola est un film sur l'Amérique, mais au Vietnam.

Pour mettre ensemble quelques images de l'Amérique, Coppola a choisi le lieu où ces images tuaient : le Vietnam.

Ces images, ce sont celles d'une civilisation industrielle - capitaliste ultra-développée. A la fois les gadgets technologiques (autos, transistors, télévision) et la barbarie des mystiques irrationnelles (Jim Jones, Charles Manson, les « tueurs fous » de carnaval). Pour aller de l'une à l'autre, des images intermédiaires : les girls culs-nus de *Play-Boy*, le surf sur les côtes californiennes, la défonce au LSD.

Et puisque ce film tente de relier quelques images entre elles, il ordonne logiquement comme un voyage, un itinéraire. Willard, le colonel américain, est chargé par l'état-major US à Saïgon, de remonter un fleuve jusqu'au Cambodge pour retrouver et liquider le colonel Kurtz, un soldat américain devenu fou...

Ainsi Willard et ses hommes remontent le fleuve à travers la jungle, dans une vedette blindée, et ils traversent toutes les situations qu'a connues l'armée américaine au Vietnam. Sur les rives, les ponts, le théâtre de la guerre — comme on dit — présentent une suite de scènes qui, toutes, expriment la même horreur.

L'Amérique au Vietnam, c'est ainsi un village vietnamien qu'on rase pour permettre à des champions de surf d'exercer leur sport ; c'est la musique de Wagner, beuglée par les haut-parleurs des hélicoptères qui apportent la mort ; c'est l'enivrante odeur du napalm ; c'est le spectacle de music-hall pour les soldats, le massacre d'une jonque de paysans, parce que les soldats ont peur, etc. Ce voyage, c'est à la fois le moyen de voir ce qu'il en était de cette guerre américaine et la démonstration de son absurdité et sa folie. Au terme de sa remontée, Willard aura donc perdu toute croyance en sa mission ; Kurtz — devenu un dieu vivant dans les ruines de temples bouddhiques — n'a fait que pousser à son comble la logique de cette guerre. Willard le tue... et prend sa place !

 « Mais, dès samedi dernier, à Cannes, des plumitifs qui ont en cené le film de Cimino sont en très en traces pour lester de *désamorcer* ce discours pourtant sans ambiguïté : Coppola ayant fait référence à Joseph Conrad et « Heart of Darkness », on s'efforce de transformer *Apocalypse Now* en un « voyage mental », on s'efforce d'y retrouver la structure religieuse de *Rencontre du 3e Type* où le personnage principal se défaisant progressivement du réel, du contexte, de la société, pour partir avec les extra-terrestres ! Symptôme du désarroi d'une société, ce dernier film proposait une solution de salut dans l'au-delà (Dieu ou les Martiens). Coppola achève, au contraire, son portrait de l'Amérique dans la caricature de la religion. Les cérémonies — montrées comme celles des « sauvages » dans *King Kong* — qui sont celles des sectes à la Jim Jones.

L'équivoque du film c'est cependant son caractère spectaculaire : évoquer l'horreur avec de telles images, c'est, notons notes, faire de l'horreur un spectacle esthétique. Coppola a beau dire : « ce n'est pas un film sur la guerre, le Vietnam, c'est la guerre le Vietnam », il met de la splendeur à montrer l'attaque d'un village où meurent les gens. Cette contradiction surmontable seulement en dehors du cinéma industriel hollywoodien, sera peut-être fatale au film. Le problème est le même — en plus petit — avec *China Syndrome*, efficace dénonciation d'une énergie audacieuse soumise au profit, *Le Tambour*, de Schlöndorff, *Sibiriade* de Mikhalkov-Kontchalovski, etc.).

Pour relier ces images entre elles...

Les joies du surf sur une plage californienne.

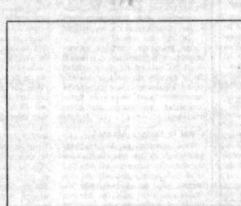

Les beautés à peine vêtues du club « Play-Boy ».

Jim Jones et ses disciples, une nouvelle spiritualité.

...il faut passer par celles-ci

François Albera, "*Apocalypse Now*: l'Amérique au Vietnam," cinema column, *Voix Ouvrière*, May 25–26, 1979

Un Premier Mai au cinéma (conte)

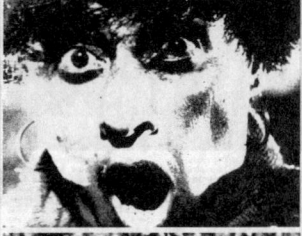

Le Premier Mai de cette année-là, comme la pluie recommençait à tomber, j'étais allé voir un film américain sur la guerre du Vietnam. Le réalisateur qui était un peu italien et russe, je crois, avait commencé à la General Motors où l'on apprend à monter les films, en assembler les pièces de manière à ce que les histoires roulent dans le bon sens. Puis il avait ensuite passé à la TV où — comme il disait — il s'était fait la main en tournant des spots publicitaires.

Justement, là, je me disais qu'il eu la main un peu lourde.

Je me rappelais le début de « Comment photographier ? », en Marabout-Flash : ce qui compte avant tout, c'est le cadrage, pour réussir une photo, c'est de « mettre en vedette le sujet dans le cadre que constituent les bords de l'image ». Mais là, il me semblait que cette mise en vedette de quelques stars s'accompagnait de mise à l'ombre ou dans l'ombre.

Et si les bords du cadre découpaient au lieu d'encadrer simplement ? Si cet encadrement divisait ? Le beau Serge disait bien que ce qui comptait, c'était le hors-cadre. Aussi, lui qui connaissait la musique et la peinture (notamment celle de Picasso), multipliait les angles de vues. Et puis, oncle Jo avait décidé que les cadres décideraient de tout, et Boris s'était mis à rentrer dans le cadre à Serge, qui fut mis sur la touche.

Mais cette idée qu'il y avait un reste de l'image me turlupinait. On pourrait donc lui demander son reste ou partir sans. Les restes, les déchets, généralement, ne posent que des problèmes d'évacuation. Comment s'en débarrasser ?

Avant la guerre, et pendant, alors que régnait le peintre en bâtiment, les images étaient toujours bien cadrées et bien composées à l'intérieur du cadre : ça ne faisait pas un pli.

On a su plus tard que, si l'opérateur d'actualité, Adolf Cimino, avait légèrement tourné la tête et fait pivoter sa caméra, on aurait vu des juifs battus, insultés, des cadavres entassés qu'on avait parfois du mal à évacuer.

D'ailleurs, comme aujourd'hui on a l'art d'accommoder les restes, le meilleur copain de Cimino avait montré ça dans Holocauste. De nouveau, tout était cadré, sauf que, ce qui était, c'est ce qui ne l'était pas avant. Il manquait toujours quelque chose aux Galeries Lafayette. Un nouveau reste.

Resnais, lui, avait vraiment filmé des déchets, des ruines, puisqu'il ne restait que ça ! Il était trop tard pour filmer ce qui n'avait pas à l'être. L'herbe repoussait autour des fours crématoires et déjà les architectes et les gardiens étaient lavés de leur crime. Les torchons ne manquaient pas...

Quand ce sera le moment, me disais-je dans la salle obscure, un cinéaste filmera, comme pour de vrai, une famille vietnamienne dont la petite-fille, un jour, aura été brûlée par le napalm, tandis que son frère apportait des vivres aux partisans.

Pour l'instant, le cinéaste cadrait obstinément la belle tête burinée et virile de Denis Rot, comme si un plan plus large aurait dévoilé des parties honteuses, comme si un autre angle aurait foutu par terre tout le plaisir du spectateur.

J'avais lu, dans une revue sérieuse, un entretien avec ce cinéaste. Il disait qu'il avait tourné son film en été, et comme on devait savoir que c'était l'hiver, il avait fallu dénuder les arbres et bien s'en tenir aux angles et aux cadrages prévus pour ne pas se trouver « enfacé... de l'été » !
Hi ! Hi !

Et puis, à la sortie, j'ai parlé un peu avec mon voisin, que j'avais vu — me semblait-il — l'après-midi au cortège. Il avait une casquette FOBB. Il avait l'air un peu ému et je lui ai montré la photo de cette petite fille de Truang-Bang. Il m'a alors demandé de vers qui elle courait, cette petite fille nue. Qu'est-ce qu'il y avait, en somme, entre nous et elle ? Ce photographe, lauréat du Prix P..litzer (je n'osais pas le lui dire !) et en quoi montrer cette image-là n'était pas faire tout simplement le contraire de Cimino et Hitler, mais pas autre chose ?

Je le regardai s'éloigner et demeurai pensif.

François Albera

et soudain

François Albera, "Un Premier Mai au cinema (conte)," cinema column, *Voix Ouvrière*, May 3, 1979

more inquisitive mind from taking a counter view, and seeking out films only available at this kind of event. When you see Dariush Mehrjui's *The Cow* (1969) in Venice, an original Iranian film which had been banned in its own country, followed, the next day, by Marcel Hanoun's *Spring* (1971), this gives you pause for thought. It casts a whole new light on the order established by advertising, the media, and so forth. What's more, festivals offer the opportunity to meet filmmakers—in 1973 I met Theo Angelopoulos in Cannes, in a bar, just after I had seen Μέρες του '36 (*Days of '36*, 1972) in the Directors' Fortnight selection. I bumped into Rocha again there; I met Nagisa Ôshima (and his actress from *In the Realm of the Senses*, 1976). Your admiration for a particular film and the way you feel about it make these meetings so intense that some things are heightened—for example, a particular film that overpowers all others and, in a sense, relegates them to oblivion.

Through Angelopoulos I began to write for *Synchronos kinimatographos*, edited at the time by Michel Demopoulos and a group of Athenian Althusserians and Lacanians who were living under the Greek military junta. I made a point of meeting up with them until democracy returned—at which point they cheered up and abandoned politics. Athens was where I met Jean-Marie Straub and Danièle Huillet who were holding a retrospective at the Goethe Institute. That was a decisive encounter.

In Cannes I met up with Monica Galer, a ciné-club friend from Geneva, who took me to Rotterdam where she was helping Hub Bals. He was organizing a festival and it turned out to be exactly my kind of festival at that time—an incredibly enriching experience. Bals was programming films that he liked without worrying about whether they were "world premieres" or not. He had an "arthouse" distribution circuit and used this to support his festival. He charged nothing for hospitality—we were put up in boat cabins in the harbor, the films were screened in a kind of enormous, multi-story Cultural Center—our only expense was that we had to contribute intelligence and taste. A photographer took portrait shots of all the participants and made enlargements that Bals hung throughout the festival spaces. There was, for example, a graphically creative daily newspaper—I later used this as inspiration for *Pardo News* in

Locarno. In Rotterdam the emphasis was far more on independent cinema, which, with its wider scope, was, to my mind, a surrogate for "experimental cinema," including it, but not limiting itself to it.

In Rotterdam we saw films by Johan van der Keuken and actually met him (I had previously met him in Lyon and he has since become a close friend), Peter Greenaway with his short films (was he really making "experimental" cinema before *The Draughtsman's Contract* [1983] catapulted him into commercially distributed cinema?). We saw the complete works of Robert Frank (which bowled me over),[10] films by Frans van de Staak, the latest films by Stephen Dwoskin, Boris Lehman, and films by Marguerite Duras, Raymond Depardon, Raoul Ruiz, Robert Kramer, Jean-Pierre Gorin, etc. It was a very stimulating atmosphere, just right for meeting people and making friends. This is where I recruited most of the filmmakers that I later invited to ESAV as guests.

Bals asked me to do some prospecting for him in the USSR as I had been going there since 1975, with the support of *V.O.*, as part of a project involving the publication of texts by Eisenstein, and I had made some friends there. This proved to be a matter of some concern to the Swiss Federal Police who called me in a few years later to interrogate me about my alleged spying—I aroused even greater suspicion as I'd also gone to Bulgaria, to a FIAF Congress! Bals also invited me to write about films for his journal *Kwartaal*, and his catalogue. One thing led to another and I started writing for *Skrien*, the Dutch magazine for which, incidentally, Van der Keuken wrote.

In Rotterdam I met David Streiff, the new director of the Locarno Festival. He was a photographic historian (his thesis was on Gotthard Schuh) who had taken over from Moritz de Hadeln. He asked me to work with him as part of the "commissione artistica," the selection committee. When I was on this committee I tried to make sure that well-known "research" (if not experimental) films by people like Alexander Sokurov, Kira Muratova, Joseph Morder, and Catherine Breillat were included in the competition—these were some of my "victories"—and that films such as *Class Relations* (1984) by Straub and Huillet were screened on the Piazza. I was also responsible for *Pardo News*, the festival's daily paper which was set up around that time. This gave us the opportunity to have fun and play around creatively with graphics, photographs, and texts. The staff involved included students and former students from the Ecole des beaux-arts, such as Françoise Bridel, Denis Corminbœuf, Claudine Després, and Véronique Goël, who I recruited, and a few outsiders such as Fausto Pluchinotta and Boris Lehman, as well as Frédéric Maire. Our main idea was to invite festival participants to contribute to the newspaper by submitting articles (Daney), drawings (Dwoskin, Mario Botta), or photographs (Arnaud Claass). We paid rather less attention to films screened on the Piazza, which tended to be chosen to attract a large public, than to research films, a Hans Richter exhibition, or retrospectives, to the great chagrin of the festival president, Raimondo Rezzonico.

I had the opportunity to organize two retrospectives in Locarno: on Boris Barnet in 1985, with Roland Cosandey, and on Lev Kuleshov in 1990, with the filmmaker's granddaughter, Katja Khokhlova, and Valérie Posener; each retrospective was accompanied by a catalogue and an exhibition. Barnet was an amazing discovery, despite the fact that Buache had shown Barnet's *The Girl with a Hatbox* (1927) at the Cinémathèque suisse on several occasions. It was here that I discovered Soviet comedy (overshadowed by epic cinema) and a school of actors unique in the world, in the tradition of Vsevolod Meyerhold's biomechanics.[11] Kuleshov was already well known, albeit for the wrong reasons—essentially for his "effect."[12] However, an issue of *Film Culture*[13] by Stephen Hill devoted entirely to Kuleshov sufficed to intrigue me and spur me to find out more. I had met Aleksandra Khokhlova in Moscow, and we decided to translate Kuleshov's writings into French and publish them for the very first time.

In those days the Locarno retrospectives explored new filmmakers such as Ozu Yasujirō, Alberto Cavalcanti, and Mikio Naruse. They did not seek to celebrate conventional values. Over time a genuinely innovative publishing activity grew up, although that was ultimately brought to an end by Marco Müller, who was the festival director from 1991–2000.

Just like Rotterdam, Locarno offered an opportunity to meet filmmakers, and this largely informed the approach I took in my cinema courses.

I'd now Ecole des arts visuels (today the Haute école des arts visuels, HEAD) and the University of Lausanne. When I left school in 1968 I went on to study philosophy (and then the science of language) at the Humanities Faculty in Lyon. In 1974 I began working at the Arts décoratifs and then at the Ecole des Beaux-Arts in Geneva. While I was still in Lyon, I was summoned to Geneva by Claude Richardet—whom I had met previously in ciné-clubs—on the grounds that I had a university degree in cinema—a thesis entitled "The Aesthetics of Eisenstein," supervised by Henri Maldiney. I had taught for a year at the Humanities Faculty of the University of Lyon, replacing Jean-Louis Leutrat, a tenured lecturer on sabbatical leave, and I had also taught at the Institut d'Etudes Politiques. Richardet had got his uncle, André Chavanne, to persuade the Department of Education (which he directed) to support a project for a Centre d'animation cinématographique in Geneva. This was the beginning of the CAC—which has now fallen into oblivion because its history has been rewritten by his successors. It was set up with the help of Richardet and François Roulet, a friend of Alain Tanner who had been involved in theater in La Chaux-de-Fonds and gone off to Algeria after it had won its independence. He worked at the Algiers Cinémathèque, where he produced some very original and talented posters. When Houari Boumédiene asked the "pieds-rouges," the left-wing French militants, to leave Algeria, and closed down the Cinémathèque, which Langlois had helped set up, Roulet returned to Switzerland. After a spell at the Patiño Foundation—an important Genevan cultural institution for contemporary art and research cinema—he became the artistic director of the CAC along with Richardet, Jean-Francois Rohrbasser, and myself. Rohrbasser, who had learnt what he knew through ciné-clubs, then took over programming the Patiño Foundation cinema before going on to direct La Bâtie Festival de Genève, and later joined the Cultural Department of the City of Geneva. We had met at the Interjeunesse Ciné-Club and he introduced me to the journal *Travelling*—he also pioneered the teaching of cinema in secondary education. We were very close friends.

As far as public education is concerned, my university degree was deemed sufficient to provide the CAC with a pedagogical dimension, which was part of its mission statement. At the time I was immersed in semiotics—Christian Metz, Umberto Eco, Yuri Lotman—it seemed to offer a rational framework for an introduction to the "language of cinema." Soon after I arrived, Rohrbasser and I jointly put our names to an introductory outline for courses in audiovisual education for the Education Department. CAC was created, in a sense, to include the teaching of cinema in the introductory media studies courses (general cinema, general theater, etc.) offered at lower secondary school level in Geneva. In short, it was a kind of "successor" to the ciné-club movement and introduced cinema into education. This venture was "crowned" in 1990 by the creation of a Chair in History and Aesthetics of Cinema at the University of Lausanne. Geneva had let the opportunity to develop this type of teaching pass it by.

Indeed, secondary education firmly believed in the introduction of media studies into its teaching practice and set up a whole production and distribution apparatus with TV-CO. This was not unrelated to the introduction of practical courses designed to train directors at the Ecole des Beaux-Arts.

Since I wasn't paid by the CAC, I was taken on as a teacher for the introductory courses. I have very good memories of this experience. I showed the school pupils films that may not have been strictly experimental (although there were some by Dwoskin) but they were fairly "challenging"; for example *Night and Fog* (1956) by Alain Resnais, and *Blood of the Beasts* (1949) by Georges Franju, etc. Shortly afterward, the Ecole des arts décoratifs—then under the expert direction of Roger Fallet—wanted to set up a cinema course for graphic design students. I took this course, which was open to students from the Ecole des beaux-arts where courses on audiovisual practices focusing on slide projection were provided. They were delivered by Claude Humbert, a specialist in "slideshows"—they have since fallen into oblivion, but seemed very promising at the time. All the exhibitions in the 1960s used this technique and had batteries of carousel slide projectors (like the 1964 Swiss National Exhibition). As mine was the only cinema course, it was very well attended and I had to split the class into two groups. That is how I ended up teaching at ESAV.

I even gave theoretical classes, one on the semiotics of the image and another on the history of the cinema, while continuing to teach the graphic design students at the Arts décoratifs. The course director, Charles Affolter, from Basel, a hard taskmaster in typography and a warmhearted man, indeed a militant Communist, was an invaluable interlocutor. That was in 1974–1975.

Then, in 1976–1977 I was invited to participate in the semester examination board at the Humbert workshop, where the practical introductory class in 16mm cinema was taught by Erwin Müllenstein. He had followed courses at the Hochschule für Gestaltung in Ulm led by Max Bill. There was a Department of Cinema Design led by Alexander Kluge in Ulm, but I don't think that Müllenstein was a member. He was totally neo-concrete and made his students produce little colored squares, which they then had to film. These experiments into the reciprocal relationships between colors depending, for example, on how they were placed, or combinations of shots, could potentially have led to "experimental" cinema, but they remained extremely didactic and descriptive and left the students feeling utterly unsatisfied. During the deliberations, some of the students—Pierre-Alain Besse, François Musy, and Philippe Scheller—challenged what they saw as a sterile approach. The board included filmmaker Francis Reusser, and school director Michel Rappo. All I had seen of Reusser's work was *Biladi, une révolution* (1971), a film that he made for the PLO in Palestine, which I had trashed in *Le Peuple*. He had been a Maoist militant in Lausanne, and I had also been militant in Lyon, yet, without mentioning this to each other, we both demonstrated solidarity with the students. This obviously caused a "crisis" in the workshop! However, this happened after May '68, when Rappo had been appointed to the Beaux-Arts precisely because it had been caught up in significant protests in 1968 fueled by the conservative approach of its former director, Mr Palfi. Rappo renamed the school ESAV to reflect the new direction he intended it to take. He set up a fairly original system designed to stimulate "creativity," a bit of a fetish word at the time, through a system of relatively independent workshops run by artists of some repute. He brought in Silvie and Chérif Defraoui, people who were working in what was briefly called "mixed media," and Gérard Musy for sculpture, an iron sculptor whom I had known as a drawing teacher during my time at Florimont, and who had become a friend. Rappo shook up the institution and broke down its pre-established categories (painting, engraving, etc.). He was very receptive to the way we challenged the institution and was so open that he asked us to try an experiment, to organize a two-day trial to show what we could do and see if it might be of interest to the students. We got together with Daniel Wilhelm, who knew Reusser from some political groups in the Vaud, and who lectured on theory (Jacques Lacan, Roland Barthes, Claude Lévi-Strauss) at the school. We put together a workshop using the working principles on which Reusser and I would later base our practice—Wilhelm decided not to continue along this path. My role was as the theoretician, Reusser was the practitioner.

We wanted to build bridges between theory and practice rather than perpetuate this kind of division. When Reusser explained how to operate lenses and described depth of field, I would talk about how important these had been in the history of cinema. Then we would watch some extracts after which we would plunge into experimenting in practice. It was incredibly stimulating because I learnt about all these techniques—lighting, editing, sound recording, etc.—at the same time as the students, and Reusser was introduced to films on things like the history of cinema, aesthetic doctrines, and texts. That was our method. Buache, a close friend of Reusser's, lent us films.

FB   What kind of films?

FA   I remember a few titles from these two trial days—*The Fall of the Romanov Dynasty* (1927) by Esfir Choub, *Mein Kampf* (1960) by Erwin Leiser, *Triumph over Violence* (1965) by Mikhaïl Romm. I had suggested talking about how we could use newsreels—which later became commonplace under the name of "found footage." At that time, this was called "montage film" and we examined it in depth. Lots of films had been made from archival material, such as *To Die in Madrid* (1963) and *Le Temps du Ghetto* (1961) by Frédéric Rossif—both great films made by editing documentary footage. Not to mention television. These films actually reconnected with what had been common practice in the 1930s, in the USSR (Choub), France (Brunius), Germany (Dudow, Blum) and the United States (Hurwitz in particular). They were practices that had become denatured by their "popularization" in American propaganda productions during the War (as directed by Frank Capra). This practice was closely related to militant cinema and its return in 1968 and later (with ciné-tracts and the like), and led us to readdress the issues raised by this kind of approach. Over the course of these two days we constantly asked ourselves whether we could use images shot by Nazis and make them say "something else." Can the meaning of an image be changed by changing a caption? There were a number of issues up for discussion—for example, the fact that the only images remaining are those of the victor, and we never have the point of view of the vanquished. These were the kinds of discussions we had. It was incredible to see how many of these "Godardian" or "Markerian" issues had already been alive prior to the Second World War. There were all kinds of experiments that had been completely forgotten because they fell outside of commercial circuits and had been obscured by 30 years of Cold War.

The students enjoyed this approach and it provided a platform for the Cinema/Video class that Reusser and I ran. Our first students came from the earlier cohort and they could, if they wished, continue to follow Humbert's slideshow courses, while Müllenstein was put in charge of something else at the institution as he was, in fact, an interior designer.

From the outset, we mixed up all the different levels, we combined, as I have already said, theory and practice, and we invited filmmakers and technicians whom we already knew. In the first year, Alain Tanner, whom Reusser knew well and I had met on more than one occasion, wrote about his films. Godard and Anne-Marie Miéville over from Grenoble, set up house in Rolle and were looking for people to talk to. Godard was in the middle of "mourning" his political phase and still deeply worried about this—that is what made us think about working together. He hadn't yet made *Sauve qui peut (la vie)* (*Every Man for Himself*, 1980), which, to my mind, marked the end of this period. He had made, or was about to make, his television series, *Six fois deux/Sur et sous la communication* (*Six Times Two/On and Under Communication*, 1976) and then *France/tour/détour/deux/enfants* (*France/Tour/Detour/Two/Children*, 1979). These were works that fell within the remit of film criticism, a questioning of the nature of cinema, which, thanks to Miéville, now addressed issues of feminism and ecology. At the same time, he was trying to make films in the United States with Zoetrope Studios in San Francisco, just as Francis Ford Coppola was wanting to make European auteur films. That was why Wim Wenders made *Hammett* (1982) with Zoetrope. Werner Herzog did something too. Godard wanted to, but he never quite managed. In fact he was trying to get what he wanted without falling for Coppola's game, and Coppola was trying to make a Godard without being "taken for a ride" by him. Godard went back and forth between Hollywood and Rolle with all kinds of film projects (one on the Hollywood Mafia, *Bugsy*, I think). He tried to keep alive the concerns that he was exploring with the Dziga Vertov Group about film as a tool of political criticism with movies such as *Letter to Jane* (1972), for example, and *Here and Elsewhere* (1976). At the same time, video was booming and this preoccupied him greatly—as did all the technical innovations that he had always wanted to experiment with, appropriate, and turn to his own personal ends. He had opened a studio behind Cornavin station in Geneva, in Rue de Montbrillant, next to Pierre Binggeli, the Sony agent in Switzerland who became the video expert for his projects, which included a history of cinema and television in pictures and sound.

In his Cinema/Video class he also organized a group project with Miéville, Tanner, Reusser, and Loretta Verna, who was finishing ESAV at the time, which was to produce four films with light equipment like Super-8, or video, and which, once transferred to U-Matic, were to be delivered in this format to Télévision Suisse Romande. This was a revolution, because nothing met the criteria set at that time by the PTT in terms of standards, wavelength, etc.[14] U-Matic, which was considered to be a semi-professional format, was not accepted by television. Since today we broadcast films taken on mobile phones, this might seem unbelievable. We had to fight to have this kind of image made with lighter equipment than that used by Swiss television accepted. Our contract was to produce four programs, plus an additional one with John Berger introducing the different authors, so a series, and to produce it for a reasonable price. It was called *Écoutez voir* (*Hear See*). Godard did not participate directly, but he was always in the background, as one of his "struggles" consisted of trying to persuade television stations to buy non-professional work at standard rates (per minute). This was a way of keeping his "production unit" going, as operating costs were lower than for institutional production, and he could use the difference to do something else. That was essentially his reasoning at the time he made *À Bout de souffle* (*Breathless*, 1960). The thing was that he didn't actually sell his work, and therefore failed to make a profit. Four little films plus one, about which I wrote in *Cinema*, Martin Schaub's Zurich journal. I titled the article "The Gang of Four."

I'm telling you this to give you an idea of what we understood by "experimentation." Our approach was more down to earth (experimenting with what particular devices could do, and with things like sound-image relationships, lighting, and editing); we were not formalist in the sense of *New Forms in Film*, but rather bound up with sociopolitical issues rooted in the criticism of images and sounds.

My memory of this time of intense activity is mainly of connections between lots of different sectors, and of all the different people to whom we could go for help. One source of inspiration, obviously, was Godard, who had embarked on his history of cinema and television which was to become *Histoir(e)s du Cinéma* (1988–1998). He had got involved in this in his classes in Montreal, and had followed it up by looking for sponsors and interlocutors. At that time he had signed a contract with the International Film Foundation in Rotterdam to produce ten videocassettes and deliver a number of classes there. He looked for financial partners to bring his project to completion. He did that right to the end. Locarno was another link in this chain. He was awarded a prize there in 1995 for the centenary of cinema without even presenting his *Histoir(e)s du Cinéma*, which were not yet complete, or providing an exhibition as planned. Then Skira took over the production of part of the work on the book, which finally ended up with Gallimard, and so it went on.

In 1978, Godard suggested to Buache and myself that we meet up once a month to talk about the history of cinema, and our recorded conversations could serve as "raw" material for his classes in Rotterdam. We met once or twice and I also went to his studio with some students. Then, in February 1981, at his request, I took part in one of these classes where he showed four reels of four different films taking the first reel of the first film, the second of the second and so on, alternating them with reels from *Every Man for Himself*. There was Eisenstein's *The General Line* (1929), Buster Keaton's *Cops* (1922), Luchino Visconti's *La Terra trema* (1948), and Andrzej Wajda's *Man of Marble* (1977). During the screening these different reels complemented each other perfectly. We all had a discussion in front of an audience about the effects of this editing. Why should this fairly random assemblage create a whole that worked both narratively and thematically? In his view, it was because all the films were of broadly the same length and adopted similar dramatic editing and tempo continuity—when you substituted one film for another while respecting the position of the sequence in the film, it all worked narratively. Furthermore, all four of these films, he said, filmed people working—peasants in the fields, a removal man, fishermen, a mason, etc.

Michael Witt, an English academic, recently put together a unique version of *Every Man for Himself*, a projection-performance. His research prompted me to recall this astonishing story to which I should also add the Special Cinema broadcast that Godard made for Swiss television under the title *Spécial Cinéma—Cinéma Spécial*. This was yet another version of *Every Man for Himself*, packaged within the hijacked structure of a TV broadcast with an interview with Godard by Jean-Michel Defaye, and one with Isabelle Huppert by Godard along with extracts reedited differently.

I obviously found this kind of experiment in which I was personally involved incredibly stimulating. It fitted perfectly with the courses I gave at ESAV and I used it in them.

It also fitted perfectly with what I was doing at *V.O.* and *Tout va bien* where, on more than one occasion, students helped out (photographs, surveys) even going as far as creating works. This led to a film and photo reportage on the production of the newspaper, which, at that time, was about to move from typeset to offset: from a text written by an editor by hand, to the printing process, to distribution by an old militant who filled newspaper dispensers every morning. Part of this photo reportage was published in the newspaper. It also fed into the programming of the university ciné-club in which we, and a number of students, played a role. The principle of contrasting films gave rise to a series of programs alternating fiction films and documentaries (which strongly displeased the columnist at *La Tribune de Genève*). Indeed, current "historians" at the university ciné-club have completely airbrushed this out, in a sense censored it, on the pretext that this period was "ideological." This can be seen in the leaflet published by the Cultural Activities Section at the University of Geneva and the short film by Vania Jaikin Miyazaki, *Nice Times*. For example, in 1979, on the occasion of Van der Keuken's visit to the school, we showed two of his feature films (*The New Ice Age*, 1974, and *The Flat Jungle*, 1978) as part of the season entitled "A 'Real' Cinema," in which we challenged the divide between documentary and fiction. Chris Marker's *Letter from Siberia* (1957) was set against the series *Kino-Pravda* (1923) by Dziga Vertov, Chris Marker's *Sunday in Peking* (1956) against *The Shanghai Document* (1928) by Jacob Bliokh, Vertov's *Enthusiasm* (1931) against *La bataille des dix millions* (*Cuba: Battle of the 10,000,000*, 1971) by Marker, and so forth.

This food for thought and our practical approach led to an important breakthrough, a different way of reviewing cinema. It was Godard who launched the idea of a review starting with the images but not commenting on them—the image first, then the text and not the other way around. He had already told us, in Locarno in 1968, that *Cahiers du Cinéma* was obsolete.[15] His experience within the Dziga Vertov Group had fueled his rejection of all "academic discourse" about film. He now insisted on starting with images and sound—as many of his films and TV broadcasts of that time do in exemplary fashion (especially *Six fois deux/ Sur et sous la communication*, 1976). There were four or five of us—Philippe Gavi, Robert Linhart, a Maoist intellectual working in a factory, Miéville, and myself, and some "correspondents" such as Gorin and Elias Senbar. We met up regularly, although never all together, to discuss these ideas. How should an image be constructed? What do you see in an image? These questions were at the core of *Six fois deux/ Sur et sous la communication* and the film *Ici et ailleurs* (1976), and we now had to tackle them in essay form. Finally Godard went to *Cahiers du Cinéma* on his own and wrote a letter to each of us to tell us that we were not to launch a journal. This was issue no. 300 of *Cahiers du Cinéma*,[16] which is not reprinted in Godard's "complete" works. It was a fascinating issue with photomontages and the publication of a report on Mozambique (which had already been published in *V.O.*).

All these experiences informed my teaching and work as a critic because I was writing at that time both for *Tout va bien*, an alternative-left weekly, and for *V.O.*, which published *Tout va bien*. I was also responsible for its cultural pages. I did "Godardian" pages, including some with Reusser and Jean-Bernard Menoud (Godard's cameraman). The full effects of these discussions with Godard were clearly apparent in a full page that I wrote on *Apocalypse Now* (Francis Ford Coppola, 1979) when it was released at Cannes. It included three empty frames in the place of illustrations with captions, to make the reader reflect on the stereotypes conveyed by and contradictions inherent in this film which, on the one hand, purported to oppose the Vietnam War, but which had gone to set fire to forests, to "rerun" the Vietnam war elsewhere, to refilm it and play at being soldiers! This was a kind of criticism by action. Undoubtedly, the editors and readers of *V.O.* initially wondered whether we had forgotten to insert the images. But they let me do it. There were ten or so of these unusual columns—one on *Les Petites fugues* (1979) concentrated only on the fact that Pipe hung his photographs on his wall.

In fact, and this is the problem when it comes to talking about this whole period, I was working at that time as part of a network, to use current parlance. I took part, I moved between all these different points of view, brought them together, divided them up differently, whether I was at the Ecole des Beaux-Arts, at festivals, writing criticism, in everything I did. It even went as far as my private life— everybody who had lived through May '68 was trying to do things differently, such as organizing communities and collectives. This approach was basically centrifugal—any connection that could turn up did. I invited Van der Keuken to ESAV to give our students a workshop, and as he had worked with Herman Ertzberger, an architect who had designed a Montessori school in Holland, two lecturers from the School of Architecture, Georges Descombes and Alain Léveillé, with whom I used to meet up at that time, invited him over to their school. One thing led to another, and he went to the Pont de la Bâtie to film a shot of the confluence of the rivers Rhône and Arve to be the "cornerstone" of a potential film about Geneva (which he came back to film for *I love $*, 1986). That little film became quite an important work for architecture students and lecturers. I also worked with him on a book, *Aventures d'un regard*, which was finally published by *Cahiers du Cinéma*.[17]

Two students at that time, Besse and Musy, went to work with Godard; when we invited Ruiz, Patrice Cologne left with him, and worked as his cameraman on several films; when I brought over Dwoskin, Véronique Goël left with him.

When I invited Nekes, Van der Keuken, Moullet, Straub and Huillet, and Ruiz, they would stay for at least two weeks, share their films, talk about them, and run practical workshops with the students. Then they would come back to have a look at things like the editing. It was very different each time. Straub and Huillet didn't shoot films with the students, but they did talk in depth about their working methods. They ended up recruiting a student to be an assistant on *Too Early/Too Late* (1982).

Even the relatively brief visit by Henri Alekan (courtesy of an invitation by the Cinémathèque suisse) was recorded and ended up in a film shot by Boris Lehman (*Travaux d'approche*, 1986). Some of what he had said was included as a voice-over. Half a day with Manoel de Oliveira led to a film by MacCluskey where he was having a conversation with Buache in the Montreux hotel that he insisted on visiting because that was where Nabokov had stayed.

Our guiding principle was to foster independence, which I mentioned a moment ago when talking about Godard. We wanted to train "independent producers," certainly not specialists (such as editors, sound engineers, and directors); we wanted everyone to be able to carry out different duties and help their colleagues. This, in a nutshell, was our teaching approach.

FB That presupposes a different teaching system. You talk about independence but did that apply to production tools as well?

FA Yes. There were other tools that we needed to be able to use—Super-8, video, because it's affordable, with, as the final format, 16mm, which is more expensive, but still affordable in certain circumstances. The 16mm works made in the classes were either group films, or films made for the completion of studies. What we wanted was to be capable of doing all the different jobs, and also of coping on our own. We wanted to be as capable of producing a script as a sound report. In any case, that was our thinking. We wanted to train independent producers who were free to do what they wanted.

Another very central idea at the school, introduced by Rappo, was that of multi-disciplinarity. A lot of people followed Daniel Suter's animation courses and combined graphic design with cinema. That is why I really liked the work produced on this course (Georges Schwizgebel had completed it a few years previously). At that time, the Annecy Animated Film Festival was a showcase for some quite remarkable experiments in animation: Walerian Borowczyk and Jan Lenica, people from Eastern Europe (Jiří Trnka, Jiří Brdečka), the Japanese, etc. It was a rare moment in this kind of cinema as it reached beyond the Disney standard to reconnect with Lye and McLaren, and was in tune with developments in contemporary painting and drawing. Take, for example, Alexandre Alexeieff, Gisèle and Ernest Ansorge, Zbigniew Rybczyński and many, many more! Here too, this kind of film experimentation was stillborn with the rare exception. This was due to disciplinary boundaries and market demand. It has now completely disappeared or has become marginalized (at L'Abominable, near Paris, there are people still doing this kind of thing); we are beaten over the head with the very over-rated Miyazaki, who offers comic books "light." Suter himself was marginalized within the school and his class was ultimately dropped in much the same way that all classes involving practical experimentation (such as engraving and carving) were dropped in favor of "concepts" and "design." These magical notions are completely backward looking when it comes to the relationship between artists and their materials. In any case, these classes have now been turned over to practitioners. Back to the division of labor.

In short, while remaining within cinema, the students followed options in animation, engraving, drawing, photography, etc. Some went to the Defraouis, as Françoise Bridel did for her main studio practice, and to me for her options.

However, in terms of social recognition, institutional pathways, and legitimation, art was clearly in a much better place. It received federal commissions, for example.

FB   Were there not also limitations imposed by the spaces where work could be presented? Such as the Centre d'art contemporain, which could also serve as a place for exchange.

FA   Yes and no. As I said, the art world was better suited for those types of production. We were able to show films in the classes—and, within a few years, in an all-format projection room where we could organize evening events. Not to mention the support of the university ciné-club which also ran practical activities (in Super-8 and video) mainly with the help of former students. The works are not likely to have circulated widely outside Geneva, in fact highly unlikely. In any case, these were not venues that legitimized art as was the case with the visual arts. The problem got worse over the years. When, in 1990, I left for the University of Lausanne, I felt increasingly out of touch with my students because, bewilderingly, as far as I could see, they no longer wanted this "independent producer" approach, they didn't want to be like Lehman, or even Van der Keuken, and fight for the means that would give them independence. They wanted us to give them the means to be able to enter the system. Cinema's main problem is the dominant cinema-television system. If you do something different at an art school, you have no social space, no structure, once you leave. So you have to find a strategy and that's quite difficult. You remain marginalized, as no equivalent to the art market exists for this type of work. People making artists' videos are not in competition with people working in television. They are in the world of art. There are not many of them. However, the world of art has a whole recognition system. Marie-José Burki started with us (she doesn't mention this on her CV) and then went to work with the Defraouis. When she left them, she could access federal grants, exhibition areas, places where her art could be recognized. These were not marginal places—they were supported by federal institutions tasked with disseminating Swiss art abroad (Pro Helvetia in particular). Cinema had no place there. It is clear that if Burki had produced the same type of work within our circuit, she would not have enjoyed the same kind of career. Cinema Spoutnik and similar independent film venues hardly give you a leg up in this profession. Nor do the tiny festivals that abound from Marseille to Brussels and Bourges, and nor do collectives in apartments. This is, in a sense, the "bohemian" model, and it no longer operates nowadays. People disappear, they give up. Once, when you were shown at the Centre d'art contemporain, or Galerie Dioptre, or even at Galerie Andata/Ritorno, you were on the path to recognition. There were federal commissions for artists. There was never any such thing for cinema—the only thing that matters is "commercial" cinema and the profession buys into that. Everything must meet television and advertising standards. Nowadays, even cultural television channels such as Arte choose to "format." Nobody says so, for fear of being shunned by producers and programmers. We standardize length, time static images, blank spaces, even words, and these standards are adhered to by the illiterate (very often in the literal sense of the term). There are obviously some exceptions, some filmmakers with legitimate status outside of the accepted channels or television such as the Gianikians who act as an alibi and offer a degree of immunity. Even Van der Keuken and Lehman have had their edits "corrected" courtesy of Thierry Garrel (not the worst). Straub was flatly rejected.

Indeed, our "independent producers" approach was rooted in the social climate of the years between 1968 and 1978, and presupposed that a group dynamic could be created outside academia and the official art schools in which cinema found its place. At that time, in Geneva, there was a whole "counterculture," with collectives and squats (take the Grottes neighborhood, for example). The same was true for the Netherlands—you can see it in Van der Keuken's films of the time—and in other countries like Germany, and in Zurich. *Tout va bien* was a journal that reflected this mindset, as did the Bois de la Bâtie Festival at the beginning, and other alternative venues. But all that just fizzled out, everything went back to the way it had been before. That was also what happened to the avant-garde in my understanding of the term—these are moments that occur at particular points in time when a collective movement questions established norms. You can either choose to subsist in a utopian community or become a reformist like Daniel Cohn-Bendit. You can see this problem again today with movements like Nuit debout in Paris. You cannot remain isolated if your main aim is to invent new ways of doing things, of being together and sharing. And in this respect, I think that the Cinema/Video class played an important role for its participants. Not, however, in terms of "capitalizing," and I must admit that this was not a major concern then as it is today when you teach students how to sell themselves, to promote themselves. This is a philosophy of creating and socializing artistic production—either through entering the market system (monetarily through galleries and collectors, or symbolically through museums and representative cultural institutions such as Pro Helvetia) or through searching for an individual audience, indiscriminately, and requiring limitless support from it.

    The filmmakers that I used to invite to run practical workshops and show their films shared this kind of social mindset. While they were not always exemplary in themselves, they did set an example in the way that they procured the "means to pursue their politics" for themselves. Similarly, they strove to remain independent of the commercial system and make films that engaged with social and ideological issues head on (like Van der Keuken, whose filmography—unfortunately overlooked nowadays by "programmers" of cinemas, festivals, television, etc.—comprises a series of lucid forward-looking observations and thoughts about ecological, economic, social issues in the late 20th century; or Kramer, or Hanoun), or based on their own experience (such as Lehman, Morder, and Luc Moullet). They taught their students to make do on shoestring budgets, not through resentment, but through technical intelligence. This inventiveness was shown to full effect by, for example, Ruiz or Ken Jacobs, in a memorable experience that proved a stimulus to some students.

This is what distinguished us from Yves Yersin's approach at the École cantonale d'art de Lausanne (ECAL) which started at around the same time. He adopted a professional approach. Teaching staff were recruited to ECAL from La Fémis in Paris and from Prague. That's what Bern liked, and consequently that is what they funded, indeed disproportionately compared with our own budgets (limited to grants to produce 16mm diploma films).

Can this type of independent cinema find an outlet today if we do what people like Philippe-Alain Michaud and Erik Bullot suggest, and try to include it in museums, exhibitions, and galleries? Maybe we should look at this idea a little more closely to see whether it accommodates people other than recognized cinema celebrities such as Chantal Akerman, Agnès Varda, Abbas Kiarostami, or institutional celebrities such as Bullot and Alain Fleischer. A whole group of people—outsiders really—from Portugal, Greece, Belgium, France, came to the mini festival organized by Lehman in Verbier in 2015 ("Rencontres au sommet") and the one this year (2016) in Fisenne in the Ardennes ("Rencontres sous les pommiers") to which he invited his friends and acquaintances. I am not sure that this is the best approach nowadays—it is more a hangover from the way things were in the past than a foretaste of how they will be in the future.[18] I still prefer it to dreary festivals with no defined identity or sense of daring, whose main aim is to host television events and sell films, to hit the headlines, and see part of their programs snapped up by hundreds of smaller festivals throughout the world who choose their films over the Internet (on Vimeo) by title alone.

In any case, it is unfair, and maybe that's an understatement, to use completely different criteria to assess visual and audiovisual works that are fully comparable and even similar in type depending on whether they fall into one subcategory of symbolic production or another. This is because a system exists governing the flow and valorization of different kinds of "merchandise."

For around 15 years, as part of the selection committee in Locarno, I fought to bring independent cinema to the festival. It was difficult. We showed *Mémoire d'un juif tropical* (1988) by Joseph Morder—a Super-8 blown up to 35mm. It was magnificent. However, even someone like Tanner was against it being shown. The first film by Sokurov, *The Lonely Voice of Man* (1979), which finally became available in 1986, led Renato Berta to say that it wasn't cinema. We showed Straub on the Piazza Grande, in the face of outright hostility on the part of President Rezzonico (who was an art collector or rather art investor), but we did not and could not fight to show experimental cinema as you understand it. When Robert Frank was screened on the Piazza, it was *Candy Mountain* (1988), not *Cocksucker Blues* (1972).

We made a constant effort to show different, where possible experimental, works that involved collaboration with other people. As I used to go to Lyon regularly—where I was still teaching at Sciences-Po—I kept in contact with Rey, a lecturer at the art school, who was responsible for the program at the Espace lyonnais d'art contemporain. This space is located in the Perrache train station, not the most welcoming of venues.

On several occasions I borrowed films from him and lent him others, taking them back and forth by train in my luggage (this reminds me of a film by Brian Eno, a static shot of skyscraper facades that changed color depending on the light—magnificent). We had meetings at Galerie Dioptre, Rue de la Servette; Jean-François Lyotard, Claudine Eizykman, and Guy Fihman came along, I met them there—and have met up with them regularly since. The long collaboration and dialogue I enjoyed with the Patiño Cinema was especially important. My brother was responsible for the contemporary music and dance program, while Rohrbasser covered cinema. Several filmmakers who came to ESAV had retrospectives at the Patiño Foundation (van de Staak, Fredi M. Murer), not to mention the cinema's own events that we attended (including "Cinema and Music," such as *Man with a Movie Camera* accompanied live by Pierre Henry, and *Paradis* by Philippe Sollers filmed live by Alice Fargier).

FB Were the group films shot in the classes ever shown publicly?

FA No, or only on rare occasions. Some ambitions were never fulfilled. Either because the filmmakers would have had to stay for longer than two weeks, or because they weren't able to come back. The discussion between Van der

Keuken and the students had led to the topic of the city "Center and Periphery." Teams of two or three students divided up the geographical areas to be tackled and came back with what they had filmed on Super-8 or video and then discussed it with Johan. That led to a kind of sociological mapping of the canton. A vast editing plan was even drawn up, but it was never completed. Indeed, once the design and filming were complete, there wasn't a great deal of energy left for editing. To tell the truth, that was the most difficult stage and we were maybe a little over-ambitious to think that we could ever have got that far. Some films were actually completed, including *Travaux d'approche*, which came out of a workshop by Lehman.

In the early days, we expected great things of Ruiz. He had agreed to come over to do the course for one year and put on one of his own plays, *Au Théâtre ce soir*. He wanted to stage it at the Saint-Gervais Theater, film it, and then make a film to sell to television. He had constructed a very coherent system, but it never came to fruition, partly due to him. He was constantly putting off his visits and dividing his time between too many things. He was busy elsewhere. He only came in fits and starts in the end. Nonetheless, it was exciting. He would spend eight hours talking to the students without drawing breath, inventing stories and virtual films. Finally, a film was shot as an exercise—they had to imagine that they were in a lighthouse with a light that revolved, creating moments of light and moments of dark. In the dark, a murder took place (like Michael Snow's *Wavelength*, but using different equipment). He decided to film it in the classroom and use craft resources such as putting water on the ground to get reflections—very simple things often with impressive visual effects. He displayed all his inventiveness in special effects with pieces of string. However, there was a gap between his initial ambition, a stage play to be shown on television, and the final result.

Having said that, I don't think it was a particularly bad thing that he didn't end up with a finished product. The filmmakers who came created a stimulating dynamic for the students. It was less about finished products than the processes themselves. Hearing Ken Jacobs talk about creating 3D with a Super-8 camera, and taking the tram to try it out and film between Moillesulaz and Carouge;

to hear Nekes explain editing frame by frame, and see him demonstrate it with animation devices picked up in flea markets; to hear Straub give detailed explanations of the camera positions in *The Death of Empedocles* (1987) was much more exciting and educational than any minor finished film, because the films would have been finished before they were ready.

During one of Straub and Huillet's many visits there was a memorable evening event at the University of Geneva, in May 1984. Straub and Huillet had spent an entire week there, and had showed their most recent films including *The Death of Empedocles*. I had suggested to Annie Lefèvre that we show it in the Piaget room at the university ciné-club, and the screening created quite a stir. In all my innocence, I had invited Jean Starobinski and [George] Steiner from the university—I thought that they might be interested in discussing Straub's "reading" of Friedrich Hölderlin's play with him. However, when Bernhard Böschenstein, a professor in German who I did not know, heard that we were going to show this film, he phoned Annie Lefèvre to say, "I insist on coming to denounce the Straubs' cinema, which is a complete fraud. This film is an attack against Hölderlin." There were verbal fisticuffs between Straub and Böschenstein. Böschenstein ended up leaving the scene on the brink of collapse while Steiner, on the pretext of having frequented the Factory, called Straub a fascist and blamed me for this attack on his colleague. Situations such as these were commonplace at the time. These people felt that commitment to their work was all that mattered, that they should push the limits. There is Lehman who lives cinema, films everything he eats, everyone he meets, and so forth. Everything is documented, everything can be used for the film because the film is his life, his "script" is the people he meets and what happens in the street; then there are Straub and Huillet and Van der Keuken, whose approach is totally different, but no less enlightening for the students. These are people for whom cinema is not a day job that you leave, and go home in the evening to put your feet up. In this sense, it is a little like experimental cinema, like Mekas constantly filming his movie journal, and Brakhage filming his baby and the grass in his garden.

FB   This was happening at the same time as conceptual and post-conceptual art, which had a fairly high profile at the Ecole des Beaux-Arts, in the person of Lawrence Weiner, for example.

FA   Yes. In this sense, retrospectively, I have some regrets. There was very little dialogue, although I had a very good relationship with Catherine Quéloz, who lectured in "theory." Indeed, her companion, Douglas Beer, who was registered for the Defraouis' class, used to come to our classes and made some films there despite having started out doing hyperreal paintings. There was a kind of competition with the Defraouis in the School. There was no hostility, but there was a kind of power struggle, or more precisely a struggle for influence. In 1980, there was considerable interaction when Dennis Oppenheim came to install an immense sculpture in a room at the Musée d'Art et d'Histoire with the help of students.

FB   As far as working methods were concerned, there could have been some mutual support?

FA   We could have met up more frequently. After I left the Beaux-Arts for the university, I worked for two years with Jean-Christophe Royoux and Christine van Assche at Beaubourg on an exhibition that we called *Nouvelles modalités du récit dans les arts visuels* (*New Narrative Modes in the Visual Arts*) to use Royoux's terms. The idea was to bring together issues in art, cinema, theory, and practice. For me, it was a bit like a follow-up of the Cinema/Video class. We had planned to mount a major exhibition, the director was in favor, but with the Centre Georges-Pompidou being what it was, it fell through, and all that was left was a series of talks in the "Revues Parlées" series. Nevertheless, we did manage to invite André Gaudreault, a historian of early cinema who talked about cinema of the 1900s, along with Benjamin Buchloh and Annette Michelson. We always had two things, two approaches, and we had to choose people who didn't normally have the opportunity to talk to each other, and yet who were still able to find some common ground. It was the same idea of contrasting points of view, of montage.

Christine van Assche was a curator at the Centre Georges-Pompidou, but she was marginalized by the heavyweight departments, because new media were deemed to be second-rate by the other curators. The director of the Georges-Pompidou was very keen on our proposal, but it had to go through all manner of committees and evaluations where we were torn to shreds. Cinema was Jean-Loup Passek's prerogative—nothing, as far as he could see, was cinema if he wasn't part of it. Jean-Michel Bouhours, who was responsible for experimental cinema, also wanted to put his oar in. Everyone felt a lack of ownership and, consequently, nothing happened. However, it was interesting to have a brief exchange of views about the issue of exhibited cinema. Especially as van Assche had organized a "rerun" of the event at the Galician Center of Contemporary Art in Santiago de Compostela, where these talks from different perspectives had another airing.

FB   "Exhibition cinema" was the term that Royoux used at the time. Were there any plans for a book?

FA   This was a term that we had actually agreed between the three of us. At the time, I tried to give this idea some historical depth by studying the issue of "exhibiting cinema," which dates back to about 1920. In actual fact, cinema has always been exhibited. In 1900, from a technological perspective, and soon after through models of sets, costumes, photographic enlargements. One of the high points was *Film und Foto* (FiFo) in Stuttgart in 1929 (organized by the German Werkbund) with a Soviet pavilion designed by El Lissitzky and Sophie Küppers, and, later, the Basel FiFo (Georg Schmidt, Peter Bächlin, Werner Schmalenbach) in 1943. The issue over the exhibition of cinema disintegrated with the practice of installations and the institutionalization of exhibitions about cinema, which are legion and largely illustrative. The interesting thing was, perhaps, that earlier a number of filmmakers—precisely those that I have talked about at length, the people that I invited to ESAV (and who later came to the University of Lausanne)—used films that ran continuously in a linear fashion much like any other film, and sought to incorporate exhibition issues. They either edited images to come and go between different series, disrupting the narrative flow and spatializing the time of the film, or they fractured continuity through long static shots, 360° panoramic shots, or they employed repetition.

As was often the case, the "anticipation" of a device or formula using resources that predate its emergence, and the potential that it had at that time, is more interesting than any achievements or standardization afforded by a new technology once it has been developed. My experience of graphics (at the newspapers I already mentioned and at *Pardo News* in Locarno) when you had to cut up images with scissors and stick them together with glue, seems a lot more creative than what you can do with Photoshop. The same goes for cinema and the "tabular" cinema of Vertov and Godard; and even, in a sense, Marker's films shot on celluloid, compared with his CD-ROM, *Immemory* (1998).

[1] P. Adams Sitney, "The New American Cinema Exposition," *Film Culture*, no. 46 (Autumn 1967), p. 25–26.
[2] *Le Peuple La Sentinelle* was a French-language daily paper affiliated to the Swiss Socialist party. François Albera, "From Protazanov to Bruce Conner," *Le Peuple La Sentinelle*, September 16, 1967.
[3] Gregory Battcock (ed.), *The New American Cinema: A Critical Anthology*, Dutton, New York 1967.
[4] Sheldon Renan, *An Introduction to the American Underground Film*, Dutton, New York 1967.
[5] Parker Tyler, *Underground Film. A Critical History*, Grove Press, New York 1970.
[6] Gideon Bachmann, "On the Nature and Function of the Experimental (Poetic) Film," *Film Culture*, vol. III, no. 14 (November 1957).
[7] Jonas Mekas, "The First Statement of the New American Cinema Group," *Film Culture*, no. 22–23 (Summer 1961), p. 130–133.
[8] *Travelling J*—from issue 23 in 1969 it was called simply *Travelling*—was a Lausanne-based journal founded by Marcel Leiser, and published until 1980 (58 issues). Marcel Leiser directed the film journal until 1975.
[9] "Entretien avec Alain Tanner," *Cahiers du Cinéma*, no. 273 (January–February 1977), p. 38.
[10] See the issue of *Les Cahiers de la Photographie* devoted to the work of Robert Frank: "Robert Frank, la photographie enfin," *Les Cahiers de la photographie*, 11/12, Spécial 3, Paris 1983.

[11] Vsevolod Meyerhold (1874–1940) was a Russian theater director. He developed biomechanics as a system of actor training in order to widen the emotional potential of theater and express thoughts and ideas that could not be easily presented through the naturalistic theater of the period.
[12] Lev Kuleshov (1899–1970) was a Russian filmmaker and film theorist. He was known for his use of editing in order to create a synthetic space.
[13] Steven Hill, "Kuleshov—Prophet Without Honor?" *Film Culture*, no. 44 (Spring, 1967), p. 8.
[14] The PTT (Postes, Téléphones, Télégraphes) was the name of the state-owned Swiss telecommunications company, which became two separate entities, La Poste and Swisscom, in 1998.
[15] See *Cenobio*, which published a little-known interview with Godard: Freddy Landry, "Les entretiens de Locarno 1968. Entretien avec Jean-Luc Godard," *Cenobio (Rivista mensile di cultura)*, Lugano, vol. XVII, no. 6, 1968, p. 419–426.
[16] *Cahiers du Cinéma*, no. 300 (May 1979).
[17] Johan van der Keuken, François Albera (eds.), *Aventures d'un regard, Cahiers du Cinéma*, Paris 1998.
[18] It has to be said that the second edition took an unexpected turn with the participation of Jean-Pierre Thorn, Jan Vromman, Claudia von Alemann, Emil Weiss, Claire Angelini, and Franssou Prenant, which was very "in sync" with current social and political events.

Appareil photo Vélomoteur

Les Petites Fugues

Le film d'Yves Yersin et C. Muret développe une fable : celle de l'aventure du valet de ferme Pipe qu'un vélomoteur et un appareil photo conduisent à découvrir le monde. Cette aventure, cette fable, ce personnage qu'est Pipe, renvoient ou éclairent une situation générale : la campagne, les rapports humains, sociaux, le travail, l'aliénation.

Pipe, ouvrier agricole un peu « simple » joue un rôle de révélateur en même temps qu'il se transforme un peu. En quelque sorte apprenant d'abord à VOIR grâce à son vélomoteur (escapade au-delà des lieux qu'il arpente durant sa journée, — évasion —, rencontre avec l'inconnu, fuite), il se met ensuite à CIRCULER à l'aide d'un appareil photo. Cette inversion des deux, fonctions est intéressante et peu relevée : c'est après avoir vu le monde que Pipe se met à le photographier et à l'organiser en série et en récit.

Ce à quoi Pipe renvoie, le monde qu'il révèle par sa naïveté, c'est celui d'une ferme vaudoise, exploitation familiale que guettent les acquis économiques de ce type d'entité précapitaliste : spéculation immobilière, monoculture, productivité, rentabilité, etc. La famille (et les deux ouvriers agricoles, Pipe et Luigi) est traversée et éclate sous la pression des rapports sociaux. La table du repas, lieu de rencontre de tous les habitants de la ferme va être le théâtre de cette dégradation et de cette dispersion : renvoi de l'immigré italien, départ de la fille, dispute entre père et fils. Cette imagerie, celle du début — celle que Pipe ne fixera pas car son travail de photographe n'a pas pour but d'enregistrer des souvenirs mais de comprendre un processus —, elle est devenue à la fin : impossible.

Yersin a construit son film à partir d'un parti pris sensualiste : le micro capte les bruits, des crissements ou des souffles ; la caméra des matières, de la lumière, des couleurs. La scène où Pipe le nez au vent écoute, observe et hume le paysage en un panorama de 360 degrés montre bien la démarche du film. De même la découverte charnelle du vélomoteur, la visite à la fabrique de chocolat : pour Pipe comme pour Mao, on connaît les poire en la goûtant. Ce parti pris des choses peut à l'occasion déséquilibrer le film dans sa narration et surtout emporter avec lui une équivoque naturaliste que les scènes lyriques (envol du vélo, poursuite du planeur sur la montagne) contredisent.

Un peu à la manière des cinéastes québécois — disons J.-P. Lefebvre — Yersin fait un cinéma qu'on peut qualifier avant tout d'ATTENTIF : durées, atmosphères, ambiances sonores, gestes de la mère pétrissant la pâte... Ce film — raccourci plusieurs fois pour des raisons d'exploitation commerciale — pourrait durer des heures, rien ne s'y opposerait. En même temps, ce film sait évoquer la haute sur les herbes hautes, rien ne s'y altitude avec l'emportement poétique d'un Dovjenko.

(Classic 1)

Donner à voir ou...

La photographie comme preuve d'une réalité : perdue ou à retrouver. Elle représente quelque chose d'absent, en tient lieu. Ces trois personnages de films montrent au spectateur la photo, preuve de l'objet perdu (L'homme de marbre), du crime (M. le maudit), preuve que l'image déchirée doit être reconstruite (L'amour en fuite).

Tout le film de Truffaut est le recollement de parties éparses d'un puzzle — Antoine Doinel, personnage de fiction qui a une histoire en film depuis Les 400 coups — connaît dans L'Amour en fuite la fragmentation et la réunification. Comme lui-même recolle les morceaux déchirés de cette photo de femme trouvée et à retrouver.

La photo prouve : depuis celle des Communards dans leurs cercueils, parue en première page du Figaro pour rassurer les bourgeois, celle du mouchard, celle des flics aux carrefours, dans les supermarchés.

Pipe au contraire, le naïf des Petits fugues ne photographie pas pour prouver (affirmer une deuxième fois la réalité de quelque chose) ou pour thésauriser (les souvenirs), mais pour apprendre quelque chose du monde qui l'environne. Ainsi le voit-on ici organiser en roman les photos de la ferme et de ses habitants, un roman pour inventer le monde.

...apprendre à regarder

François ALBERA

François Albera, "Donner à voir ou apprendre à regarder," cinema column, *Voix Ouvrière*, May 10, 1979

FESTIVALS

From a Debate over a Playground to the Meeting Point for Swiss Video Art: The International Film, Video, and Performance Festival VIPER
Gabriel Flückiger, Siri Peyer, and Fred Truniger

Translated from the German by Steven Lindberg

Cover of the catalogue for *Viper '90. 11 International Film- und Videotage*, Lucerne, October 23–27, 1990

Video Art in Switzerland in the 1970s

In the 1970s, video art was represented in Swiss institutions only in isolated cases. In the context of education, the university courses on the "Aesthetics of the Mass Media: Television,"[1] taught by René Berger, the director of the Musée cantonal des Beaux-Arts in Lausanne from 1969 onward, and the Atelier des Mixtes Médias, founded in 1972 by Silvie and Chérif Defraoui at the École supérieure d'arts visuels in Geneva (ESAV), are regarded as the first signs of the developments to come. In May 1972 Galerie Impact in Lausanne organized the exhibition *ACTION/FILM/VIDEO*, in which 73 films and videos were presented with equal billing. Two years later, in October 1974, the same group organized a small eight-day festival, *Impact Art Video Art 74—8 jours de vidéo* at the Musée des Arts Décoratifs in Lausanne.

In Basel, from the mid-1970s on, gallery owners Diego and Gilli Stampa regularly presented exhibitions and events around video art.[2] In 1974 art curator Adelina von Fürstenberg founded the Centre d'Art Contemporain in Geneva, where she occasionally also showed videos by international artists such as Bruce Nauman, William Wegman, and Vito Acconci.[3] However, the first exhibition dedicated entirely to video works in the art context was not held until April 1977: *Vidéo* at the Musée d'Art et d'Histoire in Geneva. In his foreword to the catalogue, the cocurator, Martin Kunz, along with Adelina von Fürstenberg, called on Swiss museums—which had not yet founded their own video departments, unlike American museums, which had long since been doing so—to finally establish even the "most primitive facilities" in order to be able to show video art regularly.[4] At the time, art historians regarded video as a complex and "difficult-to-convey" art.[5] The daily media claimed that, in contrast to the established medium of film, the aesthetic of video was unserious and sometimes emphasized the fact that video art was in any case viewed primarily only by a young audience.[6]

In western Switzerland, René Berger added the first video to the collection of the Musée cantonal des Beaux-Arts in Lausanne—Jean Otth's *Limite E*—as early as 1973, but that was not followed up with the regular exhibition and acquisition of videos.[7] Not until 1980 did institutional acceptance and hence the visibility of video works change as museums in German-speaking Switzerland began to include videos in their holdings as well: the Kunsthaus Zürich from 1979, the Kunstmuseum Basel from 1980, and the Kunstmuseum Bern from 1982. The *Schweizer Kunst '70–'80: Regionalismus/Internationalismus* (1981) exhibition at the Kunstmuseum Luzern, which was intended as an up-to-date survey, also included an extensive video program with contributions from Jean Otth, René Bauermeister, and Alex Silber.

Video art moved into the spotlight in the wake of specialized festivals. Fundamentally much more dynamic and agile than institutional formats for exhibitions, festivals enjoyed an international boom in the 1980s.[8] In Switzerland that decade saw the founding of the VideoArt Festival in Locarno (1980–2001), the Semaine Internationale de Vidéo in Geneva (from 1985), the Videowochen im Wenkenpark in Basel (1984, 1986, 1988), and the Krienser Filmtage (1980–2006), which from the fifth festival was known as the Film-Video-Performance-Tage Kriens, and finally, from 1985 onward, VIPER. In 1980 the Solothurner Filmtage, founded in 1966, first began including Super-8 films and videos in its program in order to permit an "open and representative survey" of Swiss film.[9]

"Murmuring of Insiders": The Founding of the Krienser Filmtage in the Spirit of the Early 1980s

Until the mid-1980s, video art was often produced in self-organized, non-institutional contexts. In order to jointly acquire technological methods and to fund infrastructure, artists formed collectives and networks.[10] At the end of the 1970s, for example, in addition to the Videoladen, there were at least three other video groups in Zurich (Videogruppe Altstadt, Videowanderkino Zürich, Videoabteilung Filmkollektiv), the Mediengenossenschaft Container TV in Bern, and the Video Genossenschaft Basel VGB in Basel. In late 1977, the Vereinigung für den unabhängigen Film (VuF; Association for Independent Film) working group was founded in Zurich; it worked to gain recognition in cultural policy for small-format film and video and to integrate them into the program of the Solothurner Filmtage. After its founding, the VuF relocated to Basel, where the filmmakers' initiative, Filmfront, formed around it, bringing together community video activists and video artists, and publishing 34 issues of the film journal *Filmfront* between 1978 and 1988. The video art networks also included various art-video clubs that actively supported the dissemination of video art by offering opportunities to play new videotapes by Swiss and international artists: Megaherz in Zurich, Einhorn and Fata-Morgana in Basel, and the KUCK-Club run by Luigi Kurmann in Lucerne.

The Krienser Filmtage arose out of this self-organized and youthful spirit of a group of politically active and culturally inclined people. From the outset there was a focus on independent film. Pius Felder, Beat Linder, and Valerian Maly started the Filmtage shortly after they had critically monitored public discussions around the use of a playground in the suburbs of Lucerne, which led into the production of a Super-8 film. In the spirit of the youth uprisings that were budding again in Swiss cities in the early 1980s, a need was felt to "organize something ourselves" and show films that could not be seen anywhere else.[11] The vacant Kino Scala, which had been an adult movie theater, was made available to the festival's founders by the community. The event's premiere in 1980 showed 14 feature and documentary films. They included, among others, older films by Daniel Schmid, for example *Heute nacht oder nie* (*Tonight or Never*, 1972), and the experimental documentary film *Chicorée* by Fredi M. Murer (1966), alongside recent productions such as the documentary *Guber – Arbeit im Stein* (*Guber: Work in Stone*, 1979) by Hans-Ulrich Schlumpf.

In the program for the second festival in 1981, the organizers explicitly wrote that they were particularly interested in films that did not meet with a response in commercial venues.[12] They were still showing primarily 16mm films—the Solothurner Filmauswahlschau (Solothurn Selected Film Screening) constituted a substantial part of the program—as well as Super-8 films and videos and, two years later, artistic performances. The presentation of the group's own Super-8 films and videos about Kriens at the second Filmtage makes it clear that the program was also open to amateur productions. Coorganizer Angelo Rota wrote in the Basel journal *Filmfront* that interested parties should meet in Kriens two weeks prior to the festival in order to develop new works together that could then be shown as part of the festival.[13] It was only with the third festival that the focus shifted away from Swiss filmmaking and toward experimental film and video art, which also changed the direction in terms of subject matter. The videos reporting on the alternative public sphere that dominated in 1981 and 1982—such as *Züri brännt* (*Zurich is Burning*, 1980) by Videoladen Zürich, *Zivildienst in der Schweiz?* (*Civilian Service in Switzerland*, 1980), by Zivildienstgruppe or the *AJZ-Reportage Tel Quel/Es herrscht wieder Frieden im Land* (*AJZ Reportage Tel Quel. There Is Peace Again in the Country*, 1981) by Videogenossenschaft Basel—were largely replaced from 1983 onward by videos from the art world. The festival now showed works by Rebecca Horn, Lisl Ponger, Anna Winteler, and Gilbert & George, as well as Christoph Rütimann from

Lucerne. Luigi Kurmann, who at the time was partly responsible for the program, justified the shift in interest by saying that the festival wanted to provide a platform for all forms of artistic activity that "did not have it easy on the Swiss art scene."[14] Characteristically, the festival in 1983 opened with a performance *Trois pièces faciles* (*Three Easy Pieces*) by John M. Armleder.

What was the festival, which in its early years saw itself as a catalyst for productions that were overlooked in the existing structures of distribution and institutional presentation, aimed at now? Charles Moser—the founder of Video One, a video production company in Aarau, and longtime director of the art class at the Hochschule Luzern—remembers that the early years had been a "murmuring of insiders."[15] Indeed, in 1986, for example, the daily press reported that, apart from the local audience, those attending were primarily "filmmakers who were presenting a film."[16] In the case of the early festivals, that could be explained primarily by the nature of the program, which, although it had thematic sections and clear selection criteria from 1982 onward, also had a forum for rejected entries and open screens on which amateur filmmakers could present their works as part of the festival. The informal roots of the festival are evident from the fact that, as a rule, throughout the 1980s, new works by video artists that were not yet finished, or other films that their makers had brought with them to Lucerne, were spontaneously shown *hors programme* at one of the two venues after the festival's final regular performances. In the early years, the Krienser Filmtage were characterized by the huge curiosity of the organizers and a youthful impetus "to just do something for once."[17]

First Successes, 1985–1995: Networking, Move, and Restructuring

This insider character had not been intended. Admission prices had deliberately been kept low to attract as wide an audience as possible, and encourage an active "culture of discussion" among the audience, organizers, and filmmakers in public forums.[18] In 1985, attendance figures of 1,000 over six days were described by the organizers as "below expectations."[19]

That year the festival had moved to Lucerne and changed its name to VIPER Film Video Performance Tage Luzern.[20] The festival received financial support for the first time from both the Canton and City of Lucerne and federal cultural funding. At the time, the budget had grown to 45,000 Swiss francs, but the organizers worked on a volunteer basis.[21] A year later, the organizers introduced an innovation to the program that recalled the origins of the festival: the Video-Werkschau Schweiz (VWS) section of the program offered, for the first time anywhere in Switzerland, a survey of current domestic video, and hence in some cases political productions as well. Of the 51 works submitted, a jury selected 31 and presented them in the main program using a large-format projector. In addition, the submissions that had been rejected by the jury could be seen in a video library—an opportunity that apparently attracted great interest.[22] The festival was thus able to offer a curated presentation, and satisfy the desire to present all of the video work under the principles of transparency, completeness, and integrative commitment. This egalitarian attitude was still indebted to the spirit of the early American film cooperatives and the Film Forum in Zurich (1966–1970), which would, if requested, include all films by any filmmakers in its distribution structures.

The reality did not immediately meet the ambition, as reviews in the press in 1986 confirmed. The films shown in the official program would, in the view of the journalist Walter Ruggle, have already been "eliminated in the selection phase" at the Solothurn Filmfestival.[23] The dominant influence of Solothurn led to the restructuring of the festival in Lucerne in 1987 in order to present it "with a new image." It would no longer offer a survey of Swiss filmmaking[24]; instead, the festival had annual thematic focuses—above all in the form of international retrospectives: Alexander Kluge; short films from West Germany; experimental films by women; parallel cinema (USSR); an homage to Rudy Burckhardt; found footage; avant-garde film and music videos; Lars von Trier; Peter Mettler. In parallel with this increasing internationalization, however, one can also see an effort to present the finest examples of Swiss film and video within this international context. A conceptual focus on experimental and artistic film and video also meant that the organizers decided to show only performances that worked with visual media. At the same time, more video actions and installations were shown.[25]

This time the festival did not fail to garner recognition: in 1989, the press compared the significance of the Video-Werkschau Schweiz for domestic video production to that of the Solothurner Filmtage for films.[26] In addition, the organizers were able to strengthen the role of the festival and they could also support artistic production not just by presenting and publicly discussing the works, but also for the first time by organizing a competition and offering prizes: the Sony Prize, which awarded a semiprofessional Video8 camera, and the VIPER Prize, in the form of 1,000 Swiss francs. The anniversary festival in 1989 was a great success: with an attendance of 4,100, the audience was four times that of the early years.[27]

These days it might seem strange to offer a camera as a prize, but it shows that shooting video in the 1980s was an expensive and by no means as yet popular technology. It represented challenges not only for the producers, but also for the viewers. For example, art historians Gioia Dal Molin and Patrizia Keller reported of the Swiss Art Competition—organized annually by the Swiss Federal Office for Culture—that, until 1985, the art commission had no way to view the videotapes increasingly being submitted, and so they were automatically included in the second round. Even winning a prize did not guarantee that a video would be presented to the public: because of a lack of infrastructure at the exhibition site, as late as 1988 video works might only have been shown at the opening of the winner's exhibition, or no video installations might have been included at all. Video placed demands even on professional viewers. For example, in 1988 a member of the committee left the jury meeting for the Swiss Art Competition, "because watching the videotapes took too long."[28]

Without a doubt, one important function of the festival was that of creating international networks, and an autonomous Swiss scene for experimental film and video that emphasized cooperation, and included the nomination of existing self-organized, national video contexts, and the professionalizing of educational work. For example, beginning in 1984, film and video from the Forum des Jungen Films

Berlin, the Experimentalfilm-Workshop Osnabrück (now the European Media Art Festival, EMAF), the Österreichisches Film Fest Wels, the Whitney Biennial, and the Marler Video-Kunst-Preis were presented, and several editions of the Unabhängiges Video Schweiz (UVS) sampler of independently produced Swiss art videos (Vereinigung für unabhängiges Videoschaffen; 1984, 1987, 1990, 1994) were prominently screened.[29] In the case of the European Media Art Festival EMAF in Osnabrück in particular, there was an informal exchange that was later institutionalized for a time: in 1996 the two festivals jointly organized an international competition, and from 1998 to 2001 the VideoGalerie, a video library in which a selection of the prizewinning works could be seen, was jointly organized, with festivals in Palermo and Split.[30]

Over the course of the 1990s, the festival increased its connections to educational institutions, especially with the video class of what was then the Schule für Gestaltung Luzern. Students designed the trailers for the VIPER festival. Charles Moser recalls that the festival was the most important event of the year for students of the video class: "VIPER is here, and we are involved and doing something with them."[31]

Another important development began at the Internationale Kurzfilmtage in Oberhausen in 1988, when Cecilia Hausheer, who was a coorganizer of VIPER at the time, met Christine Noll Brinckmann, who had been appointed professor of film studies at the University of Zurich. In 1989, Hausheer became assistant to Brinckmann's chair at the university, and invited her to program the Experimentalfilme von Frauen, 1960–1989 (Experimental Films by Women, 1960–1989) retrospective for the festival's tenth anniversary. That collaboration greatly influenced the festival's subsequent development.[32]

"School of Innovative Seeing": Film Studies, Multimedia, and the Emphasis on the Discourse of the Festival Program in the 1990s and its Decline after 2000

VIPER's heyday was during the 1990s. Attendance figures increased continuously. From a "murmuring of insiders," the event transformed into an annual meeting where attendance "went without saying," and not just for those interested in or studying film, video, or art.[33] Even a national medium such as Swiss Television reported on the festival on the main news programs in the mid-1990s, discussing the significance of the festival as a communicator, not only of experimental films, but also of technological developments.

The most important factor in the festival's internationalization was the presence of filmmakers at the international retrospectives for which Cecilia Hausheer was responsible. Throughout these years, a component of film studies was increasingly present, as both the film studies professor Noll Brinckmann (in 1989), as well as students such as Fred Truniger, Annette Schönholzer, and Daniel Wildmann, participated in the festival in the 1990s. In Hausheer's case, her programming of the festival and her teaching at the university complemented each other.[34] The festival had its own annual publications on the special programs, which were published by Zyklop Verlag, and covered the entire spectrum of the festival both geographically and temporally. That publishing house had been involved in the Krienser Filmtage since 1982, and had been founded by Christophe Settele, who later directed the festival. Settele and Thomas Imbach coedited a publication on the films of Werner Nekes in 1986,[35] after which Settele published an issue on the films of Bruce Conner on the occasion of the retrospective on the history of found-footage film in 1992, which, following the festival, accompanied a program of Conner's films that toured various Swiss cities.[36] That same year, a larger publication on found-footage film in German and English that is still one of the most important publications on the subject today was published.[37] A retrospective of music videos in 1993 and 1994, in cooperation with the Filmmuseum Frankfurt and the Long Beach Museum of Art, was accompanied by a publication on the history of the music video that also served as a catalogue for the exhibition *Sound & Vision* at the Seedamm Kulturzentrum in Pfäffikon, and for the film programs in four Swiss cities.[38] Finally, in 1995 the festival published a monograph to accompany the retrospective of Peter Mettler's films that opened at the Planetarium of the Verkehrshaus in Lucerne.[39]

As part of these retrospectives—and in some cases also other sections, such as the special program for the tenth anniversary of the Video-Werkschau in 1995—audience discussions were supplemented with lecture series and actual symposia: internationally renowned film scholars such as Heide Schlüpmann, Bill Wees, William Moritz, and David E. James were invited to give lectures in the late 1980s and early 1990s as were, in later years, proponents of Internet art and activism such as Rachel Baker, Margarete Jahrmann, Geert Lovink, and Tilman Baumgärtel. From 1996 onward, finally, scholars and curators of various stripes such as Saskia Sassen, Andrew Ross, and Catherine David took part in discussions on the technological developments in and commercialization of art.

The ambition to present trends in unconventional and innovative approaches to the media of film and video[40] and offer a "school of innovative seeing"[41] was retained in the second half of the 1990s, whereby early on the problems of the status of experimental film and video and their integration into the art world were addressed.[42] Later— influenced by the nascent networking of displays, media channels, and distribution forms—the focus shifted to the "future of visual communication." Accordingly, the full spectrum of visual design was taken into account, the program refined, and—under the new director, Conny Voester, from 1995 on—supplemented by "multimedia" programs, symposia, and an Internet café with a video and CD-ROM library that was "always overflowing well into the night."[43] These additions and thematic focuses were always undertaken with the intellectual ambition to shed a critical light on social developments—an impetus that had been the driving force of the festival since 1986, when the organization of the festival was associated with a "culture of resistance" that did not see artistic production as separate from social reality, but rather as having direct influence on it.[44]

Publications, exhibitions, and film programs in various Swiss cities, and cooperation with local and international institutions were expressions of the conviction of the festival's organizers that a festival of experimental film could only become socially relevant if it tried to inform audiences both locally and internationally. Under the direction of

Christophe Settele, with programming assistance from Cecilia Hausheer (special programs and retrospectives) and Erika Keil (Videowerkschau Schweiz and the international competition), within ten years VIPER had grown from being a marginal event into a festival with a national and international reputation. For several years it played the role of a Swiss trading center for ideas on visual and technological culture, and at the time often determined the direction taken by visual artists. The festival had become a relevant hub in the international network of experimental filmmaking. This perspective was not just shared within a small community, as became clear when the festival moved from Lucerne to Basel in 2000. When the limits on public funding in Lucerne had been reached and resources became insufficient, the festival's director, Conny Voester, decided to move to Basel, where the Canton of the City of Basel and the Christoph-Merian-Stiftung were offering subsidies three times higher for a period of four years.[45] Basel made this offer of enormously increased funding in the hope that the location would become a lighthouse for its strategy to make Basel the most important city in Switzerland for developments in the field of new media culture.

Basel's strategy did not work as far as the festival was concerned for several reasons. The move occurred at a time when, essentially, VIPER was still moving from being a film festival that featured structures that were clearly conventional while at the same time including discursive contributions, to a media event explicitly shaped by discourse. The associated shock to the festival's organic structure, which since 1995 had already entailed changing part of its audience, as well as the loss of the established foundational structure of volunteers in Lucerne, not easy to replace in the new location, confronted the festival's organizers with big problems.[46] The festival had once spoken to an audience that was truly interested in innovation in cinema, that is, in visual forms of artistic expression, but now it was speaking to one that could be equally enthusiastic about a discourse on artistic and scholarly discoveries. The reform of the festival's apparatus from a (communal and social) space of cinematic and discursive experiences to a (sometimes rigorously individualized) attendance of symposia and exhibitions, as well as a shift in subject matter in the direction of internet art and interactive installations was a crucial step, and probably from the outset it was not sufficiently communicated to the public by the festival's organizers. The program—film screenings, computer installations, and symposia—evolved in several directions; these new subject areas required increased funding for technology, and the festival was also competing in a completely new context with events such as Ars Electronica in Linz and Transmediale in Berlin, and it could not keep up on the international stage. The director of the festival changed several times. Rebecca Picht and Annika Blunk took over as directors in 2002: two women whose roots were not in experimental film. Repositioning the experimental film festival as a media festival failed and, with no manifestation at all in 2005, VIPER presented a greatly reduced, and final, 25th festival in 2006. Thereafter, the festival's public funds and support from foundations were axed.

[1] The courses covered, among other topics, the Swiss pioneers of video art from the Impact Group around René Bauermeister, Jean Otth, Janos Urban, Muriel Olesen, and Gérald Minkoff. See Irene Schubiger, "La vidéo, je m'en balance," Irene Schubiger (ed.), *Reconstructing Swiss Video Art from the 1970s and 1980s*, JRP|Ringier, Zurich 2009, p. 141.

[2] From the mid-1970s, Diego and Gilli Stampa represented video artists at Art Basel. From 1977 to 1979, in collaboration with the Kulturinitiative in Basel and the Videozentrum Zürich, they organized public video workshops with the participation of Klaus vom Bruch, among others, recorded artists' performances on video and showed video sculptures in their gallery.

[3] Esther Maria Jungo, "Schweizer Video: Ein Blick zurück," Esther Maria Jungo, Katarina Rusnakova, Marina Smolenicka, Peter Meluzin (eds.), *Video, vidim, ich sehe: Slowakische, tschechische und schweizerische Videokunst*, Kunstmuseum, Thun 1995, p. 14–22.

[4] According to Kunz, the exhibition, organized by Adelina von Fürstenberg at the Centre d'art contemporain, was also shown at the Galerie Stampa; see *Vidéo*, exh. cat., Musée d'Art et d'Histoire, Association Musée d'art moderne [AMAM], Geneva 1977.

[5] Eva Keller "Notizen zur Videokunst in der Schweiz," Ursula Wittmer (ed.), *Videoinstallationen Szene Schweiz*, exh. cat., Benteli, Bern 1994, p. 8–10.

[6] Klaus vom Bruch interviewed by Siegmar Gassert, "Video Art: Die Kunst der elektronischen Bilder," Basler Zeitung, December 21, 1981.

[7] Press release for the *Making Space: Forty Years of Video Art* exhibition, Musée cantonal des Beaux-Arts, Lausanne, October 18, 2013–January 5, 2014, http://www.musees.vd.ch/fileadmin/groups/16/documents-pdf/dossiers-presse/MCBA_PressRelease_MakingSpace_light.pdf (last accessed March 2020).

[8] Cecilia Hausheer in conversation with Gabriel Flückiger and Siri Peyer, December 8, 2015.

[9] Urs Berger, "Solothurner Filmtage mit Super-8 und Video," *Filmfront*, no. 8 (1980), p. 34. The complete series of *Filmfront* can be accessed at blog.zhdk.ch/sfex.

[10] Charles Moser in conversation with the authors, February 5, 2016. Charles Moser cofounded the company Video One with Heinz (Tello) Frutiger in Aarau in 1980.

[11] Valerian Maly in conversation with Siri Peyer and Gabriel Flückiger, March 18, 2016.

[12] Program of the second Krienser Filmtage, 1981.

[13] *Filmfront*, no. 10 (1980), p. 23.

[14] Luigi Kurmann, "Video, die Künstlerherausforderung," *Vaterland*, December 2, 1985.

[15] Charles Moser in conversation with the authors, February 5, 2016.

[16] Walter Ruggle, "Die Probleme der Eigenständigkeit: 7. Film-Video-Performance-Tage Luzern," *Tages-Anzeiger*, November 4, 1986.

[17] Valerian Maly in conversation with Siri Peyer and Gabriel Flückiger, March 18, 2016.

[18] Coorganizer Thomas Imbach quoted in Luigi Kurmann, "Video, die Künstlerherausforderung."

[19] "Vielfältige Bilderflut im 'Panorama,'" *Luzerner Neusten Nachrichten* (LNN), December 30, 1985.

[20] VIPER stands for Video-Performance.

[21] Luigi Kurmann, "Video, die Künstlerherausforderung."

[22] Walter Ruggle, "Die Probleme der Eigenständigkeit," *Tages-Anzeiger*, November 4, 1986.

[23] *Ibid.*

[24] This was explicitly justified with the argument that that role was already being played by the Solothurner Filmtage; see the VIPER program for 1987.

[25] *Ibid.*, p. 78.

[26] Anonymous, "'Viper '89': Die 'Solothurner Filmtage' des Videos," *Kultur 2*, supplement, November 1989. Found, without further details of its source, in the Schweizerisches Kunstarchiv SIK-ISEA.

[27] Anonymous, "Vom Experiment zur Verbundenheit im Schaffen," *Der kleine Bund*, November 4, 1989.

[28] Quoted in an unpublished lecture manuscript by Gioia Dal Molin and Patrizia Keller. Lecture at the Schweizerisches Institut für Kunstwissenschaft, SIK-ISEA, Zurich, June 29, 2015.

[29] The video sampler was intended as an anthology of artistic videos from Switzerland. The jury, composed of members of the Unabhängiges Video Schweiz association and experts in the field, chose current video art from Switzerland for each edition of the sampler.

[30] VIPER festival catalogue for 1998, p. 86.

[31] Charles Moser in conversation with the authors, February 5, 2016.

[32] Noll Brinckmann in conversation with Gabriel Flückiger and Fred Truniger, August 3, 2015.

[33] Charles Moser in conversation with the authors, February 5, 2016.

[34] Cecilia Hausheer in conversation with Gabriel Flückiger and Siri Peyer, December 8, 2015.

[35] Thomas Imbach, Christoph Settele, Gurtrug Film (eds.), *Werner Nekes Retrospektive*, Zyklop, Zurich 1986.

[36] Christoph Settele (ed.), *Bruce Conner*, Zyklop, Zurich 1992.

[37] Cecilia Hausheer, Christoph Settele (eds.), *Found Footage Film*, VIPER/Zyklop, Zurich 1992.

[38] Cecilia Hausheer, Annette Schönholzer (eds.), *Visueller Sound: Musikvideos zwischen Avantgarde und Populärkultur*, Zyklop, Zurich 1994. The exhibition ran from September 14 to October 23, 1994.

[39] Salome Pitschen, Annette Schönholzer (eds.), *Peter Mettler: Making the Invisible Visible/Das Unsichtbare sichtbar machen*, Bilger, Zurich 1995.

[40] VIPER catalogue for 1991, p. 1.

[41] Christoph Settele in the 1994 VIPER catalogue.

[42] Christoph Settele, "Einleitung," 1992 VIPER program.

[43] Alexandra Stäheli, "VIPER 21: Fakten und Fiktionen," *Neue Zürcher Zeitung*, January 29, 2001.

[44] VIPER catalogue for 1986.

[45] See, among others, the "Kulturzeit" broadcast on 3sat, October 27, 1999.

[46] Cecilia Hausheer in conversation with Gabriel Flückiger and Siri Peyer, December 8, 2015.

› INDUSTRIAL FILM

Between Avant-Garde and Sponsor: Kurt Blum's Industrial Films around 1960
Thilo Koenig

Translated from the German by Steven Lindberg

Fritz E. Maeder shooting at the FIAT plant, Turin, 1960

Bern photographer Kurt Blum (1922–2005) was a self-taught filmmaker.[1] His cinematic work is confined to a few years from 1960 to 1971, during which he made sponsored films that display a considerable degree of autonomy. Blum founded his own Studio für filme (Studio for Films), which he ran in collaboration with the Basel advertising agency cR, founded by Jürg Schaub and Horst Kepka, in the early 1970s.

Blum's film work concentrated on documentaries and cultural films; his only feature film was made in 1967, for which he shared a directing credit with his cameraman of many years, Fritz E. Maeder: *Rabio: Gedankenwelt eines Strafgefangenen* (*Rabio: A Prisoner's Ideas*).[2] As early as 1960, Blum had made a widescreen industrial film about an Italian steel company: *L'uomo, il fuoco, il ferro* (*The Man, the Fire, the Iron*).[3] This film, together with a triple projection on the subject of steel production commissioned for the Swiss National Exhibition in 1964 (Expo 64) in Lausanne, are the focus of this essay.[4]

Blum went freelance as a photographer in 1953. He was one of the young Swiss photographers who wanted to set off on a new aesthetic path after 1945, and who formed artists' groups to that end. Thanks to the director of the Kunsthalle Bern, Arnold Rüdlinger, Blum had come into contact with contemporary art and artists' circles in Bern early on.[5] As was typical of that era, Blum was experimenting with positive and negative luminograms; he used flashlights to create abstract, Art Informel-like traces of light in a dark room.[6] Blum saw himself "always as an artist," and he "battled fiercely for photography to be recognized as an autonomous artistic medium."[7] He fought likewise for film, including sponsored film, to be seen as a form of the author's artistic expression.

Genoa

Blum's first professionally produced film resulted from a commission for photographs. Eugenio Carmi, an Italian abstract artist who, since 1956, had been a design consultant to Cornigliano SpA (Italsider from 1961; currently ILVA), the state-owned steel works in Genoa, and was responsible for the corporate identity and the company art program,[8] contacted Blum in 1958. He told him that his company was looking for a renowned photographer in order to publish a book of photographs of Genoa, but at the same time was interested in photographs to illustrate its own printed materials, which went beyond the usual industrial documentation.[9] Cornigliano SpA was pursuing a new kind of corporate and public relations policy to promote a modern "corporate image,"[10] as well as an ambitious cultural program, including numerous commissions for many artists and intellectuals.

Blum's book of photographs, *Immagini di una città* (*Pictures of a City*),[11] was still in print in 1958; it concludes with two photographs from the neighboring steelworks in the vicinity of Cornigliano, where Blum had repeatedly been taking photographs in parallel with his photographs of the city.[12] This gave rise to an idea for a second book about the factory itself, published in 1959 as *Immagini di una fabbrica* (*Pictures of a Factory*).[13] Blum's interest in a series of photographs in book form was primarily focused on the visual spectacle of steel production, and did not seek to offer a narrative illustration of the sequence of operations. In addition to the distinctive industrial landscape of the factory area, he was interested primarily in the magic of the action, in forms, materials, and symbols in smoke and in glowing and flowing material and sparks. Many of his photographs were broken down into sharp contrasts and deliberately photographed using only existing light, often backlighting, and dark industrial spaces—even though this sometimes resulted in blurring caused by motion, and the dominant presence of black. Blum compressed space by using telephoto lenses, and incorporated atmospheric cloudiness. He often showed an interest in traces of Art Informel, for example, when flying sparks *burned* abstract, virtual *light drawings* onto the negative. This corresponded to his artistic context in the contemporaneous avant-garde.

The visual and acoustic impressions of the steelworks left a lasting impression on him, and early on Blum considered making a film as well, which he hoped could better capture this vital and almost demonic scenery. He had also shot color slides in the factory,[14] and he transferred these visual experiences to the concept of a color industrial film in widescreen format, which he offered the company as early as February 1959, and in which the focus would be entirely on more abstract shots. Cornigliano SpA already had a tradition extending back to 1926 of presenting itself in films, but they tended to be didactic documentary films about steel production.[15] Over the course of the year, Blum and his cameraman Maeder shot a 16mm color test film with an anamorphic accessory lens for CinemaScope.[16] Blum had already narrowed his focus to close-up details of production processes with red-hot irons, flames and flying sparks, distorted reflections in water, sheets of metal rolling by, and monochrome shots.

The Fiat factory in Turin was persuaded to help finance the film. In December 1959 Blum sent an "Exposé für einen subjektiven Experimentalfilm über Stahl und Eisen"[17] (Exposé of a Subjective Experimental Film on Steel and Iron) to the director of Cornigliano SpA along with a film notebook of 16 pages intended to illustrate "in photographs several scenic possibilities" of the planned film.[18] For the illustrations, Blum used black-and-white photographs taken for the steel book cut down to a narrow horizontal format to simulate the effect of CinemaScope.[19]

From this alone, it is clear that Blum's starting point was his enthusiasm for the strange industrial backdrop, whose "visual language" he wanted to show:

> As a visual artist, this landscape impressed me so much that I immediately had the idea of capturing on film this fascinating process of manufacturing steel, but not in the way to which we have been accustomed until now, as a pure documentary film, but on a subjective, artistic level.

He was clearly unwilling to settle on a narrative or didactic message in advance:

> It is not my intention to present to viewers a film on steel; rather, I want to open up for them a world of the magic of the material that until now has been perceived only as something rigid and solid.

On the contrary, Blum emphasized, he was pursuing an "avant-garde idea"; it was an artistic film in which the footage shot was merely the raw material for a dramaturgy that would not be formulated until the editing stage. He wanted to try

> to shut out the third dimension—depth. As a result, we obtain a two-dimensional, graphic image. The use of lines and movement should follow strict graphic and aesthetic principles. In order to be compared with visual artists, the film should not be too abstract, like a Mondrian, nor too impressionistic, like a Renoir, but should instead remain in the artistic sphere of a Kandinsky.

"Naturalistic shots like those the documentary film uses" were to be avoided or, where inevitable, were to be "employed artistically" by means of colored lights, filters, frosted glass, time lapses and slow motion, panning, unusual camera angles, and telephoto and macro photography.

Filming was to be entirely with existing light, and music was a leading element; it can "fuse color, rhythm, and statement into a harmonious whole." Blum left it open as to whether a specially composed film music, jazz, or old masters would be part of it. The rhythm should "climax in an ecstatic final chord."[20] At the same time, Carlo Vito Fedeli, the director of publicity for Cornigliano SpA, wrote an Italian exposé with similar arguments in which he spoke of an editing "collage."[21]

During the run-up to the film, Blum wanted to ensure he had as much freedom as possible when making it, and he emphasized his spontaneous approach and editing process:

> It is not possible to write a detailed film script because it evolves with the circumstances of the moment, through colorful impressions, rhythmic articulations, in short, through a conglomeration of forms, colors, and rhythm.[22]

With advice from Carmi, Blum and Maeder filmed the footage for *L'uomo, il fuoco, il ferro* in Genoa and, to a lesser extent, in Turin in 1960. Although Blum had already made it clear that he was not interested in giving an account of the manufacturing process from the raw material to the finished product, he was nonetheless required to shoot motifs that the sponsors themselves found important. The Fiat factory did not want a "subjective" art film so much as they wanted to see their products. Consequently, Blum and Maeder also filmed Fiat automobiles and jet engines in the Turin factories.[23]

In spite of Blum's advance explanation of his working method, the sponsors apparently demanded more concrete points of reference for the overall form early on, so Blum and Maeder produced an editing plan during the montage phase that contained more narrative elements that followed the production process more closely than would be the case for the finished film. The planned opening sequence was a long shot of the factory, with two shots of Fiat cars listed. All that remained of this in the final film was a brief and highly abstract tracking shot. The document also contains marginal notes with directions for the colors: passages dominated in turn by red, white, and blue.[24] There are also a few surviving pages with black-and-white photographs that probably represent an even earlier handwritten draft for the sequence, and show some more narrative sequences: for example, an initial sequence with exterior shots and a transition from the outside to the inside—including close-ups of a fire-spitting "spook from hell" that were intended to give the impression that "the viewers themselves were standing in 'lava.'"[25]

In the end, however, Blum seems to have succeeded with his free concept: the final ten-minute film follows a purely visual dramaturgy of crescendo and decrescendo with colors systematically alternating, usually between dominating warm red tones and cool blue ones. Color filters in front of the occasionally-needed lamps or lenses made fire, white-glowing iron, and sparks seem bright red; views through windows or of cold processes seen in daylight in the factory were automatically given a blue cast by the technique of using reversal tungsten film without filters.

Central elements of *L'uomo, il fuoco, il ferro* include the music and original noises on which the editing was based. In three sections, the driving, almost hammering piano music of Sergei Prokofiev[26] alternates with at times staccato-like machine noises from original recordings, employed independently of the images as well. The film opens with a shower of sparks seen close up, abstractly filling the screen, followed by blurrily flickering colored light against a black background, before the image transitions into work at the factory. During the running shot, an anamorphic lens with a red filter was rotated 90 degrees from the center of the image vertically to horizontally and then shifted upward, briefly revealing three converters glowing white and shooting sparks.[27] Following this introduction, the first section of the film shows close-ups of blast furnaces; the workers are often recognizable only in outline and are seen more as elements integrated into the processes than as active individuals. In the second section, the film transitions into brighter, more open spaces with original sounds and predominantly cold colors, with views of glass roofs, crane shots, red-hot ingots, and a roll of sheet metal being removed from the machine. The images and sounds are edited in such a way that an apparent correspondence between the sounds and motifs results: for example, loud, rhythmic alarms are not related diegetically to the close up of the red warning light although they seem to belong together, and instructions are heard, distorted, over the loudspeakers. The third section, with a faster piece of music, closes the circles of motifs by returning to the red-hot cast products and their transportation, and to the spark-spraying processes. The focus here is above all on visually highly reduced shots in the foreground, sketchy movements of a few visible elements, such as red-hot, linear steel forms in a black space. Many images are compressed by perspective, elements overlap, schemas push their way in front of the firelight that is the preferred light source and, in some cases, edits are shorter. The film ends in a furious climax of images and music, with a spectacle of red sparks similar to that at the beginning, and makes a symbolically coagulating flowing form the effective endpoint.

Time-lapse photography was used for crane shots that would otherwise have been too slow. According to Maeder, two scenes were staged for the shooting entirely separately from the work process. The sequences of industrial production were ultimately not reproduced in the film. Even more so than in his photographs, Blum emphasized isolated, purely visual phenomena. In contrast to his book on steel, in the film he did not show the manufacturing facilities or situations that were clearly present even once, and virtually no recognizable products could be seen. Instead, the resulting image is of an almost volcanic, archaic, steel *creation*, a kind of apotheosis of primitive forces of sublime, almost supernaturally abstract beauty.

At the 21st Venice International Film Festival that same year, Blum's film received a Special Jury Prize in section XI, International Exhibition for Documentaries and Scientific, Cultural, and Recreational Films. While Blum enjoyed a certain success with this film, however, which had a long run as a cultural film in cinema preshow programs and was also frequently screened alone, it nevertheless fell prey to the harsh criticism of the then young philosopher Gianni Vattimo, who in 1962, using the example of the book *Immagini di una fabbrica* in particular, updated the famous quotation from Bertolt Brecht in the 1920s, that a simple "representation of reality" says less about reality than ever before; a photograph of modern industrial plants "yields nearly nothing about these institutions. Actual reality has slipped into the functional."[28] Vattimo harshly condemned Blum's book and its doubtlessly suggestive, aesthetic-abstract photographs—representative for his critique of the "new mythology" of Italsider's cultural policy and its neocapitalist philosophy as a culturally open, "enlightened" industry. They were images that, rather than showing something of the reality of labor, made the factory a visual "spectacle" for those who saw it only in photographs. The atmosphere of the book (and, one could add here, *L'uomo, il fuoco, il ferro* as well) was, according to Vattimo, the hygienic-optimistic ideology of an "industrial design," purged of its true conditions, that tries to conceal, and all but "exorcise," the human suffering in industrial society. Even though Vattimo acknowledged that Italsider's cultural policy was serious and ambitious and had certainly had a relatively exemplary character, he nevertheless emphasized the risk of a "rhetoric of the humanized factory" in which technology, ethics, and aesthetics supplemented one another perfectly.[29] But apparently not all intellectuals shared this criticism, for Italsider went even further in 1963 with *I colori del ferro* (*The Colors of Iron*), a book that prominently featured an introduction by Umberto Eco, and color photographs by various artists that are highly detailed with abstract graphics that show the influence of Art Informel as well as Pop and Op art. Eco's essay assessed the current significance of "materia" (matter) and the "objet trouvé" (found object) seen through the artist's eye and isolated in a photograph, in contrast to the idealistic idea of artistic "creazione" (creation).[30]

Shortly after filming *L'uomo, il fuoco, il ferro*, Blum returned to Genoa with Maeder and shot the unfinished film *Signale* (*Signals*), an action that may have been prompted by Carmi.[31] Here Blum showed in a rapid montage only traffic signs, license plates, traffic lights, billboards, control instruments, panels, and dashboards in close-up, often with zooming or as tracking shots, or filmed off a television screen, and finally details of moving vehicles. Whereas *L'uomo, il fuoco, il ferro* was still very much in the context of an abstracting camera eye in the style of Art Informel, *Signale* points rather to Blum's other artistic interest: Pop art[32]—

perhaps here too Carmi's new interest in the technical mechanisms of control in art was also being brought to bear.[33]

In his 1960 film, Blum had revealed himself to be an avant-garde filmmaker working in a sponsorship context, but his "symphony in steel" (*Symphonie in Stahl* is the German title of *L'uomo, il fuoco, il ferro*)[34] was certainly also of its time. The relationship between the editing and sound montage, and the forms of symphonic composition already had various precursors and parallels,[35] such as the Swiss industrial film *Symphonie der Arbeit* (*Symphony of Labor*) by Werner Dressler and Kurt Früh (Switzerland, 1937),[36] and Alain Resnais' prizewinning sponsored work *Le Chant du styrène* (*The Song of Styrene*, France, 1958). One contemporaneous example of the parallel use of music and images in industrial films with no commentary is *Stahl: Thema mit Variationen* (*Steel: Theme with Variations*, Germany, 1960) by Hugo Niebeling for the Mannesmann production company, which likewise had no voice-over, but only the accompaniment of electronic music by Oskar Sala.[37] Above all *Technik: Drei Studien in Jazz* (*Technique: Three Studies in Jazz*, Germany, 1961), a film made by Hans H. Hermann from leftover footage from an advertising film from 1958 on the history of the Krupp factories, was edited directly to three concertante jazz pieces by Martin Böttcher with no accompanying commentary. Here too Hermann was seeking an analogy between the contemporary "technical" musical jazz form and modern industrial production.[38]

These films did find new forms to convey the interplay of image and sound and dispensed with an explanatory voice-over, but they remained largely didactic and presented human labor as a skilled, modern industrial activity with comprehensible processes. By contrast, in his film on steel Blum carefully avoided such informational content and hence obvious advertising value, and thus ultimately straddled the two sides: the sponsors and the cultural critics.

Swiss National Exhibition—Lausanne 1964

One revealing example of an unredeemed artistically autonomous film concept in the pragmatic business world was the project Blum developed for the Iron Group section of the Swiss National Exhibition 1964 (Expo 64) in Lausanne, commissioned by a consortium of Swiss ironworking industries represented by Von Roll AG in Gerlafingen.[39] Having seen the Italian film on steel, the company had approached Blum with the idea of producing a film on the process of making steel, from the molten iron and scrap metal to the finished product. In an early exposé,[40] Blum outlined the concept for his idea for the film, while at the same time distinguishing it from his earlier film on steel, to which he referred here as an "experimental film": "The primary idea cinematically and in the sequence of images [in the case of *L'uomo, il fuoco, il ferro*] was not iron's path precisely followed through the factory"; rather, it was the images that had been, not so much subject-related, but instead "brought into a rhythmic sequence. By contrast, the film for Expo 64 should introduce the visitor to the course of a manufacturing process." Blum had agreed with the Von Roll company that a special "film room," which enabled an approximately ten-minute-long multiple projection to be shown, should be built. Three screens in a CinemaScope format of 4.9 by 11 meters were placed as a triangle with a two-meter opening in each corner,

> onto which a film can be projected simultaneously from each of the three corners of the triangle always in harmony with the sequence of images of the two others [...] On entering the triangle, visitors to the pavilion find themselves in a pure cinematic space in which they can move freely at will.

Because a spoken commentary could distract from the overall effect, it was agreed, Blum continued, to have

> a noise commentary, background noise of factory bruitism, which, though "nonrepresentational," would accompany incomparably more effectively the images, movement, and color, supporting and even guiding them.

Each of these three films should "form a self-contained unity," whereby when projected simultaneously "one image becomes the main image, for example, when the glowing clump of iron under the press is shown once in a long shot and twice in close-up from two different perspectives." By "purely cinematic, visual, and acoustic means" the visitors are initiated into the industrial process. Unlike in panoramic multiple projections, the three independent films were supposed to run synchronously, but in every shot each would in turn supplement or follow the others; actions or movements could also move out of one film and into another[41]; analogous to the changing main image, a stereo soundtrack would always dominate.[42] The exposé also specified split-screen sequences in which individual CinemaScope shots were divided into three images by a masking and by multiple exposure of the film, so that there could be as many as nine individual shots in parallel.

Perhaps the company wanted to ensure that this approach resulted in a film that would in fact be usable for promotion. Blum, presumably in collaboration with Peter Schmidlin Advertising of Basel, developed a shooting script with all of the shots laid out in detail in order to show the images of typical processes of steelmaking that were to be projected simultaneously, including the sorting and packing of the finished products, and an illustrative final image of flowing steel; the sheets for the single shots have information about the images of the three cameras and the dominant color of each, the original sound to be recorded, and the content of the message. It was, however, once again emphasized that this plan pertained only to the shots, not to the final editing of the films.[43] The filming was to take place in the steelworks of Von Roll in Gerlafingen and of Von Moos in Lucerne with shorter sequences in Drahtwerke AG in Biel. Blum also took 35mm color slides as preliminary studies when he visited the factories.[44]

In 2005 Blum reported that, prior to filming, he was supposed to sign a statement stating that he would deliver a "valuable and important film," and even shortly before his death was angry about this. How was he supposed to be able to sign such a statement given that he filmed "subjectively" and spontaneously? While shooting the film, he reported, a company manager had come by and specified certain tracking shots they wanted, which Maeder and Blum "filmed," but without starting the camera.[45] As far as one can tell from the material in the surviving versions, here again Blum showed either details, or more compositional motivated views of aspects of the production that did, however, remain broadly comprehensible; in particular, Blum had largely dispensed with purely abstracting, aestheticizing shots.

Blum's advanced conception for this triple CinemaScope simultaneous projection seems remarkably contemporary compared with the other film projects for Expo 64. It is all the more astonishing that his concept in particular should not have been implemented by the sponsors. Since the 1950s—and some much earlier pioneer films—there had been several approaches to multiple projections including 360-degree panoramic movies. Not only were films omnipresent at Expo 64, but panoramic and multimedia projection technologies were particularly often represented in many sections.[46] For example, for its 360-degree projection on the world of Swiss trains, *Rund um Rad und Schiene* (*Around Wheel and Rail*), the Schweizerische Bundesbahnen (SBB, Swiss Federal Railways) used Disney Company's Circarama technology exclusively, with nine separate synchronized projections on moving screens 83 meters long.[47] The 70mm promotional film for the Swiss Army, *La suisse vigilante* (*Vigilant Switzerland*), was projected onto a giant triptych screen of 420 square meters.[48] In the Industry and Commerce sector, the multiple projection *Les impératifs de l'activité industrielle et artisanale suisse* (*The Imperatives of Swiss Industrial and Artistic Activity*) was shown as a large-format triptych with five additional round screens showing case studies to supplement and provide depth to the subjects displayed on the central screens.[49]

The directors of the Expo 64 accepted Blum's film *Eisen* after it was viewed by the film jury on January 29, 1964, and emphasized its "above-average quality."[50] Because only one film is mentioned, it is unclear whether this assessment was of the three films that Blum and Maeder had submitted, or of a revised version made specifically for the exhibition. Without discussing their intentions with Blum, the sponsor abandoned its concept for the installation and apparently had the three films reedited entirely and the content structured differently, resulting in three independent cinematic narratives. The person responsible at Von Roll AG, Vice Director Ulrich Kappeler, was ambivalent about this in his report on the presentation at Expo 64.

There had been considerable discussion of the film in the Iron Group section; the exhibitors' association had wanted to build a "self-contained film theater," but because it would have distracted from the architecture, "the group's project was changed—wrongly, as it later turned out."[51]

All three individual films start out with red-hot molten iron, but they address very different production processes. Other indications of a radical reediting are possibly the facts that the title sequence does not mention the filmmaker, the films have slightly different running times, and considerably shorter ones than those that had been planned by Blum and later edited with Maeder in an elaborate synchronous montage of finished versions (approximately six minutes rather than the original ten).[52] Each film has its own (original) soundtrack, the three screens were placed separately in the room, and the films were projected asynchronously, which according to Maeder resulted in unflattering overlapping of the soundtracks.[53]

No "Red Desert"

After his failed concept for Expo 64, Blum finished just one more industrial film: *ARFA Röhrenwerke AG, Basel/Schweiz* (*ARFA Pipe Mills Corporation, Basel/Switzerland*; Switzerland, 1966).[54] This commissioned promotional information film with descriptive commentary in a voice-over that was written entirely by the company follows the exact procedure of processing the rolls of sheet steel that are delivered, all the way to finished pipes and their shipping; considerable room is devoted to inspecting the materials, the milling of the pipes and sleeves, and development work at ARFA. There are only occasional flashes of Blum's earlier attention to the visual attractions in the factory, such as details of machines at work or brief close-ups of welding with sparks flying. The only truly cinematic device that stands out is a long aerial tracking shot across the entire pipe production line, which shows once again in a linear overview the process that had previously been described by the commentator and shown in detail in individual shots.

Just how much self-censorship was involved when he was working on commissioned projects can be sensed from his proposal for an instructional film on road construction planned in 1965 for the Losinger company, for whom Blum would later publish a book of color photographs.[55] In this paper, which apparently served as an internal exchange of ideas between Stalder, who was presumably a joint author, and Blum, the sequence of subjects, the visual aesthetic, and possible shots were sketched. The subject was supposed to lead "with all the important phases of the making of a street" from the preparatory work to the finished roadway, and end with a "street symphony" with "(possibly edited to music) forms, lines, and planes of streets and bridges." Certain artistic features were certainly planned:

> Also in the color, complete freedom: black-and-white, real color, leaving out intermediate tones, colored.
> Sound: mix of electronic music and real or heightened noise. Counterpoint between: objective-subjective, concrete-abstract, perhaps lyrical-factual.
> The different parts should, in each case, start out from the whole and show specific aspects of the stages of production.
> People should always appear throughout, giving orders, pressing a lever, turning a wheel. For the rest, a world of machines that has saved people from drudgery.[56]

It was, however, decided not to distort the theme: Blum and Stalder had presumably discussed whether *Il deserto rosso* (*The Red Desert*; Michelangelo Antonioni, Italy, 1964), with its dramaturgy of color and the leitmotif of a foggy northern Italy, could serve as inspiration. But Stalder came out against it:

> I would be afraid of a *Deserto rosso* landscape for two reasons. We shouldn't adopt it just because it is strange. This landscape has a specific, pessimistic, nihilistic statement in Antonioni (from *Il grido* onward). But we want to discover in technology precisely values that have been submerged until now: beauty, truth. Moreover, the word "building," which should also be exploited in the film dramaturgically, is the exact opposite of what Antonioni means.[57]

In a kind of anticipation of their sponsor's arguments, they clearly decided against too much aesthetic autonomy and opted for the applied use of film, which also seems realistic in view of earlier experiences.

In his practice of sponsored industrial films, Kurt Blum never again enjoyed a freedom of the artistic, cinematic self-realization comparable to that which he had enjoyed in Genoa. From 1962 to 1971 he made several more films about culture and travel commissioned by the Swiss Tourism Center, Swissair, and Swiss Post,[58] which were located between thematic documentary features and very free, even experimental realizations. But his ideas of form did not always conform to the interests of the sponsors. In general, openness to autonomous solutions seems to have been greater around 1960.[59] Moreover, in the late 1960s the important opportunity to screen cultural films prior to the main feature disappeared. Blum recognized these limits and was ultimately not interested in teamwork and the elaborate conceptual planning necessary for film production.[60] He therefore abandoned the medium of film.[61]

[1] Martin Gasser (ed.), *Gegenlicht: Kurt Blum, Fotografien*, exh. cat., Fotostiftung Schweiz, Limmat, Zurich 2012.
[2] Kurt Blum & Fritz E. Maeder, *Rabio: Gedankenwelt eines Strafgefangenen*, 35mm, black-and-white, 35 min., camera: Fritz E. Maeder.
[3] Kurt Blum & Eugenio Carmi, *L'uomo, il fuoco, il ferro* (Switzerland, 1960), 35mm, color, CinemaScope, 10 min., camera: Fritz E. Maeder; production: International Golden Star of Italy. Lichtspiel/Kinemathek, Bern (ed.), *Werkschau Kurt Blum: Filme und Interview*, DVD, Lichtspiel/Kinemathek, Bern 2011.
[4] *Acier von Roll: Vom Schrott zum blanken Stahl – Vom Rohstahl zur Schraube – Schmieden von Stahl*, 3 films (Switzerland, 1964), 35mm, color, CinemaScope, each ca. 6 min., camera: Fritz E. Maeder.
[5] Sylvie Henguely, "Kurt Blum und die Kunstszene," Martin Gasser (ed.), *Gegenlicht*, p. 163–86.
[6] *Kurt Blum, Fotoexperimente*, exh. cat., Kunstmuseum, Solothurn 1997.
[7] Martin Gasser, "Aus der Dunkelheit geschält – ein Vorwort," *Gegenlicht*, p. 12.
[8] Fabio Bettonica, *Your Hands! Your Head! Your Eyes! Eugenio Carmi, An Artist in the Factory*, Target, Genoa 2006; Carlo Fedeli, *Carmi e l'acciaio*, Genoa 1990, films on DVD.
[9] Interviews with Eugenio Carmi in Milan, January 9, 2012, and January 8, 2014; *Kurt Blum e l'Italia*, exh. cat., CCS, Centro culturale svizzero, Pro Helvetia/Galleria Cons Arc, Milan/Chiasso 2004.
[10] Carlo Vinti, *Gli anni dello stile industriale, 1948–1965: Immagine e politica culturale nella grande impresa italiana*, Marsilio, Venice 2007; Willy Rotzler, "italsider: Das graphische Profil einer Gruppe italienischer Stahlwerke," *Graphis*, no. 101 (1962), p. 288–303, p. 370–372.
[11] Kurt Blum, *Immagine di una città*, C. M. Lerici (Forma e vita 2), Milan 1958.
[12] Thilo Koenig, "Kurt Blum in der Fabrik," Martin Gasser (ed.), *Gegenlicht*, p. 75–92.
[13] Kurt Blum, *Immagine di una fabbrica, Pictures of a Factory, Images d'une usine*, Fretz & Wasmuth, Zurich 1959; K. Blum, *Lebendiger Stahl*, Fretz & Wasmuth, Zurich 1960.
[14] "Vier junge Schweizer Photographen: Kurt Blum," *Camera* (Lucerne, Switzerland), vol. 39, no. 2 (1960), p. 31–46.
[15] *Italsider: Catalogo cineteca*, Italsider, Genoa 1962, n. p.
[16] "Probeaufnahmen für 'L'uomo ... '" Lichtspiel/Kinemathek, *Werkschau Kurt Blum*. In 1958 Maeder had previously worked on a Cinerama widescreen film on the Swiss railway, with shots divided into three projections (according to telephone conversation with Fritz E. Maeder, March 27, 2012, and joint viewing of the Blum films and an interview at the Lichtspiel/Kinemathek in Bern, January 17, 2014).
[17] [Kurt Blum], "Exposé für einen subjektiven Experimentalfilm über Stahl und Eisen in Gemeinschaftsproduktion der

Firmen CORNIGLIANO S.p.A. Genua und die FIATWERKE, Turin," typescript [1959], n.p. [p. 1, 3, and 4], Lichtspiel/Kinemathek archives, Bern.

[18] Kurt Blum to Director Gian Lupo Osti, carbon copy of letter, December 21, 1959, Lichtspiel/Kinemathek archives, Bern.

[19] "Filmskizzenbuch über einen Film von Stahl und Eisen" (Sketchbook for a Film on Steel and Iron), Lichtspiel/Kinemathek archives, Bern. Illustrations in Martin Gasser (ed.), *Gegenlicht*, p. 88–90.

[20] [Kurt Blum], "Exposé," p. 1–4.

[21] [Carlo Vito Fedeli], undated typescript (ca. 1959), p. 1–4, Fedeli archives, Lavagna/Genoa; emails from Carlo Fedeli to the author, January 12 and 20, 2012, telephone conversation with the author, April 1, 2012.

[22] [Kurt Blum], "Exposé."

[23] According to Fritz E. Maeder, interviews in 2012 and 2014.

[24] Anon. [Fritz E. Maeder, by his own account], *Fuoco d'acciaio*, undated typescript [1960], Lichtspiel/Kinemathek archives, Bern.

[25] Untitled, p. 10, Lichtspiel/Kinemathek archives, Bern (unfinished).

[26] Excerpts from a sonata and the Toccata in D Minor, Op.11, by Sergei Prokofiev.

[27] Anon., *Fuoco d'acciaio*, editing script, marked in two places: "anamorphic lens reversed."

[28] Bertolt Brecht, "The Three-Penny Trial: A Sociological Experiment," Richard W. McCormick, Alison Guenther-Pal (eds.), *German Essays on Film*, trans. Lance W. Garmer, Continuum, New York 2004, p. 111–132, esp. 117.

[29] Gianni Vattimo, "Uomini come machine: Human relations e rapporti di produzione," *Sipra*, vol. 1, no. 3 (August 1962), quoted in Carlo Vinti, *Gli anni dello stile industriale*, p. 300–301.

[30] Umberto Eco, "Introduzione," Eugenio Carmi, Carlo Fedeli (eds.), *I colori del ferro*, Italsider, Genoa 1963; Margit Staber, "Die Farben des Eisens," *Graphis*, vol. 20, no. 112 (1964), p. 140–145.

[31] Kurt Blum, *Signale* (ca. 1961), 16mm, color, 4 min. (camera: Fritz E. Maeder), Lichtspiel/Kinemathek, *Werkschau Kurt Blum*. The film fragment has no title sequence.

[32] Martin Gasser, *Gegenlicht*, figs. on p. 82–83, 115, 118–120.

[33] Umberto Eco & Duncan Macmillan, *Carmi*, L'Agrifoglio, Milan 1996.

[34] "L'uomo, il fuoco e il ferro/Symphonie in Stahl," *Der Filmberater*, vol. 25, no. 7 (1965) p. 109–110.

[35] Walter Ruttmann, *Berlin: Die Sinfonie der Grossstadt* (Germany, 1927); Dziga Vertov, *Enthusiasm/Donbass Symphony* (USSR, 1930); *A Symphony of Steel* (USA, 1933); *Steel: A Symphony of Industry* (USA, 1936); Ulrich Kayser, *Feurige Hochzeit: Eine Sinfonie in Stahl und Eisen* (Germany, 1951; in color).

[36] Werner Dressler & Kurt Früh, *Symphonie der Arbeit*, Lichtspiel Videoportal, Dokumentar (online); first version of the film *Hände und Maschinen* (1938); Yvonne Zimmermann, "Industriefilme," Y. Zimmermann (ed.), *Schaufenster Schweiz: Dokumentarische Gebrauchsfilme, 1896–1964*, Limmat, Zurich 2011, p. 354–355.

[37] Electronic music, again by Oskar Sala, was first used in the snow film by Kurt Blum and Alexander Seiler, *Auf weissem Grund* (1962). Electronic music was often used in industrial films of the period; see Peter Donhauser, "Musik, Ton und Sprache im Industriefilm," *Ferrum: Nachrichten aus der Eisenbibliothek*, no. 76 (2004, "Das Unternehmen im Bild – Das Bild vom Unternehmen: Zum Industriefilm der Eisen- und Stahlindustrie"), p. 14–23.

[38] Dirk Schaefer, "Heavy Metal: Vom Stahlwerk ins Studio; Musikalische Experimente im Industriefilm um 1960," Beate Hentschel, Anja Casser (eds.), *The Vision Behind:*

Technische und soziale Innovationen im Unternehmensfilm ab 1950, Vorwerk 8, Berlin 2007, p. 31–33; Peter Donhauser, "Musik, Ton und Sprache im Industriefilm."

[39] Ulrich Kappeler, "Fer – Eisen – Ferro: Die schweizerische Eisenindustrie an der Expo," *Von Roll Werkzeitung*, no. 4 (July 1964), p. 103–105.

[40] [Kurt Blum], "Stahlfilm für die Expo 1964 in Lausanne" (Steel Film for Expo 1964 in Lausanne), typescript, March 1, 1963, Lichtspiel/Kinemathek archives, Bern.

[41] *Ibid*.

[42] According to Fritz E. Maeder, interviews in 2012 and 2014.

[43] Peter Schmidlin Advertising, "Expo64/Gruppe Eisen/CinemaScope-Film," project proposal, n. d. [ca. 1963], Lichtspiel/Kinemathek archives, Bern.

[44] Martin Gasser (ed.), *Gegenlicht*, p. 91.

[45] Kurt Blum interviewed by David Landolf, December 1, 2005, Lichtspiel/Kinemathek, *Werkschau Kurt Blum*.

[46] "sb," "Bewegte und bewegende Bilder. Anmerkungen zu einigen Dokumentarfilmen an der Expo 1964," *Neue Zürcher Zeitung*, no. 2566, noon edition (June 12, 1964), p. 7; C.V. Zimmermann, "Expériences de cinématographie au service de l'Exposition et de l'industrie suisse," *La Liberté* (Fribourg) (July 4, 1964), clip; Pierre Frey et al., *Expo 64: Le printemps de l'architecture Suisse*, Presses polytechniques et universitaires romandes, Lausanne 2014.

[47] *Rund um Rad und Schiene*, director: Ernst A. Heiniger. Thomas Schärer, "Das Circarama-Abenteuer der Schweizerischen Bundesbahnen," *Expo 64: Memoriav Bulletin*, no. 21 (September 2014), p. 16–17; Lukas Piccolin, "Ausweitungen des Blicks: Von gemalten zu bewegten Panoramen," *Expo 64: Memoriav Bulletin*.

[48] *La Suisse vigilante*, director: John Fernhout; Severin Rüegg, "Codename 'Gartenschirm,'" *Expo 64: Memoriav Bulletin*, no. 21 (September 2014), p. 14–15.

[49] *Les impératifs de l'activité industrielle et artisanale Suisse*, director: A + B Film AG (Georges Alexath, René Boeniger); ms, "Experiment für einen Expo-Film," *Neue Zürcher Zeitung*, no. 2940, noon edition (July 19, 1963), p. 5.

[50] Letter from Dr. P. Ruckstuhl to U. Kappeler, Vice Director of von Roll AG, Gerlafingen, copy of typescript, January 29, 1964, Lichtspiel/Kinemathek archives, Bern.

[51] Ulrich Kappeler, "Fer – Eisen – Ferro," p. 105–106.

[52] The films are in the archives of Lichtspiel/Kinemathek, Bern, and the Cinémathèque suisse, Lausanne. When watching the films with the author on January 17, 2014, Maeder confirmed that these versions have nothing to do with the versions they submitted at the time.

[53] According to Maeder, they only learned of the changes two weeks before the exhibition opened (telephone conversation with the author in 2012).

[54] Kurt Blum, *ARFA Röhrenwerke AG, Basel/Schweiz*, 16mm, color, 10 min., camera: Fritz E. Maeder, Lichtspiel/Kinemathek, *Werkschau Kurt Blum*.

[55] Losinger & Co. AG (ed.), *Losinger, 1917–1967*, Losinger, Bern 1967.

[56] Stalder to Kurt Blum, typewritten letter, October 18, 1965; script/proposal for a film about Losinger, n. d. [1965], n.p. Lichtspiel/Kinemathek archives, Bern.

[57] *Ibid*.

[58] List of films in Martin Gasser, *Gegenlicht*, p. 249–250.

[59] Yvonne Zimmermann, "Auftragsfilm versus Autorenfilm: Zur Geschichte einer Beziehungskiste," *Cinema*, no. 51 (2006), p. 109–118.

[60] According to Fritz E. Maeder, interviews in 2012 and 2014.

[61] I am sincerely grateful to Fritz E. Maeder, Carlo Vito Fedeli, Eugenio Carmi, and all at Lichtspiel, including David Landolf, for all their assistance.

Kurt Blum and Fritz E. Maeder at the editing table, post 1963

ON THE MARGINS

An Avant-Garde of Amateurs? The Cinematic Experiments of Jaques Dutoit, Georges Dufaux, and Hans Haldenwang
Vrääth Öhner

Translated from the German by Steven Lindberg

Jaques Dutoit, *Lisi Strates*, 1986 (Switzerland)
16mm film, 22 minutes

One of the avant-garde's tendencies that remained largely without consequences is a predilection for the amateur or, more precisely, a certain (romantic) idea easily associated with the figure of the amateur. Indeed, this sentiment was reciprocated by amateur film. It was described in great detail by Maya Deren in a collection of notes, essays, and letters that was published in 1965 as issue 39 of *Film Culture*. However, even before Deren, a series of filmmakers including Joris Ivens, Robert Flaherty, Stan Brakhage, Ernst Schmidt Jr., as well as Swiss filmmaker Werner Ott, had articulated the same idea, namely, that independence from economic constraints enables amateurs to develop their individual creativity freely and thereby contributes to the aesthetic development of cinema. In Deren's words:

> Instead of envying the script and dialogue writers, the trained

actors, the elaborate staff and sets, the enormous production budgets of the professional film, the amateur should make use of the one great advantage which all professionals envy him, namely, *freedom*—both artistic and physical.[1]

The utopian core of Deren's reflections is a legacy of the idealist philosophy of the 18th century and the bourgeois culture of the 19th. They are contradicted not only by the empirical experience of family films and the sociological theory of the culture of leisure, which locates the amateur in a triangular relationship between the professional realm and the public,[2] but also by well-established writings on the history of film. In the context of American avant-garde film, for example, Jan-Christopher Horak has drawn attention to a historical paradox that reflects Deren's remarks about the amateur.[3] When Deren published her notes, and especially at the time when they assumed their full importance—that is, after P. Adams Sitney had begun his history of the American avant-garde film of 1974 with Deren[4]—the close relationship between amateurs and avant-garde artists that had certainly existed in the 1920s and 1930s had long since broken down.

The 1950s avant-gardists proclaimed themselves to be independent filmmakers, actively engaged in the production of "art," while the earlier generation viewed themselves as cineastes, as lovers of cinema, as "amateurs" willing to work in any arena furthering the cause of film art, even if it meant working for hire.[5]

According to Horak, the newly acquired self-image as an independent filmmaker was tied to a kind of "professionalization" of avant-garde film production, supported by institutions such as film cooperatives, state programs (in the United States also by private foundations) providing funding for film, teaching positions at universities, and through the creation of new screening opportunities in museums, archives, and media centers.

This development was complemented by the cinematic production of amateurs who were organized within the framework of clubs and associations.[6] Already by the 1930s this production had gradually begun to abandon its initial openness to experimental forms, due in part to well-known economic and, especially in Europe, political conditions. It had progressively become a relatively autonomous parallel culture with its own umbrella organizations, national and international competitions, and aesthetic value judgments, which were increasingly based on what Noël Burch has called the "Institutional Mode of Representation," or IMR.[7] Amateurs had not, however, completely abandoned their penchant for the experimental forms of the avant-garde. Despite the differences that always existed "between the experimental impulses of amateurism and the avant-garde," amateurs retained, at least to some extent, their enthusiasm for avant-gardism throughout the entire film era.[8]

It is no coincidence that Ian Craven made this observation in the context of animated film, that is to say, in a genre that film historians had marginalized for almost as long as they had neglected amateur film, and that, because of its specific production conditions, remained close to the practice of amateurs and experimental forms of cinematic expression. Although animated film required a strict work discipline and basic graphic or drawing abilities (and hence precluded participation by many amateurs), it also liberated amateurs from numerous restrictions and imponderables associated with the production of live-action movies—the caprices of weather that make filming outdoors difficult, problems with potentially unreliable personnel in general and actors in particular, and the costs, even for simple shootings, of set, costumes, and makeup. Animated film offered both dominant factions within the amateur film movement—those enthusiastic about technology and those focused on aesthetics—an equally broad field of activity. Moreover, "its oft-celebrated liberations from the laws of physics, the constraints of reduced physical resources, and the very indexicality of the photographic sign"[9] provided solid grounds for legitimizing the abandonment of the conventions of (live-action) film and giving free rein to the imagination instead.

Against this backdrop, it is hardly surprising that two Swiss amateur animated filmmakers, Hans Haldenwang and Georges Dufaux, gained recognition as early as 1978 as a result of their inclusion in Bruno Edera's *Histoire du Cinéma suisse d'animation* (*History of Swiss Animated Film*), admittedly under the label "Les dilettantes" (The Amateurs).[10] According to Edera, both men belonged to an elite of ambitious amateur filmmakers in the decade from 1968 to 1977 who had made a crucial contribution to the evolution of the Swiss animated film. It is worth noting in this context that, in their primary professions, both Haldenwang and Dufaux pursued activities that to some extent had a close relationship to animation—Haldenwang worked as a retoucher for the Conzett & Huber publishing house, and Dufaux as projectionist for various Swiss cinemas and for the Schwarz Film AG laboratory in Ostermundigen.

While one could, at least, speak of some exchange on the margins between amateur production and experimental forms in the realm of animation, in the case of the live-action movie the situation is far less clear. As only an ever-decreasing fraction of amateur production has been archived, the state of these archives remains problematic. Amateur film has a formal diversity that has been repeatedly observed in random samples and case studies (to trace their history would require separate research projects each lasting several years), and conceptual reflections, which are still in their early stages, permit merely speculative statements about the relationship between amateurism and cinematic experiments.

It is indisputable that both amateur and avant-garde filmmakers shared a critical distance from commercial film, worked under similar conditions, and used the same smaller film formats. Yet the split between experimental films assigned to art institutions and those that are cinematic experiments—there were doubtless experiments in the realm of the amateur film as well—effectively prevents the study of the latter. Although the study of the cinematic work of amateurs has clearly increased over the past decade, and has led, among other things, to amateur film being cast both as an autonomous, semipublic mode of communication alongside the private home movie, and as the public mode of commercial and artistic film,[11] the distinction between the avant-garde and the experimental impulses of amateurism still centers around the difference between art and nonart that grew out of the "professionalization" of avant-garde film production after the Second World War.

Just how problematic this distinction has become in the meanwhile is demonstrated, among other things, by Jacques Rancière's reflection on the aesthetic regime of the arts. According to Rancière, the dissolution of the boundaries between art and life (the central signature of the aesthetic regime) not only makes every conceivable avant-garde movement possible, but also reverses every rule that allows a distinction to be made between art and non-art.[12] The determination to cling to this distinction (not least by the proponents of the avant-garde themselves) may have been connected with the need to emerge as an art movement. That should not, however, obscure the fact that every rule determining inclusion or exclusion already bears the sign of its provisional nature. In that sense, this essay attempts to illustrate this point with reference to three filmmakers—the aforementioned animated filmmakers Haldenwang and Dufaux, and the independent filmmaker Jaques Dutoit of Biel—in order, if not to eliminate, at least to call into question the common distinction made between the avant-garde and the experimental impulses of amateurism.

Art Film versus Animation

"Cinema. Ci-ne-ma! Hmm. I love cinema. I don't like a lot of films. Fewer and fewer. I love intimacy, simplicity, that which sends me back to myself." Dutoit's short film *Lisi Strates* (1986) begins with these words, which are certainly meant to be understood as programmatic, spoken by a woman off camera. *Lisi Strates* is a subjective portrait of a woman, about 40 years old (played by Lisi Skorpis), who is searching for herself. Dutoit presents this search via loosely connected shots of his protagonist outdoors, in a snowy landscape, on the shore of a lake, but also inside, in a stairwell, in her living room, in the bathtub, in bed. We see her naked descending a wooden staircase, typing on a typewriter, confiding her thoughts to a notebook. The sequence of moving images is interrupted again and again by stills, by black-and-white and partly yellowed photographs of a young woman, a man holding a small child, a girl, a teenager. On the soundtrack, the aforementioned woman's voice is heard as a kind of inner monologue about the things she loves, about feelings when touching, about waiting, about the myth of the father, about the familiarity of skin, and finally about farewell and death. In several places a second voice joins in a dialogue with the first; occasionally music is heard briefly, while the rest of the soundtrack consists of acoustic events such as the sound of walking in snow, wheezing, the noise of the city in the distance, or the sound of silence.

Lisi Strates was in fact the fifth film directed by Dutoit. While earning his living teaching Latin and Greek at a secondary school in Biel, Dutoit had previously made the short films *Matière grise* (*Grey Matter*, 1969–1970) and *E soixante-dix* (*E Seventy*, 1970–1971) with his students and colleague Luc Monnier, the experimental documentary film *Trait d'union* (*Hyphen*, 1980–1981) with financial support from the Ministry of Education of the Canton of Bern, and the short film *Oser* (*To Dare*, 1983) at his own expense. In addition to producing these films, Dutoit was active as a film critic for the *Journal du Jura* among others, organized film screenings in Biel, was a member of various juries (in Nyon and elsewhere), and also very active in theater. In 1984 the Cinémathèque française presented a first retrospective of his films, followed by the Cinémathèque suisse a year later. *Lisi Strates* premiered at the Apollo cinema in Biel on May 10, 1986, was presented as part of the Solothurner Filmtage festival, and was also widely shown in various Swiss cities and abroad.

Although Dutoit made films with passion and not for commercial reasons, it is difficult to describe him as an amateur, although in his application for funding for *Lisi Strates*, he wrote "autodidacte" (self-taught) on the official form of the Federal Office of Culture in response to a question about any special training in film that he might have; in a conversation with Fred Truniger and myself in September 2013 he described himself as a "cinéaste marginal" (marginal filmmaker), and strongly believes that it is possible to make films independently. Contrary to the usual practice in amateur production, he worked with professional camera people and editors on all of his first five films. Paradoxically, only after he retired and could devote himself full-time to filmmaking, did he begin to operate the camera himself. In the case of *Lisi Strates*, he even worked with Marcel Hanoun, who was briefly internationally famous before falling back into oblivion, a man who, as late as 1970, was called the most important and the most interesting French filmmaker since [Robert] Bresson by Jonas Mekas.[13]

In other words, the reference to the art of film with which *Lisi Strates* begins would in essence have been unnecessary. Even without it, the film would have easily been identifiable as an example of art cinema or of European auteur film. The way Dutoit presents his theme—by means of fragmentary and sometimes repetitive shots of his protagonist, assembled without any hierarchical structure, and ignoring the chronological order of the narrative as well as mixing up time so that past and present flow together indistinguishably—does not so much recall Bresson or Jean-Luc Godard, whom Dutoit cites as role models, but rather narrative styles that were already present in *Matière grise*, his first film.

As Dutoit himself has said, the aesthetic strategy he pursues in his films aims at a "deconstruction of narration," although it never goes so far as to completely dissolve the figure described in favor of the description. This may have to do with Dutoit's interest in the incidental and ordinary qualities of everyday life, an interest that dominates *Lisi Strates* as well as *Matière grise* and *Trait d'union*. Even if Dutoit removes (deconstructs) the various layers of the protagonist's self layer by layer, they remain connected to one another through their existence in the everyday, and the sensitivity of the figure, and this sensitivity thus stands for the spiritual aspect of the protagonist's search for herself. What is most important about this search is that it is triggered by everyday situations and routines, neither of which result from the omnipresence of death nor lead to a coherence of a self, but which instead produce a "poetics of life" that (to paraphrase Jacques Rancière) quite simply results from the fact that any tiny emotion can produce a "vertiginous acceleration" that enables an ordinary woman of around 40 to "experience the abysses of passion."[14]

If the deconstruction of narration that Dutoit pursues in *Lisi Strates* could be called experimental, based on its formal efforts to adopt common narrative styles, the experimental quality of his works differs quite fundamentally from Swiss underground film experiments that focused on the structure of the apparatus of the cinema. One of the most important exponents of this movement, HHK Schoenherr, only met Dutoit after *Lisi Strates* was screened in Solothurn, even though Schoenherr's films also use the quotidian as a recurring point of reference. However, Schoenherr breaks down everyday life into a series of sequences of images that constantly recur, so that the cinematic rhythm of time is similar to musical structures (for example, in the *Play* series, 1967–1969), whereas Dutoit's cinematic thinking finds both its foundation and its boundary in its form of narration.

This boundary of (classic) narration, with its goal-oriented plot and its necessity and probability, is also what enables us to view animated film (especially when produced by amateurs) from experimental points of view. In this context (although given the aforementioned archival situation, it is impossible to generalize) it would appear to be the case that while, in animated films, the experimental approaches of amateurs effortlessly undermine conventional narrative logics, only in rare cases do they employ the methods of structural or abstract film. When Georges Dufaux animated pasta (*À la Carte*, 1976) or nuts, bolts, and ball bearings (*Space Gambler*, 1979), the entry, arrangement, and disappearance of the materials that function as "leading actors" were determined by precisely calculated associations with references to things outside the film: in *Space Gambler*, the synthetically produced noises of shots on the soundtrack evoke the violent logic of early video games; in *À la Carte*, it is the anthropomorphic or zoomorphic shaping of egg pasta that evokes additional associations with industrial production and hence with industrial film and—given the synchronized movement of the pasta to extradiegetic music—with a stage performance.

This appeal to "real life," or at least to easily understandable similarities, may be indebted to contemporaneous dominant forms in the visual culture of the animated film or cartoon (animated pasta, for example, was part of the standard television advertising repertoire); it may also testify to a penchant on the part of amateurs for forms that Hans Scheugl and Ernst Schmidt Jr., in their *Subgeschichte des Films*, categorized as belonging to the "naive film"—"grotesques," for example, or "permutations."[15] One such grotesque, Hans Haldenwang's *Hair* (1969), even referred directly to the underground film or Expanded Cinema of the time—first the film shows a strip of film being smeared with paint, treated with acid, hammered, scratched with a brush, and finally stepped on and thrown in a toilet. Then we see the results of these actions—a film entitled *Hair*, which both presents the materiality of the film stock by means of a mechanical and chemical treatment of the emulsion, and also affirms the acoustically produced reference via the soundtrack, on which we hear "Donna" from the musical *Hair*, and also via occasional live-action shots of women's faces.

If Haldenwang's *Hair* was conceived as a means to make a statement about contemporaneous underground film, the ambiguity of that statement could scarcely be over exaggerated—the expectation induced by the grotesque form at the beginning is clearly countered in the second part of the film. Not only does his film within a film bear the same title as the logically superordinate "framing" film, it also shows that Haldenwang had the technical abilities and the imagination needed to treat the emulsion in such a way that the result could be mistaken for an avant-garde experiment with the materiality of film. If it were not for the grotesque frame story and the musical reference, and had Haldenwang not processed the soundtrack in the same way as the film stock, there would be no grounds for making any a distinction between *Hair* and a material film.

Conversely, the distance created by the frame story and the selection of music from experimental forms illustrates the relationship between a relatively autonomous culture of amateur filmmaking and the avant-garde movements that operated at the same time. It is remarkable first, that the materiality of film and an internationally successful musical would be considered to be on an equal footing. Thus, a performance such as *Underground Explosion*, presented as a subcultural *Gesamtkunstwerk* at the Volkshaus in Zurich on April 18, 1969, could be seen to occupy the same cultural level as a Broadway musical that was sold as socio-critical pop musical that toured for two and a half years in German-speaking countries following its premiere in Munich on October 24, 1968. Apart from that, it is just as revealing that Haldenwang, who was active for decades in the Amateurfilmclub in Zurich, received first prize for *Hair* in the club's members-only competition in 1969. We can, of course, only speculate about the reasons for this prize, but a number of factors suggest that it was recognized for its ostentatious ability to playfully break down the tightly drawn lines dividing the genres of the grotesque and the materiality of film, the avant-garde and the amateur.

This mastery of all the technical (animation) possibilities of the cinematographic apparatus that can be seen here is, as I have tried to show elsewhere, one of the key signatures of amateurism.[16] The appropriation of abilities that are distributed across a number of specialized agencies (script, camera, sound, music, editing, production) in the production process of the film industry forms the basis for recognition in the world of amateur film. Further, the very attempt to transcend the results of the industrial production process—namely, the isolation of individuals from themselves—by assuming as many specialized activities as possible, is an obstacle to creating a niche for oneself in the contemporary art field.

Haldenwang's and Dufaux's films seem to confirm the thesis in that they indeed display a certain virtuosity in dealing with the cinematographic apparatus. Haldenwang's animated films are immediately striking for their diversity of animation techniques. In *Der Maler* (*The Painter*, 1968), *Zirkus* (*Circus*, 1968), and *Neanderthal Man* (1971) he still employed the classic cutout animation techniques that were widespread in amateur film. After the mechanical manipulation of the film stock in *Hair*, he experimented with figures that he scratched into a layer of plasticine (*Fingerübungen*, *Finger Exercises*, 1971), wet remnants of fabric (*Orpheus in der Unterwelt*, *Orpheus in the Underworld*, 1973), plasticine figures (*Fussballspieler*, *Soccer Player*, 1974), wool thread (*Wollfiguren*, *Wool Figures*, 1974), and iron filings (*Waterloo*, circa 1975). In *Plastinade*, 1977, lines drawn directly onto the film stock were echoed by the lines drawn in plasticine.

Haldenwang's work shows an evolution toward increasingly abstract forms (*Plastinade*, for example, represents a pure motion study and is strikingly reminiscent of Étienne-Jules Marey's chronophotographic experiments), while Dufaux's films are characterized by the animation of ever-new materials: toy figures (cowboys and Indians) in *Wild West* (1971), toy cars in *Wroom* (1972), Play Flixies in *Flexy-Flixies* (1974), electronic parts in *Made in Hongkong* (1975), shell casings in *Juckpulver* (1977), and batteries in *Rencontre avec Ucar* (1982). Although it would, in Dufaux's case, also be possible to speak of increasing abstraction insofar as the children's toys of the earlier films are replaced by everyday objects in the later ones, the experimental dimension of his work is more evident in the invention of narrative contexts for the materials used. Whereas initially Dufaux still employed toys to parody the popular culture genres in which they originated (the Western in *Wild West*, for example, or motor sports in *Wroom*), the shell casings in *Juckpulver* are embedded in a far more complex context that both triggers associations with militarism, and parodies typical clichés about Switzerland (mountains, cows, and alpenhorns).

In connection with early cinema, Tom Gunning once spoke of the pseudomorphic similarity of early cinema to avant-garde film as a surface deceit that conceals a number of internal differences.[17] In contrast, the similarities between the experiments of amateurs and those of the avant-garde do not seem to be found as much in surface visual phenomena as in the methods, in the development of genuinely autonomous forms of cinematic expression. Whereas Dutoit's short films are on a par with contemporaneous productions in European auteur film, the cinematic experiments of both Haldenwang and Dufaux can be read as experimental films only against the backdrop of the particular context in which they were produced—amateur or animated film. The fact that Haldenwang's films regularly received prizes in national and international competitions, and that Dufaux won the Audience Award for *Wild West* and *Made in Hongkong* at the Solothurner Filmtage speaks volumes about the films' added value in terms of quality compared with common forms of animation (in the amateur film section and beyond). Visually, they are worlds apart from the cinematic experiments of the avant-garde. In terms of method, however, they are similar to what Kurt Kren during his American exile described as follows: "I am not like some other artists who, once they have found their 'groove' constantly repeat the same thing; instead I want to invent something new over and over again, something new for me as well."[18]

[1] Maya Deren, "Notes, Essays, Letters," *Film Culture*, no. 39 (1965), p. 45.
[2] Robert A. Stebbins, "The Amateur: Two Sociological Definitions," *The Pacific Sociological Review*, vol. 20, no. 4 (October 1977), p. 582–606.
[3] See Jan-Christopher Horak, "The First American Film Avant-Garde, 1919–1945," Jan-Christopher Horak (ed.), *Lovers of Cinema: The First American Film Avant-Garde, 1919–1945*, University of Wisconsin Press, Madison 1995, p. 14–66.
[4] See P. Adams Sitney, *Visionary Film: The American Avant-Garde, 1943–2000*, 3rd ed., Oxford University Press, New York 2002.
[5] Jan-Christopher Horak, "The First American Film Avant-Garde, 1919–1945," p. 14–15.
[6] See Patricia R. Zimmermann, *Reel Families: A Social History of Amateur Film*, Indiana University Press, Bloomington 1995.
[7] Noël Burch, *Life to Those Shadows*, University of California Press, Berkeley 1990, p. 2.
[8] Ian Craven, "Accommodating Avant-Gardism? Amateur Animation and the Struggle for Technique," http://eprints.gla.ac.uk/122807/1/122807.pdf (last accessed March 2020), p. 15.
[9] Ian Craven, "Accommodating Avant-Gardism?" p. 7
[10] Bruno Edera, *Histoire du Cinéma suisse d'animation*, Cinémathèque suisse, Lausanne 1978, p. 107–109.
[11] See Ryan Shand, "Theorizing Amateur Cinema: Limitations and Possibilities," *The Moving Image*, vol. 8, no. 2 (2008), p. 36–60.
[12] See Jacques Rancière, *Aesthetics and Its Discontents*, trans. Steven Corcoran, Polity Press, Cambridge 2009.
[13] See Philip Cartelli, "Quotidian Melancholy: Marcel Hanoun's *Une simple histoire*," *Senses of Cinema*, no. 65 (December 2012), http://sensesofcinema.com/2012/feature-articles/quotidian-melancholy-marcel-hanouns-une-simple-histoire (last accessed March 2020).
[14] Jacques Rancière, "Der Wirklichkeitseffekt und die Politik der Fiktion", Dirck Linck et al. (eds.), *Realismus in den Künsten der Gegenwart*, Diaphanes, Zurich 2010, p. 145.
[15] See Hans Scheugl, Ernst Schmidt Jr., *Eine Subgeschichte des Films: Lexikon des Avantgarde-, Experimental- und Undergroundfilms*, Suhrkamp, Frankfurt am Main 1974, p. 633–646.
[16] Vrääth Öhner, "Fragmentierte Spezialisierung: Zu den technischen Bedingungen der Einbildungskraft im frühen Amateurfilm," *ZfK: Zeitschrift für Kulturwissenschaft*, no. 2 (2014), p. 51–60.
[17] Tom Gunning. "An Unseen Energy Swallows Space: The Space in Early Film and Its Relation to American Avant-Garde Film," John Felt (ed.), *Film before Griffith*, University of California Press, Berkeley 1983, p. 355.
[18] Hans Scheugl. "XPRMNTL." *Kolik Sonderheft Film*, no. 14 (2010), p. 134–138, available online: https://scheugl.org/website-von-hans-scheugl-startseite/texte-von-hans-scheugl/xprmtl-experimentalfilm-und-avantgardefilm-als-begriffe/ (last accessed March 2020).

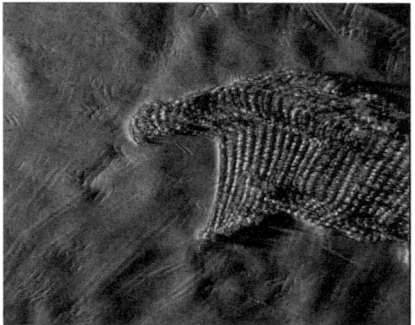
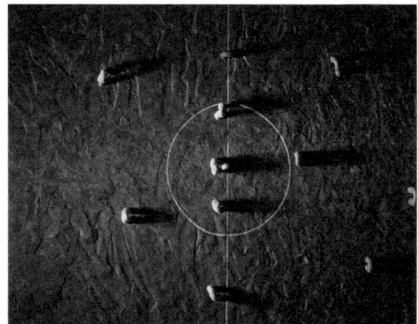

Hans Haldenwang, *Plastinade*, 1977 (Switzerland)
16mm film, 4 minutes

Georges Dufaux, *Wroom*, 1972 (Switzerland)
16mm film, 5 minutes 35 seconds

Hans Haldenwang, *Fussballspieler*, 1974 (Switzerland)
16mm film, 7 minutes 15 seconds

Georges Dufaux, *A la Carte*, 1976 (Switzerland)
16mm film, 4 minutes 45 seconds

Cléo Uebelmann, *Mano Destra*, 1985: Coldness and Cruelty
*François Bovier and
Christian Giuliano Tarabini*

Translated from the French by Miranda Stewart

Cléo Uebelmann, *Mano Destra*, 1985 (Switzerland)
16mm film, 53 minutes

The links between feminism, gender identity claims, and social representations of minorities on the one hand, and film and video on the other, are many and varied and, in fact, relatively under-researched in Switzerland.[1] Many have been rooted in activism and the use of light video equipment, as the Portapak was already on the market in 1969 in France and neighboring countries. In 1971, the Vidéo Out collective, led by Carole and Paul Roussopoulos, devoted a tape to the militants of the Front homosexuel d'action révolutionnaire (FHAR)[2]: the idea was to give them a platform to speak freely, and use a Nagra deck to amplify what they had to say—a Portapak linked up to a Nagra could be used to film the militants' struggles and demands, as well as individual speakers. Mixed-gendered collectives were also active in the struggle to legalize abortion. This was the case of the Filmkollektiv in Zurich, which made

Lieber Herr Doktor (1977, 16mm) directed by Hans Stürm. The purpose of this film was to make vital information available to rural communities. As was frequently the case with counter-information cinema, the debate structured the film. The camera unflinchingly filmed an abortion head on; the scene was then screened for the inhabitants of the Canton of Glarus, and the ensuing discussion was filmed. The second part of the film contained interviews with women reflecting on their experiences of abortion. It was left up to viewers to come to their own conclusions, now in full knowledge of the facts.

As can well be imagined, sexual relationships, gender preferences, and romantic relationships rarely feature in this type of film. The filming of intimate situations requires an *alternative* cinema practice. A clear example of this, albeit in a resolutely male context, can be seen in Stan Brakhage's films *Window Water Baby Moving* (1959) and *Thigh Line Lyre Triangular* (1961),[3] documenting the birth of his children. Some film experiments took place in the United States in the 1970s—Carolee Schneemann, for example, asserted her female perspective in performances and films that shunned Viennese Actionism and Brakhage's expressionism,[4] and Barbara Hammer developed a lesbian cinema of a communitarian bent.[5] Very few films in Switzerland tackled sexuality from an alternative perspective or showed homoerotic relationships.

Let us look now at one such film that has been elevated to the status of a cult movie[6]—a more appropriate term would be a "forgotten" work: *Mano Destra* (1985, 16mm) by Cléo Uebelmann.[7] While the secondary literature on lesbian cinema contains some references to this film,[8] there is, to our knowledge, only one article devoted exclusively to *Mano Destra*.[9] It places Cléo Uebelmann's approach within the context of Deleuze's study of the writings of Leopold von Sacher-Masoch and sees it as a strategy seeking to postpone the sexual act, based on a "contract" between the dominatrix and the submissive partner.[10] It should be mentioned that this is an art film or, at least, a "dilettante" film: certainly *Mano Destra* shows bondage sessions, but it also includes an exhibition and a talk by its protagonist and filmmaker, who plays the role of dominatrix in her own film.

The soundtrack alternates between silence, the sound of footsteps, and music from the underground scene of the time—*The Velvet Tales*, an album by The Vyllies,[11] a Swiss dark-wave group of three women. The contrast between silence and this cold, electronic music sung by women's voices, sometimes with the addition of the noise of what is meant to be the public at an exhibition or the sounds of threatening footsteps, is a perfect complement to the film's fascination—or irritation, depending on the spectator's point of view and preferred interpretation.

The *Genialer Dilletanten* Festival and the Cinema of Transgression

Mano Destra, which is not a feminist film in the sense outlined above, finds its place in the Gothic rock scene[12] and post-punk music more generally,[13] as the film's aesthetic clearly falls within this movement. In Germany, the Neue Deutsche Welle, a genre of minimal mechanical music with electronic influences as played by groups such as Die Tödliche Doris, D.A.F., Die Krupps, Trio, Malaria and Palais Schaumburg, and Grauzone in Switzerland, provided *Mano Destra* with an aesthetic reference point. Indeed, Cléo Uebelmann's reference points are closer to this musical counterculture than they are to contemporary art although, when she is actually mentioned, her work inevitably tends to be placed in the art context.[14] The film has as much in common with the Genialer Dilletanten Festival, founded in Berlin in 1981 to showcase industrial, punk, and post-punk music, as it does with the visual arts, which also appear at this festival. Significantly, Neue Deutsche Welle is part of an anti-consumerist, anti-imperialist movement, advocating support in principle, albeit in muted tones, for feminist demands and transgressions of gender boundaries through deliberate provocation. From this perspective, a figure like Lydia Lunch, muse of the New York "No Wave" scene, who sang with groups such as Teenage Jesus and the Jerks and 8 Eyed Spy, and underground cinema actress directed variously by Vivienne Dick, Richard Kern, Nick Zedd, Beth B and Scott B, is a legendary cultural reference—she loved to use shock and excess as a strategy and to flaunt her sexuality. Indeed, she played the dominatrix in *Black Box*

(1978) by Beth B and Scott B, a film denouncing torture. "The Cinema of Transgression" was a term coined by Nick Zedd to refer to a micro-community of trash filmmakers who put on screenings as part of performances and concerts.[15] The Cinema of Transgression was happy to be marginal and sought an alternative community. Cléo Uebelmann's all-woman group The Dominas, on the other hand, asserted its independence and self-sufficiency.

Cléo Uebelmann Group—The Dominas

Cléo Uebelmann's film opens with a photograph of the director as a dominatrix, followed by a shot of a staged performance with her group The Dominas in a car, sporting a flag with the emblem of this women's group. Then comes a series of static shots filmed in natural light against the backdrop of an industrial factory, with its pipes filmed from different perspectives. The setting is clearly delineated—we are in an underground space that resonates with the aesthetics of industrial music and signals a break with the social conventions that apply outside this confined space (as in Sade, if we take Annie Lebrun's reading,[16] space is divided and all bridges to or communication with the outside world are cut off). The last shot in this series shows the director herself inside this industrial world, merely as part of its setting; however, her face is erased by overexposure, and as such, she represents a *role* rather than a person. The next sequence focuses on a room set aside for sadomasochistic practices (hereinafter S&M), to the soundtrack of a first song by The Villyes. The song "Ahia" is intercut with the sound of women's high heels, which leads to very specific feminist readings of the music around fetishism, the partial object, the fragmented body, and so on. Next comes a series of descriptive shots of equipment used in S&M. Within the film, a slide of the dominatrix, namely the director herself, is projected. The sequence then concentrates on the preparation of instruments of pleasure, and the following shots construct a dominatrix character from the world of Gothic rock. From the outset, the androgynous stereotype of the dominatrix is constructed and set against the film's opening static shot, in which the director poses as if for a fashion shoot. Logically, this is followed by a variety of shots of the submissive partner in bondage, and these alternate between static shots of the setting and panoramic shots of the areas where the action takes place. There is hardly any variation in the film—the same elements are reproduced and reassembled at will. It should be noted that her second, shorter film, *Museum of Modern Art* (1986–1988), takes this first S&M film experiment further. In this later film, classical music replaces dark wave. The lack of change and the modulations are all part of the core principles underpinning *Mano Destra*: no action is intended, no sexual act will be shown explicitly, no form of violence represented apart from bondage itself and the dominatrix situation. The dominatrix is regularly filmed with a slightly low-angle shot which highlights not so much her empowerment, as her position as a dominatrix. Following Deleuze's thoughts on Sacher-Masoch's work, we could argue that the S&M relationship relies on a "suspension of the act" which here is transposed to the screen literally—not only is the narrative suspended radically, but the body of the submissive partner is held in the air by a rope-and-pulley system. Waiting and contemplation are key to this film, and the sexual act, or indeed any act, is forever deferred.

In this respect, one of *Mano Destra*'s effects is particularly noteworthy. When the dominatrix and the submissive partner are simultaneously present within the frame, the shots are systematically static—as if they had been shot by the director herself, who also determines the framing. When the submissive female is included in the frame there may be the occasional camera movement that we could attribute to the director-camera woman; similarly, when the dominatrix is filmed, the camera reframes and occasionally scans the neighboring space, with the shots being potentially actioned by the submissive partner. The effect this creates (whether Cléo Uebelmann is indeed shooting the film or otherwise) is a kind of reciprocity of gaze and desire, where the submissive partner could potentially film the dominatrix who is in charge of the mise-en-scène, and yet who ostensibly takes a step back. If we follow this line of argument, the camera is used to alternate positions of power and mise-en-scène, thereby disturbing the immutability of roles governed by hierarchies within the patriarchal system—dominant/submissive, leader/led, oppressor/

oppressed, etc. which S&M rationale tends to reverse
without, however, radically challenging the nature of these
power relationships.

There are further elements that destabilize the ritual thus
staged. The first involves a change of context as now the
filmmaker falls within the field of contemporary art. Birgit
Hein notes that Cléo Uebelmann is self-taught, and that
she creates unusual and anonymous exhibition situations:

> Cléo, born in 1962 in Luzern, Switzerland, acquired
> her knowledge as photographer/filmmaker herself [...]
> In her own style of exhibiting she rented empty store
> fronts in which she would show mounted photographs,
> to be observed only through the shop windows. With
> such exhibitions she remained totally anonymous.
> She did not know who her audience was, but she did
> know that each person would find themselves placed
> in a voyeuristic situation planned by her.[17]

From the start of the film, the dominatrix role is placed at a
distance through a projected image, effectively a constructed
representation. This is followed by several sequences that
displace the S&M session through the context of the
exhibition and the talk. An initial destabilization is produced
by the soundtrack—during an S&M session, when the
submissive female is attached to a chair, we hear the noise of
a public now located outside the film world; a new actantial
model is included in the film and sends spectators back to
their own roles as both voyeur and public. This non-diegetic
sound is then motivated with the film showing the hanging,
by the artist, of a series of S&M photographs taken from
the film and exhibitions preceding the film, explicitly
alluding to the contemporary art scene (all you can hear on
the soundtrack is the Vyllies, followed by direct sound).
The noise of the public, which returns when the filmmaker
comes on stage as the presenter in an exhibition context,
is now included in this film world. Photographs of the
dominatrix and the submissive female are intercalated in
the scene, literally showing the fixity that threatens the film
and is at the basis of the S&M ritual. By moving from an
intimate relationship (nonetheless mediated by the camera)

to a public context, Uebelmann cast a veil of indeterminacy over everything relating to the self-staging of lesbian sexuality and the field of representation, or in this specific case, contemporary art. The voyeurism and fetishism nurtured or even heightened in the film, are here diffracted through a variety of contexts involving the public in different ways (the space of the film, photographs filmed full frame or hanging on the wall, slide projections, and even, at one point, the portrayal of an exhibition and a talk). The film has explicit sexual connotations and partially activates a number of peepshow codes; however, it also places these codes at a distance particularly through its dramatization of gendered constructions and assertion of their difference from heterosexual norms. By leveraging different mise-en-scènes, the film destabilizes the reifying gaze related to peepshow scopophilia. *Mano Destra* thus moves from a mode of representation where the female body is reduced to a commodity or to a fetish, to a critical mode of exhibition not devoid of subversive, deconstructive, or political intent. Arguably the purpose of the talk is to theorize, through the effect of mise en abyme, the semiotic and film work on which this film is predicated. Through this decontextualization and recontextualization of the female body and dominatrix rituals, *Mano Destra*, a film characterized by heightened theatricality and the use of different media constructs, manages both to perform and to parody the construction of gender identity. It is not simply a "fetishist" film; it also delivers a critical commentary on the theater of sexuality and the "ob-scene" (in Bataille's sense of the word), as the talk scene shows. This displacement is further highlighted by a shot that is difficult to classify, one that refers to an *elsewhere*—the noise of the public continues over a view of an exotic building behind palm trees. This is the only outdoor shot in the entire film—is it to be interpreted as the projection of a fantasy, or as a criticism of exoticism?

From a Bondage Film to Artist's Book

There is a publication based on the film that could be deemed to be queer cinema: Cléo Uebelmann Group—The Dominas, *Mano Destra*. This book, partly composed of frames taken from *Mano Destra* and *Museum of Modern Art*, and partly from photographs exhibited by Cléo Uebelmann, underscores the displacement described above by reconfiguring the film in a fixed form and placing it in an art context. In her selection of images, Cléo Uebelmann further highlights the principle of juxtaposing scenes without connectors, which governs the editing of this film: bodies (dominatrix, submissive female), objects, and decors are all arranged without seeking to create a narrative. In her introduction to this book of photographs, Birgit Hein unequivocally includes Cléo Uebelmann's film in the underground scene that overlaps with experimental cinema, countercultural spaces, and galleries specializing in film, such as P.A.P. (Progressive Art Production, Munich and Zurich). It should be remembered that Birgit Hein, along with Wilhelm Hein, was responsible for choosing the cinema program for XSCREEN in Cologne,[18] which, from 1968 screened artists' films alongside porn films and actionist films performed by Otto Muehl and Günter Brus, and the montages created by Kurt Kren from these outrageous performances. In this case we might be tempted to view this film from a feminist perspective—under this reading, Uebelmann would be appropriating performance as a practice, and inverting it or, at least in this instance, displacing the relationships of male-female domination that have characterized happenings and actionist performances. However, *Mano Destra* clearly fits within a queer perspective, which raises questions over the performativity of identity rather than gender, which here come to the same thing—the use of leather, whip, links to "male" imagery, high heels, and stockings hardly contribute to problematizing the stereotypes attached to "female" imagery. In any event, Birgit Hein places *Mano Destra* both within the category of avant-garde or experimental cinema by citing *Fireworks* (1947) by Kenneth Anger and *Meshes of the Afternoon* (1943) by Maya Deren as precedents, and within that of contemporary art when she talks of the minimalism of the 1970s. She highlights the sense of waiting and eroticism which emerges from this film:

> In *Mano Destra*, time, which almost appears to stand still, is physically felt. "An essential element of masochism is waiting." (Deleuze) Cléo, as Domina, waits in extreme calmness and composure; she

watches over her victim, who has handed herself over to her. In this way every movement acquires extraordinary meaning: a turn of the head; certain movements of the hand to arrange ropes; a glance toward the camera, and the minimal motions of the bound woman, whose face one never sees [...]

For me the Domina, above all, radiates an incredible eroticism [...] *Mano Destra* also touches upon a taboo: the masculine in a feminine sexuality. It is unbelievable the vehement indignation that the film brought out precisely in women [...] All objects in *Mano Destra*, from the rope to the saddle to the boxes, attest to a very clear and certain consciousness of form, so that one can also call Cléo a sculptress.[19]

Birgit Hein relates this tendency toward androgyny—the masculine within "female sexuality"—in the case of the dominatrix to a desire for self-effacement and anonymity on the part of the author, which is part and parcel of the S&M world.

It would be counterintuitive to look at *Mano Destra* as a feminist film, as we have already argued. However, it is a film which, in its juxtaposition of heterogenous contexts thereby modifying the value of its "signs" (fetishized and fragmented bodies, private and public submission rituals, and a generalized aesthetic of suspension and deferment), "destabilizes" both the representation it portrays and its own discourse. In an interview, Maria Klonaris and Katerina Thomadaki, feminist filmmakers whose work explores androgynous identity, comment on the ambiguity of this film. They couch their reservations in the following terms:

> Cléo Uebelmann's film dates back to 1985 and was considered for submission to the first Rencontres [internationales Art Cinéma/Vidéo/Ordinateur] [...] However, the sadomasochistic relationships between two women and the power relationship involved in the sadomasochistic relationship gave us pause for thought. Furthermore, the way the dominatrix was presented was very much from a fashion perspective as her immaculate outfit had a touch of the model about it. Possibly even a model for sadomasochistic fashion.[20]

Mano Destra makes clear reference to the German and American music and art scenes. It is part of the postpunk world that likes to provoke, but it is also somewhat complacent, in the sense of a "sadomasochistic fashion model." Yet, aesthetically speaking, and in its construction of a point of view and affirmation of political intent, Uebelmann's film is remarkably radical in its form (tightly framed shots using meticulous black-and-white photography, precise composition, and staging of the decor and equipment) and consistent in the construction of meaning (significance), which eschews all sexual normality and questions the phallocentric position of the spectator and the sociocultural beliefs underpinning the couple as purveyed by the cinema industry and mass media.

[1] On this point, see Brigitte Blöchlinger et al. (eds.), *Cut. Film- und Videomacherinnen Schweiz von den Anfängen bis 1994: eine Benstandsaufnahme*, Stroemfeld, Basel 1995.

[2] On this point, see Brigitte Blöchlinger et al. (eds.), *Cut. Film- und Videomacherinnen Schweiz von den Anfängen bis 1994: eine Benstandsaufnahme*, Stroemfeld, Basel 1995.

[3] In 1959, Jane Brakhage turned her camera on her companion, with a sequence inserted at the end of the film. That, however, did little to alter the perspective adopted in *Window Water Baby Moving*. In *Thigh Line Lyre Triangular* (1961), the filmmaker's subjectivity is celebrated—Brakhage painted directly on the film stock to express his feelings when his daughter was born. There is no room here for female subjectivity; it should, however, be noted that in these cases Stan Brakhage was giving voice to a subjective viewpoint that was his alone.

[4] *Fuses* (1964–1967) explores the relationship between Carolee Schneemann and James Tenney, by contrasting a female gaze with a male representation of sexual relationships in a film that runs counter to Brakhage's expressionist lyricism. See Carolee Schneeemann, "The Obscene Body/Politic," *Art Journal*, vol. 50, no. 4 (Winter 1991), p. 28–35.

[5] It is often argued that *Dyketactics* (1974) was the first lesbian film. See Barbara Hammer, *Hammer! Making Movies Out of Life and Sex*, The Feminist Press, New York 2010.

[6] Lux, which rents out 16mm copies, argues that *Mano Destra* has achieved cult status among the S&M underground (Karen Smith, film description, https://lux.org.uk/work/mano-destra).

[7] In 2013, Uebelmann's film was nominated for the PorYes feminist pornographic movie award in Berlin. On this occasion, Claudia Gehrke spoke about this film in what is one of the main commentaries remaining (it has been partially reconstructed given the retrospective nature of her presentation). Claudia Gehrke noted that the film was initially screened in 1985 at the first (segregated) congress on female S&M in Cologne (Secret Minds, in January 1986, if the works that reference it can be trusted) and focused on the film's attempt to deconstruct patriarchal society.

[8] Cherry Smyth, "The Pleasure Threshold: Looking at Lesbian Pornography on Film," *Feminist Review*, no. 34 ("Perverse Politics: Lesbian Issues," Spring 1990), p. 152–159; B. Ruby Rich, *New Queer Cinema. The Director's Cut*, Duke University Press, Durham/London 2013, p. 24; Claudia Gehrke (ed.), *Frauen und Pornografie: Essays zur PorNOdebatte*, Konkursbuch Verlag, Tübingen 1988, p. 143; Beverley Zalcock, *Renegade Sisters: Girl Gangs on Film*, Creation, London 1998, p. 100.

[9] Annette Brauerhoch, "Die kalte Domina. *Mano Destra* von Cléo Uebelmann," in Eva Hohenberger, Karin Jurschick (eds.), *Blaue Wunder. Neue Filme und Videos von Frauen 1984 bis 1994*, Argument Verlag, Hamburg 1994, p. 186–201.

[10] Annette Brauerhoch cites Deleuze's introduction to the work of Sacher-Masoch on various occasions. See Gilles Deleuze, *Présentation de Sacher-Masoch*, Minuit, Paris 1967. We should note at this point the contractual principle underpinning masochism, which is diametrically opposed to that of sadism. "[T]he masochist should fashion the woman into a despot, that he should persuade her to cooperate and get her to 'sign.' He is essentially an educator and thus runs the risk inherent in educational undertakings." Gilles Deleuze, "The Language of Sade and Masoch," *Masochism*, trans. Jean McNeil, Zone Books, New York 1991, p. 21.

[11] This EP album contains "Ahia," "The Sky Is Full of Stitches," "Agrainir," and "Exquisite Carcass."

[12] In 1976, Ellen Moers coined the term "female Gothic" to refer to those women writers who, since the 18th century, had pursued Gothic literature. See Ellen Moers, *Literary Women*, Doubleday, New York 1976.

[13] See Gavin Butt, Kodwo Eshun, Mark Fisher (eds.), *Post-Punk Then and Now*, Repeater Books, London 2016.

[14] See Lux's film presentation and Claudia Gherke's talk at the PorYes awards ceremony.

[15] Orion Jericho [Nick Zedd], "The Cinema of Transgression Manifesto," *The Underground Film Bulletin*, 1985.

[16] See Annie Lebrun, *Soudain un bloc d'abîme, Sade*, Jean-Jacques Pauvert, Paris 1986. Deleuze tends to make a clear distinction between sadism and masochism. In *Mano Destra*, space is split (an underground passage leading out of the heteronormative world); conversely, the relationships between the two women are located within an intersubjective space, which is poles apart from the world of Sade.

[17] Birgit Hein, "Vorwort," Cléo Uebelmann Group—The Dominas, *Mano Destra*, Verlag Claudia Gehrke, Tübingen 1986, n. p. (trans. Patricia Lech).

[18] See Wilhelm and Birgit Hein, Christian Michelis, Rolf Wiest (eds.), *XSCREEN. Materialen über den Underground-Film*, Phaidon, Cologne 1971.

[19] Birgit Hein, "Vorwort," Cléo Uebelmann Group—The Dominas, *Mano Destra*, n. p.

[20] Angueliki Garidis, "Pour une écologie des Media. Entretien avec Maria Klonaris et Katerina Thomadaki," 1998, http://www.artmag.com/rencontre/astarti/astarti2.html (last accessed March 2020).

Imprint

EDITED BY
François Bovier, Adeena Mey,
Thomas Schärer, Fred Truniger

EDITING & EDITORIAL COORDINATION
Barbara Biedermann, Clément Dirié

COPY EDITING
Clare Manchester

PROOFREADING
Clare Manchester, Miranda Stewart

DESIGN CONCEPT
Gavillet & Cie, Geneva

DESIGN
Nicolas Leuba, Nicolas Eigenheer

PRINT AND BINDING
Musumeci S.p.A., Quart (Aosta)

TYPEFACE
Genath (www.optimo.ch)

PHOTO CREDITS
Page 6: Photographs by Max Reitmeier; p. 18: © Clemens Klopfenstein Archives; p. 46, 60, 65, 120, 196: HHK Schoenherr Archives at Lichtspiel/Kinemathek, Bern; p. 66, 79: © Temenos/Courtesy of Robert Beavers; p. 94: Courtesy of Clemens Klopfenstein; p. 124: Hans-Jakob Siber Archives; p. 131, 135: Edi Stöckli Archives; p. 148: Courtesy of Bernd Fiedler and Balz Raz; p. 163: Courtesy of Reinhard Manz; p. 170, 188–189: Kunsthalle Bern Archives/© Getty Institute; p. 177, 188: Kunsthalle Bern Archives; p. 204–205: © ETH-Bibliothek Zurich/Photographs by Hans Baumann, Comet; p. 246, 269: © Virginie et Philémon Otth; p. 288, 293: Photographs by Bernd Jansen; p. 310–311: Serge and Doris Stauffer Archives, Graphische Sammlung der

Schweizerischen Nationalbibliothek Bern, Bern; p. 378, 395:
Archives Lichtspiel/Kinemathek Bern; Fotostiftung
Schweiz. Martin Gasser

All rights reserved. No part of this publication may be
reproduced, stored in a retrieval system, or transmitted,
in any form, or by any means, electronic, mechanical,
or otherwise without prior permission in writing from the
publisher.

© 2020, the authors, the photographers, and JRP|Editions
Printed in Europe

Published by
JRP | Editions
www.jrp-editions.com

In co-Edition with
Les presses du réel
www.lespressesdureel.com

ISBN 978-3-03764-550-5 (JRP | Editions)
ISBN 978-2-37896-157-2 (Les presses du réel)

Distribution

JRP | Editions publications are available internationally at selected bookstores and from the following distribution partners:

GERMANY AND AUSTRIA
Vice Versa Distribution GmbH
www.viceversaartbooks.com

FRANCE
Les presses du réel
www.lespressesdureel.com

SWITZERLAND
AVA Verlagsauslieferung AG
www.ava.ch

UK AND OTHER EUROPEAN COUNTRIES
Cornerhouse Publications HOME
www.cornerhousepublications.org

USA, CANADA, ASIA, AND AUSTRALIA
ARTBOOK | D. A. P.
www.artbook.com

For a list of our partner bookshops or for any general questions, please visit our homepage www.jrp-editions.com for further information.

This volume is published with the IPF-Institute for the Performing Arts and Film, Zurich University of the Arts (ZHdK). It is the 18th volume of its subTexte series.

The subTexte series of the IPF-Institute for the Performing Arts and Film is dedicated to presenting original research within two fields of inquiry: Performative Practice and Film. The series offers a platform for the publication of texts, images, or digital media emerging from research on, for, or through the performative arts or film. The series contributes to promoting practice-based art research beyond the ephemeral event and the isolated monograph, reporting intermediate research findings, and opening up comparative perspectives. From conference proceedings to collections of materials, subTexte gathers diverse and manifold reflections on, and approaches to, the performative arts and film.

Documents Series 29:
François Bovier, Adeena Mey,
Thomas Schärer, Fred Truniger
[eds.]
Minor Cinema:
Experimental Film in Switzerland

This book is the twenty-ninth
volume in the "Documents" series,
dedicated to critics' writings.

The series was founded by
Lionel Bovier and Xavier Douroux.

Also available

DOCUMENTS SERIES (IN ENGLISH)

Raymond Bellour, *Between-the-Images*
ISBN 978-3-03764-144-6 (JRP | Ringier)
ISBN 978-2-84066-513-7 (Les presses du réel)

François Bovier & Adeena Mey, *Cinema in the Expanded Field*
ISBN 978-3-03764-433-1 (JRP | Ringier)
ISBN 978-2-84066-823-7 (Les presses du réel)

François Bovier & Adeena Mey, *Exhibiting the Moving Image*
ISBN 978-3-03764-388-4 (JRP | Ringier)
ISBN 978-2-84066-822-0 (Les presses du réel)

Gabriele Detterer & Maurizio Nannucci, *Artist-Run Spaces*
ISBN 978-3-03764-191-0 (JRP | Ringier)
ISBN 978-2-84066-512-0 (Les presses du réel)

Hans Ulrich Obrist, *A Brief History of Curating*
ISBN 978-3-905829-55-6 (JRP | Ringier)
ISBN 978-2-84066-287-7 (Les presses du réel)

Tomáš Pospiszyl, *An Associative Art History*
ISBN 978-3-03764-517-8 (JRP | Ringier)
ISBN 978-2-84066-982-1 (Les presses du réel)

Alice Rawsthorn, *Design as an Attitude*
ISBN 978-3-03764-521-5 (JRP | Ringier)
ISBN 978-2-84066-984-5 (Les presses du réel)

Chantal Pontbriand [ed.], *Parachute: The Anthology (1975–2000): Photography, Film, Video, and New Media*
ISBN 978-3-03764-382-2 (JRP | Ringier)
ISBN 978-2-84066-758-2 (Les presses du réel)